HOUSES OF THE NORTH YORK MOORS

Frontispiece [14] Arden Hall, Arden with Ardenside, from S.

ROYAL
COMMISSION
ON THE HISTORICAL
MONUMENTS
OF ENGLAND

HOUSES
— OF THE —
NORTH YORK
MOORS

LONDON · HER MAJESTY'S STATIONERY OFFICE

OTHER PUBLICATIONS BY THE
ROYAL COMMISSION ON THE HISTORICAL MONUMENTS OF ENGLAND

Liverpool Road Station, Manchester: an historical and architectural survey
(Manchester University Press, 1980)

Northamptonshire: an archaeological atlas (RCHM, 1980)

Early Industrial Housing: the Trinity area of Frome (HMSO, 1981)

Beverley: an archaeological and architectural study (HMSO, 1982)

Pottery Kilns of Roman Britain (HMSO, 1984)

Danebury: An Iron Age Hill Fort (RCHM, 1984)

Liverpool's Historic Waterfront (HMSO, 1984)

Rural Houses of the Lancashire Pennines 1560–1760 (HMSO, 1985)

Rural Houses of West Yorkshire 1400–1830 (HMSO, 1986)

Workers' Housing in West Yorkshire 1750–1920 (HMSO, 1986)

318100

Printed in the United Kingdom for Her Majesty's Stationery Office
Dd238890   C33   7/87   54135

LIST OF CONTENTS

CHAIRMAN'S PREFACE

THE RIGHT HON. THE EARL FERRERS

The North York Moors are best known as a popular tourist area, although they have previously attracted little attention from architectural historians.

The initial reaction of a visitor to the region is normally one of admiration for the beauty of the scenery rather than for the interest of the architecture, but a closer inspection of the older buildings reveals that they constitute a major historical canvas which illustrates the former way of life in the towns, in the villages and in the countryside.

This volume, by the Royal Commission on the Historical Monuments of England, is the product of an extensive investigation of rural houses and farm buildings and of houses in the market towns of Helmsley, Kirkbymoorside and Pickering. It is hoped that this study will prove to be of value, not only to those who are familiar with the region, but also to the many who are interested in domestic architecture or social, economic and agrarian history.

FERRERS

ACKNOWLEDGEMENTS

The Commissioners desire to express their acknowledgement of the good work of their executive staff in the preparation of this book. The authors, who also investigated the buildings, were Mr D. W. Black, Dr I. H. Goodall and Mr I. R. Pattison; Dr R. M. Butler wrote Chapter 1 and also assisted with research and editorial work. Mr J. T. Smith provided valuable assistance and advice. Investigation in the field was also undertaken by Mr J. C. Heward and the late Mr J. E. Williams. Dr B. E. A. Jones was primarily responsible for documentary research. The photographs were taken by Mr T. E. Buchanan and the drawings are by Mr A. M. Berry. Mrs J. Bryant undertook editorial work until her retirement in 1985. The preparation of the final text was by Mrs D. J. Turner. Assistance with photography of the preliminary survey was provided by Mr A. D. Perry, Mr R. A. C. Skingle and Mr P. M. Williams. The Commission's Air Photography Unit undertook some aerial photography. A number of plans in Chapter 6 were traced by Mr F. R. Raines.

The Commissioners are very grateful for assistance given by the staff of the North Yorkshire County Record Office, the Borthwick Institute of Historical Research, the Library of the University of Hull, the York Central Library, the York City Archives, the Yorkshire Archaeological Society, the Whitby Museum, the Whitby Literary and Philosophical Society and the Public Record Office. Thanks are also due to the following who generously gave help: Mr Barry Harrison, Mrs Barbara Hutton, Mr Raymond Hayes, Mr John McDonnell and Mr John Rushton. Professor J. E. Hemingway provided advice on geology and Mr W. G. Simpson reported on dendrochronology. Messrs Brierley, Leckenby, Keighley and Groom allowed free access to their collection of architectural drawings, and Mr G. Lealman and Mr P. Robinson allowed historic photographs from their collections to be copied.

The survey could not have been carried out without the co-operation of owners and occupiers of the buildings visited. They are too numerous to mention individually but special thanks are due to the following for permitting access to properties on their estates: The Earl of Mexborough, Viscount Downe, Viscount Ingleby, the late Lord Derwent, Lord Feversham, Lady Clarissa Collin, Mr H. N. Constantine, Mr S. M. Foster, Mr J. H. V. Sutcliffe, the Duchy of Lancaster, the Forestry Commission and the National Trust. Sources of illustrations other than from photographs or surveys by Royal Commission staff are as follows: Borthwick Institute of Historical Research, Fig. 60; Brierley, Leckenby, Keighley and Groom, Figs. 16, 17; Lord Derwent, Fig. 22; R. H. Hayes, Fig. 208; G. Lealman, Figs. 25, 207; North Yorkshire County Record Office, Figs. 21, 158, 284; Ordnance Survey 6 in.:1 mile maps (1st edition), Figs. 203–5, 281; F. C. Rimington and J. G. Rutter, Fig. 19; P. Robinson, Fig. 13; J. Tuke, Fig. 143; Welburn Hall Special School, Fig. 14; Yorkshire Archaeological Society, Fig. 55.

EDITORIAL NOTES

The numbers in square brackets throughout the text refer to the List of Buildings Recorded, which includes all buildings discussed in the book. They are listed by civil parishes in alphabetical order. The names and boundaries of the parishes are those effective after April 1974.

In the List buildings are located by national grid references. In the countryside outside villages, six-figure references are considered to be sufficient to identify houses and farms, most of which are individually named on the OS maps to 1:50,000 or larger scales. In villages, eight-figure references have been given to allow buildings to be identified more precisely. In the three market towns an exact address by street and number is considered to provide an adequate location.

The whole of the survey area is shown on the OS 1 inch Tourist Map of the North York Moors, and on the 1:50,000 series sheet numbers 93, 94, 100 and 101.

Unless stated otherwise, plans of buildings are of the ground floor and to the scale of 1:300. Where more than one floor plan is shown, the lower floors are to the left or below the upper floors. The plans have been arranged so that the main entrance or the front faces the foot of the page. Plans generally show the state of a building as it was when recorded, though occasionally recent features such as inserted partitions, doors and windows are omitted.

On plans, walls belonging to the earliest recognizable phase are shown in black; walls of later phases are indicated by a sequence of hatching as indicated below. The phases are relative and not indicative of specific dates or periods though occasionally one or two phases have been omitted to suggest the elapse of a considerable period of time between two phases.

■	earliest work	▨	third phase	▨	sixth phase
▨	first phase	▨	fourth phase	☐	latest phase
▨	second phase	▨	fifth phase	▨	separate phases not distinguishable

Conventions used on the plans:

PE	pitching eye	st	position of former stair	bl door	blocked door
W	window over	fp	fireplace		
p	pantry	tr	trap door		

An arrow on a staircase indicates the direction of the upward flight. Dates on plans indicate positions of inscribed datestones. Where crucks are indicated, the positions of the feet of the blades are shown.

INTRODUCTION

The North York Moors constitute a well-defined upland region, the only one in England which extends to the eastern seaboard. The boundaries to north and west, formed by steep slopes, are particularly clear cut; to the south the transition from the dip slope of the Tabular Hills to the Vale of Pickering is less dramatic but nevertheless clearly defined.

The survey area chosen by the Commission does not exactly correspond with either the natural boundaries of the region or with those of the National Park. For a number of reasons, such as assigning place-names and co-ordinating with archives, the survey was conducted on a parish basis, and the precise boundary of the survey area was determined by the boundaries of the outer ring of parishes; consequently, the western limit of the area excludes the extreme fringe of the plateau and the steep scarp slopes, where there are virtually no farmsteads in any case, but extends two or three kilometres into the Vale of Pickering on the south.

The survey area lies entirely in the county of North Yorkshire and measures about 55 kilometres from east to west and 33 kilometres from north to south. It includes 80 civil parishes, which provide the primary system by which place-names have been assigned. The town of Whitby, which is of such interest that it is worthy of a separate study, lies immediately outside the survey area. The coastal settlement of Robin Hood's Bay, though within the boundaries of the area, was also excluded from the investigation. A few country houses, though occasionally alluded to in the text of the book, were not included as they are best considered as part of a study covering similar houses over a wider area. They include Duncombe Park, Ebberston Hall, Hackness Hall and Wykeham Abbey. For similar reasons, the important medieval castles at Helmsley and Pickering are only referred to in respect of certain aspects of domestic accommodation.

Systematic investigation of buildings in the region commenced in Ryedale in 1977 as the first stage of an intended Inventory of the county of North Yorkshire. The project was subsequently redefined on thematic lines as an enquiry into the nature of domestic building in the North York Moors region. A preliminary survey was undertaken in which an attempt was made to take a single photograph and make brief notes from external evidence of every house and farm indicated on the first edition of the Ordnance Survey 6 inch to 1 mile map, surveyed in 1848–54, though a few of later date were also photographed. From this non-intensive record of over 4000 buildings, a selection of about 800 was made for more detailed investigation, and those have, on the whole, formed the basis of the discussion in this volume.

The record cards prepared by the Commission's staff contain plans, photographs and detailed descriptions of buildings investigated, and form a corpus of information which supplements the contents of this volume. They may be consulted at the National Monuments Record, Fortress House, 23 Savile Row, London, W1X 1AB, from which copies of the photographs, which are Crown Copyright, may also be obtained. Descriptions of the monuments enumerated in the List of Buildings

Recorded were omitted from this publication for lack of space. This descriptive list is available from the National Monuments Record and copies have been deposited at the following locations where they may be consulted on application; the Reference Department, Central Library, Museum Street, York; the Yorkshire Archaeological Society Library, Claremont, Clarendon Road, Leeds; the North Yorkshire County Record Office, Northallerton, and local libraries in the region.

CHAPTER 1

THE NORTH YORK MOORS

BACKGROUND AND DEVELOPMENT

The natural environment

The North York Moors are now best known as an area of wild upland beauty between three agricultural vales and the sea, attracting ramblers and naturalists from far afield. As Whitby and Scarborough have changed from being commercial ports to flourishing holiday resorts, tourism has brought to the knowledge of a wider public such places as Farndale and Dalby, once remote and unfrequented. In the villages and dales many old farmhouses, cottages and barns remain, buildings of interest to the architect and social historian, though the ancient way of life they once sheltered, little changed from the 16th to the early 20th century, has all but vanished. Its most significant aspects and the influences which have affected it most profoundly are touched on in this chapter.

The area studied in this volume is 55 kilometres east to west by 33 kilometres north to south, bounded on the east by the North Sea, on the west by the Vale of Mowbray (the northern extension of the Vale of York), on the north by the lower slopes of the Cleveland Hills, stretching northwards to the Tees, and on the south by the Vale of Pickering (Fig. 1). Most of this

Fig. 1 North-east England, showing extent of area surveyed

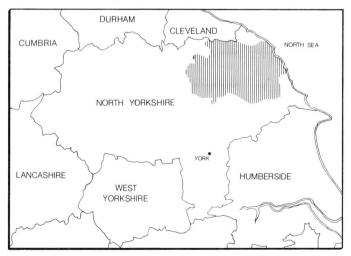

block is high moorland, rising from 50 metres above sea-level at its southern edge to over 430 metres on Urra Moor, dissected by a series of south-flowing streams. The Derwent, only 6 kilometres from the sea at East Ayton, bends south-westerly and eventually flows into the Ouse, receiving on its course the Rye and other tributaries draining the moors. In the northern part of the area the Esk flows east from Westerdale through Eskdale to reach the sea at Whitby, joined from the south by smaller becks. In the north-western corner of the moors, the Leven flows westward from near Kildale to the Tees below Yarm.

Most of the moorland consists of middle Jurassic sandstone with occasional cappings of gritstone on the highest hills (Fig. 2). To the south these rocks are overlaid with oolitic and shelly Corallian limestone, forming the Tabular Hills, flat-topped with a scarp to the north and gentler slopes to the south. Ice action in the last glaciation deepened pre-existing valleys and determined the line of the present water courses. Newtondale and Forge Valley were cut by meltwater from ice in Eskdale gouging deep channels as it flowed southwards to the extensive lake then filling the Vale of Pickering, which, blocked by ice and glacial deposits near the coast, drained through the Kirkham Gorge towards the Ouse.

Among the sandstone strata are thin seams of poor-quality coal, and earlier rocks below contain deposits of iron ore, jet and alum-bearing shales. All these minerals were exploited by man, the jet being used for ornaments from the Bronze Age and the iron being smelted on a small scale from the late Iron Age, but their fullest utilization awaited the 19th century.

Before human interference started to affect the vegetation some 10,000 years ago, the area was covered with a forest of birch and hazel. Extensive clearance progressively led to the rapid loss of fertile soil and resulted in the open heather-clad moorland and peat bogs of the northern parts. Limited regeneration of the forest produced oak, ash and alder woods in the dales and along the northern slopes of the Tabular Hills, to survive until the 17th century as the Forest of Pickering. The present pattern of land use, with arable cultivation on the limestone plateau, cow pasture in the valley bottoms, sheep pasture on the moors and some woodland, had already been long established by the 14th century. Since then, the marshes south of Pickering have been drained and exploited, more land has been

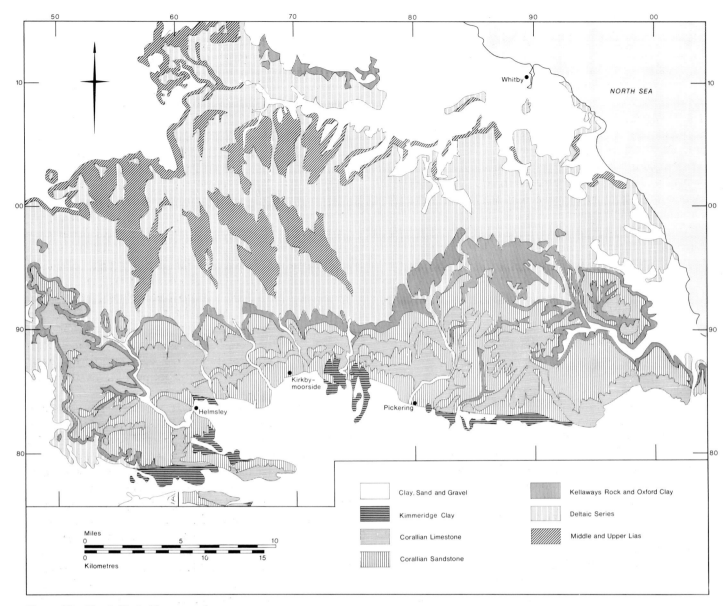

Fig. 2 The North York Moors: geology

ploughed, though often only to revert again to pasture, and plantations of conifers have, since 1920, been added to the remnants of the deciduous forest.

The North York Moors, formerly known as Blackamore, meaning 'black hill moor', although entirely within the North Riding of Yorkshire from before 1066, have always been split between several administrative areas. For civil purposes, the area was divided between the wapentakes of Ryedale (around Helmsley), Pickering Lythe (from the River Seven in Rosedale to the sea), Whitby Strand (the old territory of Whitby Abbey), Langbaurgh (north of the Esk–Derwent watershed) and Birdforth (a small area in the west). Ecclesiastically, it fell into the deaneries of Rydall (Ryedale and Pickering Lythe) and Cleveland (Langbaurgh and most of Whitby Strand) with part of the coastal strip in Dickering Deanery. Twenty-six ancient parishes, some of huge extent, included some forty townships, most of which later became civil parishes (Fig. 3); their boundaries often perpetuate pre-Norman divisions and may even represent estates or territories already delineated in the second millennium BC by lines of burial mounds and later by linear earthworks. Much of the region, including all the moorland dales, falls within the North York Moors National Park, set up in 1952, with planning restrictions on unsuitable building and on drastic changes in land use.

4

The historical background

MEDIEVAL SETTLEMENT

The Domesday Survey of 1086 is the first document to give any idea of the extent of settlement in and around the moors, previously only mentioned by Bede as 'steep and remote hills which seemed better fitted for the haunts of robbers and the dens of wild beasts than for human habitation' (Colgrave and Mynors 1969: 287), among which the monasteries of Hackness, Lastingham and Whitby were founded in the 7th century. In its entries for Yorkshire, the survey mentions some seventy places on the lower and more fertile land in the valleys of the Derwent, Esk and Rye, where finds of earlier date show that human settlement had long been concentrated. During the late 11th and 12th centuries, several religious houses were founded and endowed with land all over the area; their charters and records mention many names, both of minor settlements and natural features, the majority of these being of Scandinavian origin, as were until recently many words in the local dialect.

Many of the villages and manors in the area are described in the Domesday Survey as 'waste', whether because they had not yet recovered from the ravaging by William I's army in 1069 or because they were still unexploited and of little value to their lords. The plans of many of the villages along the northern edge of the Vale of Pickering suggest that they originated as street settlements at the spring-line below the limestone hills along roads running north to the woods and moorland pastures and south to the marshes and meadows beside the Rye or Derwent. An original north–south alignment, visible at Allerston, Ebberston and Wombleton, has often been modified by the growing importance of the east–west road which links the string of villages: Middleton and Snainton consequently now stretch along this road. A corresponding arrangement can be seen on the southern side of the vale. Among these street villages are several set around a rectangular or oval green, manifestly the result of deliberate planning. This phenomenon has been studied with no firm conclusion as to when these plans originated (Allerston 1970; Sheppard 1974, 1976). At most of the best examples, such as Appleton-le-Moors, Cold Kirby, Hutton-le-Hole, Newton on Rawcliffe, Nawton, Old Byland and Spaunton, the principal medieval landowner was a religious house and their rearrangement might be due to their 12th-century monastic lords. At other places a more complex plan has resulted from the agglomeration of distinct but neighbouring settlements or from the addition to an original core of new groups of houses or farmsteads. Pockley (Taylor 1983: 139) and Thornton Dale are examples of the amalgamation of three or four separate settlements. Elsewhere, as at Cropton, Hawnby, Levisham and Sinnington, the village seems to have moved away from the parish church, while Kirkdale church has no nearby settlement.

The three towns of Helmsley, Kirkbymoorside and Pickering had all existed as important settlements before the Norman Conquest, with churches serving a wide area. In the 11th century a castle was built to dominate each of these communities. By 1201 the king had founded a borough beside his castle at Pickering, as had the baronial family of de Ros at Helmsley. These boroughs may have been intended to attract supplies and goods to military and administrative centres rather than as urban communities. During the 13th century other lords obtained grants of markets at Egton, Kirkbymoorside, and Thornton Dale. Whitby may have been an urban community in the 11th century, since the abbey possessed a market, borough and port there from soon after its refoundation c. 1080. The plans of Helmsley and Kirkbymoorside are simple: three roads meet in a large market-place, later partly infilled, near the church and the castle is somewhat farther away. Pickering has a more complicated T-shaped arrangement with most of the town on the east side of the Pickering Beck (Figs. 203–205). Theories of its development are affected by the possibility that a mound on Beacon Hill was the motte of a second Norman castle west of the beck and by the planned appearance of the part along the east–west road with its parallel back lanes. The building of a railway beside the stream has further confused the layout. The borough was apparently centred on Burgate running north towards the castle; Helmsley too had a Borough Gate, a name originally referring to the market-place but later given to other streets.

The settlements of the area were dependent on agriculture, even if the value of ironstone was realized early at Levisham and in Rosedale. The widespread grants of land to monasteries may have been partly intended to ensure the redevelopment of a devastated or unexploited area and so enhance the value of adjoining lay property (Hodgson 1980). The Cistercian houses of Byland, Fountains and Rievaulx, the Augustinian canons of Guisborough and Kirkham, the Gilbertines of Malton and the Benedictine monks of St Mary's, York, established granges, compact farms organized as units, as in Bilsdale, divided between Rievaulx and Kirkham, and in the marshland (Marishes) south of Pickering, also exploited by the small nunnery at Yedingham and the Templars' preceptory at Foulbridge. The other nunneries at Arden, Baysdale, Keldholme, Rosedale and Westerdale, like the Grandmontine priory at Grosmont, were founded later and poorly endowed. Many of the monastic granges specialized in sheep rearing for wool production. In the 13th and 14th centuries much valuable raw wool, a principal element in England's foreign trade, was collected from the area and sent to York or Hull, being purchased by Flemish and Italian merchants. In 1368 an Ebberston dealer had over 2700 sheep, 16 sacks of wool, over £200 in his cash box and debts owed by other local sheep farmers (Waites 1963–6).

An attempt to estimate the agricultural prosperity of the area from tax assessments shows that in 1292 and 1318 the wapentakes of Pickering Lythe and Ryedale, though less prosperous than the Vale of York, were assessed more highly than Whitby Strand or East Langbaurgh. In 1342 Pickering parish contributed to a tax of a ninth on corn, wool and lambs, 'more than all the Moorland parishes put together and almost as much as the total Ninth for the Coastal Plateau' (Waites 1972: 143).

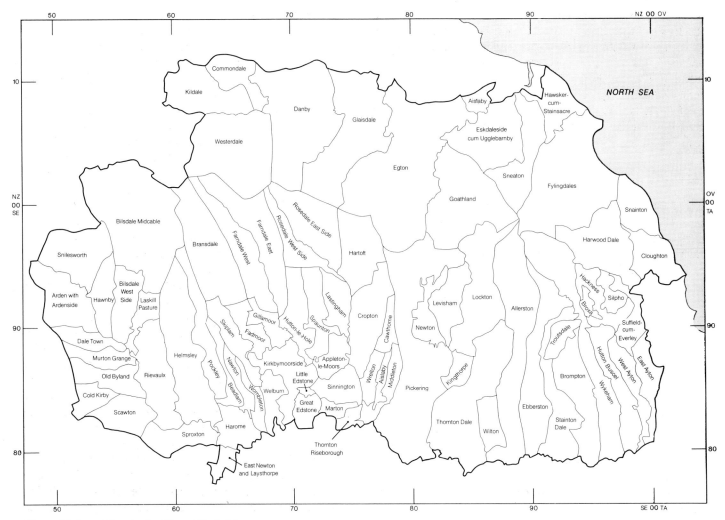

Fig. 3 Civil parishes in the North York Moors

Rievaulx Abbey's granges in the Marishes contributed over a sixth of Pickering's total. Though the Vale of York suffered heavily from Scottish raids and the monks of Malton and Rosedale fled to Bridlington, the Vale of Pickering was spared after the defeat of the English army near Byland in 1322 because its representatives promised to pay a ransom and surrendered hostages. Earlier in that year the lord of Pickering, Thomas of Lancaster, had rebelled, been defeated at Boroughbridge and executed. Edward II rebuilt Pickering Castle, intending to retain it as a royal stronghold. The Black Death of 1349 also affected the population of the moors, considerably reducing the communities at Rievaulx and Byland, where 13th-century prosperity had resulted in splendid churches and domestic buildings, as also at Guisborough and Whitby.

Much of the North York Moors was regarded as forest, reserved as hunting grounds for the king, where hart and hind, boar and falcon were protected. Place-names with the Anglian 'wood' and 'weald' or the Scandinavian 'skew' or 'thwaite' indicate the greater past extent of woodland, among which the villagers of the Tabular Hills pastured sheep and pigs. In 1267 the royal Forest of Pickering was granted to the earls, later dukes, of Lancaster, though already the borough of Scarbo-

rough, founded in 1181, had been exempted from forest law. To the north the de Brus family of Egton and Danby had a forest in Eskdale and to the west the abbot of St Mary's, York, was granted the wood between Dove and Seven. Over thirty medieval deer parks in the area belonged to a variety of lords, from the abbots of Byland and Whitby to the barons de Ros of Helmsley with four; the best documented park is Blansby, north of Pickering (Rimington 1970–8). Records of duchy administration and proceedings in the forest courts (Turton 1894–7) give some idea of life under forest law. Red and fallow deer were plentiful until the 16th century among the numerous oaks and ashes: both venison and timber were frequently presented as gifts and poached or felled by local inhabitants. In the more fertile parts the woodland was constantly being nibbled away by assarts or clearings, like that around the abbot of Whitby's cowhouse at Goathland. There were also small industrial developments, including a quarry for millstones and tombstones on Cloughton Moor and iron prospecting in the Rosedale area. Salmon fishing in the Esk and Derwent was a privilege granted to gentry. However, the forest was still wild and secluded enough for hermits to seek its recesses, as did Edmund in Farndale (pre-1115), William of Dalby in Flaxdale (1323), and the austere Cistercians coming from Clairvaux to settle beside the Rye in 1131. Eventually, the confusion of the Civil War, when no regulations to protect deer and timber could be enforced, led to the disappearance of the game and further felling of the remaining oaks. A survey of 1661 (Turton 1894) shows how little was then left. The enclosure of Pickering in 1785 finally sealed the end of the forest, though since 1920 extensive planting of softwoods has again spread green on the map over much of the ancient hunting domain.

THE 16TH AND 17TH CENTURIES

At the dissolution of the monasteries, their estates came into the possession of prominent local families. The Challoners obtained Guisborough's property, the Cholmleys most of Whitby's, the Manners much of Rievaulx's lands, and the Bellasis family those of Byland and Newburgh. The great manor of Helmsley also came to the Manners, earls of Rutland, as heirs of the barons de Ros, and eventually to the Duke of Buckingham, who was also granted the Neville manor of Kirkbymoorside with its hunting lodge and park, forfeited to the Crown after the Rising of the North in 1569. The combined Helmsley, Kirkby and Rievaulx estate was bought in 1695 by Sir Charles Duncombe, a London banker, whose descendants, later earls of Feversham, thus owned over 39,000 acres in the west part of the moors and dominated the area. To the east the Cholmleys built up a smaller estate, based on Whitby, Fyling and duchy land in the Forest. To the north Danby was divided in 1655 among 168 sitting tenants, though the Dawnays retained the lordship of the manor and the castle.

These widespread changes in ownership caused the Crown, the Duchy of Lancaster and the other lords to have their estates surveyed; a series of these surveys survives from c. 1550 onwards, giving information on tenancies, acreages and rents. Thus there are surveys of the 1550s for the former Whitby Abbey estates of Goathland and Harwood Dale, of 1576 and 1610 for Kirkbymoorside, of 1609 and 1649 for Rosedale Priory's former possessions, of 1637 and 1651 for Bilsdale, and of 1651 for the Honour of Pickering (Willan 1932–4). Much of the land was then held by tenants occupying less than 15 acres, a state of affairs that on the conservative duchy and former Rievaulx estates had probably existed from medieval times. Units of 5, 6 and 10 acres seem to be medieval relics, as do terms of tenancies: in Bransdale the farms of Lofthouse and Motehouse were held for a broad arrow head and suit at the manor court. In Rosedale holdings were larger and more like modern farms, remaining little changed between the 17th century and the sale of the estate in 1829. Other details are given besides names of tenants and the extent and terms of their holdings: in Fadmoor there were two hemp garths, in Gillamoor a water-driven fulling mill, in Bilsdale in 1642 some 6000 oak and 1740 ash trees.

The first description to survive of places in the area, brief and limited though it is, was made by John Leland c. 1540. He remarked that most of the route from Scarborough to Pickering was by hill and dale 'most plentiful of corn and grass but little

wood in sight'. His notes on Pickering church and its dilapidated castle are accompanied by mentions of the extent of the parish 'to the very brows of Blackmore' and of Blansby Park, more than 7 miles in compass but not well wooded. In c. 1605 a visitor touring Sir Thomas Chaloner's lands, seeking potential mineral wealth, described Blackamore, 'which, by the ploughed lands and ruynes of houses in many places, seems to have bin well inhabyted, but nowe, in six or seven myles together, you shall scarcely fynd a house, except in a dale; the reste is heath, and a rouste for heath-cockes'. It might be ploughed and produce oats 'which benifyte for wante of industrious people is utterly loste, for in truth the skirts and wastes of the moor are in a manner desolate' (Nichols 1853: 407).

A dispute between two of the new owners of Byland Abbey land in 1598 produced the first large-scale plan of any part of the area, drawn by Christopher Saxton and showing Old Byland village with houses around a green, three open fields, cow pasture and boundary dykes. The oldest inhabitants recalled in evidence the abbot's flocks of sheep and boundary marks between his Wethercotes Farm and neighbouring properties (Beresford and St Joseph 1979: 159–61). Previously, even leading statesmen like Lord Burghley had had to manage with crude sketch maps, such as those surviving of the Yorkshire coast and Scarborough harbour (e.g., Rowntree 1931: 179, Fig. 40a), but Saxton's general map of the county in his atlas of 1579, followed in 1611 by Speed's more detailed map of the North Riding, show rivers, hills, villages and parks for the use of the administrator, landowner and traveller.

The people of the moors were affected by the two northern rebellions of 1536 and 1569: local supporters of the Pilgrimage of Grace were executed and the Earl of Westmorland's Kirkbymoorside estate, whence 114 tenants had followed him in the Rising of the North, was forfeited. The recurrent epidemics of the early 17th century were carried even to the isolated communities of the area: at Thornton in 1638, nineteen people, twice the usual annual average, died in seven weeks. Helmsley and Scarborough Castles were held for the king during the Civil War but Pickering was too ruinous to be considered worth garrisoning. Both fortresses surrendered to Parliamentary forces after sieges. After the king's defeat the royal and episcopal estates were sold, resulting in new surveys, giving a good idea of the state of Pickering Castle and showing the conservatism of the Church as a landowner, uninfluenced by southern agricultural theorists. After the Restoration the Duchy of Lancaster, the Archbishop and Dean of York all recovered their former possessions in the area.

Pockets of Catholic recusants persisted in Eskdale, on the Cholmley estates and around Gilling Castle and Newburgh Priory. Nicholas Postgate was a missionary priest for many years in the Egton area, before his execution in 1679. George Fox visited the area in 1651: his preaching resulted in meetings at Kirkby and Pickering. Disquiet felt by the government and bishops led to the making of reports on these nonconformists; the most comprehensive of these, the Compton Census of 1676, gives a rough idea of the numbers and distribution of population in the moors. It can be compared with the records made for the collection of the Hearth Tax from 1662 to 1689, giving the number and approximate size (from numbers of hearths) of houses in each township.

The hearth tax returns give a profile of the number of households in the region, including those chargeable and not chargeable, as well as an indication of the number and distribution of the upper social classes from peers down to vicars. They record the labouring classes, artisans, tradesmen and husbandmen by Christian names and surnames, occasionally mentioning a trade or craft. The upper social classes are recorded with added titles, as master, gentleman, esquire, sir or lord. The 1670 hearth tax for Yorkshire (Purdy 1975) reveals 0.3 per cent of all recorded households in the North Riding of Yorkshire as being of peers, baronets or knights, 0.3 per cent esquires, 0.05 per cent gentlemen. A further 2.3 per cent were masters, including small freeholders, yeomen, more substantial tenant farmers in the countryside and more prosperous tradesmen and manufacturers in towns. There were also a few clergy. Within the Moors region the proportions are still lower.

Relative prosperity is indicated by the number of hearths. In the whole of Yorkshire the North Riding had the highest proportion of houses with only one or two hearths and the lowest proportion with multiple hearths. In the North York Moors the figures were even more extreme. The majority of parishes in the region had more than three-quarters of their chargeable houses with only one hearth, and many had over 80 per cent. Cold Kirby and Pockley had 100 per cent.

Social and economic influences

THE YEOMEN

The farmhouses studied in later chapters were mostly occupied by yeomen, smallholders whose livelihood depended on cattle and sheep with some arable devoted to oats, rye and, later, to wheat. From the late 17th century onwards, the wills and inventories of their possessions, listed room by room, are a valuable source of information about the inhabitants of the North York Moors. Over 630 of such documents have been examined for the purposes of this study, dating between 1690 and 1780. Most are of yeomen, with their widows (63), and weavers (26) the other most numerous occupation. Less common are butchers (4 in each of the three towns), cordwainers or shoemakers (4 in Helmsley, 2 in Pickering), carpenters (2 and a cooper in Kirkbymoorside) and mariners or fishermen, found in the coastal parishes of Fylingdales and Hawsker. These documents provide details of the number of rooms in the moorland farmhouses, their contents, and of the farm animals and implements.

A yeoman's household goods were seldom valued by his neighbours on his death at more than £10, his purse and clothes at perhaps £3 and his husbandry gear at about £2, but his wealth lay in his 'quick goods' or livestock. Comparison between the average values of items in yeomen's inventories for Eskdale and the southern dales (Bilsdale, Farndale and Rosedale) show that up to 1730 the southern farmer was the richer but then there was little difference between averages for the two areas. Cattle constituted 36 to 40 per cent of the total value, sheep 18.7 per cent and horses about 7 per cent. The average yeoman had 8 to 12 cattle, mostly milch cows, a pair of oxen for ploughing and draught, one horse for riding, 25 to 52 sheep in Eskdale or 60 to 72 in the southern dales, a pig, a few beehives and sometimes some chickens. These averages may conceal flocks of up to 540 sheep and herds of 40 cattle, but one horse was the norm and more than four exceptional. Husbandry gear was usually limited to a waggon, a coup or cart, a plough and one or two harrows. It might also include sleds, yokes and teams (ox harness) and such tools as a gavelock or crowbar. Generally its value was only 4 to 5 per cent of the total, less than the deceased's clothes and ready money.

In Bilsdale, Helmsley and Kirkbymoorside, for which many inventories survive, the 18th-century yeoman's goods and livestock averaged £82 in value, a total often considerably reduced by debts and funeral expenses. In Pickering the average was only £25. However, legacies of £20 or more, even though payment was usually spread over several years, show that they expected a good return from their cattle, sheep and corn. Nevertheless there is a striking contrast between even a gentleman in Helmsley with a ten-roomed house and possessions valued at £510 and the area's principal landowner. When Thomas Duncombe Esquire died in 1741, he left legacies of £45,000, the Duncombe Park Estate, lands in Nottinghamshire and Leicestershire, houses in York and a mansion in Grosvenor Square. Most of his yeomen tenants had only £5 in their purses when they died and, as they conscientiously endeavoured to remember every relative in their wills, their legacies were in shillings rather than pounds.

When the smallholder of the moors made his will he was usually 'weak in body but of sound mind and memory', for he had put off this duty until struck down by his last and fatal illness. Rarely did a man describe himself as 'of perfect health of mind and body' or 'in old age'. The almost invariable opening 'In the name of God, Amen' with formal references to the Church of England and the Protestant religion seem conventional, but only two exceptions were noted: a request to be buried in a meeting-house yard and a legacy to a Nonconformist congregation. Bequests to the poor of a parish occur occasionally; one man left £5 to be divided among 'such of my neighbours as my executor shall apprehend most to want assistance'.

Usually yeomen in the North York Moors left their goods to their widow or eldest son, or died intestate with the same result. However, in one will the youngest of five sons was bequeathed all his father's land 'in consideration of his long and continued service and benefits done to me and his mother in our old decayed age after all my other sons left me'. A testator normally assumed that his widow would continue to run the farm with the help of a son until she married again. Meanwhile, she must have house room, fire and elding (fuel), clothing, and pasture for her stock. Sometimes her part of the house is specified: a parlour at the low end and half the garth behind. In other cases the eldest son, as principal heir, must build her new rooms or even a new house. If William Benley's widow and son could not agree to live together, 'he shall put up a chimney in the milk-house and she to have the chamber over it to live separate from him'. John Richardson of Brompton instructed his son 'to erect a house for my wife to enjoy for her life betwixt the end of my barn and the house where my daughter lives and a little piece of my hempyard to the south is to be taken off in a line from the north end of the said house'.

Of the houses in which possessions were listed and rooms named, just under half (246) consisted of two rooms – a fore-house and parlour – or three, with a dairy or chamber in addition to the normal two. A quarter had five rooms, the accommodation being increased by either two parlours or two chambers, and a fifth had four. Only forty-two had more than six rooms, most being in Helmsley, and there are occasional mentions of cellars, garrets and shops, usually meaning the workrooms of weavers or smiths. Outbuildings are usually assumed as present and only mentioned in the standard phrase 'corn in the house and corn in the barn', but the waggons and husbandry gear would have required shelter, as would the oxen which pulled them. It is rare to have an entry like 'in the yard a colehouse and coles, a hogsty and a hog, a necessary house'. The incidental mention in a will of 'the wain house' and 'the beasthouses' suggest that such buildings were more common than the inventories reveal.

Furniture in the yeoman's few rooms consisted of the same standard items, with every farmhouse similarly equipped. In the forehouse, the only heated room, used for cooking and eating, were a table on frames, a form, a few chairs, a long settle, and usually a dresser with pewter plates, wooden trenchers and pottery vessels. A clock, presumably of long-case type, was fairly usual. The fireplace had reckons (hooks for hanging cook-ing-pots), tongs, a kettle, a pot and a pan. The parlour seldom had more than a bed and bedstead, a linen chest and a couple of chairs. The chamber was similarly furnished but might contain corn or tools to be kept dry, though some chambers were solely reserved for storage. If there was a spinning wheel, a looking-glass or a chest of drawers, it would usually be in the parlour. The dairy or milkhouse held a churn, a kimlin or tub, skeels or milk pails, several bowls and stands to support them. The existence of this dairying equipment may imply the pre-sence of a milkhouse, even if it is not specifically mentioned.

Town houses had similar furniture but often had more parlours and chambers with a corresponding increase in beds and chests. Round or oval tables, corner cupboards and silver plate might be found there more frequently than in the country-side. The more detailed inventories of residents of Helmsley and Kirkbymoorside include lists of the stock in trade of men who might describe themselves as yeomen but clearly carried on business as weaver, haberdasher, draper or chapman: one such yeoman had 1532 hats worth £100. Weaver's looms, brewing equipment, smith's and carpenter's gear are the tools most frequently mentioned. A whitesmith at Rievaulx left to his three sons his best anvil, a grindstone, a vice made by one of them and 'all the iron and steall which is in the shop'.

The most detailed inventories of those examined for the area are of innkeepers at Helmsley and Hutton Buscel (see Chapter 6), a master mariner at Fylingdales, and a grocer at Rievaulx, all in houses with more than eight rooms but with goods ranging in value from £32 to £509. At Fylingdales in 1757 Phathuel Harrison, master and mariner, had a house with three ground-floor rooms, three above, garrets and a cellar, containing 4 beds, 6 tables, 16 chairs and less usual possessions: 26 books, a picture of 'The Taking of Cape Britain', 27 pistols and muskets, a drum and drumsticks, a coffee mill and 98 empty bottles. John Brusby of Rievaulx had in 1762 a house with three rooms on each floor, a cellar, warehouse and stable. Most of his personal estate of £168 lay in his stock as a grocer or chandler of soap, sugar, treacle, tobacco, wax, hams and Manchester ware. Mr Isaac Storm of Robin Hood's Bay by his will of 1763 left his nephew a set of mahogany furniture, consisting of bedstead, dining tables, escritoire and bookcase, and framed mirrors. His servant, Aggy Day, was to have the less valuable furnishings, clothes, food, fuel, cows, calves and hay.

Such well-furnished houses stand out as exceptions among the workaday farmhouses, as do unusual legacies among the normal gifts of clothes and small sums of money. Examples are a black silk negligee left with 18 pairs of sheets and £160 in cash by a widow at Hutton Buscel, or 'one old broad called by the name of Oliver broad and one other piece called a broad noble' (antique gold coins), left with silver spoons, tankard and watch by an innholder at Helmsley. Sometimes furniture was to stay with a house as heirlooms, no doubt because they were fixtures, like a close bed and cupboard in a house at Gillamoor and a clock, panelling, shelves and press at Howlwoods, Helmsley.

Few people possessed any books other than 'a great Bible' and perhaps a prayer book, though a house carpenter in 1783 had 'three volumes of the Dictionary of Arts and Sciences'. If the ability to sign their wills is evidence for their literacy, under half the yeomen in the area, and even fewer of their wives, could write. However, the proportion signing gradually increased during the course of the 18th century. The printed will forms supplied to seamen on warships, as for HMS *Newark* in 1686 or *Defiance* in 1750, had only small spaces where a gentleman's son from Spaunton and a fisherman from Fyling-dales entered details of their heirs and scanty legacies.

A yeoman of Bilsdale or Danby might consider himself wealthy enough, with fat beasts in his closes and good horses in his stable, to leave a long will with complicated provisions for passing on his goods to his large family; his neighbours, men of similar standing, might value his possessions at £80, a labourer's pay for several years. Yet his house would show few signs of comfort or culture, for there was seldom more than one change of bed linen or tablecloths, few cushions, books, pictures or musical instruments, and only rarely even one warming-pan. He and his family ate rye bread and oatcake off wooden tren-chers and pewter plates, stewed or roasted their meat over an open peat fire in iron pots or on spits, and drank their ale from earthenware mugs or pewter tankards, for china cups and teapots appear nowhere among their household goods.

In 1750 many of the townships along the southern edge of the region either still retained open fields or had possessed them not long before; a few showed no sign of having had them just before this date. This last group included Rievaulx and Wykeham where, in the presence of an abbey, they may never have existed, and Cawthorne, Kingthorpe and Skiplam, all shrunken villages perhaps enclosed earlier. The position was different further north, in the tributary dales of the Esk, Rye and Derwent, where open fields were the exception at this date. The landscape of these dales, with small to moderately sized fields in the dale bottoms, sometimes larger on the moorland edge, has changed little since 1750, but that of the then unenclosed parishes is very different, the open, hedgeless lands of the open fields having given way to regular, hedged fields. Moorland enclosure acts were more numerous than others in this southern area, and their provisions were both compulsory and permissive. The period 1750 to 1850 was one of great agricultural expansion in the region, but it was not consistent, depending a great deal on the stimulus of an enclosure act to give it momentum. The principal motive in the majority of cases was to permit reclamation for agricultural purposes and then improvement. Grouse-shooting rights became of value only in the 19th century (Chapman 1961, 1976).

Enclosure had a number of effects on buildings. By rearranging former open fields into self-contained private land units, or by dividing formerly common but uncultivated land into private property, it generally resulted in either the immediate or gradual establishment of new isolated farmsteads out in the fields away from the village. A social consequence of enclosure was to reduce smallholders eking out the produce of their plots to wage labour (Hobsbawn 1969: 102), and this, coupled with the need for extra labour on the new farms, caused a growth in the number of cottages, principally in towns and villages. These cottages appear both as purpose-built dwellings and as conversions of former farmhouses made redundant by enclosure farmsteads.

Particular examples of enclosure can be studied. Three, in Pockley, Helmsley and Beadlam, are on the Helmsley estate held by Charles Duncombe from 1803 to 1841. Pockley Grange [437] stands on what in 1785 was part of Pockley Common but which by 1822 was a farmstead comprising two parallel ranges of buildings. High and Middle Baxtons Farms, Helmsley [239, 240], stand on what in 1792 was called Baxtons Pasture. They were established by an enclosure award of 1816 under acts of 1806 and 1814, and both appear on a map of 1822. At Beadlam an act of 1817 and award of 1819 deal with moorland enclosure. Most of the land was owned by the Helmsley estate, and a plan of 1818 shows the divisions intended for the whole. These differ little from those on a map of 1819 but for the extent of afforestation. Charles Duncombe seems initially to have intended combining the area into one centrally placed farm, but by 1854 there were three farms, Higher, Middle and Lower Farm, Beadlam [22, 23], all but Lower Farm evidently starting as isolated farm buildings which subsequently became self-contained farmsteads.

From the late 18th century, sources of information increase greatly in quantity and quality, including the first national census returns, reports on agriculture, industry and health, better statistics on crime and poverty, fuller newspaper reports on social and political movements, and the first Ordnance Survey maps, surpassing in accuracy and detail anything previously available, even Thomas Jefferys' map of 1775. For the North York Moors, the agricultural writers, Arthur Young (1770), William Marshall (1788) and John Tuke (1800), historians of Whitby (Charlton 1779; Young 1817), Ryedale (Eastmead 1824) and Cleveland (Ord 1846), together with Canon Atkinson's memoir of life in Danby (1891), add life and colour to the statistics. Recent studies of the social history of North Yorkshire in this period (Hastings 1981, 1982) have used these varied sources and are the basis of the following paragraphs.

In 1800 a third of the North Riding of Yorkshire was uncultivated land, of which about half was in the eastern moorlands where approximately a fifth of the riding's total population of 160,000 lived. They were largely employed in agriculture on small farms devoted to raising sheep and cattle, the small amount of arable being used for oats and some wheat. During the previous thirty years the open fields of the Vale of Pickering had been enclosed: the resulting landscape with hedgerow trees led one observer to complain that 'at a little distance the Vale has the appearance of an uncleared forest' (Salmon 1981: 47). The agricultural labourer of the area had better conditions than in the south of England with a more varied and nutritious diet, including more milk and cereals, and wages over a third higher. Though to Tuke and Atkinson housing seemed poor and uncomfortable, the average number of people in a house in Ryedale and Pickering Lythe wapentakes was only five, even if a tenth of families shared accommodation.

The labourers of the area were better provided with access to education than those of most agricultural counties in the Midlands or south: in 1818 Ryedale and Pickering Lythe each had fifty schools, providing one place for every two or three children though few were large or of the architectural distinction of Lady Lumley's at Thornton Dale (c. 1666). By 1851 day schools in the Helmsley area were attended by 56.2 per cent of children and by 45.7 per cent in the Pickering area, though schooling was sacrificed to farm work in harvest time or whenever there was an opportunity to earn any money. By this time their parents' literacy, judged from signatures in marriage registers, was higher: 77 per cent of men and 60 per cent of their wives.

Emigration of North Yorkshiremen hoping for a better life overseas started in the 1770s and settlers went from Danby and Westerdale, from Lastingham and Rievaulx to Canada and the United States, resulting in the place-names of Pickering, Whitby and Burlington Bay in Ontario, whence emigrants wrote describing their new life in glowing terms. Others seeking work settled in Whitby, which grew to have a population of 10,000 by 1800 and was by 1830 still the ninth port in England according to registered tonnage (it had been the sixth in 1706), with some 280 ships and over 2500 seamen. Trades connected with the sea

– such as sailmaking and shipbuilding (about twenty-five ships were built there a year) – were better paid than any in farming. Two farmer's sons achieved fame by sailing from Whitby: James Cook from Marton in Cleveland and William Scoresby from Cropton. Firkin tubs of butter from Eskdale and Cleveland had been exported through Whitby at least from the 17th century, a trade being replaced by 1800 with that of the export of hams and bacon, also for the London market.

In 1801 about 9 per cent of the North Riding's total population were receiving poor relief, but bad harvests and a fall in agricultural prices led to a sharp increase so that by 1831 perhaps a quarter were living in poverty. Expenditure on poor relief rose correspondingly until the North Riding spent the seventh largest amount of any English county for this purpose. Riots, arson and machine-breaking in Norfolk and Lincolnshire caused by the dismal condition of agricultural workers perhaps encouraged North Yorkshire landowners to greater efforts in help for the poor, supplementing the charities of long-dead benefactors, as Lady Lumley's in Thornton or Samuel Rabanke's in Danby. Labourers themselves also contributed to friendly societies providing members with sick allowances and funeral payments; by 1802 these existed in Helmsley, Kirkbymoorside and Pickering. However, less was spent from public funds on the poor in the North York Moors than elsewhere in the riding, due to the reluctance of small farmers and tenants to help those they regarded as feckless. In most larger villages a small workhouse was established, as at Fylingdales, housing the helpless poor and aged, but outside relief was preferred.

THE COMING OF INDUSTRY

During the late 18th and early 19th centuries, rural industries briefly flourished in the moors and as rapidly declined. Iron-working on a small scale had been practised intermittently from the late Iron Age and the monasteries of Guisborough and Rievaulx operated forges to utilize the ironstone found on their lands. Some twenty medieval ironworking sites, identified from mounds of slag, are known in the area; 13th-century smelting hearths have been excavated at Baysdale and Goathland. In the 1570s the Earl of Rutland developed the monastic forge at Rievaulx into a large-scale industrial enterprise with a blast furnace producing some 280 tons of iron in 1624; it continued in operation until 1674. From 1836 ironstone was mined at Grosmont and from 1856 to 1926 rich seams were worked on both sides of Rosedale, producing 1500 tons a day in 1873, while smaller mines were opened in Newton Dale and on Blakey Ridge.

Although coal working is recorded near Dalby in 1342 and in Hartoft parish in 1583, the thin seams were not generally exploited until about 1770, when they were mined at several places in Bilsdale, Bransdale, Danby and Farndale. The coal was worked from shallow pits: the largest group was on Rudland Rigg in Farndale West, where over 225 are arranged in parallel rows. The nearby pits at Harland Head were worked until 1926. Much of the coal was sold to lime burners on the Tabular Hills and returning carts carried back lime to improve the poor moorland soils. Lime was exploited by farmers for use on the land and from the 18th century was a constituent of mortar. It was produced on a larger scale for public supply at a few places, such as Lockton (Young 1817: 818).

The shales of the Upper Lias rocks were quarried to produce alum near Guisborough from 1607, but the main alum works were on the coastal cliffs at Boulby, continuing until 1867. There was also production further south, on the Fylingdales cliffs and inland near Sleights. The Eskdaleside works, founded by John Yeoman in 1764, provided the wealth for his purchase and rebuilding later in the century of Woodlands [4]. In most of the small dales, lines of small heaps mark the level where jet outcrops. In Bilsdale Midcable parish, for instance, Kyloe Cow Beck is only one of fifteen sites of jet workings. Such shallow, small-scale mines were worked from about 1850 until 1900, often by unemployed fishermen, and the raw material made into ornaments by craftsmen in Whitby, the main centre of the industry.

The abundant limestone and sandstone of the region has long been used for building; small disused quarries appear near many isolated farms on the first OS 6 inch maps. Larger quarries at Appleton-le-Moors and Thornton Dale are still worked. The gritstones of the moors were used for querns and grindstones, as on Spaunton Moor. Clay pits were dug in the 19th century south of Pickering and Kirkbymoorside, supplying brick and tile works as at Kirkby Mills. Glass was made for a time (c. 1570–93) at Scugdale in Rosedale by French immigrants. The peat bogs of the high moors were used as a source of fuel from medieval times, and within living memory 'most houses in the dales burnt nothing but turf and peat' (Hartley and Ingilby 1972: 81); it was still dug at three places in Danby and Egton in 1979.

Weaving of woollen cloth had long been a local cottage industry and there was some linen weaving both in Cleveland and in the Kirkbymoorside and Helmsley area, where it had been encouraged by the Duncombes. By 1817 Whitby had three firms with 109 looms manufacturing 5000 yards of sailcloth weekly, much in demand during the naval wars. By this time hemp growing was probably unusual, since flax could be imported in quantity through Whitby, Stockton and Hull. Bleach mills existed in 1818 at Commondale, Glaisdale, Kildale, Lease Rigg in Egton, at Costa Mills near Pickering and at Ellerburn. Attempts to introduce cotton spinning near Loftus failed, and by 1823 the linen and woollen weaving industry of the North York Moors had been destroyed by West Riding competition.

During the early 19th century, horse-wheels providing power to drive threshing machines, were introduced to the dales. These relieved men from the laborious work of threshing with flails, still used in places up to the 1930s. As machinery was gradually introduced on local farms, small foundries were established, often by millwrights, to make such wheels and threshing machines, iron ploughs, and later, turnip cutters, mowing machines, kitchen ranges and frying pans. Implement makers established at Whitby and Wrelton by the 1840s were followed by three firms at Pickering and others at Kirkby. Iron ploughs were also produced at Fangdale Beck in Bilsdale from 1874 to 1925, at Ruswarp, Ugthorpe and Wombleton. One firm, Russells of Kirkbymoorside, still operating at the time of the survey as agricultural engineers, was started in the 1850s by a blacksmith from the Thirsk area. They repaired threshing machines and water mills, made drills and vehicles, and more recently manufactured harvesters and elevators.

As well as introducing machinery, progressive landlords and farmers experimented with new crops. Both open fields and extensive common moors were enclosed during the 18th century, as at Lastingham in 1788 and Pickering in 1789. Potatoes were first seen in Kirkdale in 1715 and turnips were introduced c. 1770. By 1801 the newly introduced rape occupied a third of the acreage in Harome and Wykeham parishes, supplying an oilseed mill at Kirkby which operated from c. 1795. Tobacco was grown in Ryedale in 1782, presumably because supplies from America were interrupted. More fruit trees and soft fruit bushes were planted in gardens and small orchards in the less exposed villages on the edge of the Vale of Pickering; a gooseberry show at Egton Bridge has been an annual event since 1800. Rabbit farming was tried as a way of utilizing the poor moorland pasture and extensive warrens existed for a time at Allerston, Scamridge, Troutsdale and elsewhere; similar experiments were made on the thin wolds soils of the East Riding.

THE GROWTH OF COMMUNICATIONS

During the 18th century the road system of the area was considerably improved, enabling its products of wool, cloth, cheese and corn to be moved more easily to the local markets and further afield to the ports of Whitby and Hull. The principal road serving the area runs along the north side of the Vale of Pickering, linking Helmsley, Kirkby and Pickering to Scarborough as it passes through the string of similarly sited villages. The moors are skirted on the east by a coastal road from Scarborough to Whitby, on the north by a route from Whitby to Guisborough and on the west by that from Thirsk to Stockton. They are crossed by a major road from Whitby to Pickering and by lesser roads up Bilsdale to Stokesley and up Rosedale to Castleton and Danby. Because of the nature of the terrain, split by steep-sided valleys running north–south for up to 20 kilometres, east–west communications across the moors were non-existent. Most routes followed the ridges between the once boggy and wooded valleys and, though steep and narrow, enabled farmers from Danby or Egton to travel south. In some places tracks were paved for the use of panniermen or pack animals. Hambleton Street along the western lip of the scarp down to the Vale of York was an important route in the 18th and 19th centuries for Scottish drovers bringing cattle to markets in Malton or York. The names given to two stretches of road, Saltergate near the Hole of Horcum, mentioned in 1335, and Chop Gate (chapman's road) in Bilsdale, recall their use by salt merchants and pedlars.

To improve the principal routes turnpike trusts were set up, first for the road from York to Scarborough via Malton in 1752,

followed in 1764 by that for the road from Whitby to Lockton Lane north of Pickering, in 1765 by the Malton to Pickering road trust, and in 1768 by the York to Oswaldkirk turnpike, linked to Helmsley by a road built by Thomas Duncombe. Here, as elsewhere in Yorkshire, new bridges were provided, many designed by John Carr, as at Hawnby, Helmsley and Rievaulx. Before the construction of the turnpike road on a new line to the west, Whitby was relatively inaccessible: 'all the roads lay in a state rough, rugged, uneven; it was dangerous for a man on horseback to come into the town in the Winter season . . . but more so for any laden carriage to approach the place' (Charlton 1779: 338). The Cholmleys of Whitby were the principal agents in getting this road built, as was Lord Fairfax for the York to Oswaldkirk road. These improved roads enabled regular diligence and mail coach services to run between Whitby and York. The lesser roads were still maintained by parishes; Tuke considered the condition of those in southern Ryedale to be very poor in comparison with the well-drained parish roads in Cleveland.

The first railway in the area, designed by George Stephenson and opened in 1836, ran from Whitby to Pickering, with carriages drawn by horses or, up steep inclines, by cable. This new transport facility enabled an American skipper recalled home at Whitby in 1841 to reach Liverpool on the same day to catch a trans-Atlantic steamer (Granville 1841: 197). Steam replaced horse-power in 1847 and, though the line was closed in 1965, it has been operated from Pickering to Goathland since 1969 by the private North York Moors Railway Company. The line from York to Scarborough via Malton, opened in 1845, still operates as does that along Eskdale from Middlesbrough to Whitby, but routes from Kirkbymoorside to Pickering, Seamer to Pickering, and Scarborough to Whitby, opened respectively in 1875, 1882 and 1885, only functioned for some seventy-five years. Other routes never completed were the Lastingham and Rosedale Light Railway (1902) and a line from Brotton to Glaisdale (1875). A mineral line laboriously constructed along the moor tops from Easby to Rosedale climbed to 427 metres: it was opened in 1861 to serve the prospering ironstone mines and closed in 1929. A narrow gauge tramway in the dale was abandoned by 1879. Light railways also operated from 1915 to 1920 on Brompton and Wykeham Moors to move felled timber before reafforestation.

Canals might not be expected, in view of the topography, yet one was projected from Whitby to Pickering and another from Scarborough to Helmsley. The Derwent Navigation, set up by an Act of 1702, was flourishing by 1793, with thirty-five ships employed in carrying coal to Malton, and later extended to Yedingham Bridge. A short cut beside the Esk at Whitby enabled ships to reach a mill. Otherwise the narrow, fast-flowing becks were used to power corn mills, some later used to produce paper, as at Ellerburn, or for fulling, but there was no possibility of navigating the Esk or the upper Derwent. However, from 1747 onwards remarkable watercourses were made to supply villages in Ryedale with fresh water from springs up to 20 kilometres to the north. Joseph Foord, a surveyor of Kirkbymoorside, laid out these open clay-lined channels carrying the supply across the northern scarp of the Tabular Hills to Carlton, Gillamoor, Griff, Helmsley and other places. The last of these watercourses still in use was replaced by piped water in 1960.

The development of the region in the 19th century

LANDOWNERS, LABOURERS AND FARMING

The Duncombe Park Estate had been extended by six generations of the family from the nucleus bought by the London merchant Sir Charles Duncombe in 1695 until, in 1873, when the 'new Domesday Book' of owners of land was published, William Ernest Duncombe, Earl of Feversham and Viscount Helmsley (d. 1915) owned 39,312 acres with a gross rental of £34,326 (Landowners 1873). In Yorkshire this estate was only exceeded in extent by that of Lord Londesborough, spread over the three ridings, and rivalled by that in the Wolds acquired since 1750 by the Sykes family of Sledmere. The mansion of Duncombe Park had been built in 1718 to replace the ruined Helmsley Castle and set in an extensive deer park. In the late 18th century Arthur Young had commented unfavourably on the estate, observing that 'the roads Mr Duncombe has made in this country are in the true style of magnificence', but noting the 'surprising smallness of the farms which compose this gentleman's estate'. All were capable of very great improvement, even to doubling the rents. He felt it worthy of remark that 'the husbandry of these farmers is universally bad; their fields in a slovenly condition, and of so little encouragement to them is the lowness of their rents, that many large tracts of land that yielded good crops of corn, within thirty years are now overrun with whims, brakes and other trumpery. The farmers are a poor wretched set of people'. He urged raising rents, 'first with moderation, and if that does not bring forth industry, double them. But if you would have a vigorous culture go forwards, throw fifteen or twenty of these farms into one, as fast as the present occupiers drop off. This is the only means in such cases to improve husbandry, and consequently to promote population' (Young 1771: Vol. 2 76–88). The Duncombes did subsequently put money into enclosure in this area, notably on the limestone plateau running east from Helmsley to Nawton, but they left the villages to decline. These villages, particularly Pockley, Beadlam and Harome, contain, or did before recent rebuilding, more single-storey, stone-walled, cruck-built, thatched former longhouses than perhaps the whole of the remainder of the region. Though heavy death duties in the 20th century caused the sale of outlying parts and the house has recently been used for a school, the estate still remains a dominant landholding in Ryedale.

Other large landowners in the area in 1873 were Sir Digby Cayley of Brompton with 7785 acres, the Revd J. R. Hill of Pickering with 7632 acres and Sir Harry van den Bempde Johnstone of Hackness (later Baron Derwent) with 7238 acres.

Viscount Downe owned Wykeham Abbey and with his lady held 35,725 acres in the North and East Ridings, but his principal seat was Baldersby Park, near Thirsk. Another twelve people or organizations had estates of over 1000 acres in the North York Moors, including the Rosedale and Ferryhill Iron Company with 2231 and the Duchy of Lancaster, once pre-eminent in Pickering, but now with only 1144 acres.

Three landed gentlemen, contrasting in personality, have left autobiographical material concerning the district. William Marshall of Pickering (1745–1818) had farmed in Surrey, worked in Norfolk and the West Indies and promoted the foundation of the Board of Agriculture. His *Rural Economy of Yorkshire* (1788) contains a useful account of conditions in the Vale and moorlands and ideas for improvements. A farm at Beck Isle, now a museum, was modified for his agricultural training college. George Osbaldeston of Hutton Buscel (1786–1866) bought the Ebberston estate in 1807 for £50,000 and enlarged the house built in 1718 by Colen Campbell. His main interests were hunting, shooting and horse racing. Debts from these expensive hobbies absorbed the income from the estate, where he fruitlessly sought coal deposits, and he was forced to sell it in 1848 for £190,000 (Cuming 1926). His neighbour at Brompton, Sir George Cayley (1773–1857), made copious notes on farming matters, improved his estate, experimenting with whale blubber as fertilizer and promoting agricultural allotments and cow insurance schemes for poorer labourers. He is best known for his scientific interests and as an aeronautical pioneer: the first successful man-carrying glider conveyed his hesitant coachman across Brompton Dale in 1853. Sir George was MP for Scarborough, organized an agricultural society for the Hackness area and helped to found the British Association and the Regent Street Polytechnic (Pritchard 1961).

The great agricultural depression of the 1880s shook the structure of rural society and created a feeling of unending calamity (cf. Mingay 1977). Some idea of farming conditions in the area following the depression and before recent recollection is provided by two general surveys, one more from the point of view of landowners and agents (Haggard 1902: 242–380), the other concerned with the living conditions of labourers (Rowntree and Kendall 1913). Rider Haggard found Yorkshire more prosperous than other parts of England and his informants reasonably hopeful. At Sinnington the many smallholdings of about 20 acres had weathered the depression quite well but a drift of workers to the West Riding industrial towns had depopulated such villages as Great Barugh and Salton. On the Duncombe estate each village had several cow-keepings of about 4 acres at annual rents of £8 to £10, including a cottage. Beekeeping was practised in the Pickering area to a greater extent than anywhere else in England, producing clover and heather honey from moorland flowers. Local farmers complained of a lack of labour and claimed to be willing to pay sufficient wages to keep their labourers in reasonable plenty and comfort. Haggard contrasted this with Rowntree's 1899 report on severe poverty among the working class not far away in York.

A land agent at Guisborough told him that, though cottages

had been much improved recently, their cost was 'absolutely prohibitive to allow of their being erected with any other view than to meet the necessity for them'. This observation may be set against statistics collected sixty years earlier by W. C. Copperthwaite of Malton, when a good four-roomed stone cottage with tiled roof could be erected for £35. The average cottage in Old Malton was then described as very old, roofed with thatch, occupying a large area on the ground floor and sometimes with an attic in the roof, usually rented for about 50s. per annum (Salmon 1981: 53).

Rowntree's examples of North Yorkshire farm labourers' income, expenditure and menus show that they were certainly not living in plenty and comfort. The labourer's average weekly pay was 19s.10d., well above that in Oxfordshire, where he received only 14s.11d., though below wages in Durham. Rowntree may have underestimated the contribution made by part-time work, perquisites of the job, or garden produce (mostly potatoes), but his gloomy picture of how the labourer lived is supported by detailed budgets. Most of the weekly wage went on food, largely bread and potatoes with what little meat that could be afforded going to the man of the family, so that women and children were undernourished. Some money had somehow to be saved for the annual rent of £3 10s. One farm worker clothed his four children by rearing two pigs for sale, but another was still paying off a doctor's bill incurred four years before, helped by older children out in service. None of the families studied could afford to spend more than 6d. a week on such luxuries as tobacco or postage. Books, newspapers and rail travel were beyond their means and ale was another luxury, though a farmer was expected to provide a pint or two daily for each of his workers. One man, paid 16s. a week, said that it was too expensive to go to church or chapel; their attitude towards the churches was one of 'indifference, if not half-resentful scorn'.

Rowntree describes these labourers' tiny, dark, damp, two to four-roomed thatched cottages and details their scraps of furniture. He found that the relationship between masters and men was deteriorating with the workers complaining that their employers were not interested in them, yet could buy themselves luxuries, and the farmers feeling that a cattleman who wanted a Sunday off work after two years without free weekends was being unreasonable. The dispiriting monotony which accompanied the farm workers' habitual poverty meant that no future was foreseen on the land by men who had little faith in politics to change their immemorial lot.

Recent developments

Until the 1930s each moorland dale contained a series of small farms which had existed since the 17th century, where in some cases the same tenant families had lived for centuries. The moorland farmer still lived a life which, in spite of more mechanical aids, was much more like that of his 18th-century predecessor than is that of his present-day son or grandson. Memories and records enable this traditional way of life of the immediate past to be recalled. Reminiscences and photographs can illumine such aspects as farmhouse economy, rural trades, peat cutting, thatching and transport (Hartley and Ingilby 1972; Mitchell 1981). More recently, however, great changes have taken place; moorland strays, higher pastures and isolated dale-head farms have been abandoned to heather; farms have been amalgamated, becoming fewer and larger. The total population has fallen by 11 per cent since 1901 and the number of those employed in farming has been reduced by 45 per cent, between 1951 and 1974. Since 1920 the Forestry Commission has planted with softwoods much of the medieval Forest of Pickering, some 288 square kilometres and a quarter of the moorland has been converted to forestry or agriculture since 1950. Tourism has become an important source of employment in addition to the traditional agriculture and forestry. The old farms and cottages are therefore liable to be drastically modernized and transformed.

CHAPTER 2

HOUSES OF THE GENTRY

Within the region there is little surviving physical evidence of medieval secular buildings. No more than eight or nine standing structures, some of them ruinous, appear to be earlier in date than the middle of the 16th century. To these can be added about another seventeen sites with conspicuous earthworks or where medieval fragments or foundations have been recognized or uncovered by excavation. A few houses are known only from documents, such as a capital messuage at Thornton Dale which was in ruins in 1380 (VCH 1923: 492). This paucity of actual remains is in marked contrast to the counties of south-east England where an average parish may contain at least two or three medieval houses. A comparison may be made with another northern, mainly upland, area. The county of Westmorland was systematically surveyed in the 1930s. In an area less than twice the size of the North York Moors, fifty-six secular buildings, including castles, were described as still standing to some degree (RCHM 1936). In the North York Moors the existing remains are nearly all of buildings associated with powerful interests, either magnates or monastic institutions, rather than of smaller manor houses, and this reflects the pattern of land ownership in the medieval period dominated by a few extensive estates.

The medieval period

MONASTIC GRANGES

Quite large parts of the region were monastic lands from the 12th century onwards. The principal abbeys which had possessions in the moorland area were Whitby, principally along the coastal strip, and Rievaulx, which had acquired most of Bilsdale and parts of Farndale and Bransdale by 1170, and also had a concentration of lands in the Vale of Pickering (Waites 1959–62a, 1959–62b, 1967). The sites of some granges are identifiable as earthworks, such as those of Rievaulx at New Leys and Skiplam, and there are standing remains of an aisled barn at Murton, a grange of Byland Abbey close to the western edge of the moors. An 'ancient grange house' at Rievaulx Abbey's Newstead Grange, Thornton Dale, was mentioned in a document of 1647

(Borthwick: C. C. Ab8/2) but it is only at Laskill in Bilsdale, another grange of Rievaulx, that more positive evidence of the actual form of a domestic building has come to light.

The remains at Laskill, although scanty, are sufficient to indicate a structure about 19 metres by 9 metres, with a later extension. Stone wall foundations were uncovered in 1949; these are now lost or covered up but bases for a central row of three columns are still visible. The plan is very similar to that of the lower storey of Burton Agnes Old Manor House, Humberside, and to a building excavated at Wharram Percy, North Yorkshire, which has been interpreted as a lower stage supporting a first-floor *camera* (Andrews and Milne 1979). Architectural fragments at Laskill include parts of stone vaulting and details such as a capital and fragments of external corbelling datable to around 1200. If these belong to the same building whose foundations are known, then it would appear to have been very similar not only in form but also in date to the houses mentioned above, especially to Burton Agnes where the lower storey is vaulted, though the Laskill building is much larger. There is no actual evidence of domestic use such as a chimney or latrine, but the outer wall was not completely recovered. If it was a *camera* it was certainly on a remarkable scale. Laskill Grange is not well documented, but in the Lay Subsidy of 1301 it was assessed at the comparatively low figure of 17s.5¼d. It has been suggested that the wool house of Rievaulx was at this site (McDonnell 1963: 116); an adjacent farm is called Woolhouse Croft. In 1323 Edward II spent a night at 'Glascowollehouse' (NRRS III: 225). This seems to refer to Laskill and the building conjectured above would have provided suitable accommodation for a royal lodging.

AISLED HALLS

One other building of a monastic nature of which a part survives is Foulbridge, Snainton [477]. This was the site of a preceptory of the Knights Templars until the suppression of the order in 1311, and it was subsequently handed to the Hospitallers. Within the present extensive farmhouse is the basic timber structure of an aisled hall at least three bays in length (Figs. 4–6). The aisles no longer exist, but evidence for them is provided by mortices in the outer faces of the arcade posts. The

Fig. 4 [477] Foulbridge, Snainton: hall interior looking W.

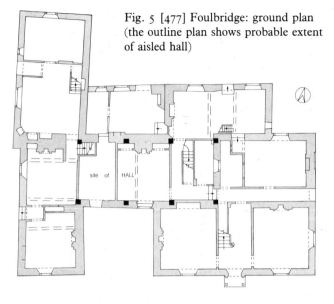

Fig. 5 [477] Foulbridge: ground plan (the outline plan shows probable extent of aisled hall)

site of HALL

outer walls were probably built of stone and part of the west wall may be original. The hall was obviously of considerable size and if the aisles were half the main span, which is a common proportion, the total width would have been 9 or 10 metres. At the west end there seems to have been a cross-wing, but nothing is known about how the building terminated at the east end.

Dendrochronology has provided a date of *c.* 1288, which places erection towards the end of the Templars' occupation (report by W. G. Simpson, 1983). An inventory made in 1308 mentioned a hall with five tables and a chamber with one great chest and two little chests (PRO: E.142/18). This hall is no doubt the same one of which remains still stand, with the chamber probably in the cross-wing.

No other aisled halls are known for certain within the region, but there is strong evidence that there was one at Canons Garth,

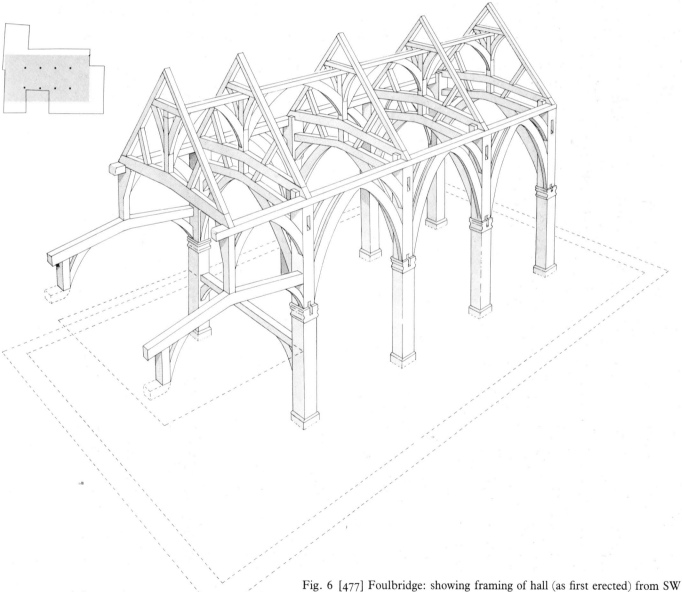

Fig. 6 [477] Foulbridge: showing framing of hall (as first erected) from SW

Fig. 7 [187] Canons Garth, Helmsley: from S.

Helmsley [187] (Figs. 7, 8). This house stands just to the north-east of the parish church and is now the vicarage; this was probably also the original use, though after the medieval period it was not in continuous ownership of the church. Its structure is of several periods, not all of which are readily datable. The earliest phase is now represented only by the roof over the central part. The roof itself is not complete, nor is very much of it now visible, but enough can be seen to show that it has features which may be dated to the late 13th or early 14th century. There are two trusses which must have covered a hall at least three bays in length. Everything below them is of later date, the stone walls being perhaps of the 17th century.

The church at Helmsley was appropriated to Kirkham Priory, so both Foulbridge and Canons Garth were built under the patronage of religious orders. They are the only two known buildings in the region to have crown-post roof trusses and they both exhibit sophisticated framing techniques. The span of the Helmsley roof is slightly more than at Foulbridge and the length of bay about the same. If both halls were actually aisled and of three bays they would each seem to have been about 10 metres square, a similar size to two other roughly contemporary halls in North Yorkshire: the Old Hall at Spennithorne and Baxby Manor House, Husthwaite (Harrison and Hutton 1984: 21). As at Canons Garth, the roof trusses at Baxby have double tie-beams separated by arcade plates, but the central truss was supported by base-crucks. The combination of base-crucks and double tie-beams is also found elsewhere, such as at 19 Thorpe-acre, Loughborough, Leicestershire (Rickman 1968: 150–3); at

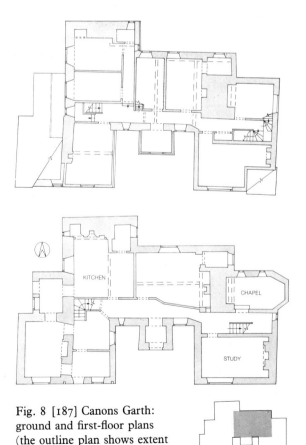

Fig. 8 [187] Canons Garth: ground and first-floor plans (the outline plan shows extent of surviving medieval roof)

18

Canons Garth, however, the details indicate that aisle posts were the probable form of construction.

The largest medieval halls in the region must have been those in the castles at Pickering and Helmsley. Both castles are now ruined and the halls represented only by foundations or low walls. At Pickering, a royal castle that passed eventually to the Duchy of Lancaster, there were two adjacent halls, though the earlier one probably went out of use soon after the later one was built (Thompson 1958). The Old Hall was built before the stone curtain wall was erected next to it in 1180–7. The foundations show that it was 15 metres by 6 metres and therefore not aisled. The New Hall, nearly twice the size of the old one, is known from the accounts to have been built in 1314–15 (PRO: D.L.29/1/3). It is said to have had a chamber within and in 1619–21 Norden referred to it as being of timber-framed ('post-and-pan') construction, and mentioned that the 'upper part . . . above the postes . . . is so ruynous' which suggests that it could have been two storeyed (Turton 1894: 27). It is difficult to reconcile this with the surviving remains which are those of a conventionally planned, though large, stone-built hall. The posts may have divided the hall into aisles as the width of 13 metres would be large for a single roof span.

At Helmsley Castle the hall stands to no more than one or two courses above ground level. There is no definite dating evidence but one distinctive feature is a boldly projecting buttress on the north-east wall, which has proportions unlikely before the 14th century. It may not be greatly different in date from the New Hall at Pickering; it was also of very similar size and was likewise placed against the curtain wall, though there is no hint here of a two-storeyed structure. With a width of 14 metres an aisled construction also seems probable, but with an aisle only on the south-west side as the three service doorways in the south-east wall are placed off-centre.

If the New Hall at Pickering was actually two storeyed, the probable form of heating would be from fireplaces in the side walls, but though there is a recess in the north-west wall it is not shaped like a fireplace and shows no sign of burning. Central open hearths would be expected at Helmsley Castle and Canons Garth, and the existence of one at Foulbridge is confirmed by smoke-blackening on the roof timbers.

Another large hall within a castle, which from its size is likely to have been aisled, was at Cropton, where immediately to the east of the motte are grass-covered foundations of extensive domestic buildings. The site has never been excavated but there appears to have been a hall about 18 metres by 11 metres with further bays at each end which are likely to have been two storeyed; extensions, probably of later date, created a building with a total length of about 50 metres. A date of c. 1290–5 has been suggested, though without any firm evidence, when John, Lord Wake, held the manor (I'Anson 1913: 344).

A possible aisled hall of a different character from the other buildings mentioned above is the so-called Manor House, Helmsley [209] (Fig. 9). Its name is not of great antiquity and the earliest known mention of it is in the 17th century as an inn. It stands directly on the street frontage of Castlegate and the actual evidence for an aisled structure is small, limited to a

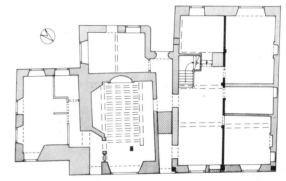

Fig. 9 [209] Old Manor House, Helmsley: from NE and plan

single post standing on a stone base. But the house stands out as being unlike other town houses and its general shape, with a roof of broad span with low eaves, has the outward appearance of being aisled. The two-storeyed, timber-framed north part may be interpreted as a double-width cross-wing, added or rebuilt in the 17th century.

MEDIEVAL MANOR HOUSES

The scarcity of medieval buildings in the region is demonstrated by the absence of any certain example of a manorial hall where the walls exist to their full height. Two houses may incorporate medieval masonry. The Old Hall, Snainton [474] (Fig. 10), has

Fig. 10 [474] The Old Hall, Snainton: from N.

Fig. 11 [56] Low Hall, Brompton: from S. and plan

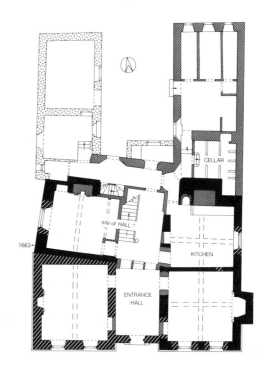

no features datable before the 18th century, but, at 0.8 metres or more, the walls are unusually thick for a house of fairly modest size, and the main range with a cross-wing at the east end could well represent a medieval plan.

Plans of the manor houses at Allerston and West Ayton have been recovered by excavation. Both had a large room, probably a hall though not positively identified as such, with a fireplace on a side wall, an arrangement that had been used at the Old Hall at Pickering Castle. Allerston has been attributed to the 13th century and the building at West Ayton is probably of about the same date and was demolished before the tower house which still stands was built over it *c.* 1400. At Low Hall, Brompton [56] (Fig. 11), a block at the core of the house is probably earlier than the 17th-century cross-wing built against it at a slight angle and could be the fabric of a medieval hall.

The most enigmatic building of the period is at the Hall, Sinnington [458] (Fig. 12), where there must have been a medieval house of some size. It caught Leland's eye for he commented that this was 'where the Lord Latimer hath a fair

Fig. 12 [458] Old Hall, Sinnington: from SW and plan

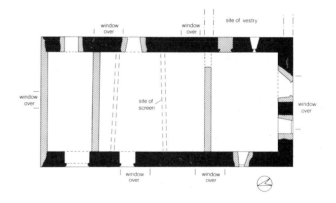

manor place'. The only surviving structure has usually been
interpreted as a hall (VCH 1923: 489), but it has some features
which are more readily explained as those of a chapel. Now used
as a farm building, it was originally erected, on the evidence of
one surviving window, in the late 12th or early 13th century.
The position and form of this window suggest a two-storey
building of a domestic nature, perhaps with a *camera* on the
upper floor. But after substantial alterations in the 15th century,
it became a single large cell divided into equal parts by a timber
screen, which also supported a floor over the north half only.
The proportions of the division are characteristic of domestic
chapels, and this interpretation of the building is strengthened
by the record of payments in 1431–2 to Richard Wright, carpenter, for making a screen and floor for the chapel at Sinnington
and to Will Carter for making holes in the walls for inserting
joists. It would have been extremely large for a chapel, being
not much smaller than the one at Helmsley Castle, and the need
for it so close to the parish church is not clear. It would be

expected that the house which it served was on a correspondingly large scale (Sheffield 1914: 255).

No fully timber-framed hall survives. Excavations on the site
of the Manor House, Harome [174], a 17th-century cruck-
framed structure, revealed evidence of earlier timber buildings,
but it is only at Welburn that there is full evidence of a
completely framed hall house with cross-wings, of the type so
frequently associated with the late medieval period.

Welburn Hall [506] now consists of a long stone-built wing

21

of early 17th-century date to which is attached a house designed in similar style, built in 1891 but partly reconstructed in 1933 after a fire (Figs. 13–17). On the site of the modern house was a timber-framed house demolished in 1890, of which good records exist, partly as measured drawings made by the architect of the new house, W. H. Brierley, and partly as sketches, photographs and a published account. The house consisted of a three-bay hall with gabled cross-wings to each side. It is not now possible to be sure of the exact size when it was built, as it had been much altered by the 18th century when the earliest records were made. The cross-wings projected very little at the front, but there may have been a greater projection to the rear, allowing two rooms within each wing. When the house was photographed in 1890, demolition had already started and some rendering had peeled off. The framing of the cross-wings was characterized by diagonal bracing which must have originally created a very strong ornamental effect, and suggests that the hall dates from the very end of the medieval period. Welburn was held by Rievaulx Abbey, but the hall may have been built about the middle of the 16th century by the Savile family to which the estate had come within a few years of the dissolution of the monastery.

Fig. 13 [506] Welburn Hall, Welburn: from S., 1890, during partial demolition

Fig. 14 [506] Welburn Hall: from S., c. 1900

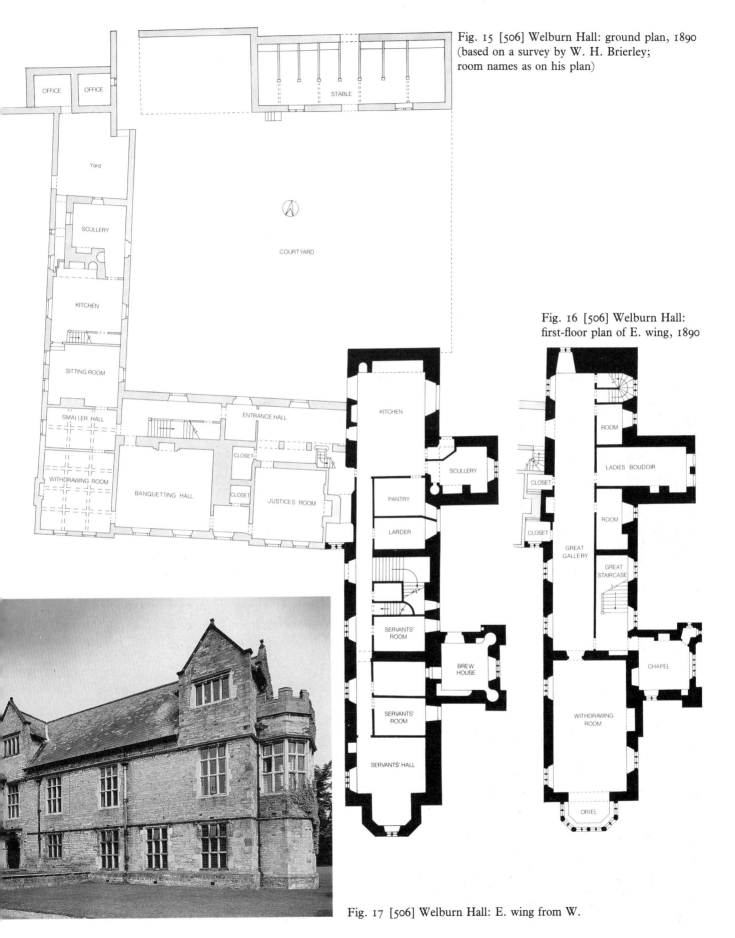

Fig. 15 [506] Welburn Hall: ground plan, 1890
(based on a survey by W. H. Brierley;
room names as on his plan)

OFFICE

OFFICE

Yard

SCULLERY

KITCHEN

SITTING ROOM

SMALLER HALL

WITHDRAWING ROOM

BANQUETTING HALL

ENTRANCE HALL

CLOSET

CLOSET

JUSTICES ROOM

COURTYARD

STABLE

Fig. 16 [506] Welburn Hall:
first-floor plan of E. wing, 1890

KITCHEN

SCULLERY

PANTRY

LARDER

SERVANTS'
ROOM

BREW
HOUSE

SERVANTS'
ROOM

SERVANTS' HALL

ROOM

LADIES BOUDOIR

CLOSET

ROOM

CLOSET

GREAT
GALLERY

GREAT
STAIRCASE

CHAPEL

WITHDRAWING
ROOM

ORIEL

Fig. 17 [506] Welburn Hall: E. wing from W.

23

The only cruck-built open hall in the region known to survive until recently was the Old Manor House, Harome [174] (Fig. 18). Possibly of late 16th century rather than strictly medieval date, it had been much altered and the precise plan lost, especially at the service end. What was clear was that the scale of the house, and of the cruck trusses, differentiated it from a normal farmhouse.

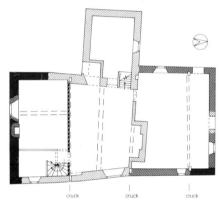

Fig. 18 [174] Old Manor House, Harome: from E., 1970, and plan

FORTIFIED HOUSES

The dominant fortified buildings in the southern part of the region were the castles at Helmsley, Pickering and Scarborough, all of which were large, extensive complexes as befitted, for the last two, their status of royal castles. In Eskdale, after the abandonment of the motte at Castleton, Danby Castle was the principal seat of the Latimers. This was a smaller castle than the three named above and, being of later foundation, was designed to a more formal concept with four ranges around a courtyard. A similar form was used at several other castles of the same, late 14th-century, period such as Bolton and Sheriff Hutton, both in North Yorkshire, and Wressle, Humberside. Danby differs from these in that the four corner towers are placed diagonally, and the courtyard is quite small. The whole of the east range was occupied by the hall and there were service

quarters to the north and chambers to the south. It was therefore compact and self-contained and there are no indications of any outlying buildings or earthworks (VCH 1923: 334–5).

At a lesser, manorial level there are remains of several moats such as Harome Hawe and Wilton where John de Heslerton obtained a licence to crenellate in 1335, but only at West Ayton are there standing remains. Ayton Castle is an isolated example in the region of a three-storeyed tower house, a type more commonly found within the border areas and in the northern Pennines [507] (Figs. 19, 20). Its actual erection is not documented but details suggest a date in the late 14th or early 15th century. At that time the manor was held by Sir John Eure, who had married one of the co-heiresses of Sir William de Aton. Eure had strong northern connections and a house at Witton, County Durham. His probable familiarity with the tower house as an architectural form makes the occurrence of the outlying example at Ayton less surprising, though that does not in itself explain why he found it necessary to erect this particular house. Ayton Castle is built of good-quality masonry and, though now ruined, it was an accomplished design with the storeys articulated by weathered string courses. It can only be speculated whether or not it owes anything to John Lewyn, who was certainly known to Eure (Harvey 1954: 167) and was the foremost designer of fortified buildings in northern England in the late 14th century.

Fig. 19 [507] Ayton Castle, West Ayton: from E., ground and first-floor plans, 1:600

Fig. 20 [507] Ayton Castle: SE ground-floor room from W.

The tower is built partly over the foundations of an earlier building. An extensive complex, thought to be of 12th and 13th-century date, was excavated to the east and south. It is not known if any of these buildings were still standing after the tower was built, but the one which was immediately adjacent to it cannot have been, as evidence would have shown on the east wall of the tower. There are unexcavated earthworks west of the tower but on this side, also, the wall has an unbroken plinth and string courses. The tower therefore appears to have been detached and did not have a hall range built against it as do some other tower houses, such as Nappa Hall, North Yorkshire (Ambler 1913: 46), and Paull Holme, Humberside, which now stands isolated but was originally attached to a hall range (Ryder and Coleman 1983). It is possible that at Ayton the tower functioned in combination with other detached buildings but further excavation would be needed to determine this.

The 16th and 17th centuries

As with the medieval period, the region does not possess a great number of surviving houses of post-medieval date which are of a status above that of farmhouse. In some villages there is nothing that can be regarded as a manor house or hall occupied by the gentry. Of the several houses built before the end of the 17th century which still exist, not one remains complete or unaltered enough to illustrate fully the original plan or appearance. Graphic evidence provides valuable information about a few other houses which have been either demolished or altered drastically. These include the house of the Cayleys at High Hall, Brompton [55], and that of the Hutchinsons at Wykeham Abbey, both drawn by Samuel Buck, c. 1720 (Hall 1979); a painting of an earlier Hackness Hall is preserved in the present house and a small but convincing sketch of the predecessor of the present Ebberston Hall appears on a late 17th-century map of the manor (Fig. 21). Hearth tax returns from the period

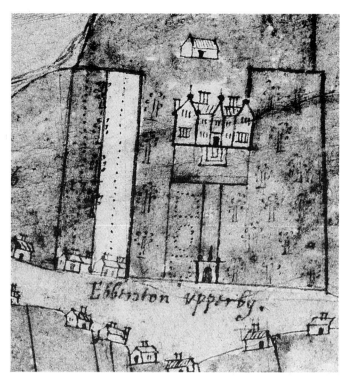

Fig. 21 Ebberston Hall, Ebberston: detail from a late 17th-century map

1662–74 provide some evidence for the size of houses which have completely disappeared: Middleton Hall, rebuilt in the 18th century, had nine hearths in 1662 and Sir Jordan Crosland's house at Harome had eight; the latter was at a now deserted moated site at Harome Hawe about 1 kilometre south-west of the village and may have had a medieval core, but the number of hearths must indicate post-medieval alterations. More enigmatic is Sir Henry Cholmley's house with sixteen hearths at Rievaulx, the site of which cannot even be identified.

THE LIFE OF THE GENTRY

Three prominent residents of the area have left personal records which give an insight into the way of life of the gentry in the late Tudor and Stuart periods. Margaret Dakins (1571–1633), by successive marriages to Walter Devereux, Sir Thomas Sidney and Sir Thomas Posthumous Hoby (married 1596), was related to many noble families (Meads 1930). The Hackness estate was bought for her in 1589 and her diary, one of the earliest surviving by an Englishwoman, was written there and on visits to York and London between 1599 and 1603. Although primarily concerned with her spiritual and bodily health, it illumines a landowner's busy life. Hackness Hall, demolished after the present house was completed in 1797, was an Elizabethan mansion with two courtyards (Fig. 22). In 1600 the household included ten male and four female servants, plus several maids of good family. Lady Margaret supervised her staff and estate, treating her servants' ailments with medicine and surgery. For relaxation, in the time left from long hours of prayer and study, she walked, fished, played bowls and a

Fig. 22 Hackness Hall from S: an 18th-century painting

musical instrument. Frequent visits to relatives and neighbours by coach or on horseback, and the reception of guests helped fill her days. She mentions disturbing rumours of plague and the sermons of the private chaplain of the puritanical household. Her husband, assiduous as a JP and in hunting down papists, was considered by a contemporary as 'a vexatious troublesome neighbour . . . who . . . having a full purse and no children . . . delighted to spend his money and time in suits'. Sir Thomas built a chapel in her memory at Harwood Dale and a monument in Hackness church but left her legacies unpaid and willed her estate to his nephew.

Sir Hugh Cholmley (1600–57) cuts a more conventional figure in his memoirs (Cholmley 1777). His grandfather had sold property in Kent to buy monastic land around Whitby, and by the 1560s 'had now so much enlarged his Yorkshire possessions that he was almost upon a level with the first Nobility of the nation'. His father had rebuilt the abbot's house at Whitby and by 1635 Sir Hugh could claim that 'having mastered my debts, I did not only appear at all public meetings in very gentlemanly equipage but lived in as handsome and plentiful fashion at home as any gentleman in all the county of my rank. I had between 30 and 40 in my ordinary family'. He describes his youth in the vanished mansion at Roxby, his repair of Whitby Abbey gatehouse where a ruined banqueting hall remains, his wife's prowess at needle-work and her careful housekeeping. His younger son, another Hugh, left memoirs mentioning supervision of alum works near Whitby.

Alice Wandesford (1627–1707) was married in 1651 to William Thornton of East Newton and lived there for over forty years, surviving her husband and all but two of her nine children, six of whom died in infancy (Jackson 1873). Her autobiography ends in 1669 and is much concerned with illnesses and accidents. Her pious meditations are written from a High Anglican stance, bitterly opposed to the Parliamentarians who had killed Strafford, her father's patron, and suppressed sacramental worship. Her life story is vivid with details of house building (East Newton Hall took six years to finish and they moved in in June 1662), finance, travel and family anecdotes. Like the other two writers, she was related to gentry all over the county, including the Cholmleys and Osbornes; Thomas Comber, Dean of Durham, was her son-in-law. Her marriage portion was £2500 and she kept a coach, possessed rich jewellery, had the great parlour at East Newton hung with family portraits, and could entertain fifty to sixty guests at its house-warming, helped by numerous servants and nursemaids. Her account of the appraising of her mother's goods, including a dispute over the value of the best bed, throws light on the way inventories were made, though her property was only valued at £174. Her love of trees preserved Newton Wood after other 'great and beautiful woods' had been felled to provide dowries for her Catholic sisters-in-law and led her to transplant planes from Hipswell 'to set in the rows and walks in the front of my house . . . For I ever took a delight both in the ornament . . . as well as the pleasure and profit of it [woodland] on my land'. Generous legacies were left to restore the Thornton aisle in Stonegrave church and to rebuild East Newton chapel.

26

Architectural development of gentry houses

THE HALL

The dominant and central feature of the medieval house was generally an open hall, extending the full height of the house with no intervening floor or ceiling between ground level and rafters. The immediate post-medieval development of the hall was the introduction of a floor into it to create an upper storey. This process was happening throughout much of England in the second half of the 16th century in two ways. One was the insertion of a floor into an existing open hall, leaving a hall only on the ground floor and creating a chamber above it. If the hall previously had an open fire it was also necessary to build a chimney for fireplaces serving both hall and chamber above.

Contemporary with the process of conversion of older houses was the erection of new ones with essentially the same form, producing a house of medieval shape with flanking cross-wings on each side of a central part which comprised a ground-floor hall with chamber over. The significant external detail which distinguishes the two is the eaves level of the hall range which in the converted open hall is usually at a lower level than that of the cross-wings. There is also frequently evidence of alteration to the fenestration to provide two storeys of windows.

So few medieval houses survive in the region that it is not possible to generalize as to how far the national trend was followed locally. The slight evidence available does not suggest early introduction of floors into open halls though new houses with halls chambered over were being built from the late 16th century onwards. The inserted floor at Foulbridge, Snainton [477], does not appear to be particularly early, and at Welburn the hall remained without an inserted floor until its demolition in 1890, though a ceiling may have been introduced below the roof structure. At the Manor House, Helmsley [209], a floor with moulded beams and joists was inserted *c.* 1700 within the possible aisled hall. The earliest reference to a chamber above a hall describes riotous behaviour by a hunting party at Hackness Hall in August 1600 (Meads 1930: 40–3). As that particular house was completely replaced by a new one in 1797, it can only be conjectured whether or not the hall in 1600 was a conversion of a medieval one.

The earliest surviving house in the region built with a chamber over the hall may be Rectory House, Helmsley [223] (Fig. 23). This is of timber-framed construction and stands in the market-place, immediately adjacent to the churchyard. It was occupied by the Earl of Rutland's agent, a post held by the Crosland family in the late 16th and throughout the 17th century. Its date of erection is not certain but 1580–90, early in the Crosland occupation, would accord with the framing style. The hall range is of two bays but there is no proper termination to the structure at the east end where it breaks off in an arbitrary manner with no truss. It has obviously been truncated and it is very probable that a further part of the house, either another bay or a cross-wing which may have passed into separate occu-

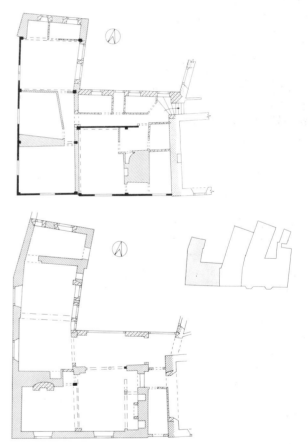

Fig. 23 [223] Rectory House, Helmsley: from S. ground and first-floor plan (outline plan shows position in Black Swan complex)

pation, has been demolished. The framing indicates that the hall was floored over from the outset to provide a chamber over. The hall occupies one full bay, with a fireplace and a wide passage behind it in the second, incomplete bay. It is evident from the position of the first-floor window in this bay that the fireplace is in the original position, which has the same relation to the cross-passage as in contemporary longhouses.

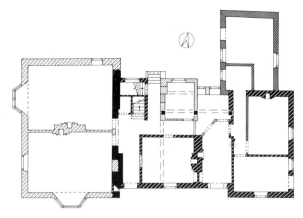

Fig. 24 [259] High Hall, Kirkbymoorside: from SE and plan

High Hall, Kirkbymoorside [259] (Figs. 24, 25), is probably a little later in date than Rectory House and was also originally timber framed, though the external walls were subsequently entirely rebuilt in stone, apart from the south gable ends of the cross-wings. There is no documentation but it may have been erected soon after 1616. The hall appears to have been built against an earlier stone building to the west, of which one wall survives. The hall was of three bays with an aisle or outshot on the north side. The surviving framing makes it clear that the floor over the hall is original but there is no evidence for partitions separating the outshot from the hall or, indeed, from the chamber over it. It is unlikely that there would have been no partition at the upper level and there may have been a non-structural partition which left no evidence after removal. It is not readily apparent which was the service end of High Hall. A chimney stack in the east bay of the hall might suggest that there was a wide cross-passage but this stack, which has been recently removed, was not old. No original fireplace can be located. At the west end of the hall an entry in the south wall is directly opposite an 18th-century staircase; the adjacent west cross-wing was rebuilt in the 19th century with large rooms, so, at a later date at least, this was the superior end of the house.

Fig. 25 [259] High Hall: from SW, c.1860

Buckingham House, Kirkbymoorside [272] (Figs. 26, 27), is reputed to be the house in which George Villiers, Duke of Buckingham, died in 1687. Though much altered and lacking any original dating features, its plan and shape are quite consistent with a date in the 17th century. Unlike the two houses discussed above, it is stone built and has a hall, with chamber over, occupying the central part between two slightly projecting cross-wings. The property is now divided; the door to the north part leads through a passage to an 18th-century staircase at the rear, a very similar arrangement to that found at High Hall. On the south side of the hall there is a fireplace against a substantial wall, leaving a space of about 1.5 metres beyond it before the cross-wing is reached. This part of the house has been gutted for a shop but the original existence of a cross-passage in this position may reasonably be inferred, providing a direct comparison with the wide passage at Rectory House. There seems to have been a passage of about the same width behind a large stack in the east bay at Welburn Hall [506], though by the 19th century it had been divided into closets and the hall fireplace moved to the back wall.

Several of the houses in the region illustrated in Samuel Buck's sketches almost certainly had screens passages in their halls, entered through storeyed porches which are significantly off-centre. In none of these houses does the passage seem to have been behind the hall fireplace. At Wykeham Abbey a chimney stack was very conspicuously placed against the front wall, and High Hall, Brompton [55], had a chimney visible above and behind the ridge which must indicate a fireplace on the back wall of the hall. Another house with a storeyed porch is titled 'Rushton Hall. The Seat of Robt. Robinson Gent.'; this cannot be identified but may be an error for Riseborough Hall, Thornton Riseborough [504], a Robinson house of which the surviving cross-wing is identical to that shown by Buck. In the sketch there is a very large stack on the opposite side of the porch to the hall, but this unusual position may be due to poor draughtsmanship (Hall 1979: 301).

The reconciliation of an entry leading to a screens passage with a symmetrical elevation was a recurring problem in the

Fig. 26 [272] Buckingham House, Kirkbymoorside: from E.

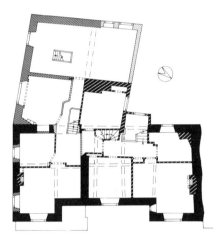

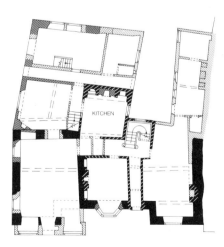

Fig. 27 [272] Buckingham House: ground and first-floor plans

design of the house in the 17th century. One solution was the E-shaped plan with a central storeyed porch. The hall could then occupy half the main range to one side of the porch with service rooms or a parlour to the other. Judging from old views, both Ebberston Hall and Hackness Hall were of this type before being rebuilt in the 18th century.

In the later 17th century the function of the hall changed as it began to be used more as an entrance hall. It then became feasible to have a central doorway providing direct entry into an axially placed hall. Newbiggin Hall, Egton [99], illustrates this significant step towards a more symmetrical plan and elevation (Fig. 28). The house cannot be dated very precisely but is probably of the later 17th century, though modified in the 18th century. It has a U-shaped plan with two gabled wings projecting boldly forward on the north side, which was the front, with a central doorway in the re-entrant. This leads into the hall which occupies the central part of the house. The staircase, of 18th-century date, appears to be an intrusion into the hall itself. If this was so, and since the front door shows no sign of alteration, any sense of a cross-passage has obviously been abandoned though the hall, from its size, was clearly still an important living area in the house. The original fireplace position is not clear. There is now only a small internal stack against the south wall opposite the door, but it does not seem convincingly original and there is no sign of the removal of an external stack, which might have been expected.

Fig. 28 [99] Newbiggin Hall, Egton: from N. and plan

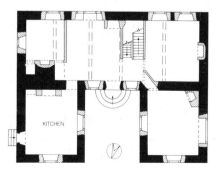

Fig. 29 [490] Thornton Hall, Thornton Dale: from S.

Fig. 30 [490] Thornton Hall: first-floor plan

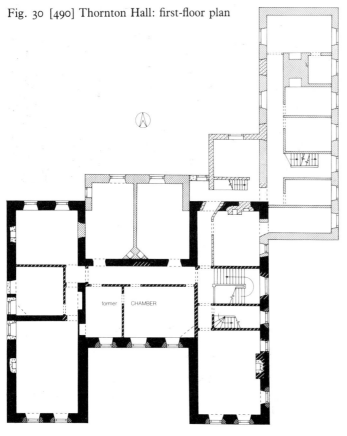

The arrangement of a hall with entry and fireplace centrally placed in opposite walls is seen more clearly at the Hall, Thornton Dale [490] (Figs. 29, 30). This house was probably built some years after 1669, when the manor was purchased by John Hill, a retired silk merchant. The decoration and fittings of the hall date from the 18th century but this does not necessarily imply that the general arrangement is different from the original. Samuel Buck's sketch of *c.* 1720 creates confusion as it is titled 'to the south', though it actually appears to show the north side, with a large chimney stack against the wall of the central range in which the hall is situated. The existing hall fireplace is on the north wall, and though there is now no projecting stack behind it, the plinth on the original external face, now within a later addition, breaks significantly at the point where such a chimney could have been torn away. A strange feature of Buck's view is the front door in the centre of the stack. If he was accurate on this point there can have been no fireplace in this position on the ground floor, but the arrangement is so peculiar that there must be considerable doubt over Buck's accuracy or whether he conflated two opposite elevations.

THE DEVELOPMENT OF THE CROSS-WING

By the late medieval period the cross-wing had become a common feature of the English hall house. It continued to be employed to contain private rooms and service quarters in houses of the post-medieval period into the 17th century, but thereafter one of the main developments of house design was its gradual elimination and the trend towards a more compact plan and shape.

At nearly all the larger houses of this period in the region there are one or two cross-wings. Six houses either have, or are known to have had, two wings, flanking the central range which contains the hall. The other houses, with only one cross-wing, are mostly not complete enough to be sure that a second wing has not been lost. The most certain evidence of houses with only one wing is in the sketches of Samuel Buck. High Hall, Brompton [55], and the house which Buck titled 'Rushton' but may be Riseborough Hall, both have a cross-wing at the opposite end of the hall to a storeyed porch, showing that they must be parlour wings. At the service end, beyond the porch, there is simply a continuation of the main range in each case.

At Rectory House, Helmsley [223] (Fig. 23), and the Old Manor House, Helmsley [209] (Fig. 9), the one wing that exists is at the upper end, which leaves the possibility open as to whether or not there may have been a second wing at the other end. But in several other houses the surviving wing is the service end, recognizable by the presence of a kitchen with a large fireplace; in these it is more likely that there would have been a balancing wing at the other end.

On the frontage of Rectory House, the gable wall of the cross-wing and the wall of the hall are flush, though the wing projects at the rear. At the Manor House, Helmsley, the whole frontage also seems to have been flush, with the proviso that the existence of an aisled hall is rather hypothetical. The bringing forward of the hall to the building line occurs elsewhere in urban situations and several similar examples of this are known among the medieval houses of the City of York, except that in these the cross-wings are jettied out at first-floor level. Buckingham House, Kirkbymoorside [272] (Figs. 26, 27), which fronts directly on to High Market Place, has two wings with a fairly small projection forward, not much more than 1 metre. At High Hall, Kirkbymoorside [259] (Fig. 24), the projection forward of the wings is less, even though the house is set within its own grounds. This seems to be an exception among houses on more open sites, and in several others the wings have a much more pronounced projection. Newbiggin Hall, Egton [99] (Fig. 28), is one of the most complete examples and here the wings are large enough to contain complete rooms, as they are also at the Hall, Thornton Dale [490] (Figs. 29, 30), where they project to both front and rear. This is quite unlike Buckingham House, where the slight projection only provides a little extra space within the rooms, prompting the suspicion that the reason for the cross-wings was more a matter of tradition and status than of practical requirements.

The extensive H-shaped plan at Thornton Dale is exceptional, but the U-plan of Newbiggin Hall, with wings projecting forward of the hall only, seems to have also been the arrangement, on a much larger scale, at East Newton Hall, and at Low Hall, Brompton [56] (Fig. 11). The single wing which survives at Church House, Ebberston [96], has indications that it also could have formed part of a house of the same shape.

The purpose of the cross-wing at the superior end of a house was to provide accommodation for parlours, with chambers over. Parlour wings seem to have been more liable than service wings to be demolished or rebuilt in later centuries, and there are only a few examples remaining. At Rectory House, Helmsley, the timber-framed wing is three bays long and there is no indication of internal partitions on either of the two floors. If this was actually so, there would have been a room about 12 metres by 4.5 metres on each floor, surprisingly large and much greater in area than the hall. This was the house of the Earl of Rutland's agent, so perhaps special administrative functions may account for the unusual plan. An internal stack was later introduced into it but there are no signs of any original fireplaces nor of a staircase. The timber-framed cross-wing, if it was such, at the Manor House, Helmsley, is also exceptional. It is of double width, expressed by twin gables towards the street, and probably extended backwards four bays, though these have been subsequently altered. Its most rational division inside would have been into four rooms on each floor. The only reference to its early history is as an inn and this function may provide the reason for the great size of the wing.

The best example of a 17th-century parlour wing is at Riseborough Hall, Thornton Riseborough [504] (Fig. 31), even though it is now a ruin and the hall range of the house has disappeared,

Fig. 31 [504] Riseborough Hall, Thornton Riseborough: from S. and plan as in 1963

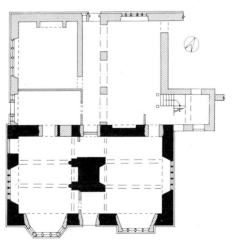

the site of it now being occupied by a block built in the late 19th century. The 17th-century wing formerly carried a rainwater head dated 1664 but this may not have been the date of erection; some of the fittings in it were earlier in style and the wing may have been built soon after it was bought by Sir Arthur Robinson, a London merchant, in 1632. The wing was of two storeys and attics, and had two rooms on each floor separated by an internal chimney stack providing back-to-back fireplaces. These parlours and chambers were quite well fitted out judging by some fireplaces and chimney-pieces that survived until recently, and they had large windows in the front and rear walls of the wing; there may also have been smaller windows in the side wall to the south-east but these were replaced by larger ones in the 19th century. Connection with the rest of the house was apparently through a lobby beside the internal stack and also perhaps directly into the south-west room. The north-east room was in the part of the wing which was forward of the hall range. If there was a staircase within the wing, it can only have been a tight, winding one beside the stack.

Though the scale is more modest than at Riseborough, the parlour wing at Newbiggin Hall, Egton (Fig. 28), was similarly planned, with a parlour to the west of the hall and another one to the north of that within the projecting wing. A direct entry from the hall to the latter room was created diagonally in the 18th century, and before that it must have been entered through the first parlour, unless some sort of a lobby was contrived. The corner fireplace in the north parlour is an obvious intrusion, though an earlier one could be blocked up. Mr Salvin was assessed for seven hearths in 1662. If that relates to the existing house, and not to its predecessor, there must have been two or three heated bedrooms.

The Salvins had held Newbiggin since the 15th century, and the 17th-century rebuilding does not relate to any particular known event in that family's history. A new and wealthy owner coming into an estate might wish to have a more pretentious house than what was already there. This is what John Hill created at the Hall, Thornton Dale (Figs. 29, 30). It must have been several years before he rebuilt the house, for he was assessed for only three hearths in 1674. Possibly the central hall range itself survives from an earlier period, as the stone walls are rendered, and Hill may only have added the flanking wings. The wings are of equal size, about 17 metres long, which is quite large enough to contain three good-sized rooms on each floor. Though the wings are identical in size, and have been much altered, it is the east wing which must have been the superior one, with windows in the long side wall as well as the gable ends. A spacious staircase was inserted into it in the earlier part of the 18th century, perhaps about 1710–20, which would have been when the house was held by John Hill II. The original arrangement can now only be a matter of speculation. Perhaps there were two less grandiose and more equal staircases, one in each wing. If the hall does survive from an earlier date, it is possible that it may have remained open through two storeys until the early 18th century, perhaps with a balustraded gallery across it linking the two wings, an arrangement which occurs up to that date in West Yorkshire.

There were wings of very much the same size as Thornton at East Newton Hall [92] (Figs. 32–34), which was built in 1656–62 for William and Alice Thornton after their marriage. The plan of the house seems to have been U-shaped but the hall linking the two cross-wings had been demolished by 1854. The parlour wing was on the east side and is now detached and completely gutted so the internal arrangements are no longer apparent. The internal length of nearly 17 metres is large enough to provide for three rooms. Various rooms are mentioned in Alice Thornton's autobiography, including the great parlour, Scarlet Chamber, Grey Chamber and study, but their precise locations in the house are not stated, though the great parlour was next to the hall.

Direct external access to the parlours at East Newton was provided by two doorways in the east wall. The wing at Riseborough Hall has a door in the south-east wall which provided a lobby entry beside the central stack; though the door is of 19th-century date, it may replace a similar earlier one in the same position. At the Hall, Thornton Dale, the present main entrance to the house is through a doorway in the east wall of the parlour wing, but this may not be original. Buck's sketch of Wykeham Abbey shows an 'extruded corner' between the hall and cross-wing, in which there are two arched doorways on the ground floor. Projecting blocks in angles of this type contain staircases in some other contemporary houses and may have done so at Wykeham, though the windows in it are not at mezzanine level.

Chambers with a high standard of fittings were sometimes provided on the upper floor of the service wing. The rooms above the kitchens at Newbiggin Hall, Egton and East Newton Hall are wainscotted, and in the latter the fireplace has a large overmantel with classical orders, indicating a room of some importance (Fig. 387). At these two houses no obvious distinction is made between the two floors in respect of ceiling heights and window sizes, but in a few of the largest houses the first floor is clearly predominant. An early example of this is the south-west range at Helmsley Castle, built in the late 1570s; on the first floor are two large chambers with panelled walls, ornamental plasterwork and transomed windows (Figs. 375, 385), whereas the ground-floor rooms are much plainer and have smaller windows. In the early 17th-century wing at Welburn Hall, the main room, a large chamber and a gallery are on the first floor and have tall windows with double transoms; the service rooms on the ground floor have lower ceilings and single transomed windows (Fig. 15). Fyling Old Hall, Fylingdales [129] (Figs. 35, 36), may represent an analogous structure, with important first-floor rooms. It was built in 1629 by Sir Hugh Cholmley, possibly as a wing to an earlier house, but the original form has been much disguised by early 19th-century alterations. The ground floor had small mullioned windows and must have contained service rooms. The first floor was taller and had mullioned and transomed windows, and it appears that the second floor, now reduced in height, may have been similar.

The position of the kitchen in most houses where it can be identified is at the back part of the service wing, its large fireplace necessitating a prominent chimney stack against the gable-end wall, as can be seen at East Newton Hall. A large stack of

Fig. 32 [92] East Newton Hall, East Newton: from W.

Fig. 33 [92] East Newton Hall: from S.

Fig. 34 [92] East Newton Hall: plan
(the two separate buildings were once linked by a hall)

Fig. 35 [129] Fyling Old Hall, Fylingdales: from E.,
ground and first-floor plans

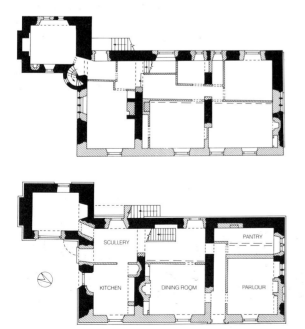

Fig. 36 [129] Fyling Old Hall: from NW

the same kind at the north end of Church House, Ebberston [96], suggests that this is a wing of a house of similar form to East Newton Hall, even if more modest in size (Figs. 37, 38). The kitchen normally has an external doorway. At East Newton Hall it is in the back wall immediately beside the chimney stack, and Low Hall, Brompton [56], has one similarly related to a large gable-end stack. The kitchen at the north end of the early 17th-century wing at Welburn Hall, and the one of about the same date added at the rear of Canons Garth, Helmsley [187], both have doorways in their side walls. At the much-altered Church House, it appears that there may have been a lobby between the external doorway and the kitchen. All these kitchens are on the north side of the house except at East Newton where the front faces northwards. Newbiggin Hall, Egton [99], is also a north-facing house with a U-shaped plan, but the kitchen is at the front of the house, occupying the north-east wing, and with an external doorway in the east wall.

Fig. 39 [63] Thirley Beck Farm, Cloughton

Fig. 37 [96] Church House, Ebberston: from E., ground-floor plan

Fig. 38 [96] Church House: section through N. end

HOUSES WITHOUT CROSS-WINGS

Several houses of the later 17th century are not very much larger than contemporary farmhouses but are superior to them because of their plans or the standard of design and quality of fittings. At Thirley Beck Farm, Cloughton [63] (Fig. 39), the house, though accompanied by farm buildings, is in its symmetry

unlike other farmhouses of the same period. The ground floor has only two rooms, parlour and kitchen, with a wide passage between them which probably contained the original staircase. The house faces south and each room has a three-light, stone mullioned window and a hearth lit by a fire-window. The central-entry plan, with the staircase opposite the front door, is precocious even for a larger house and did not become common in farmhouses until the middle of the 18th century. The exactly symmetrical elevation, though now compromised by a small inserted window on the first floor and with modern porch and dormers, represents a more disciplined concept in design that would normally be expected in a house of this size.

Thorn Hill House, Goathland [165] (Fig. 40), seems to have been similar in plan to Thirley Beck Farm. This has a door lintel on the south side inscribed 1699 and with the initials IEP, for John and Elizabeth Pierson. As the interior is gutted the plan can only be conjectured, but a fire-window near each end of the north elevation must indicate that there were fireplaces against the two gable walls. In the undated inventory of John Pierson's effects, the Hall, House, Little Parlour, Great Parlour, Great Chamber and Little Chamber are all mentioned. Opposed doors in the long walls suggest some form of a cross-passage but the elevation is less regularly disposed than at Thirley Beck Farm and the doors are not exactly central.

Fig. 40 [165] Thorn Hill House, Goathland

Fig. 41 [244] Martin Garth, Hutton Buscel

Martin Garth, Hutton Buscel [244] (Fig. 41), is another 17th-century house that has an entry between hall and parlour. The original staircase opposite the front door has now been removed but evidence for it is preserved in an old photograph. Unlike the two houses described above, Martin Garth has a third room, probably a kitchen, beyond the hall; a large fireplace has been removed from it. As at Thorn Hill House there are two pairs of cruck trusses but there is also a stone cross-wall, with the hall fireplace against it.

A rather similar plan was utilized in the 18th century at the Manor House, Cloughton [62] (Fig. 42), which was probably built in 1733, a date inscribed on a tablet on the first floor. The hall and parlour flank a passage which runs through the house, and at the north end is a third, heated room. The passage is narrow and cannot have contained the staircase but this may not have been its original width, as the flanking walls are of

Fig. 42 [62] Manor House, Cloughton

different materials, brick and stone. Many windows have been altered but those of the north room on each floor, now in separate occupation from the rest of the house, retain their original raised surrounds. Apart from such details as these windows, and raised quoins at the angles, the superior nature of the house is shown by the south room on the first floor, which has full wainscotting, three panels high, on all the walls.

THE DEVELOPMENT OF THE DOUBLE-PILE PLAN

Newbiggin Hall and Thornton Hall are both houses of traditional shape comprising a central body and projecting wings to produce either a U or H-shaped plan. At Newbiggin the main door was placed on the central axis, and the same may have been the case at Thornton. These provided access directly into the hall and not through a screens passage at one end. The halls were nevertheless principal living rooms, occupying a significant part of the total floor area. The gradual change in the nature of the hall from a living room to purely an entrance hall is one of the most important developments in house planning in the 17th and 18th centuries, and is accompanied by the desire for more formally designed symmetrical elevations. The solution adopted at Newbiggin and Thornton was hardly satisfactory, as it meant that draughts and muddy boots were introduced directly into the hall. Another changing aspect of house planning was towards centralization, not only of the entry but also of vertical circulation. This produced a close relationship between entrance and staircase, which led to a first-floor landing off which doors to the main bed chambers opened. On both floors a situation in which all the main rooms could open off a central hall or landing was facilitated by a plan with rooms in double depth.

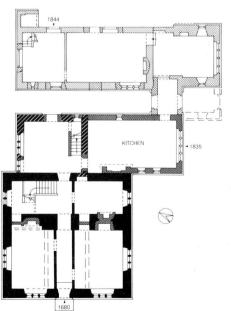

Fig. 43 [117] Thorpe Hall, Fylingdales: from SW and plan

As a double-pile house Thorpe Hall, Fylingdales [117] (Fig. 43), is precocious. Built in 1680 by a member of the Farsyde family, whose name with the date of erection are inscribed on the door lintel, it is unlike any other contemporary house in the region. It has a compact, almost square shape on plan, with a front door placed nearly, though not quite exactly, in the centre of the west elevation. The roof has two separate spans with a valley between, and their ridges run from side to side. Consequently there are double gables on each of the lateral elevations and only a small gable for a dormer window at the front. The plan originally provided for a hall and parlour at the front of the house, and at the rear is the staircase and a room that is surely too small to have been a kitchen. Thorpe Hall, while being progressive with its double-pile plan, has a traditional appearance, with three-light mullioned windows, moulded stringcourses and multiple gables, that is in no sense advanced for 1680.

Fig. 44 [14] Arden Hall, Arden with Ardenside: from SE

The up-to-date style of the late 17th century with classical detailing and proportions probably first appeared in the region at Arden Hall, Arden-with-Ardenside [14] (Frontispiece and Fig. 44). This is on the site of a priory of Benedictine nuns which in 1574 became the seat of a branch of the Tancred family. Initially, their house no doubt utilized and adapted the conventual buildings to which the new work of *c.* 1700 was added to form the principal front. There is a large, heated entrance hall with a sturdy staircase rising directly out of it around an open well (Fig. 398). The hall is entered centrally in its south wall, with a narrow window to each side; these together with a fanlight over the door provide adequate light. The size of the hall is such that it would have served purposes other than merely being the entrance and providing access to the ground-floor rooms. Ancillary accommodation, such as that for servants, remained in the earlier parts which were subsequently rebuilt.

Esk Hall, Sleights, Eskdaleside cum Ugglebarnby [105] (Figs. 45, 46), is probably a little later in date but may be the earliest surviving house in the region with a full double-depth plan with front and back rooms of equal size. It was built with a recessed centre at the front, between two slightly projecting wings, a shape that is partly reminiscent of the 17th-century house with

projecting cross-wings but which was also common in great country houses of the late 17th century, such as Belton House, Lincolnshire. The wings are not gabled or hipped; instead, a single roof slope covers both centre and wings by the simple expedient of raising the wall of the central part to three storeys. The hall, which was not heated, corresponds to the whole of the recessed centre of the front, with the staircase directly opposite at the rear, and represents a stage in the development of the hall before it simply became a passage leading from the front door to the staircase. The hall also provided direct communication with the four rooms on the ground floor. The room at the north corner was originally the kitchen but in the later 18th century the house was extended by wings to each side. The original kitchen became a breakfast room and a new kitchen and service quarters were provided in the north-east wing. The first-floor plan was similar to the ground floor, with a spacious landing at the front of the house over the hall, off which opened four bedrooms. The stair continued up to the attics, which were habitable and lit by windows in the gable walls. To make the best use of the attic space, the central valley between the two parallel ridges is raised well up above the level of the eaves.

Fig. 45 [105] Esk Hall, Sleights, Eskdaleside cum Ugglebarnby: from S. and plan

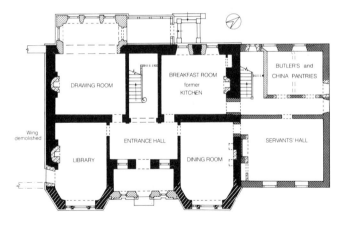

Fig. 46 [105] Esk Hall: entrance hall

Fig. 47 [6] Aislaby Hall, Aislaby: from N. and plan

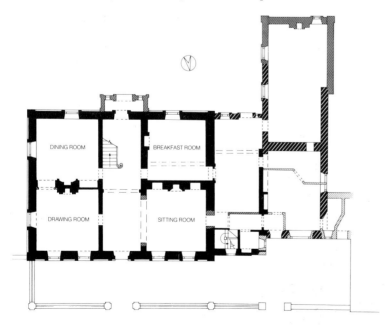

Fig. 48 [6] Aislaby Hall: entrance hall

The development of the entrance hall, which functioned primarily as a circulation space, is illustrated by Aislaby Hall, [6] (Fig. 47), which was built around the middle of the 18th century for the Hayes family. The ground floor has four rooms, all nearly square and of very similar size to each other, and on the central axis the hall extends through the house from front to back with a uniform width. The staircase is in the back part of this hall, with a doorway below the half-landing leading to the garden. With a width of over 3 metres (10 feet), the hall occupies a significant part of the floor area, but its shape, and the poor lighting of the front part solely from the semicircular fanlight over the front door, virtually precludes its use for anything other than an entrance, though, from its proportions, it was clearly designed as an entrance hall which was intended to impress (Fig. 48). It is the size and pretentiousness of this hall, rather than the size of the rooms, which distinguishes the house.

Woodlands, Aislaby [4] (Figs. 49, 50), is a double-pile house built to a less formal and regular plan. This may represent a picturesque approach in a rather mild form, for the house has also a crowning battlemented parapet, but it may also be a response to the site. On a sloping site such as this, the most desirable orientation is for the house to face down the slope towards the view, but this makes it difficult to have a reasonably spacious approach to the front door. At Woodlands a pragmatic approach to this problem has produced a formal five-bay elevation facing south and with the main entrance on the west where there was no attempt at symmetry. The house was built in the late 18th century, probably by Henry Walker Yeoman who succeeded his father in 1782 and died in 1801. The shape is not an absolute rectangle and was partly determined by parts of an earlier house on the site, which remain in the service quarters. The south front is entirely occupied by the two principal rooms, called the dining room and drawing room in a sale advertisement

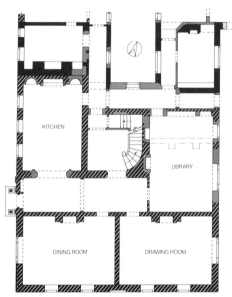

Fig. 49 [4] Woodlands, Aislaby: from SE and plan

Fig. 50 [4] Woodlands: from W.

41

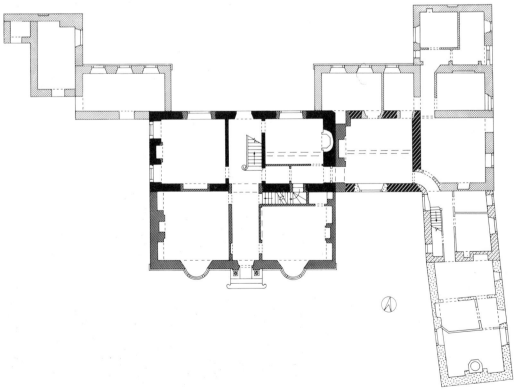

Fig. 51 [254] Kingthorpe House,
Kingthorpe: from SW and plan

of 1835; the room to the east was the library, the first mention of this use in a gentry house in the region. The entrance hall is on the east–west axis but the staircase to the north occupies a separate compartment and is not visible, as so often in Georgian houses, from the front door.

The double-pile plan achieved by growth

Though the double-pile house, by its formal nature, seems to be a self-contained entity, a number of houses of this type were created by additions to earlier houses or else arrived at their final form by a process of accretion or alternate rebuilding. Aislaby Hall, which has already been referred to, outwardly appears to be a compact, mid 18th-century, hipped-roof house with later additions on the west side. The west extension, though largely rebuilt in the early 20th century, is on the site of an earlier building, which was already there when the 18th-century house was erected. The new house included all the reception rooms and bedrooms necessary for family living but had no kitchen or service rooms, which must have been in the earlier wing.

At Kingthorpe House, [254] (Fig. 51), a rather similar plan was produced by a process of growth and rebuilding. The earliest part of the existing house is what is now the north half or 'pile' of the main block. This consisted of two rooms with a staircase between; the off-centre fireplace in the north-east room and the doorway beside it in the east wall suggest that this room may have been the forehouse in the rebuilt house-part of a longhouse, following the same pattern of development that occurred in some farmhouses in the 18th century and described in Chapter 4. The lower end was then subsequently rebuilt as a new kitchen obliterating all indications of a hearth-passage. Subsequently, the main body of the house was doubled in depth by an additional range built on to the south side of the older house and this contained a new parlour, dining room and appropriate bedrooms above. At the same time a new staircase was inserted. On stylistic evidence this upgrading to a full-scale gentry house was undertaken c. 1800 and cannot be related to any change of ownership, as the estate was acquired by Robert Fothergill in 1681 and remained with his descendants until the late 19th century; it was presumably an expression of the family's heightened social ambitions. The additional southern half of the house is clearly marked by a straight joint in the west wall and in the shape of the roof, which has a central valley and two parallel ridges of which the later one is higher. The south elevation is given elegance by two-storeyed bow windows and a pedimented doorcase. However, the entrance seems to have been on the north, as it is now, where a grand composition was created by the addition, not necessarily at precisely the same time as the other work but at about the same period, of two flanking wings with pediment-like gables. Designed for show, these wings only provide service accommodation, such as a dairy in the left-hand wing and a coachman's room in the right.

Other possible instances of development out of longhouses are at Levisham Hall [320] and at Low Hall, West Ayton [513]. A clearer example is Hawsker Hall [183] (Figs. 52, 53). This

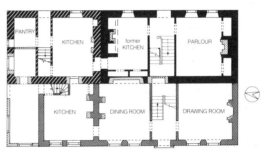

Fig. 52 [183] Hawsker Hall, Hawsker-cum-Stainsacre: from W. and plan

house has two ranges or 'piles' of different dates, each expressed externally by a gabled roof with a valley between the two. The difference is also marked by building materials, for the east half is of stone and the west half of brick, though this is disguised by rendering on the south gable wall. The house is now divided into two separate occupancies and this was apparently the situation when it was extended into a double-pile house, even though it was all in a single ownership in the middle of the 19th century.

Fig. 53 [183] Hawsker Hall: from E.

The origins are in the east half of the house, which is itself of two periods. The earlier surviving phase is the south part, which has a higher roof level. This is a central-entry house of two rooms and staircase in between. It is not strictly symmetrical as the south room, a parlour, has two windows, whereas the north room, formerly the kitchen, has only one. The latter has, against its north wall, a large hearth with heck and hearth-beam and beside this is a doorway leading to the northern part, all of which are indications that the room was the forehouse of a longhouse or hearth-passage house. The north end, of later date, has a kitchen and service rooms and must be a rebuilding of the lower end in which all traces of a hearth-passage have been eliminated. The whole is not very different in size from some farmhouses in the region but the quality of the interior fittings marks it out as being rather superior. This is evident in the panelling and bolection-moulded fireplace surround in the parlour, and even more so in the staircase which extends up to the attic; the balustrade of this has square-knop balusters which on the lowest flight are clustered three to each step.

The west side of the house is very much of a mirror image of the east side in its ultimate form. There is a parlour at the south end and, beyond the staircase, a dining room with kitchen leading off. The fittings in this part of the house indicate a date in the later 18th century. Externally, the appearance is much more appropriate to a house of gentry status than is that of the east elevation which has a rather more vernacular character. This surprising occurrence of the unit system cannot, on present knowledge, be related to any particular families but the evidence for it seems clear. It was possibly occupied by two branches of the same family. Though the house functioned as a single unit in the mid 19th century, as when it was offered for sale in 1856 and 1866, interconnecting doors having been made between the two kitchens and the half-landings, there are two principal and two servants' staircases.

CHAPTER 3

HOUSES OF THE PROFESSIONAL CLASSES

The total stock of pre-1850 houses in the region includes relatively few built for the middle class of men engaged in professional or business life. The easiest to identify and the first to emerge were houses for the clergy; the majority of these are in villages and rural areas, whereas the house of the professional man was pre-eminently a town house. There are also a number of houses of men, successful in business, who aspired to the life of the gentry and established themselves in the country. The houses are mostly in the east of the region and some were erected by men associated with the sea, among them a master mariner at West Ayton and a shipbuilder at Fyling Hall.

The houses of the clergy

Before the late 19th century, there were twenty-six ecclesiastical parishes in the region. They were generally very large, taking in extensive areas of moorland, though a few, mostly along the southern margin were relatively small.

The only surviving medieval house that may have been a vicarage is Canons Garth, Helmsley [187], which would have been built by the priory of Kirkham, to which the church was appropriated. This seems to have been an aisled hall and has already been discussed (page 18). The rectory at Middleton was mentioned in 1411 as having a hall, chambers and kitchen (Purvis 1944–7). Although there are few records and little surviving evidence of vicarage building in the century and a half after the Reformation, many of the houses described in early 18th-century terriers were probably of 17th-century date and do not seem to have differed much from contemporary farmhouses. The earliest to survive in a relatively complete state is the former vicarage of Ellerburn, now known as Old Ellers [501] (Fig. 54). In 1716 it was described as 12 yards long and 6 yards wide, the size of the existing house excluding the short byre. It is of false longhouse plan, without direct access to the byre from the cross-passage. The house remained humble throughout its use as a vicarage, and a terrier of 1817, more detailed than the earlier ones, described it as having three small garret rooms and a thatched roof; the kitchen was flagged, the parlour and pantry

Fig. 54 [501] Old Ellers, Thornton Dale: from SW

had mud floors, and none of the three rooms was wainscotted. The condition must have been very similar to that which Sydney Smith found at Foston-le-Clay on his appointment in 1806 (Holland 1855: Vol. I, 107), and the accommodation was so inadequate by the mid 19th century that the vicars of Ellerburn were living in a rented house in Thornton Dale.

The vicarage at Ellerburn may be compared with the 17th-century rectory at Kildale [247], which survives in part though much altered. This was also of one and a half storeys, but built of a superior quality of masonry, and is dated 1691 on a door lintel. Though described in 1727 as being 18½ yards long, it does not seem to have been a longhouse, as the stable, barn, and cowhouses are separately mentioned as being 28 yards long and under one roof.

Other early 18th-century terriers give the impression of houses of similar proportions. At Middleton [324] in 1716 the vicarage house was 18 yards long by 6 yards wide, about the same size as that at Kildale, with a barn mentioned separately. In the same year, Great Edstone vicarage [167] was 14 yards long with a separate barn and stable, and Levisham 20 yards in length with a barn of 16 yards, and stable and beast house together of 12 yards. At Sinnington [459], the vicarage in 1716 was the same size as Ellerburn, 12 yards by 6 yards. By 1770 it had been slightly extended to 15 yards and had a kitchen, parlour and 'another room' with earth floors, but was without chambers. By contrast, the vicarage at Lastingham [317] was 20 yards long in 1716; in 1764, when it was the same size, it had a parlour, kitchen, hall, pantry, milkhouse and four chambers, though it is possible that between these two dates a former byre had been converted.

In the towns the parsonage houses were more substantial. Though much altered in the 18th century, the vicarage at Kirkbymoorside [291] retains walls probably of 17th-century date which indicate a house rather more extensive than those in the villages; this is confirmed by a terrier of 1716 which refers to a house in the form of a letter T, 18 yards by 9 yards. The new parsonage house built at Pickering [379] in 1698, also to a T-shaped plan, was even larger (Fig. 55). A contemporary plan and the building accounts survive showing it with a 60 foot frontage and 46 feet in depth; although it does not seem to have been built entirely in accordance with the plan, the overall dimensions are almost the same. Whether or not the Kirkbymoorside vicarage followed a traditional plan form, that at Pickering marks a clear break; there are no vernacular features, but

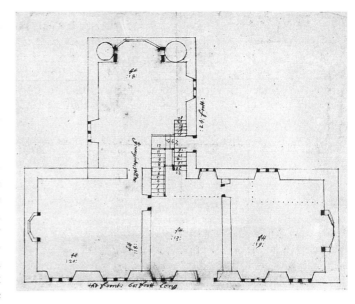

Fig. 55 [379] Old Rectory, Pickering: from SW and plan of 1698

46

a central-entry plan with a spacious, unheated entrance hall, out of which the staircase rises, a large room to each side, and the kitchen in the rear wing. There must have been at least four chambers on the first floor and the reference to 'lutheram' windows implies usable garrets. The front elevation, also, must have been up to date with six equally spaced windows of classical proportions, each with a timber mullion and transom. The rebuilding came almost immediately after the succession in 1698 of John Osborn of Chicksands, Bedfordshire, as lay rector (Crossley 1940–3).

Some vicarages, which had been built before the earliest extant terriers were made in 1716, remained with only small improvements throughout much, if not all, of the 18th century. A few were rebuilt, more particularly in the second half of the century. The small one at Sinnington, which still had no first-floor chambers in 1770, was rebuilt in 1785, though even after that it was still comparatively small at 9 yards by 6 yards. The rectory at Kildale was heightened in the 18th century but had no major alterations or additions until the second half of the 19th century. At Brompton, the vicarage was in ruins by 1777 and another house had to be acquired. The rather larger houses at Lastingham and Thornton Dale survived until the early 19th century; at the latter, in the terrier of 1809, the only real improvement recorded since 1786 was that the garrets were underdrawn.

A new rectory built at Hawnby [179] in 1733 no longer followed the longhouse plan but had a central entry between two front rooms, called in 1764 a dining room and kitchen; behind were pantry and milkhouse and a second parlour added about the middle of the century. A third room was added on the east side in 1793, when the south front was refaced and the house heightened, though it already had garrets (Fig. 56). After

Fig. 56 [179] Hawnby House, Hawnby

the vicarage at Middleton was rebuilt in 1764, its size of 15 yards by 5 yards was not very different from that of the front part of Hawnby; it had two rooms on each floor, and might be expected to have had a central entry. At Sleights, a completely new house was built for the curate of Eskdaleside in 1765 by Robert Bower, who also rebuilt the chapel at Eskdaleside at the same time. The house [103] has considerable architectural quality, in respect both of the front elevation and the internal fittings (Figs. 57, 404, 410b). The main part, fronting on to and close to the main road, is in its size and its plan quite similar to Hawnby rectory, with a dining room to one side of the entrance hall and a fore kitchen on the other; behind the latter a wing contained a back kitchen, and a similar wing behind the dining room housed a stable. On the first floor were three chambers, with two garrets under the roof.

Fig. 57 [103] The Old Vicarage, Sleights: from W. and plan (room uses as in 1857)

At Pickering the late 17th-century parsonage house was replaced in the early 19th century by a new house on a different site. This, now 25 Hall Garth, Pickering [380], was described in 1809 as 'lately erected'. It is a fully urban type of house (Fig. 58), built of brick, with the main floor raised above ground level and the central doorway approached by a flight of steps. On this floor are a dining room, drawing room and a third room. The basement has two kitchens and pantries, and on the first floor are three bedrooms, with garrets over them. The house does not have a full double-pile plan, for on each of the two main floors one room extends through the house from front to back.

Fig. 58 [380] 25 Hall Garth, Pickering: from E.

The vicarages rebuilt in the 1840s at Sinnington [459] and Great Edstone [167] both followed a small version of the double-pile plan, with large rooms at the front and smaller ones behind, these being the kitchen and offices. Similar in appearance, with hipped, slated roofs, both houses were about 11 metres by 8 metres overall; the two main rooms were called parlour and drawing room at Great Edstone, but unnamed at Sinnington. Each house had four family bedrooms, and Great Edstone also had a chamber for a servant over the scullery.

In a village otherwise of farmhouses and cottages, the vicarage at Great Edstone stands out as of slightly superior character. But virtually none of the houses in the region belong to that class of grander parsonage which occurs all over England, often standing in a large garden, and of the size of a manorial or larger gentry house; such houses are usually found where the incumbent belonged to the same social class as the squire and

was frequently actually related to him. Low Hall, Brompton, though not built for the purpose, was occupied in the 18th and 19th centuries by the vicars of the parish; many were members of the Cayley family who held the manor and whose property this house was. The rectory built at Thornton Dale in the early 1690s by Thomas Comber, Dean of Durham, who held the living, was 20 yards by 8 yards, and therefore larger in scale than other parsonages in the region. By 1764, though still with a thatched roof, it had a wainscotted parlour, hall, kitchen, back kitchen, servants' hall, and butler's pantry; the four lodging rooms all had closets, and there were two cellars. This house was replaced in 1841 by a new one, now Comber House [489] (Fig. 59), built for the Revd J. R. Hill, eldest son of Richard Hill of Thornton Hall. It is a large house to an elongated plan, with its back to the street on the north side and most rooms facing south over the garden. There were seven bedrooms, as well as a water closet, on the chamber floor. The three principal rooms were drawing room, dining room and study.

Dean Comber had used an isolated tower at East Newton Hall as a study in the late 17th century, and one was mentioned at Kirkbymoorside vicarage in 1777 and 1786. The architect's plans for Thornton Dale rectory, however, show for the first time in the region the exact location of a study within the house (Fig. 60). A room added to the east end of Hawnby rectory in 1793 may have served this purpose, a study being mentioned there in 1849. It had a separate door in the front wall, probably to permit parishioners to visit the incumbent without intruding into the family part of the house. There is no such convenient access to the study at Thornton Dale, though the position of its door close to the service quarters suggests that at least some of the visitors were admitted through that end of the house. Studies are also mentioned at Lastingham in 1853, at Sleights in 1857, where it was converted from the former stable at the rear, and at Kildale in 1862.

The professional classes in the towns

Houses for the middle ranks of society, except for the clergy, cannot be identified before about 1750. By the second half of the 18th century a small class of men had emerged who had been successful in the professions and business or, in Pickering at least, who had acquired sufficient property to justify the term urban gentry; they must have been the leading figures in their communities and demanded houses large enough to provide for their needs and to proclaim their status.

Low Hall, Pickering [384], now the Forest and Vale Hotel (Fig. 61), is a prime example of this kind of house. Said to have been built about 1787, by the early 19th century it belonged to the Mitchelson family, for whom it may have been erected. Throughout the 19th century this family was one of the principal landowners in the town and at least two of its members were magistrates. As originally built the house did not provide a great deal of accommodation, but it was enlarged considerably in

Fig. 59 [489] Comber House, Thornton Dale: from S.

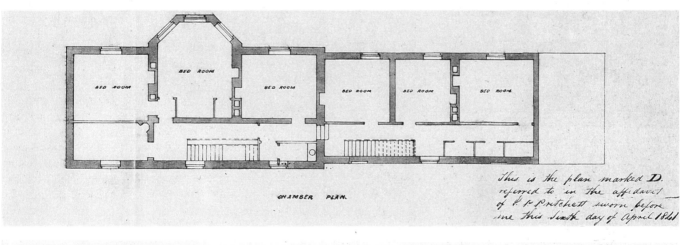

CHAMBER PLAN.

This is the plan marked D. referred to in the affidavit of J. P. Pritchett sworn before me this Sixth day of April 1841

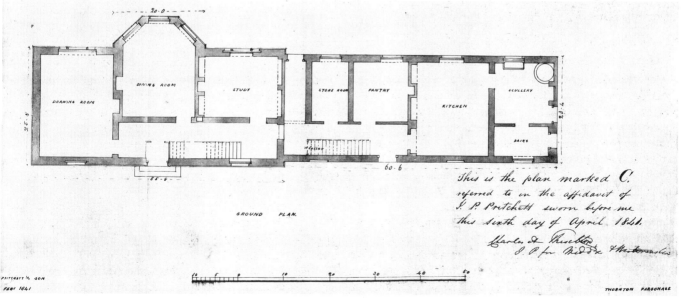

GROUND PLAN.

This is the plan marked C. referred to in the affidavit of J. P. Pritchett sworn before me this sixth day of April 1841.

THORNTON PARSONAGE

Fig. 60 [489] Comber House: ground and first-floor plans by J. P. Pritchett, 1841

Fig. 61 [384] Forest and Vale Hotel, Pickering: from NE

successive phases in the 19th century. In the main part there can have only been one principal room to each side of the entrance hall and one or two smaller ones behind, though a rear wing contained the kitchen and service rooms. There was very little land in front of the house, but its position facing along Eastgate gave it a prominent position; the facade, five windows wide, and the hipped roof conferred on it a distinction not shared by other houses in the town.

The five-bay elevation, in fact, only occurs elsewhere in the three towns in the region at Low Hall, Kirkbymoorside [265] (Fig. 62). This may have been built in 1797, a date carved on one of the roof timbers, and is in many ways comparable to its namesake at Pickering. The site is, however, quite different; the house stands within, rather than on the edge of, a large garden on rising ground and foreshadows the concept of the 19th-century villa. The front is given distinction by being built in ashlar stone and raised on a semi-basement with the front door approached by a flight of steps. Though altered, the original plan is more apparent than in Low Hall, Pickering. A wide entrance hall, extending through the house to the rear, contains the staircase. It is flanked by two large south-facing rooms, behind which were smaller and apparently unheated rooms. The basement provided spacious accommodation for the kitchen and service quarters and on the first floor were four good-sized chambers and a smaller one over the entrance hall. An extension was built in the later 19th century and the original servants' accommodation is not clearly defined. The builder of Low Hall has not been identified, but by 1823 the house was probably the residence of Francis Atkinson Esquire.

The few houses of men at the peak of the professional world were less like manor houses than the two mentioned above and had more of an urban character: in particular, they formed a more regular part of the street scene and utilized height and depth to gain adequate space.

Petch House, Kirkbymoorside [277], provides a clear statement of the kind of house demanded by a late 18th-century professional man of some consequence (Figs. 63–65). Built about 1785 for John Petch, a solicitor, it stands almost on the edge of the town in Howe End, which was then the road to Pickering. Though detached and with a garden of some size, it has an urban situation for it is not set back at all from the building line of the street, which is itself quite narrow at this

Fig. 62 [265] Low Hall, Kirkbymoorside: from S., ground and first-floor plans

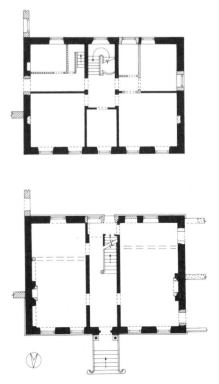

Fig. 63 [277] Petch House, Kirkbymoorside: from NW

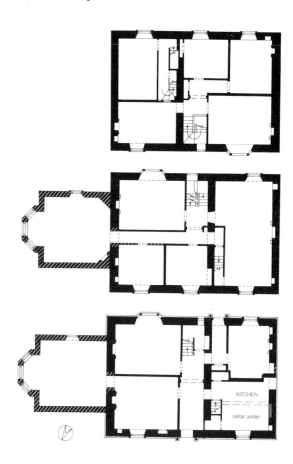

Fig. 64 [277] Petch House: ground, first and second-floor plans

KITCHEN

cellar under

Fig. 65 [277] Petch House: from S.

point. A double-pile house, it has rooms of equal depth to front and rear. Now divided, it originally had a central entry into a hall which extended through to the rear where the staircase is placed. But the rear, to the south, is the principal side of the house. This is indicated partly by the large bay window to the south-east rooms on all three floors, but more by the placing of the kitchen in the north-west corner, on the streetward side. The house is spacious, as it has three full storeys. The first floor has four chambers, one occupying the whole depth from front to back on the west side; on the second floor are a further five chambers. One of these, at the north-west corner, in the same relative position as the kitchen, has its own separate staircase from the first floor continuing up to provide the sole access to the loft under the roof. The room must have been for servants, even though they would have had to use the main stair between the ground and first floors. Though neither partitioned nor underdrawn, the loft has roof trusses designed to allow free movement within it.

As a late 18th-century house Petch House may be compared with Ryedale House, Helmsley [202], built for a brandy merchant, James Fawcett, and which is also three storeyed and stands close to the edge of the town. More specifically urban in character is 19 Bridge Street, Helmsley [200] (Fig. 66). It was probably built about 1790 by Humphrey Sandwith, an apothecary and surgeon, who sold it in 1796 to Thomas Barker, a merchant. The three-storeyed house has a relatively narrow frontage of 11 metres, originally reduced for effective living accommodation by a passage along the south side, leading to the rear. The narrow plot was utilized effectively by an L-shaped plan. The front block has three rooms on each floor, providing six bedrooms, and in the narrower rear wing was a kitchen and back kitchen. Above these were two bedrooms for servants, reached by a staircase which gave convenient access to both kitchens and a back door. Underneath the whole house is a cellar with both internal and external access. Early 19th-century additions to the rear wing may have been built by Thomas Barker as warehousing.

At a slightly lower level in the ranks of society, or in wealth, was a larger group of men, and indeed by the 19th century some women, who occupied houses characterized externally by a symmetrical three-bay elevation and internally by a central-entry plan in double depth, though usually only one-and-a-half rooms deep. In size and general arrangement of rooms these houses are not unlike the central-entry, double-pile farmhouses which also began to appear about the mid 18th century. They occur sporadically in some villages and are distinguished from farmhouses only by the lack of associated farm buildings. In the towns, there are very few in Helmsley and several in Kirkbymoorside, but they are much more common in Pickering, reflecting the pattern of land ownership by a number of small proprietors, in contrast to the other towns which were wholly or partly held by the Duncombe Park estate.

Fig. 66 [200] 19 Bridge Street, Helmsley: from SW, ground and first-floor plans

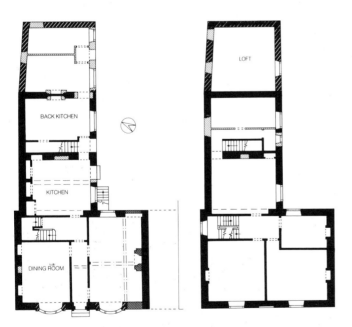

One of the earliest of these houses may be the present Estate Office, Helmsley [206], which on stylistic evidence was built about the mid 18th century; before extension in the early 19th century it was just large enough to have two rooms at the front and two smaller ones behind. The front rooms on both floors were heated, those on the ground floor probably being parlour and kitchen. Though the chimney stacks seem to be large enough for each to provide three flues, there is no direct evidence that the small rear rooms were heated. A house of similar size and of about the same date is 8 Market Place, Kirkbymoorside [281] (Fig. 67), though it was enlarged at the rear and heightened to three storeys in the 19th century. In this house one of the original rear rooms had a large fireplace which suggested use as a kitchen, though it would have been very small for that purpose.

Fig. 68 [368] 25 Castlegate, Pickering

Fig. 67 [281] 8 Market Place, Kirkbymoorside

It is not known who originally occupied these two houses but, modest as they seem by 19th-century standards, they must have been lived in by men of some consequence locally, and when built would have appeared more prominent in relation to neighbouring houses than they do now. Another house of similar size which can, however, be directly related to specific people is 25 Castlegate, Pickering [368] (Fig. 68), described in 1787 as 'newly erected'. The owner was then Richard Simpson, gentleman, and the occupier William Watson, surgeon. The plan is simpler than the two houses described above; the front door gives on to a small lobby with a straight-flight staircase directly opposite, doors to left and right leading to parlour and kitchen; there is thus no entrance passage providing direct access to the rear of the house, the two small service rooms there being approached through the kitchen.

In the later part of the 18th century, a few other houses of comparable size and type were built in the towns, such as 12 Burgate, Pickering [357], and The Green, Kirkbymoorside [261] (Fig. 69), which was developed from a 17th-century longhouse. Rose Cottage, Pickering [347], represents one of the smallest with this type of plan, having main rooms to each side of a straight-flight staircase and very narrow service rooms behind.

Fig. 69 [261] The Green, Kirkbymoorside

It was described in 1800 as 'newly built in an orchard', apparently as a speculation by Thomas Atkinson, carrier, and immediately sold to Robert Atkinson, currier.

Houses of this kind are therefore representative of those inhabited by men of gentry status, even if they were at the lower end of the range or perhaps aspiring to it, and also of professional men and those successful in business. These were not fixed, unchanging classes but ones with some degree of social movement within and between them. A central-entry house with a three-bay elevation at 75 Eastgate, Pickering [374] (Fig. 70), was built in 1786 Richard Ness, then described as a yeoman, though in his will of 1795 he was called a gentleman. In the same street is 132 Eastgate [376], built about the beginning of the 19th century, and distinguished by full-height bow windows that were fashionable at that time. The owner was William Dennis, a maltster in 1782 when he acquired the site; by 1823 his son, with the same name, was described as a gentleman and in 1851 was a landed proprietor.

Fig. 71 [201] Buckingham House, Helmsley

Fig. 70 [374] 75 Eastgate, Pickering

By the first half of the 19th century, the central-entry, double-pile house was being more widely built, particularly in the towns and occasionally in villages. The distribution is uneven, though, and reflects the differing patterns of land ownership. In Helmsley there are hardly any examples except Buckingham House [201] (Fig. 71), which acquires prominence not so much from its size, the frontage being relatively short, but from its height, above that of its neighbours, from the window proportions, and from architectural embellishments such as the pedimented doorcase and railings enclosing a strip of land in front of it. By contrast, in Pickering there are over twenty surviving houses in this category. These vary in size, the largest being represented by 118 Eastgate [375], probably the house of the Hardwick family, recorded as landed proprietors. A much smaller double-fronted house, 3 Undercliffe [402], was probably built for Christopher Lyon, who certainly owned it. He was described as a proprietor of houses in 1851, though ten years

earlier he was a miller and in his will dated 1856 was called a yeoman.

By their very nature, plans of central-entry houses do not provide scope for a great deal of diversity. A common, though not invariable, feature is an entrance hall leading through to the rear of the house where the staircase is placed, thereby providing direct access from the front door to the rear rooms. The entrance hall itself is quite narrow, being simply a passage, and the stair compartment is made wider at the expense of space in one of the rear rooms. To allow for the door to the adjacent rear room, the foot of the staircase has to be well towards the rear of the house, necessitating a dog-leg plan with a return flight on the upper half; in a very tight space there are winders rather than a half-landing connecting the two flights. Stairs of this type were apparently employed in some of the earliest central-entry houses such as the Estate Office, Helmsley [206], and Brook House, Thornton Dale [497] (Fig. 72), though in both there have been some later alterations. A better-preserved example from the second quarter of the 19th century is Ashton House, Nawton [334], which also illustrates the characteristic position of a rear entry into the back kitchen rather than below the staircase where there would be inadequate headroom.

In a house on a larger scale, or at least one with a longer frontage, a wider entrance hall could be provided with the staircase within it, rising either in a single straight flight or with only a short return flight at the upper level. It is therefore

54

Fig. 72 [497] Brook House, Thornton Dale

possible to provide a door in the rear wall of the hall. Psychologically, there is also an impression of a greater separation of the front part of the house from the rear, created by the proximity of the foot of the stair to the front rooms and by circulation between the rear rooms beneath the half-landing. The staircase also becomes more of an architectural feature within the hall. Such a plan may seem more suitable for a gentry house, since family and servants would encounter each other less frequently, and it is not surprising that it occurs at Low Hall and at Vivers Lodge (Fig. 73), both in Kirkbymoorside [265, 278]; at the latter the rear hall is even more separated from the front by a partition with an inter-connecting door. There are houses where both front rooms were parlours, but at Hill Crest, Snainton [472], a house superior enough to have a coach-house with coachman's cottage attached, one of the front rooms was originally a kitchen, though later replaced by a new one in an added rear wing.

Fig. 73 [278] Vivers Lodge, Kirkbymoorside

Some houses have no real entrance hall; instead, the front door opens into a small lobby with the staircase rising directly opposite the doors in the flanking walls to the two front rooms. Access to the back rooms from the foot of the stairs was therefore only possible by passing through the kitchen. As already noted, this type occurs at 25 Castlegate, Pickering [368], which, when newly erected, was occupied by a surgeon. Though this plan may seem inferior, and can be found in rural cottages, it is nevertheless here employed in the house of a professional man; there is, however, a degree of quality in the fittings of the parlour such as the chimney-pieces and the doors with six fielded panels. Buckingham House, Helmsley [201], provides a comparable example as, though now altered, it must have had a similar plan originally; here the superiority of the front elevation distinguishes it from its neighbours. An almost invariable external characteristic of houses with this plan is the absence of a central window on the first floor above the doorway.

The difficulty of associating the central-entry plan with any specific social group or function is illustrated by four similar houses of the early to mid 19th century in the twin villages of Beadlam and Nawton. Prospect House, Nawton [335], was built as a farmhouse as was one at Beadlam [21], though it later became the vicarage. Almost opposite to the latter is the White Horse public house [20], probably built for that purpose; the fourth is Ashton House, Nawton [334] (Fig. 74), to which a schoolroom had been added by 1853; as this interconnected with the parlour, the house must have been that of a school teacher.

The single-fronted house, only one room wide but two deep,

Fig. 75 [260] 5 Church Street, Kirkbymoorside

Fig. 74 [334] Ashton House, Nawton

with entrance hall and staircase beside these rooms, is mainly associated in the region with smaller houses and cottages. As the town house of the gentry, and of the professional and commercial classes, the type was commonly built in larger towns and cities. Only a few at this level occur in the regional towns, probably because the low density of building permitted more frequent use of the double-fronted central-entry house. The best example is 5 Church Street, Kirkbymoorside [260] (Fig. 75), of the early 19th century. Three storeys high, in brick, it stands prominently above its neighbours and was clearly built by someone who wished to express his status. Bankins, Helmsley [224] (Fig. 76), is of more modest size, though space is gained by a long rear wing. The two-storeyed front part, rebuilt in 1835, is distinguished by the quality of the masonry and the fine proportions; the total height equals that of the adjacent three-storeyed Black Swan.

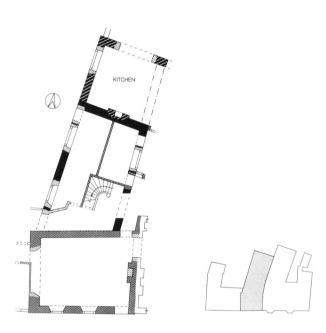

Fig. 76 [224] Bankins, Helmsley (the outline plan shows its position in the Black Swan complex)

Country houses of the aspiring gentry

The Bay Tree, Fylingdales [120] (Fig. 77), was built in 1764 by Isaac Storm, described in his will as a gentleman. He had acquired only a small amount of land on which to build his new house, which is not that of a proprietor of an estate. The L-shaped plan provides only a few rooms but these are of good size and well fitted out with panelled wainscotting and carved detail (Fig. 404). Family accommodation was limited to a parlour and a dining room, and two bedrooms above. In the wing behind are a kitchen and two bedrooms above, one of

Fig. 77 [120] The Bay Tree, Fylingdales: from SW and plan

them unheated. The house was obviously designed to signify the status of the owner. The exterior demonstrates this as much as the interior, with its five-bay wide elevation in excellent masonry raised above a high basement.

A very similar plan is at Cliff Grange, Snainton [473] (Fig. 78). It apparently dates from c.1800, a generation later than the Bay Tree, on the evidence of the fittings, though it is actually a remodelling of an earlier house of which some of the walls survive. The builder is not known, but for much of the 19th century the house was the residence of doctors, indicating a tradition of occupation by professional men. Though of L-shaped plan, it differs from the Bay Tree in that the staircase is positioned more towards the rear, partly within a projection designed for it, enabling the kitchen to be entered directly from the hall. Though not so elegantly fitted, the house is quite large, the front part three storeyed, and there is a room and not the landing behind the central window. The rear wing, though not all of one date, is long enough also to include a back kitchen with servants' bedrooms above.

Fig. 78 [473] Cliff Grange, Snainton

Fig. 79 [2] Pond House, Aislaby: from SE

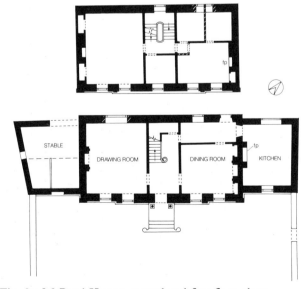

Fig. 80 [2] Pond House: ground and first-floor plans

STABLE

DRAWING ROOM

DINING ROOM

KITCHEN

fp

58

Pond House, Aislaby [2], built c.1789, provides a similar amount of accommodation to the Bay Tree, but through a different plan (Figs. 5, 79, 80). The main part of the house is two storeyed with an entrance on the central axis into a staircase hall; this is flanked by a parlour and a dining room, behind which runs a passage providing access to the kitchen in a single-storeyed wing. Though the house is three rooms long, symmetry is gained by attaching a traphouse and stable to the opposite end to the kitchen and treating its elevation as part of the whole composition. Because the kitchen is one storeyed, less bedroom space is available. Nevertheless, four bedrooms of different sizes are provided on the first floor and there are more in the attic. The external appearance, presenting a five-bay elevation with a parapet rising in the centre to form a pediment, creates an impression of a house much larger than it actually is.

High Hall, West Ayton [500] (Fig. 81), has the same amount of family accommodation as the Bay Tree but a greater number of servants' rooms, which are almost completely segregated. The house was completed in 1786 for Captain Wyville Todd, master mariner, who may have built it purely as a speculation, for he sold it almost as soon as it was finished. The plan is in double depth with dining room and parlour at the front, but all the rear of the ground floor, at a lower level than the front, is given over to service rooms; above there were three back bedrooms on the first floor originally only accessible from a stair rising from the kitchen. This positive distinction between the front and rear parts of the house is illustrated by the position of the main staircase. This is placed in the front half of the house, rising in short flights with half-landings. A similar plan occurs at Cloughton Hall [61].

Fig. 81 [509] High Hall, West Ayton: from E. and plan

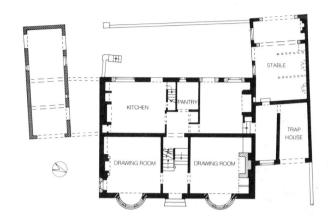

Fyling Hall and Carr View, Sleights, are houses of similar date which can be directly compared with each other, because they both adopt the foursquare double-pile plan as the most acceptable solution for a medium-sized house requiring three parlours and a kitchen. Fyling Hall [125] (Fig. 82) is not a manor house and did not acquire its present name until 1888. It was a new house on a new site built shortly after 1819 for John Barry, a Whitby shipbuilder and ship owner who had purchased land and property in Fylingdales. The house has three equal-sized reception rooms and a kitchen on the ground floor with a wide central hall containing the only staircase. The kitchen was in the north-west corner and other service rooms in the basement. The house is three storeyed and each upper floor has four equal-sized bedrooms and a smaller dressing room. Those on the second floor are of superior finishing and much more suited to family use than by servants. There are servants' bedrooms in the north wing, but this is a later addition and there is nowhere else in the original house where they could have been. The added wing contained a new kitchen, the original one becoming the servants' hall. After subsequent alterations, the entry is now at the back of the hall, which is not what would

Fig. 82 [125] Fyling Hall, Fylingdales: from SE and plan

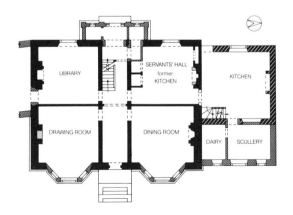

be expected when the house was newly built. Nevertheless, the ground falls steeply at the front of the house and would have made it difficult to provide a carriage drive there. The house was possibly always entered at the back so that the front could have the advantage of the view towards the sea.

Carr View, Sleights [102] (Figs. 83, 84), was built about the same date as Fyling Hall, probably for John Boulby, the owner in 1830. He was described as a gentleman (Baines 1823) but may have been another successful Whitby business man. As built, the ground plan of the house was very similar in size and shape, with the kitchen occupying the same position in relation to front door and staircase as at Fyling Hall. The only significant difference was the provision of a service stair between kitchen and hall. This similar plan was created despite different orientation and siting. Carr View faces towards and stands only a few feet away from the main road from Pickering to Whitby. In spite of the similarity of plan, the external appearance of the two houses is quite different. Though the front elevation of Carr View is marginally shorter, it is divided into five bays. It is also only two storeyed, though this need not imply a great deal less space than at the three-storeyed Fyling Hall, for Carr View has bedrooms in the attics under the roof. As at Fyling Hall, the accommodation had proved insufficient even before the mid 19th century, and additions were made on two sides to provide extra space both for service quarters and family needs. The added service wing is single storeyed, and servants' bedrooms must therefore have remained in the attics.

Fig. 83 [102] Carr View, Sleights: from NNW

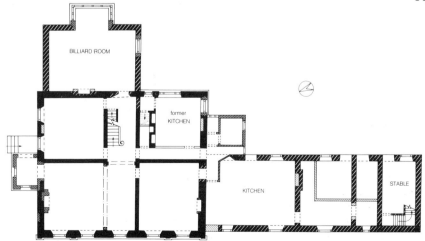

Fig. 84 [102] Carr View: plan

CHAPTER 4

FARMHOUSES

The farmhouses of the region are principally of 17th-century and later date, the majority of them standing on long-established sites, whether in village, town or countryside, others occupying positions on land more recently enclosed from moors or common fields. A few atypical ones were probably the dwellings of gentlemen or men who styled themselves as such, but most were the houses of yeomen and husbandmen and their successors. The form of these farmhouses changed significantly over the period to which they belong. At first the dominant type was only slightly removed from the typical dwellings of the medieval peasantry, but at the end of the period new houses reflected the latest and very different ideas on comfort and convenience. These changes, represented both by modifications to traditional practices and by innovations, can be studied in two separate but interrelated ways: as they are reflected in the evolving plans of farmhouses, and in the number and use of rooms. Houses have also developed as a result of partition between members of a family or because of the adoption of a 'unit system' of grouped or subdivided accommodation.

The evolution of farmhouse plans

Among farmhouses, plan was to a large extent governed by the number of rooms required and their use, and until quite late architectural display was of little importance or influence. The evolution of plan, mainly the product of changing ideas and economic and social standards, is represented by a more special-ized use and better arrangement of rooms which provided greater comfort, privacy and convenience.

In the North York Moors region, it is clear from the buildings that the longhouse plan was dominant among farmhouses in the 17th century, but that during the 18th and 19th centuries it was succeeded in popularity first by houses of linear plan and then by those with a centralized plan. The initial dominance of the longhouse is significant, since, as a house type capable of almost infinite adaptation, it exerted a powerful influence on the subsequent evolution of farmhouses. The piecemeal rebuilding and conversion which it permitted tended to discourage total

reconstruction, and this inevitably limited the ability to respond at all effectively to changing requirements; existing walls or the need to retain an earlier part of a building often led to a solution based on traditional practices. The mid 18th to early 19th century, however, was a period of more vigorous experimen-tation in an attempt to reconcile the ideals of a centralized plan with a traditional linear arrangement, and to incorporate new and changing rooms within that pattern. Some builders were able to finance total rebuilding in a more up-to-date manner but such farmhouses, like those on entirely new sites, often still reveal a preoccupation with traditional plans or only a partial assimilation of newer ideals.

THE LONGHOUSE

Excavations have shown that the longhouse existed over large areas of medieval Britain (Beresford and Hurst 1971: 107, 236–8, 263–4; Beresford 1979: 124–7), and although no example has yet been excavated in the region, it is likely to have a medieval ancestry there too. Evidence from elsewhere in North-east England supports this (Jarrett and Wrathmell 1977: 113–17, Fig. 4; Andrews and Milne 1979: 51–4, Figs. 16, 17), as does that of its surviving buildings. The longhouse accommodated both family and cattle at different ends of a single range of buildings, and in its earliest form, that of a true longhouse, both shared a common entrance. In time, however, rising standards of accommodation caused piecemeal rebuilding and adaptations which initially created false longhouses in which there was no longer common access to house and byre, but later led to the vestigial longhouse independent of its byre. These stages of evolution, identified in all their complexity among longhouses elsewhere in Britain (Smith 1963; Jones and Smith 1966–7: 23), are also represented in those of this region.

Laverock Hall Farm, Laskill Pasture [309] (Fig. 85), may be taken to show one method of evolution from true via false to vestigial longhouse, the evidence for its development being in part its own structure, and in part that of less well-developed longhouses. Different social and economic pressures might have led to any number of different stages of development, all of which can be found among surviving farmhouses. The byre might have been enlarged, demolished, replaced with another

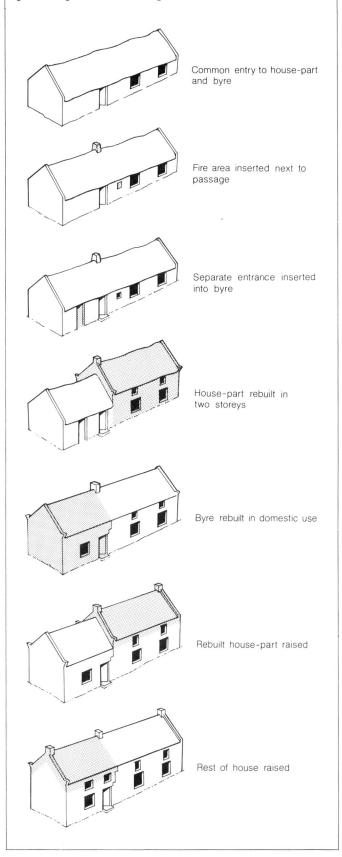

Fig. 85 [309] Laverock Hall Farm, Laskill Pasture: possible phases of development

Common entry to house-part and byre

Fire area inserted next to passage

Separate entrance inserted into byre

House-part rebuilt in two storeys

Byre rebuilt in domestic use

Rebuilt house-part raised

Rest of house raised

farm building or a domestic room, or with a combination of these two. The house-part might have been converted to a lobby-entry, central-entry or other plan, have had outshuts added or been rebuilt in double pile. A wide range of farmhouses could therefore be derived from a single house type.

The evolution of the longhouse is most clearly understood if house-part and byre are considered separately. These two parts were directly linked only in true longhouses; in false longhouses each part could, and generally did, develop independently of the other. The byre-end may be considered first, since agricultural and economic factors largely influenced its evolution, which must therefore be viewed as part of the wider development of farm buildings. The evolution of the house-part, on the other hand, is part of the broader, essentially social, development of the farmhouse, into which the discussion leads.

The evolution of the byre-end

The surviving longhouse byres, very few of them still in agricultural use, are mainly of 17th-century date, a few perhaps earlier, others certainly later. Those built in or before the 17th century were originally entered from a passage which also served as the entrance to the house, but during the 18th century social pressures led to the provision of a separate byre door, to the demolition of some byres, and to the conversion or rebuilding of others in domestic use. These later changes are clearly visible in the buildings, as also is evidence about the size and layout of the original byres, and of the arrangement of the passage which once formed the common entrance to these longhouses as a whole.

Excavations of medieval and later longhouses in North-east England have indicated that the passage was sometimes partitioned off from both house and byre, with the more substantial partition or wall towards the house. All surviving longhouses have stone walls between passage and house, and in some there is also one towards the byre. The latter walls, however, are all probably insertions contemporary with the creation of separate access to the byre, or with its conversion to domestic use. In no case does the timber partition which is likely to have created the formal division between passage and byre survive, and without it the original passage width and the position and size of the entrance into the byre can only be determined by the siting of the outer doors to the passage. These are variously disposed. In the many longhouses in which they are opposed and set next to or very close to the house cross-wall (Fig. 86), there must have been either a passage or an opening in the byre partition of sufficient width to have allowed cattle to enter safely. Some opposed doors are set away from

Fig. 86 [470] Oakwood Cottage, Snainton

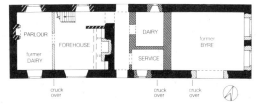

the line of the house (Fig. 87) and so imply a passage of some width. One purpose of the wide passage, observed in other longhouses (Jones and Smith 1963: 10, Fig. 2), seems to have been to keep a space next to the house wall free from farmyard dirt. It was also a solution to the problem of enabling cattle, which have laterally inflexible backbones, to turn into a byre without injury (Smith 1963: 393), although a wider byre opening and narrower passage would have served the same purpose.

Fig. 87 [141] Grange Farm, Houlsyke, Glaisdale

Staggered doors (Fig. 88) provided a more effective use of a wide passage and allowed stricter segregation of those using it; cattle could enter from the farmyard side through a door next to the byre, the other door being used only by people.

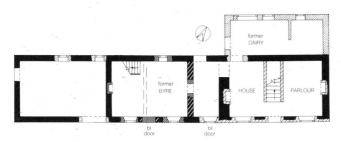

Fig. 88 [134] Highfield Farm, Gillamoor

Like passage width and door positions, byre length varied in these true longhouses, and with it arrangements for stalling and tethering cattle. In byres shorter than they were wide, cattle might have faced either the gable wall or the side walls (Fig. 89); in longer byres they would have been stalled along the building, backing on to a central drain (Figs. 88, 90). The range in the number of cattle implied by the diversity in size of byres gives some indication of the disparity in wealth of their owners.

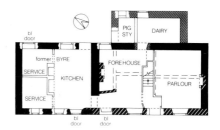

Fig. 89 [112] Laburnum Cottage, Fadmoor

This is also reflected, of course, in the nature of the accompanying house-parts, and in the type and date of alterations made to the house and byre relationship.

True longhouses, of which all of these byres originally formed part, were still being built in the region in the late 17th century, one of the latest being Glaisdale Head [162] (Fig. 137), which has a house-part dated 1690. By this time, however, the first steps were being taken towards providing separate access to house and byre, and even to the conversion of byres for domestic use, arrangements which became commonplace during the 18th century. In those houses in which the byre was retained for cattle, common access was usually eliminated in the most economical way by inserting a new external door, or occasionally two opposing doors, in the byre. Only rarely was the byre rebuilt, and if direct access from the passage was retained, it was only for the convenience of the farmer in supervising his cattle.

In long byres the new door was frequently inserted more or less centrally in the side wall, close to the cruck truss which supported the roof (Fig. 90). This alteration must have upset stalling arrangements and, even if the existing stalling was retained, the standing room of at least one animal must have been dispensed with. Sometimes more extensive alterations were

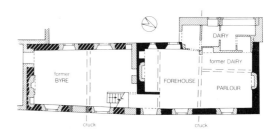

Fig. 90 [175] The Star Inn, Harome

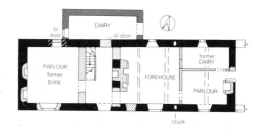

Fig. 91 [94] Peartree Cottage, Ebberston

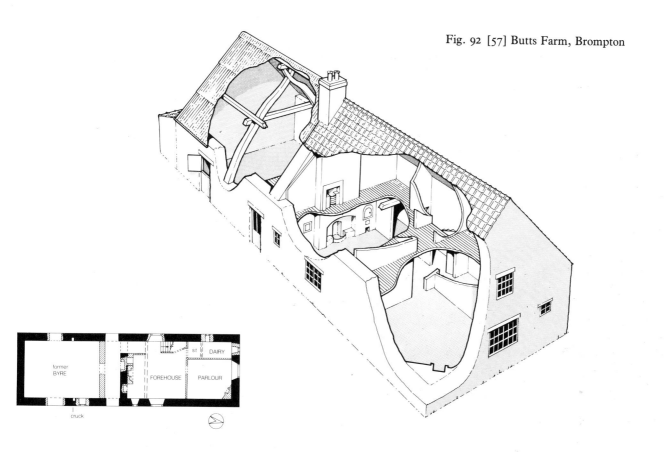

Fig. 92 [57] Butts Farm, Brompton

necessary, as well as the associated adjustments to drainage, and must have resulted in stalls set across the byre and cattle backing on to a central walk-way (Fig. 91). At times there was clearly a compromise, with some cattle facing the gable wall, others still the side walls (Fig. 92).

In short byres, doors were usually set close to one or other end of the side wall, so enabling the maximum number of cattle to be stalled across the building. Some of these doors were insertions, duplicating those to the hearth-passage (Fig. 93), but at Slidney Beck, Glaisdale [150] (Fig. 108), both sets are original and belong to a false longhouse built in the mid 18th century.

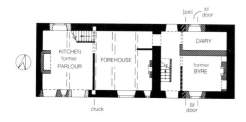

Fig. 93 [472] Cottage, West Lane, Snainton

Such measures separated man and animals, but the byre door and the smell and dirt associated with cattle were still close to the house. However convenient this arrangement was for the farmer, it was increasingly an affront to his family and visitors (Jones and Smith 1965: 55–6, 88), and to remedy it some doors were placed further from the house, generally next to the gable (Fig. 94), or occasionally in it (Fig. 105). The continuing close

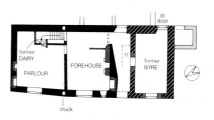

Fig. 94 [429] West View, Pockley

relationship between house and byre in the 18th century, as shown by these false longhouses, is reinforced by The Green Farm, Levisham [321] (Fig. 95), with its byre rebuilt in 1791. Anthony House, Westerdale [519], is another example, though of somewhat unconventional plan.

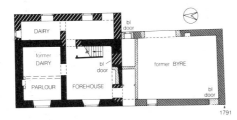

Fig. 95 [321] The Green Farm, Levisham

Most longhouses followed a different sequence of development, with cattle moved out to a new byre either adjoining the old one or elsewhere around the farmyard, the original byre being put to domestic use or rebuilt as such. Some byres, however, were replaced by other types of farm buildings, mainly during the 19th century, but there was never direct access from the house. These replacements were barns (Fig. 96), barn and byre, or stables (Fig. 117). The continuing strength and influence of the longhouse tradition is reflected in rebuilt byre-ends which combine domestic and agricultural functions (Fig. 127).

Fig. 96 [526] Fir Tree Farm, Wombleton

The evolution of the house-part

The surviving longhouses, whether of false or vestigial type, have mostly evolved from true longhouses. None is still in use as such, and though the house-parts are much altered and improved, they contain evidence for a series of stages of development. Archaeological excavations provide the background to these developments, since they have revealed medieval longhouses with house-parts of varying length and different internal arrangements. Whatever their form, most had a single open hearth in the room next to the cross-passage, and one of the first developments in the post-medieval period was its replacement by an enclosed hearth set beneath a chimney or firehood. There is archaeological evidence for this (Jarrett and Wrathmell 1977: 117–19, Fig. 5), and a few surviving buildings in the region contain signs of once having had open hearths. Spout House, Bilsdale Midcable [28] (Fig. 97), is one of these. Here smoke blackening of the roof, most intense in the middle bay of the present house-part, indicates the site of the open hearth which was succeeded, probably in the 17th century, by an enclosed hearth in the next bay east. The new hearth is not on the site of its predecessor, since this would have encroached unnecessarily on the forehouse, the equivalent of the hall in

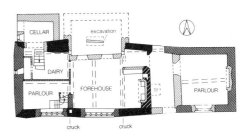

Fig. 97 [28] Spout House, Bilsdale Midcable

vernacular houses further south, and have created too wide a hearth-passage. Instead, it backed on to the existing cross-passage, the point of functional division in a longhouse, and its insertion involved the minimum of alteration. The fire in the forehouse was often the sole hearth in these 17th-century farmhouses, and the development of the enclosed hearth within its fire area frequently led to the incorporation of a fire window to light it. The absence of such a window at Spout House suggests that the enclosed hearth, itself later than the outside walls, may have been inserted before such windows had become fashionable. A number of other early longhouses also lack them (Figs. 100, 125), a factor which raises the possibility that in some of these, too, the enclosed hearth is secondary and the house-part perhaps earlier than the 17th century.

The incorporation of the enclosed hearth, with its stone fire wall backing on to the passage, was to be of great significance in the development of the longhouse, since it established a fixed structural division between house-part and byre, with the communal hearth-passage firmly in the latter. This was not of immediate importance in single-storey buildings, but as house-parts were heightened or rebuilt in two storeys and the original low fire wall became a full-height cross-wall, the distinction between it and the byre became more marked, giving the appearance of a house with its entrance in a visibly inferior part of the building.

The earliest surviving house-parts, most of them probably 17th-century but some perhaps earlier, are single storeyed with stone walls and internal cruck trusses. They vary in length from two to three and a half bays, some complete, others shortened, and although alterations have often confused evidence of the original room arrangements, it is doubtful whether any had the equivalent of the 'long hall' of some Devon longhouses (Alcock and Laithwaite 1973: 109–11). Instead, they show evidence of having had a forehouse and an inner room, or rooms, which were frequently divided from each other by partitions on the line of cruck trusses (Fig. 360). Most of the buildings, like White Cottage, Pockley [430], and Oak Crag, Farndale East [116] (Figs. 98, 99), had a forehouse which was one or one and

Fig. 99 [116] Oak Crag, Farndale East

a half bays long, although in a few houses, Broadway Foot, Laskill Pasture [314] (Fig. 100), being perhaps one of them, it may have been two bays long. These rooms, used for cooking, eating and sitting in, all have fire areas which in the one-and-a-half bay long forehouses share a bay with the hearth-passage. As Spout House indicates, however, the half bay, although part of the forehouse, was not necessarily the site of any earlier open hearth.

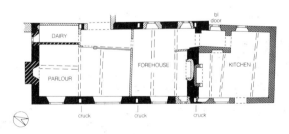

Fig. 100 [314] Broadway Foot, Laskill Pasture

The inner rooms, so-called because they lie beyond and are only reached through the forehouse, vary in length; some are of only one bay (Fig. 94), others either of one-and-a-half bays (Figs. 98, 99), or perhaps two bays (Fig. 100). Probate inventories indicate that in the 17th century they were generally parlours, serving as bedrooms or combined bedrooms and sitting rooms; some were dairies. Many one-bay inner rooms were probably not divided originally, although the end bay at Broadway Foot shows how, in the late 17th century, a dairy

Fig. 98 [430] White Cottage, Pockley

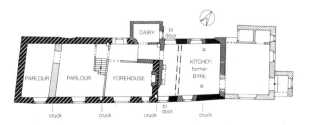

and parlour might be contrived from one; the middle bay here may have formed part of the forehouse, or have been another parlour. At White Cottage both inner rooms could have been parlours whereas at Oak Crag they may have been parlour and dairy, the latter always the smaller room.

The explanation for the diversity in size of forehouses and inner rooms must lie, as has been observed elsewhere (Jones and Smith 1964: 131–2), in the predominance of the longhouse in local society. As late as the 17th century, the architectural evidence implies that most farmers in the region, whether yeomen or husbandmen, freeholders or tenants, lived in longhouses. The difference in forehouse size, and indeed in internal detailing, are not particularly great and so are perhaps of limited significance, but there is greater variety in the number and arrangement of inner rooms. Second parlours afforded greater privacy and comfort to a family, and separate service rooms relieved other rooms of ancillary functions. Like the implications of different sizes of byre, it is probable that the number and types of room provided reflect such matters as relative levels of wealth, shared accommodation, and different relationships between generations of a family, but without documentary support there can be little certainty about this.

Most of these single-storey longhouses were probably open to the roof internally when built, although some may have had storage lofts over the inner room. Certainly, without the necessary wall height to front and rear, the roof space can only have been lit from the gable end; and in many of those which were not subsequently heightened, the forehouses must long have remained open, like that at Delves Cottage [101] (Fig. 102). Such house-parts illustrate one problem of single-storey construction in longhouses where the byre was still in use, namely that, unless placed in an outshut or created by subdivision, multiple rooms could only be built in line above the hearth-passage. The incorporation of chambers during the 17th century, however, led to a much greater uniformity and regularity of plan since it enabled functions previously catered for on the ground floor to be transferred upstairs. Longhouses with house-parts built to a two-room plan, the inner room sometimes divided, and often with a full-height cross-wall between house and byre, became customary, at first principally with a single chamber over the inner room but later and mainly during the 18th century with chambers over both rooms. Single chambers were usually entirely or substantially within the roof space, some in newly built house-parts (Fig 101), others in shortened and adapted earlier buildings (Fig. 102, see also Fig. 97). Staircases serving them usually rose within the inner room, and occasionally had their own windows as at Grange Farm, Houlsyke, Glaisdale [141], and Raw Farm, Fylingdales [118] (Fig. 87). Seventeenth-century longhouses with chambers over the whole house-part include 86, 86A Westgate, Pickering [411] (Fig. 103), where they are partly in the roof, and Caley Becks Farm, Eskdaleside cum Ugglebarnby [108] (Fig. 104), which is fully storeyed. In the manner of 17th-century farmhouses of other types, the staircases are set at the rear of the forehouse, that at Caley Becks Farm sharing a shallow outshut with the dairy.

The principal ground-floor rooms in these houses were fore-

Fig. 101 [158] House 1, York House, Glaisdale

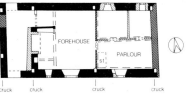

Fig. 102 [101] Delves Cottage, Egton

68

Fig. 103 [411] 86, 86A, Westgate, Pickering

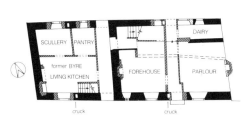

Fig. 104 [108] Caley Becks Farm, Eskdaleside cum Ugglebarnby

Fig. 105 [176] Mill Cottage, Harome

house and parlour, and even if in some houses the chambers were initially used for other purposes, all eventually came to serve as bedrooms, so relieving ground-floor rooms of this function. In these circumstances, parlours increasingly became family sitting rooms, at first commonly unheated. Some inner rooms were just parlours, others were subdivided into parlour and dairy, and it is often difficult to determine whether subdivision is original. Centrally placed gable windows, only found in 17th-century houses (Figs. 87, 92, 101), provide perhaps the clearest evidence, as at Mill Cottage, Harome [176] (Fig. 105), where they and an inserted, off-centre fireplace imply one-time subdivision. An alternative position for a dairy was in a rear outshut.

By the end of the 17th century, true longhouses with common access to house and byre had been almost entirely superseded by other house-types, one of them the false longhouse in which house and byre were still conjoined, but had separate access. Most of these latter houses were created by altering or alternately rebuilding existing longhouses, and in the 18th century the rebuilt house-parts were all two rooms long and fully storeyed. Many of these retained the traditional entry from a hearth-passage (Figs. 96, 106), but sometimes this was sup-

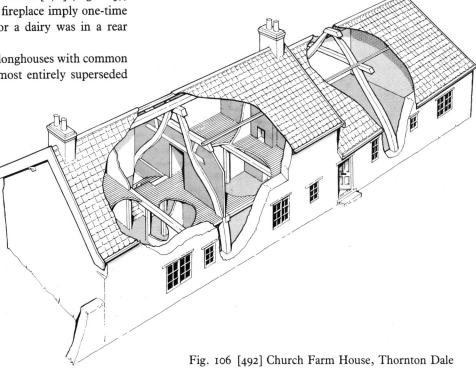

Fig. 106 [492] Church Farm House, Thornton Dale

pressed and a house-part with end-lobby entry was created (Fig. 107). The same plan was also achieved by altering some existing single-storey buildings (Fig. 90).

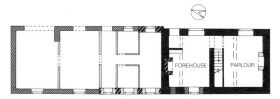

Fig. 107 [450] Forge Cottage, Rievaulx

From the mid 18th century onwards, the plans of these house-parts were influenced by trends towards more specialized room use, greater convenience, and increased personal privacy. Extra service rooms were most readily provided by the adoption of the double-pile plan, and at Slidney Beck Farm (Fig. 108) this was combined with a traditional hearth-passage in a newly built mid 18th-century false longhouse. The house is significant not only for its use of the double-pile plan, but also for indicating that close proximity between family and cattle was still acceptable then to some farmers; indeed it remained so there, as in some other farmhouses, until the 19th century when the byre was converted into a kitchen. Similar mid and late 18th-century farmhouses include Coronation Farm, Cold Kirby [65], and Bleach Mill Farm, Kildale [249].

Fig. 108 [150] Slidney Beck Farm, Glaisdale

Greater convenience and privacy were provided by another plan type which often retained the hearth-passage, but combined it with a house-part with central entry. The earliest examples include Brayton House, Goathland [163], as altered in 1740 (Fig. 144), and Red House, Glaisdale [154], as rebuilt in 1748 (Fig. 145), but similar rebuilding and alteration continued in the late 18th and 19th centuries (Fig. 89), although the separately entered byres were all ultimately replaced or converted to domestic use. These houses form part of the progress of centralized planning in farmhouses, and both they and those of which Slidney Beck Farm is typical show how aware their builders were of current developments in house design. They are yet further evidence of the adaptability of the longhouse plan to change.

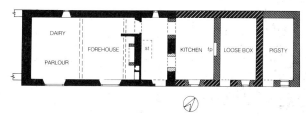

Fig. 109 [159] Highdale Farm, Glaisdale

Fig. 110 [310] New House, Laskill Pasture

Although the longhouse could be adapted to changing requirements, a number of derivative plan types were established during the late 18th and 19th centuries. Some two-room houses were built on new sites and others rebuilt on existing ones, and though some of the latter may replace former longhouses, none is the vestige of one, nor was it probably ever accompanied by a byre. Most of these houses are on small farms and differ greatly from contemporary farmhouses on larger farms. One of the most distinctive derivative plan types incorporates an integral hearth-passage (Fig 109), whereas others are merely the equivalent of storeyed house-parts entered directly through the gable wall (Fig 110), or in the front wall sometimes as an end-lobby (Fig. 111). Apart from minor variations of plan, these farmhouses differ little from the storeyed two-room house-parts of actual longhouses. The entrance, possibly no longer from a hearth-passage or in the gable wall but immediately round the corner, continues to open into a forehouse or 'house' which often still has the traditional fire area and firehood. Fire windows are rare, and though High Elm House, Bransdale [98] (Fig. 112), has one, it is set in the gable wall to avoid upsetting the near-symmetrical front elevation. Similarly, though the staircase

Fig. 111 [444] Mill House, Rievaulx

Fig. 114 [47] Low South House Farm, Bransdale

Fig. 112 [48] High Elm House, Bransdale

Fig. 113 [50] Catherine House, Bransdale

is generally in the forehouse, it may rise close to the parlour and not the entrance door, thus more conveniently serving the household (Fig. 113). The inner room is usually divided into the characteristic parlour and dairy; at Low South House [47]

(Fig. 114), the dairy is slightly built-out as if influenced by the outshuts of earlier houses. There were nevertheless variations, as at Bainley Bank Cottage, Glaisdale [149] (Fig. 430), where the dairy is conveniently set in a small outshut behind the forehouse, allowing the parlour to occupy the full width of the house.

These derived house types can frequently be matched by the standing house-parts of longhouses now shorn of their byre-ends. Some are still farmhouses, but others are smallholdings or have declined to cottage status, superseded by enclosure farmhouses or overtaken by the amalgamation of holdings. They include Nova Scotia Farm, Hawnby [182] (Fig. 115), which retains its hearth-passage, Brook Side Farm, Danby [87] (Fig. 116), which lacks one, although the end of the lintel over the former hearth-passage door survives, and a cottage in High Street, Snainton [469] (Fig. 184), once end-lobby entry but now central-entry. At Old Kiln, Helmsley [237], the dairy outshut (Fig. 117) was added when the space of the original dairy was incorporated into the parlour. Fragments of many other former longhouses survive throughout the region, particularly in its villages and towns, providing evidence not only of their wide distribution, but also their versatility in changing circumstances.

Fig. 116 [87] Brook Side Farm, Danby

Fig. 117 [237] Old Kiln, Helmsley

Fig. 115 [182] Nova Scotia Farm, Hawnby (before heightening)

FARMHOUSES WITH A LINEAR PLAN

Linear-plan farmhouses, so-called to distinguish them from longhouses and farmhouses with a centralized plan, are at least three rooms long and one or two rooms deep, either overall or along part of their length. Some are of one build, but many are longhouses alternately rebuilt in fully domestic use, and they have a variety of plans: entry into a hearth-passage, behind the hearth or away from it, into a central lobby, or into a combination of these. The definition 'linear plan' is intended to exclude those house-parts of longhouses which, though more than two rooms long and thus linear, are entered from a hearth-passage or lobby set at one end. These form part of the evolution of the longhouse, not of the linear-plan farmhouse.

The earliest of those surviving are of 17th-century date; most are of one build to a hearth-passage plan with two rooms above the passage and one below. By the early 18th century, however, more farmhouses achieved this plan by alternate development as former longhouse byres were put to domestic use; although most of these retained the hearth-passage, in a minority it was replaced by a lobby entrance. Only later in the 18th century did other plan forms challenge the popularity of these two arrangements.

The 17th-century one-build linear-plan farmhouses are of one or two storeys, or are storeyed only in part. Most have three main ground-floor rooms, some subdivided, and the houses differ in the number and position of their service rooms and in the siting of the staircase, if any. Such differences were accentuated as longhouse byres, converted or rebuilt in domestic use, were added to the domestic accommodation already provided by existing house-parts. Nevertheless, during the 18th century, greater uniformity of room arrangement was established.

Until the mid to late 18th century, the combined evidence of probate inventories and buildings indicates that the outer room, that below the passage or main door, was almost invariably a second parlour. At its most basic this plan comprised a forehouse and two undivided parlours which, the position and size of windows suggest, may once have been the arrangement at Orchard House, Harome [170] (Fig. 118), and Swiss Cottage, Rievaulx [440] (Fig. 119). Service functions, principally dairying, must have been undertaken in one of these rooms. Where there were two parlours and one or more service rooms, one invariably a dairy, the positions of the service rooms varied. One of the main factors influencing this was the date and nature of the farmhouses: in those of one build, the builder could opt for a traditional position or a new one, whereas in alternately rebuilt longhouses the number and arrangement of rooms in the existing house-part inevitably influenced new work.

A sample of rural inventories between 1689 and 1759 indicates that 42 per cent of houses with a forehouse and two parlours had one service room. In some one-build houses, probably including the 17th-century House 2 at York House [158] (Fig. 120), this was beside the inner parlour in typical longhouse manner, and the outer parlour was undivided; Stingamires, Bilsdale Midcable [25], a former longhouse, achieved a similar plan during the 18th century. In other houses, window positions imply that the service room was set beside the outer parlour,

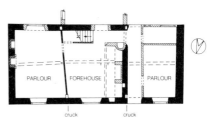

Fig. 118 [170] Orchard House, Harome

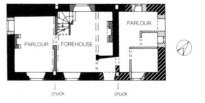

Fig. 119 [440] Swiss Cottage, Rievaulx

74

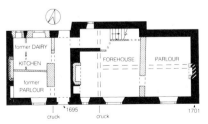

Fig. 120 [158] House 2, York House, Glaisdale

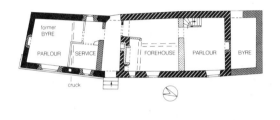

Fig. 122 [15] Cliff Cottage, Beadlam

Fig. 121 [481] Woodman's Cottage, Spaunton

Fig. 123 [530] Cruck Cottage, Wrelton

both in those of one-build (Fig. 121) and in former longhouses (Fig. 125). Service rooms between outer parlour and hearth-passage (Fig. 122) only occur in former longhouses, since this was the easiest way of subdividing an existing long byre when adaptation was preferred to rebuilding.

In the small number of inventories with two service rooms, one of them is generally a dairy, the other a buttery or pantry. Only a few such houses can still be recognized, with the service rooms in a variety of positions. At Cruck Cottage, Wrelton [531] (Fig. 123), dated 1665, it was possible to leave the inner parlour undivided by placing one service room beside the outer parlour and another in an outshut originally shared with the staircase. When the outshut was eschewed, however, both parlours had to be flanked by service rooms (Fig. 124). At Stangend, Danby [70], a former longhouse, one service room was beside the inner parlour and a second between hearth-passage and outer parlour. The reason for all these differences in arrangement must lie in the varied uses to which parlours were put. By virtue of its position, the inner parlour was more private than the outer parlour and so more likely to serve as the best bedroom or, in houses with chambers, the family sitting room. The outer parlour, because of its position near the entrance, could more appropriately have a general purpose use than that of bedroom or even sitting room. This is confirmed by the tendency to heat inner parlours rather than outer ones.

Fig. 124 [9] Rose Marie Lodge, Appleton-le-Moors

By the early 18th century, storeyed construction was the norm for newly built linear-plan farmhouses, although most long-houses converted to this plan were still single storeyed. Most of the latter had no chambers in the roof space, or only ill-lit storage lofts, but probate inventories indicate that some had a single chamber. Later alterations make it difficult to identify single chambers, although Swiss Cottage (Fig. 119) probably once had one, as Moorings, Pockley [432] (Fig. 125), has still.

Fig. 125 [432] Moorings, Pockley

In houses with two chambers, the chambers were often over the two parlours (Fig. 120). In houses with chambers overall, the staircase was usually at the back of the forehouse (Fig. 104).

The main ground-floor rooms of linear-plan farmhouses were still generally a forehouse and two parlours in the mid 18th century, but during the late 18th century the second parlour was often superseded by a kitchen as cooking was transferred there from the forehouse. Some houses were newly built with kitchens, but in far more an existing parlour, which may in turn have replaced a byre, was converted or rebuilt in this new use. The change from outer parlour to kitchen was significant in several ways, not least because it removed cooking and no doubt often eating from the forehouse, which was thus left with a changed role, not unlike a sitting room, and no longer at the centre of daily life. The change of use from outer parlour to kitchen was not necessarily as marked as it may seem, for by this time the inner parlour had become a sitting room, chambers served as bedrooms, and many outer parlours were probably general purpose service rooms. Inventory evidence lends some support to this. At Ankness, Bransdale [53], the kitchen with men's room over dated 1789 replaced the 'little parlour and chamber over' of 1752 (Inventory of George Sigsworth, 18 Feb. 1752, Borthwick). The 'little parlour' with kimlin (a wooden tub used for salting meat, kneading dough, or other household purposes), churn, milk vessel and woollen wheel was clearly more of a service room than a bedroom or sitting room; it was replaced by a room which took over some of the functions of the forehouse.

Many linear-plan farmhouses were built or rebuilt with kitchens in the late 18th and 19th centuries, but to essentially traditional plans. One of the earliest farmhouses with a recognizable original kitchen used for cooking is Crag House Farm, Danby [77] (Fig. 126), dated 1770, which is of hearth-passage plan; similar late 18th and 19th-century farmhouses include Rutland House, Harome [173], High Butterwitts, Danby [75], and House 3 at York House, Glaisdale [158] (Fig. 127). In a few contemporary farmhouses there was no formal hearth-passage, although at Harker Gates, Arden with Ardenside [12] (Fig. 128), there are opposed doors, and at Bog House, Bransdale [54], a single door. Another plan, with a central lobby entrance, already familiar from earlier two-parlour houses, occurs at Abbot Hag Farm, Rievaulx [449] (Fig. 129), and Ashberry Farm, Old Byland [344] (Fig. 130). The lobby in these houses, whether opening on to a heck, cross-wall or staircase, is always between forehouse and kitchen in the manner typical of northern lobby-entrance houses (Mercer 1975: 65–9); only in one-build houses, however, are there back-to-back hearths.

Fig. 128 [12] Harker Gates, Arden with Ardenside

Fig. 126 [77] Crag House, Danby

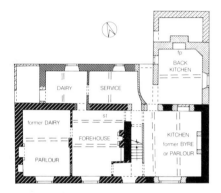

Fig. 129 [449] Abbot Hag Farm, Rievaulx

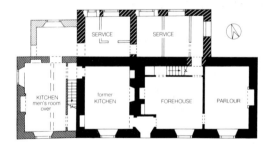

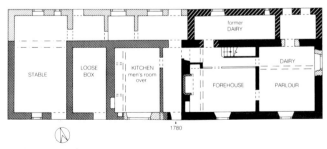

Fig. 127 [158] House 3, York House, Glaisdale

Fig. 130 [344] Ashberry Farm, Old Byland

The sequence of rooms in these houses is always the same: kitchen, forehouse and parlour. In most the original dairy is beside the parlour, a traditional position inherited in some houses from a longhouse origin. It was not a particularly convenient arrangement, however, when cooking had been transferred from the forehouse to a kitchen beyond it, since the

77

two service rooms were separated and the forehouse remained a room of passage just when it had become more of a private family room. The incorporation of kitchens indicates that the builders of these houses were aware of the specialization of room use, but were less concerned with other developments, notably convenience of plan. Such developments came to have an impact, however. At Harker Gates [12] (Fig. 128), for example, the construction of a dairy outshut not only brought dairy and kitchen closer together, but enabled the parlour to be enlarged and some through-traffic to be removed from the forehouse. At High Butterwitts [75], though a similar dairy outshut was added, the original dairy was retained as a pantry, as it also was at Low Farm, Carlton [252] (Fig. 131). The forehouse, however, was given privacy by partitioning-off a corridor, much like that in Crag House Farm, Danby [77] (Fig. 126).

Traditional plan types were quite effectively exploited in some linear-plan farmhouses built to a double-pile plan. Some, like West House, Kildale [252] (Fig. 132), are fully double pile but others, particularly those with a longhouse origin, can be double pile only in part. In these latter houses, the double-pile house-part may have accompanied a byre or, as at Hart Hall, Glaisdale [153] (Fig. 133), a second parlour, before they were replaced by kitchens. All these houses have service rooms along all or part of the rear; some added kitchens are accompanied by back kitchens, others not, like Cherry Tree Farm, Fadmoor [113] (Fig. 134). At the last farm, somewhat unusually, the double-pile element is provided by an integral outshut; in some other farmhouses (Fig. 135), added outshuts created a double-pile plan.

The continuing usefulness of traditional plan types in a period of change requires some explanation. The retention of the hearth-passage plan in the late 18th and 19th centuries was largely due to its continuing convenience, and to the fact that many of the farmhouses were alternately rebuilt longhouses in which it was less easy to break away from traditional planning. The plan was convenient where the kitchen was an outer room: it quite satisfactorily separated the working and family parts of the house, as well as providing immediate access to or from both, and to or from the front and rear of the farmhouse. The passage also relieved rooms from the draughts inevitably

Fig. 131 [232] Low Farm, Carlton, Helmsley

Fig. 132 [252] West House, Kildale

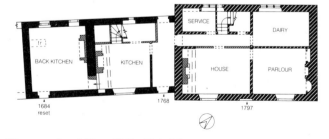

Fig. 133 [153] Hart Hall, Glaisdale

78

Fig. 134 [113] Cherry Tree Farm, Fadmoor

Fig. 135 [132] Manor Farm, Gillamoor

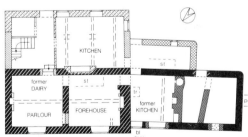

associated with a direct external door, particularly when it was combined with an opposing door. To this degree, therefore, those houses with a suppressed hearth-passage would seem less convenient, particularly when it would also have been necessary for everyone to pass through the kitchen to reach the rest of the house. Central-lobby-entry houses overcame this hardship with a front door from which kitchen and forehouse could be entered independently, and by providing the kitchen with its own external rear door. The parlours of all these houses shared the common feature of isolation from the entrance, and consequently of being entered through the forehouse. With cooking transferred to a kitchen, however, forehouse and parlour were both in effect varieties of family sitting room, and separate entry to the latter was perhaps not deemed of great importance. It was, however, already an element in the development of farmhouse plans in the mid 18th century, and it was not long before it was incorporated in various ways in linear-plan farmhouses.

Fig. 136 [166] Hunt House, Goathland

Because of its nature, the linear-plan farmhouse could not be fully centralized, but various attempts were made to achieve this. The ideal of centralized planning was to provide independent access to the main rooms of a house, enabling parlour, forehouse and kitchen to be reached from external doors, and to allow the working and family parts of the house to function separately. In linear-plan houses this was effected by providing a door from which forehouse and parlour, if not also service rooms, could be reached, as well as a separate kitchen door either from a hearth-passage or directly from outside. As is characteristic of the region, the farmhouses are either of one build or are alternately rebuilt longhouses. Hunt House, Goathland [166] (Fig. 136), was remodelled in the 1780s to a pseudo-centralized plan, and West Sleightholmedale Farm, Skiplam [463], was built as such. At the former, the centralization is superficial, since though the forehouse has its own door, parlour and dairy still open from it; at the latter the front door opens on to the foot of stairs between the forehouse and the parlour, behind which the dairy was reached by a corridor from the kitchen. Glaisdale Head [162] (Fig. 137) shows an unusual way of achieving this plan by building a two-storeyed addition

Fig. 137 [162] Glaisdale Head, Glaisdale

against the upper end, with ground-floor parlour or drawing room, fine staircase, and bedroom over, rather than converting or rebuilding the byre end. This enabled the forehouse to be used as a kitchen, and in time allowed the original parlour to be remodelled as a dining room. These houses, and others like them, may have the sophistication of separate access to the parlour, but their plans are otherwise very traditional.

In some pseudo-centralized houses, the kitchen, instead of being in line with the forehouse, was placed in a wing behind it. Examples are few, and from the front they give the impression of being true central-entry houses. At Rye Topping Farm, Brompton [59], the single-storey rear wing may originally have been a dairy or back kitchen, later converted into a kitchen; at Westwood Farm, Ebberston [95] (Fig. 138), the kitchen wing is a late 18th-century addition. In neither of these, nor any other similar house, could the kitchen be reached directly from the entrance hall. The dairy, rarely behind the parlour, is instead more closely associated with the kitchen.

Some farmhouses were also built or rebuilt in double pile but, as in those only one room deep, the degree of centralization and the disposition of the rooms varies. The houses are all of late 18th and 19th-century date, the earliest including Fryup Hall [90] (Fig. 139) and Lawns Farm [145], each with a hearth-passage, and Red House [154] (Fig. 145) without one. All have an entrance hall between parlour and forehouse, as well as a dairy behind the parlour, an arrangement which meant that the dairy could only be reached from the kitchen by passing through both forehouse and entrance hall. Such a clumsy arrangement was avoided by contriving direct access between forehouse and parlour and between dairy and kitchen: Fyling Old Hall [129] (Fig. 35), as remodelled as a farmhouse, and Winsley Hill,

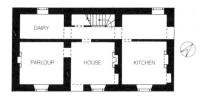

Fig. 140 [95] Winsley Hill Farm, Danby

Danby [69] (Fig. 140), are two early 19th-century examples. Both retain more or less traditional room arrangements, but each in different ways shows an awareness of circulation and of the convenience and privacy gained by linking rooms of like purpose. Nevertheless, in each the parlour could only be reached by passing through the 'house' or forehouse.

Not all late 18th and 19th-century linear-plan farmhouses had kitchens or approximated to a centralized plan. Low Wethercote, Bilsdale West Side [35] (Figs. 141, 174), and a former

Fig. 141 [35] Low Wethercote, Bilsdale West Side

farmhouse at Old Byland [341] (Fig. 161) were both rebuilt with outer parlours in the early 19th century, cooking being retained in the forehouse. In each a new service room beside the outer parlour replaced one beside the inner parlour, which was in consequence enlarged over its site. Other earlier two-parlour houses continued in use. At Cruck Cottage, Wrelton [531] (Fig. 123), and Rose Marie Lodge, Appleton-le-Moors [9] (Figs. 124, 142), new cooking ranges were inserted in the forehouses, the outer parlours remained unheated, and neither they nor their accompanying service room was converted into a kitchen.

Fig. 142 [9] Rose Marie Lodge, Appleton-le-Moors: interior

Fig. 138 [95] Westwood Farm, Ebberston

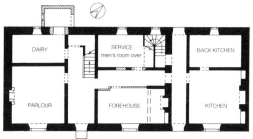

Fig. 139 [90] Fryup Hall, Danby

FARMHOUSES WITH A CENTRALIZED PLAN

Houses of centralized plan, with a central front door and rooms to each side, were first built in the region by men of gentry or professional status. Their houses (see Chapters 2 and 3), all storeyed, date from the late 17th century onwards; the earliest are one room deep, but from the early 18th century most are double-pile. Internally, a centralized system of circulation evolved, based on a combined entrance hall and staircase from which either all rooms on a floor, or at least the main ones, were independently reached. This plan established its popularity amongst landowners during the 18th century, and copybooks such as Thomas Lightoler's *The Gentlemen and Farmers' Architect* (1762) and John Crunden's *Convenient and Ornamental Architecture . . . beginning with farm-houses . . . and ascending to the villa* (1770) confirm that this was a national trend in houses of all types. From the mid 18th century, professional men and yeomen farmers adopted the plan in the region and it was also recommended locally by the agricultural writer, John Tuke. Two of his three ideal farmhouses are of such a plan, one of them not unlike some built in the region, albeit without the detailed subdivision of the service accommodation (Fig. 143). Tuke did not attempt to justify the double-pile plan, whether for its convenience of room layout or symmetrical elevation, but Laing stresses another benefit which must have appealed to all builders, whether landlord, tenant, or freeholder: 'The nearer the plan of a building approaches to a square, the greater are its conveniences, and the cost proportionally less. A square, equal in superficial extent to a parallelogram, requires less external walling, and consequently less internal finishing' (Laing 1800: vi).

The earliest examples of centralized planning in yeoman farmhouses are some former longhouses whose house-parts were converted or rebuilt in the mid 18th century. At Brayton House, Goathland [163] (Fig. 144), a central door was inserted in 1740, the interior of the house was altered, and rear outshuts were added to provide extra service accommodation; at Red House, Glaisdale [154] (Fig. 145), the house-part was completely rebuilt to a fully double-pile plan in 1748. Both were still probably false longhouses, with a separately entered byre below the hearth-passage, but each also had a parlour which could be independently reached. Red House is the more advanced of the two since it is fully double-pile and carries centralization to the extent of combining entrance hall and staircase; so, too, does Street Farm [144] (Fig. 146), built in 1749 and perhaps the earliest freestanding centralized plan yeoman farmhouse in the region. There are various differences between these houses, which indicate the experimentation at that time with the problems associated with centralizing access. At Brayton House and Red House the retention of entry behind the hearth illustrates the influence of the longhouse; at Street Farm the fire area with its gable fire window and incipient heck is one of the few indications of traditional influence on the plan.

The experimentation with plans continued through the late 18th into the 19th century, almost entirely in double-pile houses. The formal symmetrical elevation was rapidly mastered and the imperfect symmetry of some early farmhouses is almost entirely absent from later buildings. Most late 18th-century central-entry farmhouses were built on large farms, and, as well as a parlour, living room and at least one other service room, all incorporated a kitchen. Beyond this uniformity, however, there are variations in their approach to centralization. Some, like Welldale House,

Fig. 143 Farmhouse elevation and plan from Tuke 1800: Plates IV and V

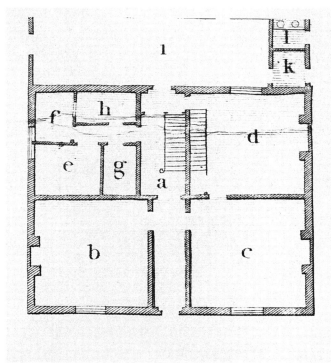

Fig. 144 [163] Brayton House, Goathland

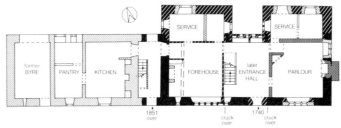

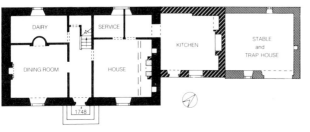

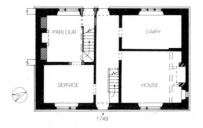

Fig. 145 [154] Red House, Glaisdale

Fig. 146 [144] Street Farm, Street, Glaisdale

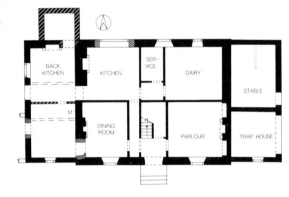

Fig. 147 [98] Welldale House, Ebberston

Ebberston [98] (Fig. 147), have little more than a lobby at the foot of the main stairs, facing the front door, and beside it an awkwardly contrived passage or corridor leading to other rooms, but others have more convenient arrangements. Although Street Farm (Fig. 146) was built in 1749 with a full-depth combined entrance and stair hall, this arrangement was little used until the end of the 18th and during the 19th century. The entrance was at times reduced to a passage, as at New Hambleton, Pickering [419] (Fig. 148), or was the same width as the stair hall, as at Demesne Farm, Fylingdales [126]. At Howdale Farm (Fig. 284), the staircase opens off the side of the full-depth hall, whereas at Foulbridge (Fig. 5) and the earlier Scawton Croft [457], there is a front stair hall. In almost all these houses, regardless of siting or orientation, the service rooms were at the rear, the family rooms at the front, and each in a different way contrived independent access to most if not all rooms. The majority had separate access to all bedrooms too, often from a spacious landing, although the men's rooms over many kitchens were frequently isolated from other first-floor rooms. The interiors of some of these larger farmhouses were fitted out to quite a high standard, with decorative plasterwork, chimney-pieces of marble or with composition moulding, as well as good staircases (Figs. 420e, 422).

Although the construction of some large double-pile central-entry farmhouses continued in the first half of the 19th century, the majority of that date are smaller. Many seem to have been built not by freeholders but by landlords and by tenant farmers; some were enclosure farms, whereas others had been rebuilt in a spirit of improvement. In many of these smaller central-entry farmhouses, most of them of 19th-century date, the front door opens on to a lobby at the foot of the stairs with the parlour to one side, the 'house' to the other, and service rooms at the rear.

Fig. 148 [419] New Hambleton, Pickering

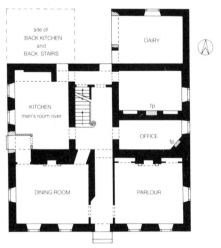

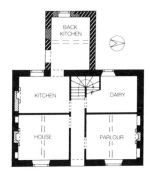

Fig. 151 [426] West Farm, Pockley

Fig. 149 [42] Smout House, Bransdale

The latter always include a dairy, and either a kitchen or back kitchen depending on whether cooking was still undertaken in the 'house' and preparation of the food therefore elsewhere (Fig. 149). Some farmhouses had a third rear room; at Griff Farm, Rievaulx [452] (Fig. 150), the attic stairs rise from this. A central passage occasionally replaced the entrance lobby, so providing separate access to the ground-floor rooms and staircase (Fig. 151); sometimes even lobby and passage were omitted (Fig. 152). The inadequacy of some of the farmhouse plans without a separate kitchen is indicated by Beck Side Farm, Danby [88] (Fig. 153), which had a kitchen added in a rear wing within a generation of its construction in 1813. These smaller houses reveal the same experimentation with plan exhibited by the larger ones, and although there are inevitable variations in the combination, arrangement and size of rooms, the basic division between front family rooms and rear service rooms was rarely, if ever, disturbed.

Fig. 152 [51] Moor Houses, Bransdale

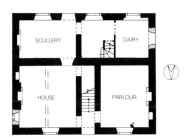

Fig. 150 [452] Griff Farm, Rievaulx

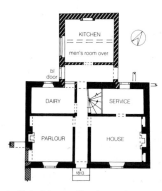

Fig. 153 [88] Beck Side Farm, Danby

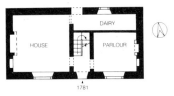

Fig. 154 [180] Mill House, Hawnby

Fig. 155 [311] Carr Cote, Laskill Pasture

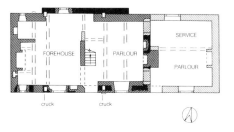

Fig. 156 [437] Pockley Grange, Pockley

Single-pile central-entry farmhouses appear on smaller, poorer farms from the late 18th century onwards, either as freestanding buildings or the result of alterations to the house-parts of former longhouses. Mill House, Hawnby [180] (Fig. 154), built in 1781, incorporates a dairy behind the staircase and parlour. At about the same time, Carr Cote [311] (Fig. 155), a former longhouse, achieved this form by remodelling, although it lacks a formal entrance hall, as does Pockley Grange (Fig. 156), a moorland enclosure farm. A few farmhouses have a single room to each side of a central door, as do Low Thwaites, Hawnby [181], and Newgate Foot, Laskill Pasture [313]. In 1851 (Census) the former was occupied by an 'agricultural labourer and pauper', the latter by a farmer of 45 acres.

Not all central-entry farmhouses have entry into a passage or at the foot of stairs; a few are of true lobby-entry plan with the door opening against a central chimney-stack. Scalla Moor House, Pickering [422] (Fig. 157), of 19th-century date, is one of these; the substitution of gable fireplaces for the original central stack highlights the alien nature of the latter. As at Beck Side Farm (Fig. 153), the original rooms proved inadequate and a kitchen was created within part of the barn. Scalla Moor House is not entirely without parallels in the region, for a similar, unexecuted design of 1827 exists for a house in Danby parish (Fig. 158), and the house at Bumper Castle is not dissimilar.

The freestanding farmhouses with symmetrical elevations, central front doors and double-pile plans, which were character-istic of the region in the early 19th century, were often part of

Fig. 157 [422] Scalla Moor House Farm, Pickering

86

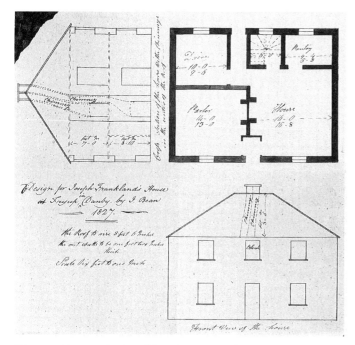

Fig. 158 Proposed plan of farmhouse, Danby, 1827

planned regular farmstead layouts (Fig. 285). They stand in marked contrast to earlier longhouses and linear-plan farmhouses which, even after development, often retained a physical link with their farm buildings, which were rarely as organized in their overall layout. John Tuke recognized this discrepancy in his report to the Board of Agriculture. He wrote of the upland farms of the North Riding of Yorkshire: 'Little can be said in praise of the arrangements either of the farm-houses or offices throughout this district; the old ones appear as if built without plan or contrivance, patched together at various times, as the circumstances of the occupier might happen to require . . . Those of a more recent date are far more commodious and compact, and the plans are daily improving, though not yet arrived at perfection; much more attention is paid than formerly to external accommodation, and some judicious plans of farmyards may be met with' (Tuke 1800: 35).

The subdivision of farmhouses

PATTERNS OF INHERITANCE

Wills made by the inhabitants of the North York Moors region survive in significant numbers from the late 17th century onwards. Most of them were made by yeomen or their widows, and the pattern of inheritance which they reveal at first conforms to the ancient arrangement by which a third of personal property was left to the widow, a third to the children, and a third, the dead's portion, as the testator pleased. This custom was still observed in the province of York during the 17th century, but

it was modified by an Act of 1695 which allowed the free disposition of property (Camp 1974: xi–xii). Usually most of those who made wills left their goods to their widow or eldest son; the same result is likely to have occurred from intestate deaths, since widow and son were next of kin. Combinations of widow and children, or other relatives, usually nephews or grandchildren, accounted for the remainder. Daughters were only occasionally favoured, younger sons still less, since normally a man expected his eldest son, if not already established, to farm his land. On let freehold property, as well as on leasehold farms, this had to be with the agreement of the landlord. In 1754 Francis Hogard of Oakhouse, Laskill Pasture, left to his eldest son, John, 'tenant right of all the housing and barn called Stoddfast Hill in Bilsdale with the consent of Thomas Duncombe', who owned the Helmsley estate from 1746 to 1779.

Modes of inheritance had different effects on the development of houses. The commonest division of buildings was the temporary one between widow and heir, as at Southfield, Kirkbymoorside, in 1724 where Thomas Fisher enjoined that his son was to allow his mother 'house room while she remains my widow'. The precise rooms to be used by the son and his mother were left to their discretion and convenience, but at times wills are more specific. In 1756 George Woodwark of Glaisdale willed that his mother should have 'the low parlour and the Chamber over it to dwell in during her natural life', and 'one bedstead and the furniture thereunto belonging standing in the low parlour'.

Even such specific bequests do not imply structural division of the house, although they at times foresaw the need for some building work. William Garbutt of Ewe Cote, Bilsdale West Side, specified in 1718 that if his widow 'be not content to have her being with my son William he shall put her up a chimney in the low parlour and let her have a cow keeping winter and summer'. Whether the separation was not only spatial but structural cannot be told, but it is a possible cause of subdivision, even if only temporary. While the terms of such wills provide reasons for the appearance of additional fireplaces, perhaps still only the second fireplace in a house, these provisions became less necessary as living standards improved during the 18th century. By his will of 1773 Frankland Coates of Red House, Glaisdale [154], left his house and farm to his son, but provided that his widow should have 'all that room on the west end of the house wherein I now dwell called the dining room and the chamber over it to dwell for and during the term of her natural life but not to sell the same'. The dining room and chamber over form part of a house rebuilt in 1749, and since each has an original fireplace there was no impediment to wife and son living separately. Indeed the growing number of heated rooms, combined as at Red House with a central entrance hall and staircase independent of the other rooms, will have eased the temporary division between widow and heir.

The 'low end' and 'low parlour and chamber over' left to widows are likely to have been the converted or rebuilt lower ends of former longhouses, houses which by development had achieved hearth-passage plans. The house of William Ward of Rosedale West Side, as revealed by an inventory of 1738, consisted of forehouse, parlour, little parlour, milkhouse and the 'west end of the house'. Ward, in his will, left his farm to his son John and to his wife for her life the west end of the house, namely 'one low room with a chamber over it and one little parlour adjoining to the said low room' and 'one little house called Bakehouse to bake in and to lie her elding in'. The house was almost certainly a former longhouse, but whether the 'west end' was the former lower end, or an addition to it, is uncertain; each part seems to have been able to function independently of the other.

THE UNIT SYSTEM

An alternative form of partition resulted from the division of a house between two heirs. In 1755 Jane Potter of Fadmoor, widow, left her freehold house and garth in Gillamoor to her two sons, and to her unmarried daughter for life the 'parlour and chamber over it adjoining to the west end of the dwelling house'. How house and land were divided is unknown, but at Castlehouses, Danby [84], there is more detailed information. In his will of 1780 Thomas Peirson left to his grandson Thomas Peirson 'the west end of half of messuage called Castle Houses, divided from east end . . .', and to his grandson John Peirson the 'east end of messuage called Castle Houses'. The present farmhouse is a longhouse which had already been alternately rebuilt in fully domestic use by 1780, the date of the will, in which it was specified that 'the door in the west side of the entry or passage in Castle Houses and the door in the chamber over the entry shall be walled up and made fast by Thomas Peirson and his brother John shall not be entitled to any part of the west end of the house'. The outbuildings, barns, stables, cowhouses, farmyard and spring of water passed jointly to John and Thomas. The will took effect on Thomas's death in 1783, and the house is still divided, each part rebuilt.

This arrangement, which resulted in a permanent subdivision, is an example of the unit system. The unit system was first recognized in Wales and was defined as 'the arrangement in a group of several small houses, each complete in itself, in place of the single large house which might be expected to result from addition or rebuilding' (Hemp and Gresham 1942–3: 98). The term was subsequently expanded by Machin (1975) to include divided buildings where each part functioned separately. Examples are now known over much of England and Wales, at gentry and yeoman levels, and though mainly between related households, also between unrelated people (Machin 1978: 117–22).

There is both structural and documentary evidence suggestive of unit systems among the gentry of the North York Moors region, at Welburn Hall and Hawsker Hall, but the majority of examples are of yeomen farmers, both freeholders and tenants.

Houses recognized as being unit systems occur both as houses joined together and as houses which are detached. They take various forms. Houses which are joined together include Castlehouses, Danby, a former longhouse which was subdivided down one side of the hearth-passage and subsequently rebuilt by each owner, becoming by development two houses set end to end. At Howdale Farm, Fylingdales [131], a similar unit system, but between unrelated owners, was established after the

sale of the farm in 1787. The farm was bought by Henry Robinson on 31 March 1787, who retained part for his own use and on 3 April following sold the 'east end of Howdale farm house, orchard on back part, moiety of turf house, moiety of open yards and well, the upper cow house, barn in open yards' to John Sedman. The property was eventually reunited in 1816, perhaps hastened by the burning down of the house in 1812, and by the fact that by then one half of the freehold was let rather than occupied by its owner. The farmstead was rebuilt to a regular plan between 1827 and 1829 by Robert Usherwood, who also let it.

Lane Head Farm, Glaisdale [146], consists of two houses set end to end, the earlier an alternately rebuilt longhouse and the whole of 18th-century date. It gives every impression of being a unit system, as evidently was Highgate House, Hawsker cum Stainsacre [185]. Although now two separate houses at right angles to each other, in her will of 1789 Ann Smith of 'Haggit How' left to her nephew George Stockton 'moiety of the new dwelling house where sister Mary Sleightholme lives, adjoining to the south end of the old dwelling house at Haggit How', and to her sister Mary Sleightholme 'her moiety of the old dwelling house, farm and freehold at Haggit How'.

Another layout has the two houses in a staggered line with overlapping corners. Scamridge Farm, Ebberston [97], has this arrangement, as does Beck Side Farm, Danby [88], where a self-contained house was added in the late 19th century to that built in 1813. The two have an interconnecting door, no doubt the reason for the overlap, and were perhaps occupied by two generations of farmers.

Unit systems consisting of separate houses are much more common than those with houses which are joined. The houses are frequently parallel, and may be set side by side as at Dean Hall, Eskdaleside cum Ugglebarnby [110], or in a staggered layout as at High and Low Wethercote, Bilsdale West Side [35]. At Prospect House, Glaisdale [147], the two are at right angles, the earlier house a longhouse alternately rebuilt in fully domestic use and just behind the south-facing, central-entry house of about 1800. At York House, Glaisdale [158], the two earlier houses, 1 and 3, are some distance from each other and are almost at right angles, perhaps to avoid one overlooking the other. If these two houses represent a unit system, and in the context of Danby and Glaisdale with its regularly spaced, individual farmsteads this is likely, so in turn do Houses 2 and 3 which are now just separate although in a staggered line. How these two houses were occupied and who farmed the land is unknown, but they seem to have been amalgamated before in turn House 1 and its land was absorbed into a larger holding. Both these unit systems are likely to date from before 1655 and the sale of the manor of Danby, which produced strict control of the total number of freeholds. House 3 bears the only date, of 1780 on the rebuilt house-part of a former longhouse. Houses 1 and 2 are stylistically 17th century, and the absence of date-stones on them, in the context of their parish, reinforces a pre-1655 date.

Danby and Glaisdale seem to have had unit systems both on land held of the manor of Danby before 1655, and on freehold land thereafter. A number of other wills relate to freehold land, but evidence from the Helmsley estates indicates that tenure by lease or at will need be no barrier to the creation of a unit system. The surveys by successive owners of the Helmsley estate, particularly those of Bilsdale between 1637 and 1827, supplemented by the 1851 Census (Ashcroft and Hill 1980), reveal considerable subdivision and rearrangement of holdings. Already in 1637 in an area consisting of the parishes of Bilsdale Midcable, Bilsdale West Side and Laskill Pasture, eight farms had divided garths from which separate land holdings were farmed, and one other had adjacent houses. Four of the nine farms were worked by members of the same family, as at High and Low Crosset, Bilsdale Midcable [26, 27], where Richard Dobson held 'one halfe or messuage called Crofthowmate', and John Dobson 'the other half messuage called Croftswaite'. At Malkin Bower, 'Christopher Bowes, John Bowes and William Bowes holds one tenement called Mawkin Bower, three fire houses, three farmes, and the said John one little hay house'. Between 1642 and 1781 a further twelve farms were divided, three of them farmed in 1781 by members of the same family, another with one name identical to that in 1642. Thus, of twenty-one farms, seven were farmed by related families and in one more an established family retained its interest. Length of time since the first creation of a unit system, coupled with lack of heirs, could explain some of the unrelated examples. At Orterley, Bilsdale Midcable [24], the farm was split into three, subsequently reorganized as two, all farmed by people with different surnames. As the subdivision could have taken place any time between 1642 and 1781, the initial undocumented division could have been between members of the same family. The number of unit systems with related families must prove the ability to provide shared inheritance, generally for two sons but occasionally three, by subdividing tenanted holdings. It may not, in Bilsdale, have resulted after the early 18th century in more than marginal intaking, but it will have ensured by its very existence more efficient farming as well as guaranteeing the landlord his rent, and the prospect in future of additional sums. This division of land supports the view that landlords raised no objections to large-scale transfers of land between farmers and changes of tenancies (Hobsbawm 1969: 99).

It remains to be discovered whether the farms were worked from a divided house or from separate houses. The evidence is generally lacking in the documents, but buildings suggest that there were often separate houses. The 1781 map which accompanies the Bilsdale survey confirms this. It is possible that at first houses were subdivided, new houses being built only when individual circumstances made it possible. At one of the farms subdivided between 1642 and 1781, Laverock Hall, both houses are former longhouses alternately rebuilt in fully domestic use. It is improbable that either was first built after 1700, and indeed Laverock Hall, Laskill Pasture [309], incorporates two 1691 inscriptions. An inventory shows the house to have had a forehouse and high and low parlours in 1728, and in 1751 its tenant left to his eldest son 'tenant right of all my houseing and farming at Laverock Hall with consent of Thomas Duncombe his steward or officer'. At Laverock Hall Farm,

Laskill Pasture [309], the house is also almost certainly at least 17th century in origin. The relationship of the two farms, with their yards facing each other across a boundary, implies the division of one garth, and occurs elsewhere, including High Wether Cote and Low Wether Cote, Bilsdale West Side [35]. The latter is of at least 17th-century origin, the former a house rebuilt in the early 19th century. Given the degree of rebuilding and amalgamation of houses and holdings, it is difficult to identify which of any two or more houses is the earliest, and which the newly created house.

All farmsteads with two houses should not be interpreted as unit systems. On some, the secondary house may be a labourer's cottage, as at Stormy Hall, Danby [82], and on others the custom of rebuilding a house on the same site was not followed. At Lounsdale Farm, Kildale [248], a late 18th-century farmhouse stands away from the farm buildings, which include a 17th-century longhouse. Similarly, at Moor Houses, Bransdale [51], a new house of 1802 overlooks the earlier 18th-century house and the farmyard. Its isolation from the farm buildings, surely the reason for its position, did not outlast the 19th century, however, since by 1900 extra farm buildings had been built close to its side wall.

Amalgamation or consolidation of holdings also produced pairs of houses, which pose few problems of identification on farms set out in the fields, but can be more difficult to interpret in villages: Beech Farm, Ainthorpe (Danby [67]), is such an amalgamation.

The use of rooms in the farmhouse

Changes in the use, number and arrangement of rooms, caused among other things by increased prosperity and heightened personal requirements, were important factors in the evolution of farmhouse plans. These changes, which were mainly concerned with segregating functions and providing greater comfort and convenience, led to the creation of new rooms and to the use of existing rooms in different ways. The principal sources for the study of these farmhouses, apart from the buildings themselves, are probate inventories, estate records and the writings of agricultural commentators. Of these, probate inventories are the most numerous and collectively the most valuable source, for though they only survive in large numbers after 1688 and become progressively less detailed in the last decades of the 18th century, they cover a period of great significance for the farmhouses of the region. They reflect the growing number of rooms noted in the buildings, although changing room functions created problems of terminology. When longhouse byres were first being put to domestic use, the room was sometimes called the 'low end' or 'low house' rather than a 'parlour'. The name 'parlour', however, did not reflect just one type of room, since it might be a bedroom, a sitting room, or even a service room, depending on date and social circumstance. Such factors must be borne in mind when considering room use.

THE FOREHOUSE OR 'HOUSE'

The term 'forehouse' is the common description in probate inventories of the main living room in farmhouses in the late 17th and 18th centuries, other names, including 'firehouse', 'dwellinghouse', 'fore room', and 'house', occurring less frequently. During the 17th and for much of the 18th century, the forehouse was principally used for cooking, eating and sitting, and often contained the only hearth in a house before the heating of other rooms became common. In 1670, as many as 70 per cent of houses in the region assessed for hearth tax had only one hearth (Purdy 1975). In the 17th century, as Spout House, Bilsdale Midcable [28] (Fig. 97), shows, the forehouse fire was sometimes still on an open hearth, which was superseded by an enclosed hearth within a fire area (Fig. 159). Cooking took place in this fireplace, at first over a fire on a hearth-stone, but later on iron cooking ranges as these developed during the 18th and 19th centuries. The contents of forehouse inventories include such implements as kettles, pots and pans of iron and brass, reckons on which cooking-pans were hung, and tongs for controlling the fire. Other cooking implements mentioned less frequently include spits, bellows and frying pans.

The use of the forehouse for eating and sitting is indicated by the furniture commonly listed in inventories, which includes tables, seating such as chairs, forms, stools and long settles, and cupboards, spences and dressers providing drawers and storage space for household requirements. The shelves of dressers (Hartley and Ingilby 1972: Pl. 34) were probably used to display the pewter plates and dishes and wooden trenchers often listed, as well as the more rarely mentioned 'delf' or 'potter' vessels. The not uncommon listing of a clock, or 'clock and case', in the 18th century further strengthens the impression of the forehouse as the main living room.

The forehouse was sometimes used for sleeping in, particularly in the 17th century, although inventory evidence for this is sparse. Nevertheless, the advantage in winter of having a bed in possibly the only heated room, or the circumstance of several generations sharing a house, must have contributed to this use. The bed could have stood in the room, have been set within a recess or outshut, or have been built in as a box bed, though none of the last survives in a forehouse. In 1696 the single-storey house of Thomas Meggeson of Stone Moor Sike, Snilesworth (Borthwick: March 1695/6), had beds in all three of its rooms, and a recess enclosed by 17th-century panelling at the rear of the forehouse in Oak Crag (Fig. 160) is probably a rebuilt and modified bed outshut. No bed equivalent to that of Ralph Pennock, described in 1738 as 'one bedstead seiled in the forehouse' (Borthwick: Jan. 1737/8), has been recognized.

Fig. 159 [28] Spout House, Bilsdale: forehouse, showing fire area

Fig. 160 [116] Oak Crag, Farndale East: forehouse, showing panelling

With the increasing use of chambers as bedrooms in the 18th century, some parlours became sitting rooms. Such a change inevitably had some impact on the use of the forehouse, removing one of its functions, but was not as far reaching as that which occurred to some in the late 18th and 19th centuries

when cooking was transferred to a kitchen. The forehouse was then no longer at the centre of household life and had become essentially another sitting room, albeit one in which food might have been eaten. These changes of use are reflected by a change in nomenclature in inventories, for though the term 'house' had been used from at least the 1690s, it occurs with greater frequency in the later decades of the 18th century as well as on subsequent farmhouse plans (Figs. 143, 285). Tuke defined the 'house' as 'the living room' (Tuke 1800: 32). 'Forehouse' and 'house' must at first have been interchangeable, but as the 18th century progressed the term 'house' was preferred. In some farmhouses, nevertheless, the forehouse or 'house' was still used for cooking (Fig. 161), which is no doubt why in a very few inventories it may instead be equated with the room called the kitchen.

The late 18th and 19th centuries saw the ultimate development of the 'house' as the dining room of a few farmhouses. In the larger farmhouses in which day-to-day cooking and eating took place in a kitchen and the parlour was a sitting or withdrawing room, it would appear that the 'house' was a family dining room. Examples of such houses are Foulbridge, Snainton [477], New Hambleton, Pickering [419], and Stiltons, Rievaulx [451] (Figs. 5, 148, 166); at Foulbridge the room has a sideboard recess.

Fig. 161 [341] House, Old Byland: forehouse, showing fire area

91

The parlour was the second ground-floor room common to all farmhouses, and though its name remained unchanged from the 17th to the 19th century, the number of parlours and their use did not. The latter varied with time and according to the type and number of other rooms in a house, and was also related to household size, income and social status. In the 17th century, parlours were most commonly bedrooms, and although some continued to be used as such, in the 18th century they became sitting rooms, dining rooms, and service rooms. The last use was generally eclipsed in the late 18th and 19th centuries as these rooms became kitchens.

Of 395 rural probate inventories examined for the period 1689 to 1799, 246 (62 per cent) have a single parlour, a further 120 (30 per cent), most of them earlier than 1760, two parlours and 11 (3 per cent) three or more. Farmhouses with a single parlour belong to all the main house types (Figs. 92, 126, 146), but those with two parlours are all either former longhouses or linear-plan farmhouses (Figs. 119, 124). In these, the parlour usually reached through the forehouse, here called the inner parlour, in inventories is named high, upper or great parlour, or merely parlour; the second or outer parlour, often below the hearth-passage or entered through a lobby, is the low or little parlour. The third parlours, all three variously called high, hither or low or little parlour, or high, middle and low parlour, are difficult to identify. While some may be rooms in linear-plan farmhouses, others could conceivably be in an outshut or wings.

Parlours generally served as bedrooms in the 17th and early 18th centuries. In farmhouses like Cliff Cottage, Beadlam [18] (Fig. 122), built with a single parlour and no chamber, this use was probably unavoidable but, on the evidence of inventories, it also occurred in some houses with two parlours. The occasional mention of chairs or a table in inventories suggests that some parlours were combined bedrooms and sitting rooms, a possible use for parlours like those in Broadway Foot [314] (Fig. 100) and Oak Crag [116] (Figs. 99, 397), which have inserted fireplaces of late 17th-century date. Although there were chambers in some 17th-century houses, they did not become common until the 18th century when their provision became a major influence on the function of parlours, encouraging the change away from their use as bedrooms. This change, however, was not inevitable. Although the chamber of Ralph Knaggs' house at Stonegate, Danby, housed a bed in 1756 (Borthwick: July 1756), the parlour also contained a bed, as well as a chest, table, chairs and linen. Inventories of the 1780s still list beds in the parlour as well as in chambers, and Tuke commented that the parlour of a typical farmhouse 'usually has a bed in it' (Tuke 1800: 32). Most of these beds were probably freestanding, although a few 18th-century built-in box beds survive (Fig. 162).

Despite this evidence, there was a marked trend in the 18th century for single parlours, or inner parlours where there was more than one, to become just sitting rooms. This is probably how the parlours in most newly built mid 18th-century and later farmhouses were used. It is implied in such houses as Street

Fig. 162 [36] 26 and 29 Brook Lane, Ainthorpe, Danby: panelling concealing box bed in parlour

Fig. 163 [154] Red House, Glaisdale: china cupboard in parlour

Farm (Fig. 146), built in 1748, in which both the parlour and chamber over it (Fig. 423a) are heated. Here, as elsewhere (Fig. 424), the status of the parlour as a sitting room is stressed by the arrangement of cupboards flanking the fireplace. During the late 18th and 19th centuries, such parlours often had good chimney-pieces, and particularly in larger farmhouses like New Hambleton [419] and Foulbridge [477], they also had moulded cornices and panelled shutters. These sitting rooms were probably not greatly used when farmwork was pressing and the kitchen was the centre of activity. Some may have served for special occasions and receiving visitors, the function noted by Francois de la Rochefoucauld who, after visiting some comparable farmers in Suffolk in 1784, wrote 'The houses are always clean and well kept . . . and they are always careful to keep one small sitting-room spotlessly clean and sometimes quite elegant. In this room they receive their guests; the tables and chairs contained in it are of well polished mahogany, the chimney-piece is sometimes of marble but generally of carved wood' (Marchand 1933: 237).

In some larger farmhouses with dining rooms, this room took the place of the 'house' rather than the parlour. In smaller houses, however, in which cooking still took place in the fore-house or 'house', the parlour seems occasionally to have been a dining room rather than a sitting room. Such use was presumably prompted by the desire to eat away from the cooking hearth, but it meant that there could be no formal sitting room unless the dining room served both purposes. Frankland Coates' will of 1773 indicates clearly that the main ground-floor rooms in that part of Red House, Glaisdale [154], which he built in 1748 (Fig. 145), were a 'house' and 'dining room'. Identification of parlours used as dining rooms is difficult, although that at Red House, significantly and unusually, has a china cupboard (Fig. 163) midway along its back wall rather than cupboards flanking the fireplace. Once cooking in kitchens became common, the forehouse or 'house' must often have served as a family living room capable of being used as a dining room if necessary. 'Dining room' rarely appears in yeoman inventories, though that of William Barker of Nawton in 1751 listed one which contained 'chairs and other implements'; other rooms were forehouses, parlour, kitchen and chamber (Borthwick: June 1751).

Another use for a parlour was as a service room. In some single-parlour houses without separate service rooms, inventories of late 17th to mid 18th-century date indicate that, as well as containing beds and a chest or two, dairying and other domestic equipment was at times stored in the parlour, if perhaps not actually used there. Other inventories indicate that in houses with two parlours, both of them with beds, the outer parlour was often used for domestic storage and general service purposes, and sometimes also for industrial activities. Indeed a number of outer parlours, variously called 'low parlour', 'low end' and 'low house', contained domestic fittings and dairying equipment only. Domestic storage is indicated by such items as chests, cupboards and presses, and general service by the presence of kimlins, baking tubs or arks, and such dairying equipment as churns, bowls and skeels. Spinning wheels and reels

are the main indicators of industrial use, and these are rarely the only contents of a parlour. This trend towards a service function for outer parlours paved the way for their conversion or rebuilding as kitchens, a common development in the late 18th and 19th centuries. Nevertheless some outer parlours continued to survive as unheated service rooms (Fig. 103), while others (Figs. 141, 161), though rebuilt with fireplaces, were not used for cooking since this was retained in the 'house' or forehouse.

As well as a 'house', parlour and kitchen, some farmhouses had other rooms; Tuke (1800: 45, Pl. II) labels one a 'study'. New Hambleton House (Fig. 148) has such extra rooms at the side; if not pantries, being heated, they could be study, housekeeper or maid's room, or some other servant's room.

SERVICE ROOMS AND KITCHENS

During the 17th and early 18th centuries, although separate service rooms were lacking in some farmhouses, many did have one such room and a few had two. From the mid 18th century onwards, more farmhouses were being built with or enlarged to incorporate at least two service rooms, while kitchens became commonplace later in the century, and particularly in that following. The need for service rooms originated in the desire to relieve the forehouse of some of its functions. Just as sleeping was transferred from parlour to chamber, and in consequence sitting from forehouse to parlour, so were dairying and related matters of storage moved to a dairy. From the forehouse, food preparation and the storage of pots, pans and food were in turn transferred to scullery and pantry, and ultimately cooking to the kitchen.

Late 17th and 18th-century inventories indicate that single service rooms were almost invariably dairies. Before the mid 18th century most of these were termed 'milkhouse' rather than 'dairy', and the few called 'buttery' clearly served the same purpose although they also contained such equipment as baking tubs and pans. Only five inventories list second service rooms other than kitchens, all in addition to a dairy. One of 1705 is another milkhouse, two of 1716 and 1791 are butteries, and two of 1753 and 1755 are pantries. The butteries and pantries both stored pots, pans and perhaps food, and they must represent the same room but with a different name, the earlier old-fashioned, the later new (cf. Barley 1963: 496).

The importance of dairying in the region is indicated by the frequency of dairies in its farmhouses. Before refrigeration and better communications made the sale of milk a practical proposition, butter and cheese must have been produced on most farms, either for home consumption or for sale as well. The contents of dairies listed in inventories confirm this, including as they do such necessary equipment as skeels, milk pails, bowls and their stands, churns, and 'lead bowls', (a form of settling dish). Those farmhouses which produced butter for sale are usually recognizable from the quantities of individual dairy goods listed. In 1753, for example, the dairy of Richard Brewster of Middleton included 2 firkins of butter, 2 churns, 27 bowls and 2 milk pails (Borthwick: Aug. 1753). A firkin was a wooden tub capable of holding 56 lb. of butter.

Cheese was also produced for home consumption as well as for sale, and in both large and small quantities. Cheese-making is most frequently indicated by the presence of the brass kettles used to heat the milk to encourage curdling; cheese vats or troughs, and cheese presses, are less commonly listed. These items occur in dairies, parlours and kitchens. Benjamin Lumley of Muscoates, Kirkdale, seems to have made both cheese and butter on some scale. His inventory of 1738 (Borthwick: June 1738) shows a dairy including 10 milking pails, 2 stands, 84 bowls, 10 skeels, a barrel churn, 2 kettles, 6 cheese vats (fatts), a cheese trough, a table and 6 butter firkins. None of these late 17th and 18th-century inventories names a separate cheeseroom, although examples of 19th-century date survive on a number of farms, including Crag House Farm, Danby [77] (Fig. 126), and Winsley Hill Farm [69] (Fig. 140), both in Danby. (For detailed accounts of dairying and cheese-making, see Brears 1972; Brears and Harrison 1979; Mason 1968; Hartley and Ingilby 1972.)

Kitchens in which food was cooked were already part of the gentry houses of the region in the 17th century, but they did not become common in farmhouses until the late 18th century. Rooms called kitchens are listed in the inventories of some yeoman farmers in the 18th century, but most seem to have been used as general domestic service rooms, and whether all were heated is uncertain. The contents of many indicate that they were used for butter and cheese-making. Pots and pans, which can probably often be identified as the cauldrons and skillets of iron and brass used for everyday cooking, need only imply food preparation in the kitchen, for in very few yeoman inventories does it, rather than the forehouse or 'house', have the reckons and tongs associated with a cooking fire. The kitchen of Benjamin Lumley contained a table, form, dishes, trenchers, pot, cheese press and a furnace in 1738, the last item probably used to heat milk for cheese-making and not to cook food. That in 1764 food was not cooked in the kitchen of Mary Deighton of Baysdale, Westerdale, widow of a yeoman (Borthwick: Mar. 1764), is certain, for though its contents, which included skeels, cans, iron pans, an iron pot and iron oven, imply dairying and food preparation, the reckons and tongs, table and chairs listed in the forehouse indicate that the food was cooked and eaten there. The kitchen of Robert Stamper of How Gill, Kirkdale, was evidently being used for cooking in 1721 since it contained a table, pair of racks, 4 kettles, a reckon and a pot of dripping, though a table and chairs in the 'house' suggest that food was eaten there (Borthwick: Sept. 1721).

Items specifically related to brewing, such as mashvats, coppers, tubs and barrels, are rarely listed either in the kitchens or the brewhouses of farmhouses except where farming appears to have been combined with innkeeping. Nevertheless, some brewing was possibly undertaken on most farms, if at times only of gale beer or mead (Hartley and Ingilby 1972: 44–5, 92).

Late 18th-century inventories lack the detail to be of value in the study of kitchens, but their implied evidence that kitchens defined as rooms used for cooking were rare before that date is

Fig. 164 [98] Westwood Farm, Ebberston: range in kitchen

confirmed by that of the farmhouses. Rooms recognizable as kitchens all date from the late 18th and 19th centuries (Figs. 126, 148), and have large fireplaces to accommodate the cast-iron ranges which ultimately developed to incorporate hearth, oven and boiler (Fig. 164). On some farms the family, servants and labourers often ate in them, not necessarily at the same table, and they still served more general service activities such as dairying, brewing, salting meat and washing. Nevertheless, they did not become universal even at this date. On smaller farms a separate kitchen was unnecessary, and the 'house' was often a multi-purpose room for cooking, eating and sitting in. Many, however, had a back kitchen for the preparation of food and for other household purposes (Fig. 149).

CHAMBERS

The chamber accommodation provided in farmhouses in the 17th century varied considerably. Some single-storeyed farmhouses originally lacked chambers and were either open to the roof or had ill-lit storage lofts reached by ladders (Figs. 98, 122); other ostensibly single-storeyed houses had attic chambers largely or wholly in the roof and lit from the gable (Figs. 92, 101), and there were also storeyed houses (Figs. 103, 123). Many such houses were still occupied in the 18th and 19th centuries, often with inserted or extended chamber accommodation (Figs. 99, 118), but from the early 18th century onwards the spread of storeyed construction resulted in a substantial increase in the number of chambers.

Probate inventories dating from the late 17th to the mid 18th century indicate that some chambers were used as bedrooms, some for storage, and some combined both functions. Such uses are found irrespective of the number of chambers listed. Those containing beds also housed chests and occasionally tables and chairs, and items in store in them included various pieces of dairying and baking equipment, cheeses, wool, corn and such agricultural items as winnowing cloths, sieves, riddles and skeps.

Despite the information provided by inventories about the number and content of chambers, few are specifically named and so capable of precise location within a house. Eight inventories dating between 1705 and 1730 are, however, sufficiently detailed and list a chamber over a forehouse or 'house' as well as over one or more parlours. Four include beds in all chambers, but in the other four they were only in the chamber over the parlour, that over the forehouse being used for storage. It may seem unusual that the latter chamber, by virtue of its position probably the warmest in a farmhouse, did not become the best bedroom. That it did not was due to the intrusive bulk of the firehood, as well as to its use as a corridor to other chambers. The parlour chamber became the best bedroom in part-storeyed houses because it could be lit from the gable wall; in storeyed houses it remained so because of its privacy and the ability to heat it using a stack shared with the parlour below. By the late 18th and 19th centuries, when all newly built farmhouses were fully storeyed, many of them to a centralized plan, there was often little but size to distinguish one chamber from another. Landings gave independent access to many of them; in the smaller farmhouses only one or two might be heated, whilst in the larger ones it was usual to heat all family bedrooms. In these larger farmhouses, if any ground-floor room determined the nature of the room over it, that was the kitchen over which men's rooms were so frequently placed.

Fig. 165 [28] Spout House, Bilsdale Midcable: chamber over parlour

Some indication of the nature of earlier chambers is provided by Spout House, Bilsdale Midcable [28]. A single-storey farmhouse, it has a parlour chamber created in the roof space in the 18th century, and a later chamber over the forehouse (Fig. 165). The latter, difficult to enter and originally very dark since it was lit directly only by a small window in the eaves, may have been used solely for storage, although in other houses similar

chambers were certainly slept in. Joseph Ford, a stonemason born in Danby parish in 1870, writes of chambers 'lit by a very small window in the roof on a level with the boarded floor'. To reach such a window meant creeping on hands and knees, and to allow room for getting into bed the bedstead had to be placed directly under the apex of the roof (Ford 1953: 63). Spout House has a box bed in the parlour chamber, but in the many other chambers without this sophistication, sleeping conditions must have been primitive. Hartley and Ingilby (1972: 11) note that when the wind blew, bits of straw fell down on the occupants, and wasps crawled in from a nest in the thatch.

SERVANTS' ACCOMMODATION

Changing agricultural methods affected the development of the farmhouse in the late 18th and 19th centuries, when a considerable proportion of the agricultural labour force of the whole North Riding of Yorkshire consisted of annually hired farm servants who 'lived in' with their masters (Hastings 1981: 59). These servants, both male and female, were unmarried and board and lodgings were part of their annual wage. This was one factor in the introduction of the farmhouse kitchen large enough to cook in and for family and servants to eat in, and which often had a men's room over it.

Not all farms employed labour, whether living in or not. The *First Report from the Commissioners on the Employment of Children, Young Persons, and Women in Agriculture* (1867: 94) states that in the North Riding of Yorkshire there was 'a class of small farmer who by himself and his children does the whole work of the farm, and rarely if ever employs a labourer or hires a lad by the year. These farms vary in size from 10 to 50 acres'. As a broad generalization, this was probably true of the North York Moors region. The 1841 and 1851 census returns for Fylingdales indicate that about one-third of the farms there were worked only by the farmer and his wife, and that about half of all farms were under 50 acres (FLHG 1976: 40, 1979: 13). In the census of 1851, almost as many farms under 50 acres in Bilsdale employed labour as did not, although sometimes farming was combined with milling or innkeeping (Ashcroft and Hill 1980: 140–70). These family-run farms are one reason for the existence of farmhouses with kitchens which have no men's rooms over them, as at Fir Tree House, Danby [89], or of kitchens with bedrooms over, reached from the main house only. Another reason lies in the number of servants employed, and whether they resided in the farmhouse. Of 105 farms listed in Bilsdale for the census, 26 had no labour outside the close family, and those employing 1, 2, 3, 4 and 5 labourers totalled 23, 32, 17, 6 and 1 respectively. Allowing for variations in numbers of non-resident labourers and resident house servants, at least half the farms would probably have had no need for special servants' accommodation.

The annual statute or hiring fairs in the region were held at Martinmas in Helmsley, Kirkbymoorside, Pickering, Castleton, Egton and Whitby (Hartley and Ingilby 1972: 16). Male and female servants were hired for indoor and outdoor work, the men to undertake farm labour of all kinds but not to the exclusion of women. Writing of the women, Tuke (1800: 315–16) records that 'the dairy is entirely theirs . . . they perform at least half the harvest work . . . [and] a multitude of lesser occupations of husbandry. At home, when the weather or season of the year does not permit the labours of the field, the women spin flax, or wool, chiefly for the use of the family'. Since farm servants living in were unmarried, separate accommodation was necessary for each sex. Evidence taken in the Helmsley area indicated that girls almost invariably entered domestic service with its obvious and unavoidable dangers, and represented some farmers as unpardonably reckless about the places where men and women servants slept (Reports 1843: 294).

On the larger farms sleeping accommodation was usually provided by creating men's rooms over kitchens, as was customary in other areas (Neave 1971); female servants probably slept in a bedroom in the family part of the house, where the farmer and his wife could exercise some supervision. Men's rooms can be recognized in farmhouses from the late 18th century onwards, early examples including Crag House Farm, Danby [77], of 1770, Ankness, Bransdale [53], of 1789, and Stiltons, Rievaulx [451]. In most of these, as in other contemporary and later farmhouses, the men's room is over the kitchen, from or off which it is reached by its own staircase; there was rarely any communication between the men's room and the rest of the first floor. Since they were directly warmed by the kitchen fire below, few have their own fireplaces. Most men's rooms occupied a full storey (Figs. 132, 148) but at times they were in little more than an attic (Fig. 134). In some farmhouses, including Crag House Farm [77] and Woodhead Farm, Danby [91], they also had access to the attics, which must have provided more sleeping and storage space. At Woodhead Farm, a glazed peep-hole in a closet off a family bedroom allowed direct supervision of the men's room.

Some attics were used to provide separate servants' accommodation for men or women. At Stiltons, Rievaulx (Fig. 166), a new servant's room was incorporated over the added back kitchen wing, and the original one over the kitchen was retained; the partitioned second floor (Fig. 167), partly in the roof and reached from the main staircase, must have been for male or female servants. At Foulbridge, Snainton [477] (Fig. 5), the men's room is over the back kitchen, and a second back stair probably led to women's rooms. The box beds built into the attics at Sinnington Lodge [460] (Fig. 168) were possibly for male servants, the females sleeping elsewhere in the house.

On smaller farms, or in smaller houses, servants' accommodation was not so formal or as separate. Farm and house servants were employed in such houses as Smout House, Bransdale (Fig. 149), although the plan gives no indication of this. They and the family all slept on the first floor, but access to the unmarried women's room was through the farmer's bedroom. Such an arrangement was not always acceptable, however, and among

Fig. 166 [451] Stiltons, Rievaulx

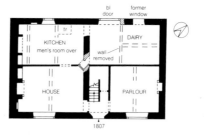

Fig. 169 [329] Shaken Bridge Farm, Murton Grange

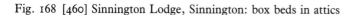

Fig. 167 [451] Stiltons: servants' rooms

Fig. 168 [460] Sinnington Lodge, Sinnington: box beds in attics

the smaller farmhouses, Griff Farm, Rievaulx [452] (Fig. 150), has back stairs rising to attics which may have served as servants' rooms, and High Leys Farm, Rievaulx [448], has a men's room over an added rear kitchen wing. At Shaken Bridge Farm, Murton Grange [329] (Fig. 169), a trap-door in the kitchen ceiling implies ladder access to a former men's room.

WORKSHOPS

In a number of late 17th and 18th-century probate inventories there are rooms called 'shop' or 'workhouse' which are clearly the workrooms of craftsmen, many of them weavers, others blacksmiths or woodworkers. From the stock, crops and husbandry gear listed, it is evident that many of these men also farmed, generally on a scale larger than that associated with just a smallholding or cow-keeping. It is, therefore, legitimate to look for such workplaces in farmhouses and associated outbuildings.

Textile manufacture from wool, flax and hemp was undertaken on a domestic basis throughout the region in the postmedieval period. Spinning, traditionally undertaken by the farmer's wife and therefore probably always secondary to farming, was the most widespread activity, and spinning wheels and reels are listed in some forty-eight rural inventories. All of those for which a specific location is given were in parlours or chambers; none was in a 'shop' or 'workhouse'. In houses with more than one parlour they were almost invariably in the equivalent of an outer parlour, in what was clearly a general purpose room alongside furniture, dairying and other equipment, and beds. In four of fifteen inventories, however, such items are missing; three list spinning wheels alone, while one also includes some cloth. In these instances the outer parlour was in effect a workroom, but it was probably architecturally indistinguishable from other parlours with multiple domestic uses.

Twenty-four inventories listing 'looms' are certain evidence of weaving; some belong to people accorded the status of 'weaver', others 'yeoman', and one a 'fuller'. In the fourteen which specify where the looms were housed, nine are in 'shops', two in 'workhouses', two in parlours, and one 'below the entry'. All the 'shops' are in houses with only a single parlour and so are probably on the site of an outer parlour or former byre; this is confirmed by the naming of one of the parlours as 'far parlour', and by mention of 'below the entry, 1 loom' (Borthwick: John

Agar, Dec. 1783). One 'workhouse' was probably a separate building, since the house has two parlours (Borthwick: Robert Skelton, Sept. 1763); in another with just one parlour (Borthwick: Robert Petch, June 1757) the 'workhouse' could have been on the site of an outer parlour. Typical entries include a shop with 'two looms and 8 lining [linen] webs [pieces of cloth taken from a loom] with some yarn and other things' (Borthwick: William Kayesley, July 1727), or the workhouse (Borthwick: Robert Petch, June 1757) with '1 loom, gears and other things belonging to her'.

Other craftsmen with 'shops' include woodworkers of various types, particularly a 'house carpenter' whose shop contained 'some small work tools' (Borthwick: John Peacock, Feb. 1724) and a husbandman, clearly a cooper, in whose shop were '22 iron hoops, 2 saws, firkin staves, ends of rods, ash wood, and other things of employment belonging the trade' (Borthwick: George Ward, Nov. 1761). Such shops are again in houses with one parlour and could be below the entry, as could the blacksmiths' shops. At the Old Forge, Pockley [431], the smithy was in just this position, on the site of a longhouse byre.

CHAPTER 5

COTTAGES

Cottages, the dwellings of people holding little or no land, are most numerous in the towns and villages of the region. The earliest are of the 18th century, and although there is documentary evidence for some before that date, none met the requirements of improved housing standards and survived the rebuilding of later centuries.

Historical evidence

Documentary references to cottages in the 17th century include those listed in the Survey of Kirkbymoorside in 1610, among them the 'little cottage of one room, lately erected by Agnes Vickers' (PRO: L.R.2/186). A more general indication of the cottager element of the population in the late 17th century is provided by the returns of the Hearth Tax, levied from 1662 to 1689, which contain evidence of the structure of society, the degree of poverty, and buildings. Households too poor to pay church or poor rates were exempt from it, as were those in a house worth £1 a year or less, and not occupying land worth more than £1 a year, or possessing lands, tenements, goods and chattels worth £10. In 1670 (Purdy 1975) 27 per cent of all households in the region were so exempt, and it seems reasonable to equate these with cottagers. The towns of Helmsley, Kirkbymoorside and Pickering, with 49 per cent, 32 per cent and 26 per cent of exempt householders respectively, contain proportionately more than the average 19 per cent exemptions for the rest of the region. Some of the households assessed with just one hearth may also have been cottages. The same three towns had 62 per cent, 61 per cent and 78 per cent of assessed households with just one hearth, compared with 73 per cent outside the towns. Nevertheless, in a not particularly prosperous region, with an economy founded on agriculture, many of these single-hearth households, particularly outside the towns, are likely on the evidence of the buildings to represent the long-houses or hearth-passage houses of yeoman farmers, rather than cottages.

Historical evidence for cottages and cottagers is not as readily available in the 18th century because probate inventories for the region, which almost all date from that period, are principally of yeomen, and only three among over six hundred examined are of men who described themselves as labourers. All three had assets comparable with those of yeomen, and they were clearly not typical cottagers, most of whom had insufficient goods to merit making a will. By the end of the 18th century, however, descriptions of cottages are available, and those in the North Riding of Yorkshire were described by John Tuke as being 'generally small and low, consisting only of one room, and, very rarely, of two, both of which are level with the ground, and sometimes a step within it'. Such situations, he noted, rendered them damp and, together with the small apartments, injurious to the health of all who lived in them, for 'in such contracted hovels numerous families were often compelled to reside' (Tuke 1800: 41). Similar low standards continued during the 19th century. An unfavourable description of the farmhouses in Egton is followed by a note 'that the cottages are rather worse' (First Report 1867: 414). J.C. Atkinson, vicar of Danby, who accompanied the Commissioner acquiring evidence, describes one of them as having a passage with a calves' pen and henhouse on one side and on the other a single living room with a clay floor, no loft, and on two sides the cubicles or sleeping places of the entire family (Atkinson 1891: 19). There were two similar cottages in Danby, each one roomed and loftless, one of them about four yards square. Neither offered any privacy to its occupants, who at one time numbered a total of twenty-three (Atkinson 1891: 22).

These accounts reflect a widespread degree of rural poverty, although they do not present a completely balanced picture since during the 18th, and particularly the 19th, century standards of cottage accommodation improved significantly. Such cottages were not particularly numerous at the time that Tuke was writing and, although there were many more by the mid 19th century, the Parliamentary Commissioners perforce highlighted bad housing as part of their investigations. The condition of the Egton farmhouses and cottages to which they drew attention was the result of neglect by the landlord, compounded by their being on an estate then in chancery. The cottages in Danby described by Atkinson were, as he wrote, typical of the 'old-fashioned, as well as old, cottages once the rule in the district' (Atkinson 1891), few of which, he observed, then remained.

Fig. 170 [532] Lora Terrace, Ruston, Wykeham

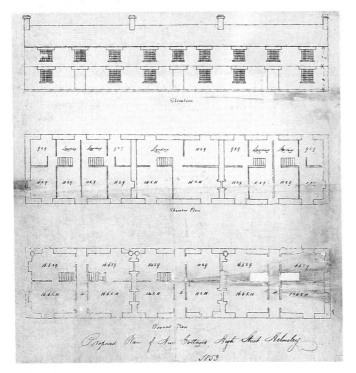

Some writers noted the improved accommodation. Although Ord described some cottages in Cleveland and Eskdale as 'small, meagre and inconvenient', he also drew attention to improvements effected by such landlords as the Turners of Kildale, and added that he must not 'tax indiscriminately the landlords with negligence or the farmers with apathy in respect to the condition of our labouring population' (Ord 1846: 87–8). In Wykeham and Hutton Buscel, Marmaduke Langley, holder of the Wykeham estate, between 1822 and 1850 built for his tenants twenty-one cottages, some single, some in pairs, and some in terraces [532] (Fig. 170). The improvements were particularly noticeable in the towns. In Helmsley, almost entirely owned by the Duncombes, a writer recalled that in 1821 the houses were low and covered with thatch but that in 1858, after the succession in 1841 of the second Baron Feversham, 'old houses have been taken down and new elegant ones erected in their stead' (Parker 1982: 18). His successors continued the rebuilding, as shown by the surviving cottages (Figs. 171, 172). There was much speculative cottage building in Pickering where property was mainly freehold, but less in Kirkbymoorside, which was only partly owned by the Fevershams.

Occupants and location

Agriculture was the dominant employer of labour during the 19th century, maintaining that importance despite population increase and a growing diversification of activity. Those engaged in it included not only farmers and smallholders but servants and labourers as well, and during the late 18th and 19th centuries many unmarried farm servants and labourers lived in, often in special accommodation (see Chapter 4). A few cottages

Fig. 171 [219] 36–46 High Street, Helmsley and plan, 1853

Fig. 172 27–51 Bondgate, Helmsley

are incorporated in farmsteads in a way which suggests that they were intended for labourers; one such example is at Stormy Hall, Danby [82] (Fig. 173), where a one-room cottage, dated 1795, was added to the end of a range of farm buildings. Several others, including one at Low Wethercote, Bilsdale West Side [35] (Fig. 174), are attached to the gables of farmhouses but do not interconnect with them. Such cottages occur both in addition to and instead of men's rooms; though some may have served different generations of a family, others may well have been provided for agricultural labourers.

Male and female farm servants who remained in the same employment on marriage generally moved out to cottages of their own, whether as tenants or owners. Tuke observed that the labouring classes of both sexes generally set out as servants in husbandry, and 'being liberally paid', were often 'able to save in a few years sufficient to enable them to marry and start as housekeepers in possession of the necessary requisites of their situation' (Tuke 1800: 318). The cottages of agricultural labourers are identifiable from entries in successive 19th-century census returns. Some of these labourers, however, might have been daytal men, so-called because they were originally paid by the day, who lived in their own cottages but often received meals or other perquisites. They might have worked for a single farmer or have travelled from farm to farm specializing in one aspect of work such as walling, thatching or mowing. Together with the smallholders, who had to take at least occasional wage work to supplement an inadequate income, and the craftsmen and cowkeepers of the moorland dales, they provided a pool of mobile labour at haytime and harvest, the periods of peak demand (Hartley and Ingilby 1972: 21).

Early 19th-century census returns show that, in the towns in particular, an increasing number of people were engaged in

Fig. 173 [82] Stormy Hall, Danby

Fig. 174 [35] Low Wethercote, Bilsdale West Side

trade, manufacture and handicrafts (Hastings 1981: 5); the occupations listed include joiner, carpenter, cartwright, stonemason, blacksmith, shoemaker and tailor, as well as butcher, baker and grocer. Any of them might have lived in a cottage, as might those employed in one of the various industries which existed in the 18th and 19th centuries, the most dominant of which were alum, coal and ironstone mining, stone quarrying, textile manufacture and leather-working.

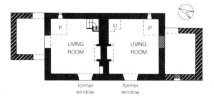

Fig. 176 [71] Clitherbeck Cottages, Danby

Fig. 175 [130] Browcote, Fylingdales

Centered on the coastal cliffs in Fylingdales and a little inland near Sleights, alum mining and manufacture resulted in the conversion of former farmhouses to cottages, as well as the building of a number of cottages, including a pair in Fylingdales dated 1769 (Fig. 175). Cottages associated with coal miners include Clitherbeck Cottages and Rose Cottage, Danby [71, 72] (Figs. 176, 177), all of which are on intakes from Danby Moor where coal had been mined since the mid 18th century. White Row, Aislaby [3], an early 19th-century terrace of small cottages, may have been erected for quarrymen at the nearby Aislaby quarries which supplied building stone locally and to the South of England. Ironstone was not worked in the region on a large scale until the 19th century. Census returns indicate that in 1851 the village of Grosmont housed thirty-nine families, and Hollins, a little to its east, twenty, all mostly of ironstone miners. Both settlements contain many pre-1851 terraces of

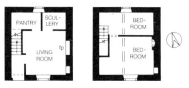

Fig. 177 [72] Rose Cottage, Danby

Fig. 178 [109] Hollins Cottages, Eskdaleside cum Ugglebarnby

cottages including Hollins Cottages (Fig. 178), and at Grosmont commercial and other facilities were provided close to the station [108, 109]. In the second half of the 19th century the further development of the industry produced a variety of such terraces, particularly in Rosedale (Hayes and Rutter 1974: 13–14, Pls. XXIV, XXVI).

Architectural features

No cottage earlier than the 18th century has been recorded, nor have any of those disparagingly described by such writers as Tuke and Atkinson. A good many of the latter are likely to have been the reduced fragments of earlier buildings, rather like the one-room, cruck-built cottage of Anne Heaton which once stood in Egton (Hartley and Ingilby 1972: Pl. 7). The surviving cottages, either conversions of existing buildings or purpose-built dwellings, include some of 18th-century date, but most are 19th-century.

Buildings converted to cottages were most frequently former farmhouses but occasionally farm buildings and other structures. The farmhouses were principally those in towns and villages, which had ceased to function as such because of enclosure and changing patterns of agriculture. Many were former longhouses, which subdivided easily and allowed multiple occupation. The original two-room house-part was frequently retained as one cottage; the nature of the conversion of the former byre-end, however, depended on its size and form, on the fate of the hearth-passage, and on the pressure for accommodation. These factors together determined whether a house was converted, or partially or completely rebuilt in cottage accommodation; the last influenced whether, on a site of sufficient size, one or more cottages might be built, while the fate of the hearth-passage affected finer details of plan.

The hearth-passage was frequently retained, albeit in a variety of ways. It was sometimes converted to a passage independent of a number of cottages, as at 63, 65, 67 West End Kirkbymoorside [306]. Such an arrangement resolved the problem of entry to the rear of a newly subdivided site, common in parts of towns and villages without back lanes or direct access from the street

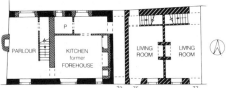

Fig. 179 [307] 73–77 West End, Kirkbymoorside

Fig. 180 [369] 55–57 Eastgate, Pickering

front. The hearth-passage was otherwise frequently retained as an entrance, but only to one cottage. When this was to the former house-part, as in cottages at Kirkbymoorside and Wombleton [307, 523] (Fig. 179), the byre-end could be converted to cottages with their own independent access; when it was to the former byre-end the house-part was free for rebuilding or conversion (Fig. 180). A common method of conversion in the 19th century, which created a double-fronted cottage with an up-to-date appearance and a potentially better arranged interior, involved the insertion of a central door in the house-part, as at 23 Bondgate, Helmsley [190] (Fig. 181), or its rebuilding with one. This removed the need to retain the former hearth-passage, although it was not infrequently kept as the entrance to a cottage.

Not all longhouses came into multiple occupation on their decline to cottage status. The house described by Atkinson (1891: 19) was clearly a former longhouse, its house-part perhaps reduced in length, as may have been Anne Heaton's cottage. In villages in particular, where there was often comparatively little

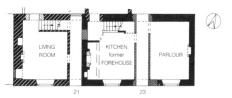

Fig. 181 [190] 21, 23 Bondgate, Helmsley

Fig. 182 [17] White Cottage, Beadlam

pressure on space, byre-ends were sometimes demolished, leaving the house-part as a free-standing cottage occupied by one family. The hearth-passage was sometimes incorporated (Fig. 182), but more often not (Fig. 183); on occasions a central door was inserted (Fig. 184).

Although former longhouses form the bulk of buildings converted into cottages, other types of superseded farmhouse were also used. A hearth-passage house, 9 Castlegate, Helmsley [207], became an unequal pair of cottages, one double-fronted, the other single-fronted, and 8–12 Bondgate, Helmsley [191], became three single-fronted cottages. Sometimes a building was demolished and purpose-built cottages were erected on its site (Fig. 185).

As well as former longhouse byres, other farm buildings were converted to cottages, including a barn behind Penn Cottage, Wombleton (Fig. 186). Documentary evidence for such a conversion includes a will of 1786 in deeds relating to 3–4 East

Fig. 183 [235] Cottage, Carlton, Helmsley

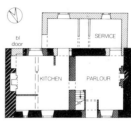

Fig. 184 [469]
Cottage in High Street,
Snainton

Fig. 185 [299] 64–68 West End, Kirkbymoorside

Fig. 186 [527] Cottage behind Penn Cottage, Wombleton

View, Nawton [332]; this required that a stable behind the dwelling house be converted into a comfortable place for the testator's wife to live in. The dwelling house itself (Fig. 187) was a former single house divided between two sons after the death in 1786 of their father, a stonemason and perhaps its builder.

Purpose-built cottages were erected singly, in pairs, or in terraces, all of them storeyed dwellings. Those of the 18th century were almost all single (Fig. 188) or pairs (Figs. 175, 189), rather than terraces of three or more contemporary dwellings. An 18th-century terrace at Pickering, 4–6 Birdgate [348]

Fig. 187 [332] 1–4 East View, Nawton

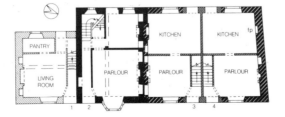

Fig. 188 [293] 8 West End, Kirkbymoorside

(Fig. 218), is of one build but the remainder of that date are multi-period, having developed from existing cottages, as at Wombleton (Fig. 189) and Nawton (Fig. 187). Terrace building was much more widespread in the 19th century, although single cottages and pairs continued to be built.

Most of the pairs and terraces are composed of single-fronted dwellings, the former usually arranged in mirror image and so presenting symmetrical elevations (Figs. 175, 194, 195). The terraces normally repeated the same plan and elevation (Figs. 177, 192, 202), except where site constrictions caused a change at one end of a terrace (Fig. 196). Double-fronted cottages occur both in villages and towns (Figs. 197, 198); in the towns a number of passage-entry and lobby-entry single-fronted cottages are combined and resemble the type. Pairs of double-fronted cottages are restricted to the towns where some terraces combine different plan forms and cottage sizes (Fig. 267). Midge Hall, Sleights [104] (Fig. 190), somewhat unusually, is a pair of cottages masquerading as a central-entry house.

The majority of cottages have unpretentious exteriors which reflect their status and date. In conversion of earlier buildings, the existing structure inevitably constrained development and sometimes resulted in unbalanced fenestration. Alterations were frequently left visible, but could be hidden by rendering. A number of 18th-century purpose-built cottages have elevations of some character (Figs. 188, 189); perhaps because of their comparatively early date as cottages, these were the dwellings of cottagers of some wealth, a few of whose probate inventories are known. Not until the middle and later 19th century were other cottages of character built. In Helmsley a few were built with Tudor detailing [205] because of their proximity to the entrance to Duncombe Park, which has a lodge of 1841 in similar style; a later terrace in Bondgate is not unlike it (Fig. 172).

Fig. 189 [521] 1–7 Carter Close, Wombleton

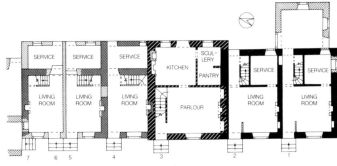

Fig. 190 [104] Midge Hall, Sleights, Eskdaleside cum Ugglebarnby

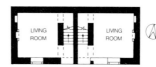

Fig. 193 [178] Daniel Steps, Hawnby

Number and use of rooms

Although no one-room, single-storey cottages now exist, there are examples with upper storeys. In these, the simplest type of cottage to survive and all seemingly of 19th-century date, the single ground-floor room must have been an all-purpose living room used for cooking, eating and sitting in; in those households with many children it would also have served as a sleeping place, additional to the first-floor chamber. The simplest version of such cottages has direct entry into the room, usually from the front (Figs. 179, 191) but occasionally from the side (Fig. 176).

Fig. 191 [454] Rose Cottage, Scawton

A short screen, not necessarily original, gave some shelter from draughts as well as affording a little privacy (Figs. 189, 192), but both were more effectively provided by entrance lobbies, often situated at the foot of stairs (Fig. 193). Sometimes the hearth-passage retained from an earlier building provided similar comforts, as at 21 Bondgate, Helmsley (Fig. 181). Parti-

Fig. 192 [135, 136] The Row and Reckon Forge, Gillamoor

tioned-off pantries of varying size are found in many cottages, often against the rear wall (Figs. 187, 189) or in an understairs cupboard (Fig. 194).

Fig. 194 [268] 30–32 Dale End, Kirkbymoorside

More spacious service accommodation was sometimes provided from the start. A single service room possibly acted as a combined scullery and pantry (Figs. 187–189), but at times these functions were separately catered for (Figs. 177, 195), sometimes by additions which upgraded earlier inadequate accommodation (Figs. 189, 192).

Fig. 195 [482] Cottages, Sproxton

In some two-room deep cottages the rear room was a kitchen in which cooking and perhaps also eating took place, leaving the heated front room free for use as a parlour, a family sitting room. It may have been used this way in 12–20 Dale End, Kirkbymoorside [266] (Fig. 196), as well as in cottages with separate pantries like 3 Carter Close, Wombleton [521] (Fig. 189), and 6–10 Pottergate, Helmsley [227] (Fig. 197). All of

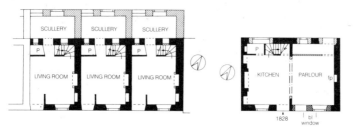

Fig. 196 [266] 12–20 Dale End,
Kirkbymoorside

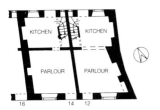

Fig. 197 [227] 6–10 Pottergate, Helmsley

Fig. 198 [441]
Alexandra Cottage, Rievaulx

Fig. 199 [522]
Rose Cottage,
Wombleton

these are single-fronted and of late 18th or 19th-century date. Similar accommodation, often better arranged, was provided in a number of double-fronted cottages of the same date; some purpose-built like Alexandra Cottage, Rievaulx [441] (Fig. 198), Rose Cottage, Wombleton [522] (Fig. 199), and Reckon Forge, Gillamoor [136] (Fig. 192), others conversions of the house-parts of former longhouses (Figs. 181, 184). As in the smaller cottages, a pantry or general service room was often incorporated, at Reckon Forge partitioned off the rear of the living room, at Rose Cottage set behind the parlour. At Ivy Cottage, Wombleton [524] (Fig. 200), where the second main room was unheated and perhaps served as a bedroom rather than a parlour, it was incorporated in an added rear outshut.

Fig. 200 [524] Ivy Cottage, Wombleton

The site of the staircase in purpose-built cottages varies, as do the detailed arrangements for internal access. In one-room cottages the stair was often set against the rear wall, and only occasionally close to the front door where it both created an entrance lobby and gave privacy to the main room. In single-fronted two-room deep cottages it was frequently next to the rear room, as at 8 West End, Kirkbymoorside [293] (Fig. 188),

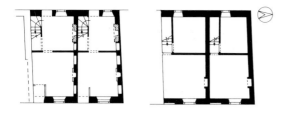

Fig. 201 [366] 12–13 Castlegate, Pickering

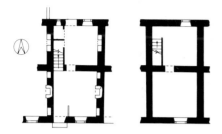

Fig. 202 [412] 93 Westgate, Pickering

and Pickering [366, 412], although it was sometimes set next to the front room, and the front door opened on to it (Figs. 177, 187). At 36–46 High Street, Helmsley [219], and 6, 8, 10 Pottergate [227], the stair is between front and rear rooms (Figs. 171, 197), in the manner more typical of town houses (RCHM 1972: lxxix, xcvi, 1981: lxxvi). At 2 East View, Nawton [332] (Fig. 187), it rises in a stairhall and so all bedrooms have independent access and privacy. In the last two positions the main living room gained some privacy, whereas in the previous ones it was a room of passage. Two cottages in Pickering show different methods of access to the stair, one from the front room, the other from the rear room. Though not of great significance to the ground-floor rooms, at first floor it implied different treatment for the two bedrooms; at 12, 13 Castlegate [366] (Fig. 201) they were separated, whereas at 93 Westgate [412] (Fig. 202) the more private front room could only be reached through the rear one. The luxury of privacy was clearly not afforded in many one-room cottages with subdivided first floors; at Rose Cottage, Danby [72] (Fig. 177), it was only enjoyed by the front bedroom, the only heated one of a pair.

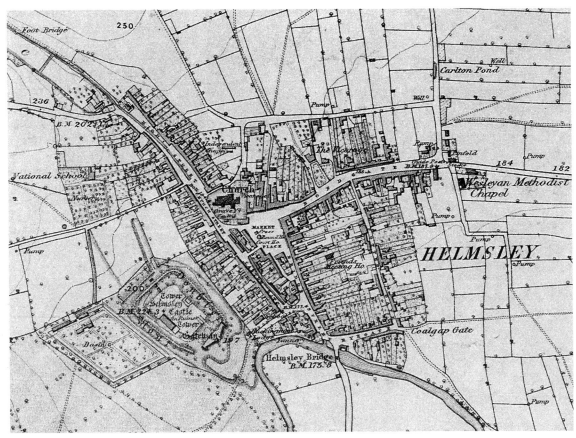

Fig. 203
Helmsley:
town plan, 1856
(from O.S. Sheet 89)

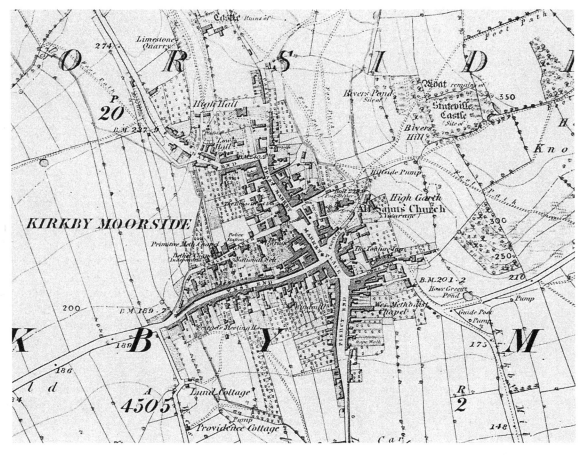

Fig. 204
Kirkbymoorside:
town plan, 1856
(from O.S. Sheet 90)

CHAPTER 6

TOWNS

The historical background

The upland mass of the North York Moors is ringed by a number of small market towns. The three within the survey area, Helmsley, Kirkbymoorside and Pickering, are concentrated in the south of the region at approximately five-mile intervals along an east–west line between the tabular hills to the north and the marshy lands flanking the Rye and the Derwent to the south. The villages of Brompton, Egton, Kildale, Sinnington and Thornton Dale once had urban ambitions of which scant evidence survives. The positions of their former market-places can be deduced, although, had their charters not survived, most would be indistinguishable from other villages which developed by the roadside or around a green which never had a market.

The historic roots of the present towns lie in the Middle Ages, and while few actual buildings survive from that period beyond castles and churches, one important element in the present appearance of the town, the disposition of houses along streets and around market-places, owes its form largely to decisions made then but not documented. The long, narrow burgage plot is characteristic not only of English towns known to have been laid out at specific dates but of others with more distant and obscure origins. With its head on the market-place or a major thoroughfare, and often with access at the rear to a back lane, it accommodated the dwellinghouses, workshops and outbuildings; in small towns those are likely to be as much agricultural as industrial or commercial.

Despite planned elements in all three towns, an earlier small settlement of irregular form may have existed in the vicinity of each church. At Helmsley (Fig. 203) the curve of the churchyard wall is continued in the land containing Canons Garth, and a site boundary to the west of the former vicarage curves across the block to the north of Bondgate. The area enclosed by these old boundaries and by the north side of the market-place may have been the nucleus from which Helmsley developed, controlling the crossing of the River Rye. At Kirkbymoorside (Fig. 204) a similarly curved lane forms one side of the churchyard and, since it leads to the site of Stuteville Castle, the earlier of the two seigneurial centres, was formerly of greater importance.

The original settlement may have grown up at the intersection of this lane and a track from Kirby Mills to Gillamoor, leading on across the moors by means of Rudland Rigg. At Pickering (Fig. 205) the church stands on a marked promontory, dominating the east–west route along Ruffa Lane which continued on the line of Market Place to the crossing of Pickering Beck near the present bridge. The site of Morcar's manor is probably represented by the later rectory site at the north end of Hall Garth, just to the east of the church, and the original settlement may have clustered around it.

Helmsley had the earliest market charter, of 1190/1, contemporary with the building of the castle, and a charter for Pickering followed shortly afterwards, in 1201. Between 1253 and 1303 six more markets were founded by royal charter in the survey area (Table 1). It is not clear whether these charters ratified an existing situation with a functioning but unlicensed market, or were facultative, with the intention of converting an agricultural settlement into a more profitable trading community.

In all three surviving towns these markets developed alongside the churchyards and, except at Helmsley, bore little relation to the first phase of planned development. At both Pickering and Kirkbymoorside the market-place was at right angles to the axis of what was probably the original village street; at the former, this street linked the existing church and the new castle along Burgate and Castlegate, and at the latter was represented by West End on the far side of the market-place from both church and castle. At Pickering the market-place developed along the existing east–west route, and although it widens slightly by the churchyard it was probably constrained by the existing street pattern, and is more linear than the other two markets, which were wedge-shaped. At Helmsley the main burgage development was on opposite sides of the market-place, in Boroughgate and Castlegate. At Kirkbymoorside the market-place was probably superimposed on the existing street pattern, perhaps reflecting the increased importance of the north–south axis following the erection of the Neville castle, with the churchyard forming its eastern boundary. Both wedge-shaped market places were gradually infilled, first by market stalls and then by more permanent shops. At Kirkbymoorside the southern end of the market-place was later encroached upon by inns.

Developments outside the burghal area differed in all three

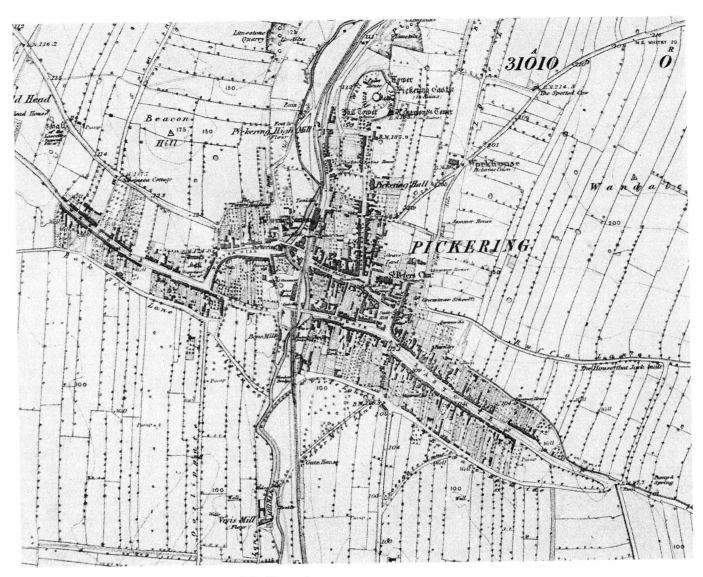

Fig. 205 Pickering: town plan, 1856 (from O.S. Sheet 91)

towns. Although the presence of a castle could act as a stimulus to the town at its gates, it could limit the options for expansion. At Helmsley the castle presented its flank to the market-place, and acted as a barrier to expansion westwards, while the river discouraged development southwards. New plots were developed along roads running eastwards and northwards from the corners of the market-place, with a new north–south road, Pottergate, running parallel to it. At Kirkbymoorside, where both castles were more remote from the centre, development took place along the north–south axis and straggled along other roads leading from the town. Pickering Castle stopped development northwards, although part of its original outer defences, known as the barbican, was incorporated in the town and divided into burgage plots. Its banks and ditches provided the only element of town defences detectable in any of the three towns. The main east–west route through Pickering Market Place was shifted southwards, probably in the 12th century, and agricultural land occupied to create planned suburbs in Eastgate and Westgate.

Differentiation of market functions is apparent in all three towns. At Helmsley, Bondgate widened distinctly towards its western end before 19th-century rebuilding. This feature can be paralleled at Kirkbymoorside in the Beast Market, now High Market Place, where the widened street is in marked contrast to the constricted entrances to Dale End, Howe End and Castlegate. At Pickering this function may have been served by the open spaces at Potter Hill and Smiddy Hill, both of which had their own cattle pounds. If cattle were kept out of the main market-place, the butchers' shops were concentrated there, with purpose-built shambles at Kirkbymoorside and Pickering. At Pickering these were supplemented by permanent butchers' shops, while at Helmsley the stalls in the market-place had been replaced with two-storey butchers' shops by the 16th century. In Kirkbymoorside the portion of the Market Place south of Church Street was known as Swine Market and used for the sale of pigs and geese.

The probate inventories of weavers and other town craftsmen from the late 17th to the mid 18th century show they were also

116

Table 1 Markers and fairs

Settlement	Charter	Market day	Fair	Duration
Brompton	1253[1]	Monday[2]	Annual	8 days
			Annual	1 day[3]
Egton	1269[4]	Wednesday	Annual	8 days
	1699/1700[5]	Tuesday	Four p.a.	1 day
			18 p.a.	1 day[6]
			11 p.a.	1 day[7]
Helmsley	By 1285[8]	Saturday	Three p.a.	1 day
	1670[9]		Fortnightly	1 day[10]
			Three p.a.	1 day[11]
		Friday	Four p.a.	2 of 1, 2 of 2 days[12]
Kildale	1253[13]	Friday	Annual	3 days
Kirkbymoorside	1254[14]	Wednesday	Annual	3 days
Pickering	By 1200[15]	Monday[16]	Annual (1291)	3 days[17]
			Two p.a. (1651)	3 days[18]
			16 p.a.	1 day[19]
			Fortnightly	1 day[20]
Sinnington	1303[21]	Monday	Annual	3 days
Thornton Dale	1281[22]	Tuesday	Two p.a.	3 days each

1 Calendar of Charter Rolls 1226–57: 434; VCH 1923: 427.
2 Market suppressed as result of plea from burgesses of Scarborough in 1256 (Cal. Pat. Rolls 1247–58: 477; VCH 1923: 552).
3 Fair of 1 day in 1770 (Owen's Book of Fairs, 6th ed.). 'Half the fair' mentioned 1656 and 1754; market toll collectors and waywardens in 1895 (VCH 1923: 427). Fair held on 12 November (Whellan 1859: 890).
4 Lapsed (Cart. Antiq. JJ, no. 8; VCH 1923: 345).
5 New grant (Pat. 11 Will. III, pt. vi, no.9; 12 Will. III, pt. iii, no.26; VCH 1923: 345).
6 Approximately 16 fairs or cattle markets and 2 hiring fairs by 1859 (Whellan 1859: 825).
7 For cattle, early 20th century (VCH 1923: 345).
8 The 'liberties and customs of the city of York' were granted between 1190 and 1200 (Clay 1893: 155). Burgesses taking tolls of market by 1276, for which £11 paid in 1285 (VCH 1914: 494).
9 Calendar of S. P. Dom. 1670, 216; McDonnell 1963: 182; VCH 1914: 493.
10 For linen webs every fortnight during 18th century (McDonnell 1963: 182).
11 For sheep (McDonnell ibid.).
12 For cattle and sheep, late 19th century (Whellan 1859: 245; McDonnell 1963: 183).
13 Calendar of Charter Rolls 1222–57: 418; VCH 1914: 251.
14 Calendar of Patent Rolls 1247–58: 385; VCH 1914: 514.
15 Calendar of Charter Rolls 1199–1216: 85; VCH 1914: 467–8.
16 Since 1619 (Honor of Pickering i, 36; VCH 1914: 468). Weekly market for corn, etc., on Mondays (Whellan 1859: 229).
17 Calendar of Charter Rolls 1257–1300: 389; VCH 1914: 468.
18 Honor of Pickering i, 93; VCH 1923: 468.
19 Monday cattle fairs monthly, plus 4 p.a. (Whellan 1859: 229).
20 For cattle on alternate Mondays (VCH 1923: 468).
21 Calendar of Charter Rolls 1300–26: 41; VCH 1923: 490.
22 Calendar of Charter Rolls 1257–1300: 257; VCH 1923: 495.

occupied in agriculture, continuing a tradition found earlier in most English towns. The dominance of the longhouse tradition even in the town centres emphasizes the rural connection, but examination of the town plans shows a functional distinction between areas where farming predominated and others where dual occupations were practised, and buildings of marked urban form were built from at least the 17th century onwards. The existence of a Burroughgate and a Bondgate in Helmsley emphasizes the distinction between the burgesses, primarily involved in trade, and the bondmen, primarily involved in farming. The working farms are concentrated outside the initial area of burgage plots along Bondgate and in Pottergate. This latter name is echoed in Potter Hill in Pickering, also away from the main market centre. In Kirkbymoorside the working farms are again segregated from the original core and earliest planned part of the town in High Market Place, the former Beast Market.

Not only the largely agricultural suburbs of Eastgate and Westgate but even the centre of Pickering remained dominated by agriculture until late in the 18th century. The basic burgage plot in Burgate, whatever the medieval use, had a frontage consisting of a longhouse comprising house and byre, with a separate barn lengthways on to the street. Barns were also present on the south side of the Market Place and in Hall Garth, where a working farm existed prior to the erection of the National School. The smaller pre-industrial town where the townsfolk 'were directly concerned in the surrounding land which they farmed daily' (Patten 1978: 39) seems to have survived later in this region than elsewhere in the country. Eighteenth-century wills and inventories show the farming interests of cordwainers, a tanner, an apothecary, a hatter and a glover in Helmsley, and a cordwainer, a blacksmith, a wheelwright, a grocer, butchers and numerous weavers in Pickering.

Commercial and public buildings

PUBLIC BUILDINGS

The principal public buildings are connected with the ancient market-places. Three market crosses survive, at Helmsley, Kirkbymoorside and Thornton Dale; a fourth at Pickering was still in existence in 1856 (NYCRO: ZPC, Lease of the Honor of Pickering).

No ancient public buildings survive in the survey area, but a tradition of tolbooths which combined covered shopping space at ground level with an upper room whose primary function was usually the administration of justice is evident in more recent public buildings. The manorial courts at Helmsley and Pickering were held in their respective castles, in the latter in a special Court House (Bulmer 1890: 953, 1005), but in Kirkbymoorside the Court Room in the Tolbooth was used for this purpose (Whellan 1859: 238). In smaller settlements the manor house served both this function and as a court for magistrates at Petty Sessions. By 1859 Petty Sessions alternating between Kirkbymoorside and Helmsley were held in the Court Rooms

of their respective tolbooths (Whellan 1859: 238, 245); in the latter this use of the upper room was new and coincided with its refitting to serve as a County Court following the County Courts Act of 1846, so that the previous setting of the Petty Sessions is unknown. At Pickering they had been held at the Black Swan and the White Swan Inn alternately, but were later transferred to one of two rival buildings erected for this purpose. By 1890 Petty Sessions were held in a Court House at the police station (Bulmer 1890: 1008).

The Helmsley Tolbooth existed by 1637, and had shops on the ground floor until their replacement by a County Court Office in the middle of the 19th century (Whellan 1859: 245), being subsequently referred to as the 'Court House in the Market Place' (Bulmer 1890: 953). It was replaced in 1901 by the Town Hall designed by Temple Moore (Fig. 206): this 'new

Fig. 206 Town Hall, Helmsley

Court House' served more general public purposes since, as well as housing the County and Magistrates' Courts, it contained a reading room and library established in 1908 (McDonnell 1963: 302). At Kirkbymoorside the Tolbooth (Fig. 207), built at the beginning of the 18th century, had shops on the ground floor, a court room on the first floor and workshops on the floor above (Whellan 1859: 238). It was rebuilt in 1872 after a fire, with a market hall replacing the shops and without the top floor (Bulmer 1890: 972). At Pickering, where no comparable market building had previously existed, two separate buildings were erected in close proximity, both designed by John Gibson. One was a privately financed project on the site of the shambles, known as the New Commercial Building (MNG: 12 Sept. 1857) (Fig. 208), with a large room for the Magistrates' meetings over a bank and a wine and spirit store. It was demolished for road widening in 1958 (Pickup 1983: 2, 54). The rival civic scheme, known initially as the New Town Hall (MNG: 1 Aug. 1857, 12 Sept. 1857) but afterwards as the Market Hall (Bulmer 1890: 1009 (Fig. 209), has a large first-floor room above four shops [345]. The Tolbooth at the vestigial urban settlement of Egton, described in 1859 as an 'old *Market House* – a plain structure

Fig. 207 [255] Tolbooth, Kirkbymoorside, 1872

Fig. 208 New Commercial Building, Pickering

Fig. 209 [345] Market Hall, Pickering

(Whellan 1859: 826) and probably demolished shortly after-wards, as no mention is made of it by Bulmer in 1890, may have been only a market hall.

Linked with the administration of justice was the provision of penalties. It has left few physical remains in towns apart from the rebuilt stocks by the market cross in Thornton Dale and three mid 19th-century police stations, which provide the principal visible evidence of crime and punishment. That at Pickering (7 Hall Garth) [378] (Fig. 210) was probably built in the 1840s, and is described in 1851 as Lock Up House, occupied by John Heslehurst, superintendent constable (census). One barred window is visible on the otherwise domestic-looking street frontage of the old police station, Tinley Garth, Kirkbymoorside [256] (Fig. 211), erected in 1851 with two cells (Whellan 1859: 238). At Helmsley the police station of 1858 replaced a circular lock-up in the Market Place, probably of the late 18th or early 19th century (McDonnell 1963: 316–17).

SHOPS AND COMMERCIAL PREMISES

Market-places provided space for the moveable stalls from which commodities and craftsmen's products were sold; such stalls preceded the erection of shops, and continued to exist alongside them. Butchers were an important element; their concentration in the market-places suggests customers not involved in subsistence farming and, as in so many other small towns, they probably occupied the first permanent stalls, here grouped together in one part of the market-place as shambles, although any early

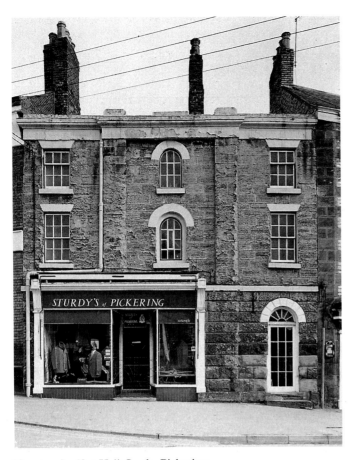

Fig. 210 [378] 7 Hall Garth, Pickering

Fig. 211 [256] Old Police Station, Kirkbymoorside

examples have been rebuilt. In Pickering some butchers may have had permanent shops as early as the 15th century; the three shops next to the churchyard at Pickering, late of John Flesshewer, mentioned in 1438/9 (PRO: D.L.29/490/7935), may on the evidence of the surname have been butchers' shops. In 1739, 42 Market Place, Pickering [391], incorporated small lock-up shops which, as they faced the old shambles and known butchers' shops which backed on to the churchyard at various dates, may well have themselves been butchers' shops. Despite this, the majority of butchers at both dates probably used permanent stalls, which by the 18th century were grouped as a free-standing unit towards one end of the Market Place. These 'pestiferous old shambles' as they were described in 1857 were probably repaired or rebuilt about a hundred years earlier, when wood from Dalby was marked out for the butchers' shops at Pickering (Rushton 1976b: 83). Another group of timber-fronted stalls, probably also built as shambles, survives in Crown Square, Kirkbymoorside [264] (Fig. 212), behind the former Tolbooth; they probably faced butchers' shops occupying the rear of the Tolbooth (Whellan 1859: 238). Thornton Dale also

Fig. 212 [264] Market Stalls, Crown Square, Kirkbymoorside

possessed, as slender evidence of its urban character, a building used as meat shambles, which stood near to the market cross (Whellan 1859: 924). In Helmsley the original stalls were probably replaced before the 16th century by permanent butchers' shops, although the argument for this depends on a continuity in use for over three hundred years until the demolition of the west side of the market-place in the mid 19th century, which then consisted almost entirely of butchers' shops. They needed little more space than a market stall; one 'little room used as a butcher's shop' in 1730 shared a yard to the rear of premises on the east side of Helmsley market-place with a barn, turfhouse, swinecot and probably a smithy (NYCRO: ZEW I 84). Little evidence remains of the butchers' activities in the buildings themselves. Meat hooks surviving in 7 Birdgate, Pickering [349], suggest that the house-part was later converted to a

butcher's shop, but of another butcher's shop occupied by Robert Cross erected to its west (17 Apr. 1815: PRO: D.L.30/399, Pickering Court Books, 1795–1815), no such definite evidence remains.

One other trade which called for specialized buildings from an early period was that of smith. The trade was not specifically urban and smithies occur both in the countryside and in the towns. In 1438/9 Walter the Smith paid 12d. as a new rent for a forge on Potter Hill, Pickering, and Simon Smith held a 'shop at Kyrkesyde' (PRO: D.L.29/490/7935): the latter was probably the 'smith's forge lying by the kirkside sometime held by William Kirkby, a bastard' in 1619 and then operated by Robert Nattress, blacksmith. His cottage on the south side of the church wall (PRO: D.L.43/11/8, D.L.42/124) must be the cruck building now 7 Birdgate, Pickering [349]; the smithy was probably adjacent, but its site is now occupied by a late 18th-century terrace, 4–6 Birdgate, Pickering [348]. As smithies are sometimes referred to as shops, their true function is not always obvious, either in Pickering or the other towns, unless described as explicitly as the forge in Kirkbymoorside market-place leased by Ralph Sowerby in 1568 (PRO: E.164/37). More specialized metalworking is implied by the brass furnace situated at Keld Head, Pickering, held by Richard Parke in the reign of Charles I. The property was occupied by the same family between 1574 and 1812, but the furnace had been converted to a barn by the latter date (PRO: S.C.12/30/15, D.L.42/124, D.L.30/399).

In the 19th century this local expertise in metalworking is demonstrated on a larger scale through its products rather than its buildings, in the shape of numerous cast-iron fireplaces and kitchen ranges which still survive throughout the region. Although some came from Malton and farther afield, most were made at Carter's Foundry at 17 and 19 Piercy End, Kirkbymoorside [287], where the cast-iron shopfront combines two shop units which frame the carriageway jointly used by the gas works and the foundry. Another member of the Carter family ran the Cyclops Foundry at Tinley Garth in the same town (Bulmer 1890: 974), and in 1851 John Carr employed three men in a small foundry in Eastgate, Pickering (census).

The occupation of baker ranked with those of butcher and smith as being among the most important in medieval and early modern towns and, like them, its physical remains are exiguous. The only surviving building known to have been used as a bakehouse, 38 Bondgate, Helmsley [196], was not built as such, having been the Green Tree Inn before its conversion early in the 19th century.

The first known shops were naturally erected facing the market-places. In 1438, and again in 1476, four of the shops listed in Pickering were next to the churchyard, and at least some of these will have been on the side fronting the market-place (PRO: D.L.29/490/7935, D.L.43/11/5). An early 16th-century list of tenants of the Manor of Helmsley (Belvoir: Misc. MS 105(3)) enumerates seven occupants of shops on the north-west of the market: no other shops are mentioned. As in Pickering, the shops were concentrated on one side of the market-place, presumably in a continuous row. In Kirkbymoorside, where only one shop is documented before the 18th century, this kind of development did not occur. Although burgage plots were laid out fronting the market-places, the earliest known shops replaced removable stalls in the market-place itself, and so began the encroachment which is particularly noticeable at Helmsley and Kirkbymoorside. In Helmsley the Borough Beck probably defined one side of the original market-place, which would make the seven shops listed there in the 16th century an encroachment. At a later period another shop was built which backed directly on to the churchyard and thus lacked the depth of a customary burgage plot. This feature also characterizes the shops on the east side of the market-place in Pickering, which also back directly on to a churchyard. Although the process of encroachment is less evident in Pickering, nine shops and the bakehouse in Pickering were significantly listed in 1651 as 'encroachments on the waste', and form the greater part of the properties so described (PRO: E.317/43).

Little can be deduced about the appearance or planning of these vanished shops. Such evidence as there is suggests that shops here as elsewhere were small; in 1661 'a house called a shoppe in Pickering Market Place' was 12 feet long and 18 feet wide (Turton 1894: 101). Some, but not necessarily all, must have been used as butchers' shops or smithies. Of the five 'shops' listed in Pickering in 1438/9, three can plausibly be explained as butchers' shops, and a fourth as a smithy (PRO: D.L.29/490/7935). The use of some of these five shops may have altered by 1476, but the presence of a chapman and a chaplain among the lessees may only indicate some form of investment in a trade carried out by others (PRO: D.L.43/11/5). The rents paid differ considerably, and although a number of factors, including the date of the initial lease, may account for the variation, it could imply that some shops had attached living quarters justifying a higher rent, but only John Kempe is specified as having one cottage and one shop. Lock-up shops certainly existed since at least the 15th century, as is evident from the number of people who held two or three shops. The 16th-century description of the shops in Helmsley as 'shops and chambers over, each shop having one chamber over' implies storeyed construction, although it is possible that the single chambers were over only part of the shop, as at God Begot House, Winchester. The planning was probably similar to rows in York, with shops one bay wide and one room deep (RCHM 1981: 225). As only one of the Helmsley shopkeepers appears as a tenant of another property, the chambers may be presumed to have provided living accommodation. By 1642 only two tenants of seven shops in 'Burrowgate' (NYCRO: ZEW IV 1/1–10) – probably the same row – had a 'house and shop' and no property elsewhere; presumably the chambers over the shop were being abandoned as living accommodation.

In this particular case the 'house and shop' seems to indicate living quarters above the shop, but this was not necessarily so, for the mention or omission of living quarters may be fortuitous. In Pickering, a list of 1619 separates the cottage of Robert Nattresse, blacksmith, from his shop (presumably a smithy), and where shop is to be interpreted as workshop, especially for a trade of this kind, living quarters above are unlikely. Conversely, the 1619 shop of Robert Parkinson had become the

house and shop of Richard Parkinson by 1651 (PRO: D.L.43/11/8, E.317/43). An early 18th-century building, 42 Market Place, Pickering [391] (Fig. 213), appears to have combined lock-up shops with living quarters for either a resident shopkeeper or the owner of the property.

Fig. 213 [391] 42 Market Place, Pickering

Despite unambiguous late medieval references to shops in the towns, it is difficult to identify purpose-built shops in the region before the end of the 18th century, not least because ground floors are so vulnerable to modernization. The architectural evidence presents two major problems in considering shops. The first problem is to discover which buildings were intended as shops and which were converted for the purpose. For example, 56 Potter Hill, Pickering [399], probably built in the early 1850s, appears as a grocer's shop in 1861; on the evidence available it may have been converted to a shop but equally the shell of the building could have been adapted to the purpose before completion. Few of the smaller shops are documented as such before 1850 and probably began as private houses. Many of these small shops, especially those outside the main shopping areas, have been reabsorbed into the living accommodation. Both processes were no doubt operating earlier than any surviving architectural evidence. Windows provide the principal clue to function. Sometimes the shop window surround has been left or a more domestic window has been reinstated, usually leaving indications that a wider opening has been narrowed. Few old shop windows survive unaltered, despite a few notable

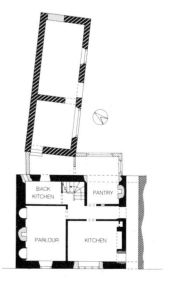

Fig. 214 [214] 8 High Street, Helmsley

exceptions such as 37 Market Place, Pickering [388], but their former appearance is known from old photographs. None of the shops identified seems to have possessed windows of a purely domestic character. Even where a projecting display window, either bowed or rectangular, was not provided, the window opening was a single fixed unit, subdivided by glazing bars, without sliding sashes or opening casements. In the later 19th century the large single panes of glass by then available were framed with pilasters, and the fascias sometimes provided with blinds. Doors and windows are sometimes treated as an architectural unit, sometimes kept separate (Fig. 214).

Where a building can be identified as a purpose-built shop, the second problem presents itself: does the present internal layout represent the original design? The answer to this question lies in the duality of function, commercial and domestic, found in most of the relevant buildings. The vast majority of surviving shops in both towns and villages are associated with living accommodation and so are split into private and public areas; some have a common entrance to the public and private areas, others provide a separate access, usually with an interconnecting

door. Subdivided buildings on wide plots usually have the shop and shopkeeper's house in line, with a separate entrance to the house, and the room or rooms above the shop providing extra living accommodation, as at 2 Howe End, Kirkbymoorside [276]. This arrangement probably had its origins in the use of outer parlours as workplaces by many local craftsmen (see Chapter 4). Where the frontage was narrower, such planning was impossible. As the commercial importance of the town centres increased, the use as living accommodation of ground-floor rooms facing the street in single-fronted buildings was gradually abandoned, for both purpose-built shops and houses converted as such. Living accommodation could be provided entirely above the shop, or where the depth of the plot permitted, partly above and partly behind. On some restricted sites a common entrance gave access to both the shop and the living accommodation. Until the late 19th century, this arrangement served both parts of 6 Market Place, Kirkbymoorside [280] (Fig. 215), then two separate properties. Both subsequently came into the same ownership, and the doorway to one became the shop entrance, the other the house entrance.

Fig. 215 [280] 6 Market Place, Kirkbymoorside

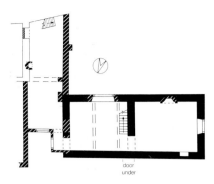

Fig. 216 [283] 14 Market Place, Kirkbymoorside

At 4 Market Place, Kirkbymoorside [279], there were separate entries for house and shop from an earlier date. An open and a covered side alley respectively provided access to living quarters behind and above the shop and to other rear premises at 14 Market Place, Kirkbymoorside [283] (Fig. 216), and 37 Market Place, Pickering [388]. As both have deep sites, two-storey buildings, with or without attics or semi-attics, proved adequate. On shallower sites, as at 4 Market Place, Kirkbymoorside [279], a three-storey building resulted.

A new type of shop, the retail shop, appeared around the beginning of the 18th century and purpose-built examples for trades other than blacksmith or butcher became more common from the last decade of the century, but most have been altered internally. In Pickering the house of a blacksmith, which had a shop at its east end in 1755, had become a 'lately erected messuage with a shop, lately a smith's shop' by 1793. This wording shows the need for cautious interpretation of legal documents. It suggests that the shop was a conversion of a smithy and structurally separate from the house, but the shop identifiable as this property at the east end of 15–17 Birdgate [350] is an integral part of a building appropriate to 1793 which has windows sheltered by the projecting canopy, one of the hallmarks of a shop. A short distance away, 33 Burgate, Pickering [360], was probably advertised as a 'freehold house in Boroughgate, roomy shop, extensive warehouse and outbuilding' with 'shelves, counters etc.' which was 'eligible for draper, grocer or druggist' (*YH:* 3 Apr. 1830) – occupations which could be combined, as by William Ashton at Burgate Chambers, Pickering [363] (Fig. 217), who was grocer, druggist and tallow chandler. Depending on the types of business, the goods could be kept in the one room used as a shop, in a separate storeroom or cellar, or in a detached warehouse.

Fig. 217 [363] Burgate Chambers, Pickering

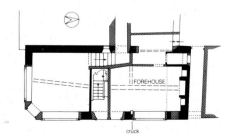

Warehouses are frequently referred to in association with shops; few survive. One such, of unknown purpose, stands behind 14 Market Place, Helmsley [222]. Another may be a four-storeyed mid 19th-century structure by the Beck, 34 Potter Hill, Pickering [397], which can probably be identified as a grocer's shop and warehouse of a corn merchant. Advertisements show that this combination of premises was common, as for example in Helmsley in 1820 and in 1822 (*YG:* 1 Jan. 1820, 5 Jan. 1822).

Nineteenth-century development includes for the first time terraces incorporating shops. What may be a slightly earlier example, the late 18th-century terrace comprising the three messuages 4–6 Birdgate, Pickering [348] (Fig. 218), cannot be shown definitely to have been built as shops, although the ground floors of two were already so used by the early years of the 19th century. The appearance of a group of buildings in Malton Gate, Thornton Dale [493] (Fig. 219), is primarily domestic, but the apparent house with flanking wings included in 1822 a new-built house lately occupied by a bankrupt linen draper, a spacious shop, warehouse, candle-house and other buildings, and two adjoining houses, one in two tenements. The shop is not obvious from the street; just possibly the word was used in the older sense to denote the workshop reached by a side alleyway, a distinctly urban form of development in so far as it achieves intensive use of the ground plot. The candle-house is also likely to have been at the rear by analogy with similar town complexes such as that on the east side of Crown Square, Kirkbymoorside [263], where the candle-house stood at the far side of the yard from the 'house and shop lately built by Mr. Fletcher and in his occupation', backing on to the churchyard.

A formal development incorporating more than one shop is first documented at 6 and 7 Bridge Street, Pickering [354], where a shared alleyway provides access to the living quarters of two shops, a separate cottage and the Primitive Methodist Chapel. The inclusion of a nonconformist chapel is significant; tucked out of sight away from the street, it is part of the wave of modest building which preceded the appearance of larger chapels in the fashionable architectural styles of the mid and late 19th century. A similar early 19th-century development in Thornton Dale [491] comprised four terrace houses, two of which included shops by 1849, a further house at the rear, and two cottages in the yard behind. A development in Pickering, 17–22 Market Place [387], otherwise known as King Street or King's Row after the builder Nicholas King, comprised seven 'recently built' messuages in 1842. None are mentioned as shops, although all now serve this purpose, and most appear as shops in an early photograph. Three of the occupants listed in the 1851 Census were tailors and it seems likely that at least some of the premises served as tailors' shops.

VILLAGE SHOPS

Shops are a distinctive feature of the urban scene but are not confined to it; the village shop comes later. The village grocers in the old sense of a general dealer were probably supplemented by travelling chapmen and pedlars (Patten 1978: 223) such as

Fig. 218 (Above) [348] 4–6 Birdgate, Pickering

Fig. 219 (Below) [493] Malton Gate, Thornton Dale

George King of West Ayton, a weaver and chapman, whose stock in 1738 consisted entirely of cloth. The minimal urban characteristics of Thornton Dale include the presence of a grocer, Thomas Plummer, by 1749 and several shops were built there during the next hundred years, following 'the typical pattern for many smaller places which lost their markets . . . to gain shops' (Patten 1978: 220). Shops were also built in places which had never had a market. The 'shop or milkhouse' of John Brusby of Rievaulx in 1762, with sugar, soap, candles and weighed tobacco, must have served as the village store. Similar evidence exists for Hutton Buscel, Lockton and Levisham.

Fig. 220 [315] April Cottage, Lastingham

Village shops are infrequently documented before 1850. One in West Ayton [512], already a shop in 1812 (NYCRO: Reg. Deeds DP, 1811–13), survives, and another in Lastingham which was 'newly erected' in 1825 may be either an existing house and shop [316], or the nearby April Cottage [315] (Fig. 220). A small number of post offices appear on the first edition OS sheets at that time, and many more appear by 1911. Traditionally the post office doubled as the village shop, but it is not clear how common this practice was before the second half of the 19th century. Where the shop came first, there will be no identification on the first edition map. The pattern that emerges is of a handful of purpose-built shops and post offices, and a large number adapted from standard house plans, some of which were converted by 1850.

INNS AND PUBLIC HOUSES

Few extant buildings in the region can be shown to have served as either an inn or alehouse before the 18th century, although inns were common in major urban centres by the 16th century and between 1600 and 1750 alehouses and private houses were

Table 2 Part of 1577 list of inns, taverns and alehouses in Yorkshire, County Durham, Cumberland and Westmorland

District	Inns	Taverns	Alehouses
York and Ainsty	86	11	171
Ryedale	17	0	140
Langbaurgh with Whitby Strand	0	0	126
Pickering Lyth Wapentake	0	2	146
Birdforth	2	0	110
Allertonshire	3	1	30

[SOURCE: PRO:SP/12/96]

Table 3 War Office list of guest beds and stabling, 1686

Locality	Beds	Stabling
Allerston	3	0
Cloughton	2	4
Ebberston	2	0
Egton Bridge	2	4
Fadmoor	1	2
Farndale	1	2
Glaisdale	1	4
Harome	4	6
Hawnby	3	6
Helmsley	60	136
Middleton (by Pickering)	1	0
Nawton	1	2
Pickering	16	0
Rosedale	1	2
Sinnington	1	2
Sleights	2	1
Snainton	3	0
Danby	5	1
Kirkbymoorside	33	60
Thornton	4	8

[SOURCE: PRO: WO/30/48]

Table 4 War Office list of guest beds and stabling, 18th cent.

Locality	Beds	Stabling
Brompton	6	6
Egton	10	20
Helmsley	14	26
Kirkbymoorside	11	22
Pickering	14	28
Thornton	5	10

[SOURCE: PRO:WO/30/50]

being upgraded into inns, often by the direct conversion of substantial private properties. Large wayside inns outside the main settlements only appeared in the later 18th century. In 1577 the region was well provided with alehouses but poorly with inns, especially when compared with York and its surroundings (PRO: S.P.12/96, Table 2). However, it seems likely that Helmsley and Kirkbymoorside in Ryedale possessed inns, although there were none in Pickering nor in most of Eskdale, including Whitby. Helmsley certainly possessed a New Inn and Olde Inn by 1637 (NYCRO: ZEW IV 1/4).

Some idea of the accommodation available for travellers may be gained from lists produced for the use of the army, enumerating the beds and stables in inns and alehouses. The data from the region may be defective in the earliest such list of 1686 (PRO: W.O./30/48, 489–520: Table 3). Of the two figures given, beds are probably the better indicator, but both show Helmsley as the most important route centre, a pre-eminence later eroded. Interpretation is bedevilled by the existence of places with similar names both within the region and elsewhere in the north of Yorkshire, so making identification of Kirkbymoorside and Thornton Dale impossible. A list of 1756 (PRO: W.O.30/49) gives totals for districts, not individual settlements, while a later list of c. 1780 (PRO: W.O.30/50, Table 4) confines itself to the principal towns of the country for billeting purposes. Although generally ignoring village inns, it includes three settlements in the area with earlier urban aspirations.

To relate documented inns to existing buildings is difficult. Several known to have existed in the three market towns have been rebuilt and problems of identification arise from changes in inn names; in Pickering, for example, the same name was adopted by inns in totally different streets, or applied to two adjacent properties, or transferred from one inn to another in the next street in the same ownership. The buildings themselves present problems. The King's Head, Kirkbymoorside [273], an old inn rebuilt by 1760, may be identical with the King's Arms described in 1752 as an 'ancient and well accustomed Inn'. In Kirkbymoorside the date 1632 on the porch of the Black Swan [285] is separated by more than a century from the first reference to it as an inn. Adjacent to it, the George and Dragon [286] (Fig. 221), in origin a cruck building, remodelled with two storeys on a three-room plan in the 18th century, had stables, barns, coach-houses and outbuildings by 1811 (NYCRO: Reg. Deeds DL, 1810–11), but the distinctive entrance to the yard, the usual hallmark of an inn, was first mentioned in 1830 as the 'building erected over the gateway at the south end of the messuage' when a rear wing providing extra accommodation was probably added. At the Crown Inn at Pickering a 'gateway

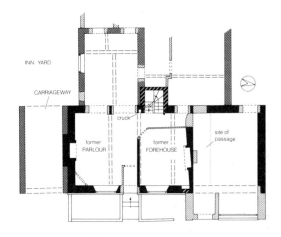

Fig. 221 [286] The George and Dragon, Kirkbymoorside

into Thomas Marshall's yard', first mentioned on 5 April 1792 (NYCRO: Reg. Deeds CJ, 1792–4), still exists between 31 and 32 Burgate, though now separated from the inn itself. The latter, at 35 Burgate [361], was the house-part of a former longhouse which retained the hearth-passage supplemented by a two-storey 17th-century rear wing, and with the rebuilt byre end in separate occupation.

The most unexpected feature of the North Yorkshire inns is the lack, prior to the 19th century, of any distinctive mode of access to the first-floor rooms. No surviving 17th or 18th-century inn has any trace of the galleries usual south of the Trent, nor is there evidence of rooms grouped around staircases. This must reflect the small size of inns in the region; all of them were far from major roads, with comparatively few travellers to cater for, and none had to accommodate numbers of people on legal or administrative business. Only with improved roads and a greater volume of traffic did anything clearly recognizable as an inn plan appear.

What may well be the earliest purpose-built inn structure in the region is the timber-framed block at the north end of the misleadingly named 'Old Manor House' at Helmsley [209]. Its history is uncertain at a number of points, but the house can be assumed to have been an inn in the 17th century, when it had a normal domestic plan, albeit one resulting from a complicated development (Fig. 9). No doubt increasing business necessitated enlargement and this was undertaken, unusually, on the site of the service rooms, by adding a block of double depth reached from the cross-passage, with a staircase near the point of entrance; although the details are doubtful, this arrangement appears to have provided at least one large and four smaller rooms on each floor, all of them, or all but one, reached directly from the staircase. Appropriately enough, this seems always to have been a superior inn in the possession, in the 17th century, of a gentry family. Not until the 19th century did such a sophisticated and up-to-date plan again appear in the region's inns.

Part of the difficulty of identifying early inns anywhere stems from the adaptation to that particular purpose, with very little alteration, of ordinary house plans. The 'Old Manor House' at Helmsley is one such, the Bay Horse at Pickering [386] (Fig. 222) another. Only by the mid 18th century did either inn achieve a distinctive plan. At the Bay Horse, as with similar buildings in southern England, a covered way or unusually wide cross-passage – for it was both – provided access for animals and vehicles from the street to the yard at the rear. A short

passage gave access from the covered way to the staircase, which led to four principal and two smaller rooms on the first floor. This was a simple and logical solution to the problem of providing many more bedrooms than were needed in an ordinary house. Otherwise the natural way to tackle this problem was by adding rear wings which could be reached directly from the inn yard where travellers dismounted or alighted from carriage or coach. The White Horse, Kirkbymoorside [301] (Fig. 223), developed like this, by stages not easy to disentangle, until it had two wings, each with a modern staircase giving access to a separate block of rooms. This was a compromise between two ideas, one that the staircase should lead by means of galleries or corridors to all rooms, the other that separate blocks of rooms had their own staircase. However, the letting rooms of the inn seem to have been in the main range facing the market-place, with the main staircase to its rear accessible from the inn yard. This kind of adaptation of a domestic plan could be carried on for a long time with extraordinarily inconvenient results. Thus

Fig. 223 [301] The White Horse, Kirkbymoorside: existing layout with room uses in 1925

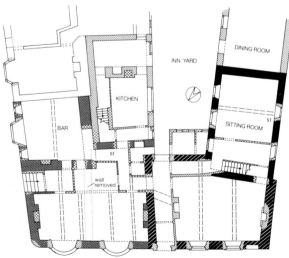

Fig. 222 [386] The Bay Horse, Pickering

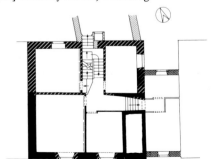

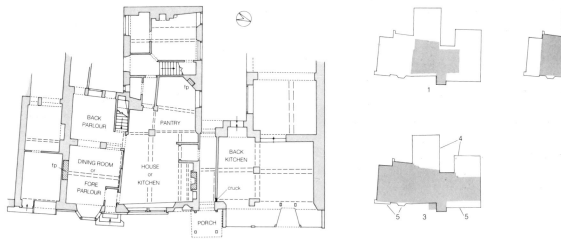

the Black Swan, Kirkbymoorside [285] (Fig. 224), has on the ground floor several passage rooms whilst on the first floor, where nine rooms of a rambling plan are reached from a single staircase, passages and lobbies of the most awkward shapes are needed. This situation had been avoided at the Old Manor House, Helmsley, in the late 17th century but such drastic rebuilding was rarely thought necessary until a hundred or more years later.

Fig. 224 [285] The Black Swan, Kirkbymoorside: 18th-century room names (the outline plans show the phases of development)

Fig. 225 [531] The Downe Arms,
Wykeham

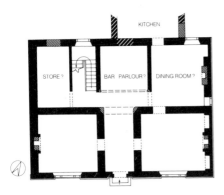

Fig. 226 [282] 10 Market Place (the former Tontine Inn),
Kirkbymoorside

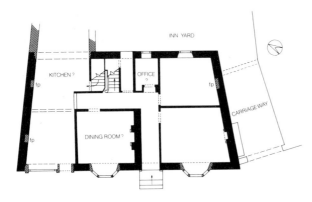

The story of inn development extends in the late 18th century beyond the towns to villages such as Wykeham where, about 1800 the Downe Arms [531] (Fig. 225) was built. It has a narrow entrance hall flanked by two principal rooms, one of which was certainly the dining room. A feature distinguishing it from a house is the position of the staircase, which is quite deliberately not treated as a display feature to be viewed from the entrance hall but is set out of sight of the entrance. Why the room to the front should not have a doorway giving access to it is not clear; perhaps this room was akin to a bar parlour, from which customers were not expected to enter the rooms reserved for travellers. In place of a staircase an unheated room of modest size faced those entering the inn; since it has a plaster cornice it must have served some public purpose, perhaps as a bar or servery. Unfortunately, the original location of the kitchen is unknown; it may have been the room to the rear of the large room to the right of the entrance, which suggests itself as a dining room. Upstairs, three principal and two or three lesser rooms provided the better accommodation, with several attic bedrooms above.

Some twenty years later the Green Dragon Inn in Kirkby-moorside was thought to have come to the end of its useful life and was largely rebuilt by the innkeeper John Atkinson 'for the reception of commercial friends'; it became the Tontine Inn and makes an interesting comparison with the Downe Arms [282] (Fig. 226). Extensive though the alterations undoubtedly were, the elevation and the plan of the rooms adjoining the street suggest that the 'thorough repair' which Atkinson announced is an accurate description because the front part has the archaic hearth-passage plan, with three rooms. Surprisingly there is no doorway from the passage-hall to the principal room (the equivalent of a residents' lounge?) to the left. Possibly this is due to a different clientele, providing for residents rather than the travellers in a hurry stopping for meals at the Downe Arms. The putative bar or servery facing the entrance is reduced to a room so small as to provide no more than a bar counter or possibly an office. To the right of the entrance two large rooms may have provided bar parlour and dining room. Upstairs an axial corridor led from the staircase, like an extended version of the Downe Arms plan, to four principal and four minor bedrooms, with two small closets in addition. So far as the present survey is concerned, this represents the culmination of inn development, with a very compact and efficient plan in which no space is wasted; the contrast with the Black Swan in the same town is extreme, yet it is the latter which has survived to serve travellers.

Purpose-built structures form a very small minority of inns, the remainder being adaptations of common house plans with innumerable variations on the hearth-passage type. Although many buildings which were called inns come into this category, the provision for travellers was minimal, no more than a bed or two, so that they hardly deserve separate treatment. The former Crown, later White Horse Inn, now 34, 35 Burgate, Pickering [361] (Fig. 227), illustrates the kind of alteration or addition that was needed: a short rear wing was added, the walls of the house being heightened to provide adequate bedrooms, and a new staircase was built to give an appropriate means of access to the three inn bedrooms. On the ground floor the principal change was the addition of a second parlour in the wing.

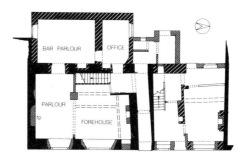

Fig. 227 [361] 35 Burgate, Pickering

Although these changes fall far short of producing a specialized plan, they must have transformed what may already have been an inn into one of a distinctly superior kind. With houses of hearth-passage type drastic change was possible without destroying the essential relationships of the plan. At Pickering the house now 1 Willowgate [415] (Fig. 228) was described as a 'messuage now used as an inn' in 1798, having adopted its new function within the previous two years. It was then a 17th-century cruck-trussed building to which an outshut, perhaps a dairy, had been added. Evidently the trade prospered and c. 1814–16, when extra stables were provided, the service rooms were replaced by a new block of double depth which provided four good rooms for travellers. At the same time a small room was added to the old house which was altered rather clumsily into four parlours. The site of the kitchen is uncertain; it may have been a detached building.

How variously buildings could be made to serve the purposes of an inn can be shown by a final example, the full architectural history of which has not been fully elucidated. The New Globe,

Fig. 228 [415] 1 Willowgate, Pickering (cruck-built nucleus to right)

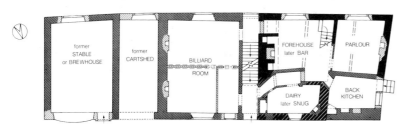
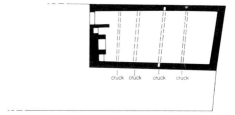

Fig. 229 [351] The Black Swan, Pickering: room uses in 1927

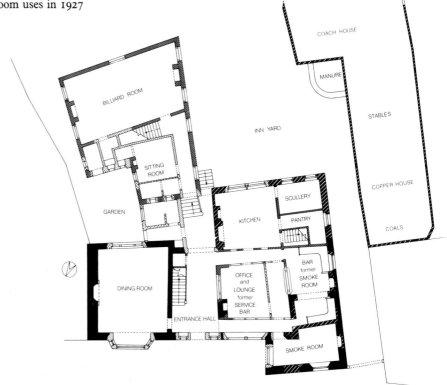

now Black Swan, Pickering [351] (Fig. 229), was an established inn by 1730 but then and for long afterwards was described in legal documents as two messuages, a fact confirmed by the disparity in plan between the two main parts of the building. It is difficult to locate the rooms listed at the sale of the contents in 1860; the principal ones were the Commercial and Market rooms, the large and back sitting rooms may have been the landlord's, and there were eleven bedrooms. The sale is of some interest as being occasioned by the removal of Monkman, the proprietor, to a 'large and comfortable house called Monkman's Hotel', a name symbolic of the increased emphasis given to the commercial trade rather than the market trade which was one of the advertised attractions of the old inn. As with several other such ventures, it is the newer establishment which has gone out of business.

Comparison of all these plans, diverse though they are in detail, establishes approximately the number of ground-floor rooms needed for an inn and may eventually, in the light of sales catalogues and literary evidence, show just how those establishments functioned. Three principal rooms were evidently essential. Taking first the older buildings derived from the regional hearth-passage plan, the most important room was the former hall or forehouse which was reached from the cross-passage; beyond the hall was a parlour with a second one opening off it, usually to the right; in the larger inns the second parlour intercommunicated with the staircase hall. The staircase could be reached easily from the entrance to the inn but faced the hall. Such an arrangement exists at the Bay Horse and the former Crown Inn (now 34, 35 Burgate), Pickering [361, 386] (Fig. 227), and can be established or inferred at the White Horse and Black Swan, Kirkbymoorside [285, 301] (Figs. 223, 224). In each case space was left for a small room adjoining or at least commanding a view of the entrance, as if for an office or perhaps one or more porters. The functions of the three principal rooms are uncertain. Possibly the one backing on to the entrance passage was a reception room equivalent to the entrance lounge of some modern hotels, and one of the parlours was presumably a dining room. A difficulty here is that it is rarely possible to locate the kitchen with certainty, although mere distance from where food was prepared and cooked would not disqualify any room from being a dining room: as late as 1925, the kitchen and dining room of the White Horse, Kirkbymoorside, were in different rear wings separated by the inn yard. The inventory of the tenant of the Crown at Helmsley in 1725 shows that it then had 8 beds, 9 tables and at least 22 chairs; by 1735 another occupier had increased these to 12, 15 and 41, with 24 pictures on the staircase, but two or three extra rooms were included in the later inventory. There were six rooms on each floor, plus garrets and a cellar, kilns for malt and lime, and outhouses.

Once an inn's trade outgrew the limits imposed by a slightly modified house, one or more rear wings were needed and with them, usually, the necessity for access from the yard. Since none of the inns of this region ever achieved any great size, the problem was not pressing; only at the Black Swan, Kirkbymoorside [285], was the principal and, indeed, only staircase removed to a wing abutting the hall in order to provide such access. There

and at the White Horse [301] the addition or incorporation of a second wing produced an unusually large plan and perhaps, in the case of the White Horse, an unusual element; for the second or west wing incorporated what was originally a free-standing building, bearing at least a formal resemblance to buildings in a comparable position elsewhere which look like some kind of public meeting or assembly room. Such a room was provided to its rear in the mid 19th century.

The plans of purpose-built inns may have been influenced by the traditional relationship between hall or forehouse and staircase, which was to its rear and not directly at the end of the entrance passage. This arrangement is evident at the Tontine Inn, Kirkbymoorside [282], the Black Swan, Helmsley [225] (Fig. 230), and also in the George and Dragon Inn, Kirkbymoorside [286], and would have been similar at the Downe Arms, Wykeham [531], but for the lack of intercommunication between the large west front room and staircase-hall. How far

Fig. 230 [225] The Black Swan, Helmsley. The small plan shows the position of the Black Swan in the complex, also including Bankins and Rectory House

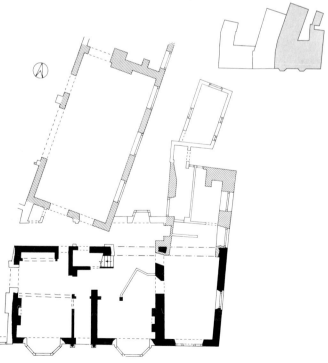

the functional relationships were dictated by adherence to custom, rather than thinking out a new solution to the problems, is a very difficult question. As the inn served both travellers requiring overnight accommodation and passers-by wanting no more than a drink or a snack, the removal of the staircase to an inconspicuous position may have been intended to guarantee the privacy of the former.

Equally characteristic is the need for a room overlooking the entrance in which, perhaps, were combined the functions of office and reception in a modern hotel; a small room at the Tontine, a large one at the Downe Arms. How the Black Swan, Helmsley, managed in this respect is not clear although space for a small room may have been provided near the staircase. An equally small room seems indicated in some other inns, e.g., 34, 35 Burgate, Pickering [361].

The differences between an inn and a private house are apparent at Ryedale House, Helmsley [202] (Fig. 231), where the relation of the three principal rooms and staircase to the entrance and of stables to house have an altogether domestic character. In 1799 it was described as a dwelling house (albeit with a large brewhouse; its predecessor had an adjoining maltkiln), and although less than twenty years later it had become an inn, the essentially domestic character remained unaltered. Similar considerations may underlie the plan of the Black Swan, Pickering [351], which has a plan quite unlike that of any other inn and was described for many years as two messuages.

A final point about inns emerges from the plan of the White Swan, Pickering [385] (Fig. 232), a building originally only one room in depth and subsequently enlarged to a double pile. One room is clearly the kitchen; in all the other three the fireplaces are set off-centre to the walls against which they lie, as if to allow space for some special function to be performed at the rear of every room. In the dining room, which may have been next to the kitchen, a sideboard or cupboards may have occupied the space and in the two front rooms a bar or serving counter

Fig. 231 [202] Ryedale House, 39–41 Bridge Street, Helmsley

Fig. 232 [385] The White Swan, Pickering: room uses in 1915

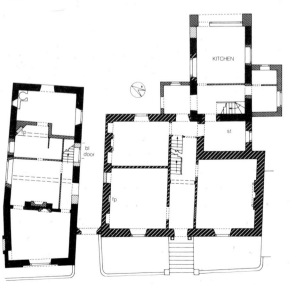

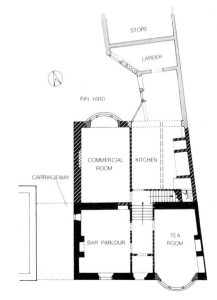

Fig. 233 [323] Saltersgate Public House, Lockton

may have been needed. It would be interesting to see from a larger sample if this positioning of fireplaces is a diagnostic feature of smaller 19th-century inns.

Little is known about inns outside the main towns prior to the middle of the 18th century. The small inn at Hawnby documented in 1686 may have been the house of John Trewman, yeoman, whose probate inventory of 1690 suggests small-scale farming activity coupled with brewing. As well as a forehouse, chamber and low parlour, the house had a lodging parlour and brewhouse suitable for an inn. The inventory of Daniel Newton senior of Brompton, innholder, in 1758 gives room names and uses, and indicates the size of the staff with its 'five servants' beds'. Thomas Skelton's inn at Hutton Buscel in 1736 had only four rooms below, two above, a cellar, brewhouse and maltkiln, plus a stable, hogsty and coalhouse. There were 22 chairs, 5 stools and a settle, but only 6 tables and 4 beds.

Communications were improved during the 18th century by the provision of new roads. Between 1750 and 1771 a network of planned or completed turnpike roads had sprung up linking York to Helmsley, and Thirsk to Kirkbymoorside via Helmsley (maps by Emmanuel Bowen (1750) and Thomas Jefferys (1771)). Pickering was linked to Whitby in 1764 with regular stage-coach services. Inns on these routes flourished not only in towns but elsewhere on the major roads. A farmstead on the route of the Whitby and Middleton Trust turnpike became the Saltersgate Inn, Lockton [323] (Fig. 233). Purpose-built inns include the Coachman, Snainton [467], fitted up as The New Inn in 1774, and the Downe Arms, Wykeham [531], of c. 1800, both conveniently situated for the Scarborough–York coach which was running by 1793 (McDonnell 1963: 281). The Milburn Arms Hotel, Rosedale East Side [453] (Fig. 234), prob-

Fig. 234 [453] The Milburn Arms Hotel, Rosedale East Side

ably purpose built in 1776, shows a trend visible in major inns from this time on by being of three storeys.

The arrival of the first railway in 1836 began the demise of the long-distance stage-coach, but horse-drawn transport became increasingly important as a link between stations and their hinterland, until as late as 1919. This accounts for the addition in the late 19th century of stables and coach-houses to The White Horse, Kirkbymoorside [301], and of extensive stabling to The White Swan, Pickering [385]. The railways, like the turnpikes before them, generated a need for extra accommo-

Fig. 235 [107] The Station Tavern, Grosmont

dation along the route. Although this was mainly satisfied by the expansion of existing inns in the towns served, it sometimes led to the creation of new inns at intermediate stations, such as the Station Tavern, Grosmont [107] (Fig. 235).

The inn buildings themselves now rarely show any trace of the occupations frequently associated with them, such as that of blacksmith. It was a useful extra service for the innkeeper to shoe travellers' horses or repair their carriages, similar to that provided nowadays by a motorway service station or a motel combined with a petrol station and car repair facilities. This conjunction is not unknown in towns but is commoner in country places. An early instance is John Page, who built the Milburn Arms Hotel [453] and appears as blacksmith on deeds of 1773 and 1778; he was probably also the innkeeper. Similarly, at the Hammer and Hand, Hutton-le-Hole [246] (Fig. 236), the Stricklands, who built it in 1789, were innholders and blacksmiths. In the towns this dual occupation occurs only in minor inns such as the Horse Shoe, Pickering [377].

Fig. 236 [246] The Hammer and Hand, Hutton-le-Hole

Fig. 238 [226] The Crown Hotel, Helmsley

Fig. 237 [389] St George's House, Pickering

As most inns brewed their own beer, it is not surprising to find James Boddy, described as brewer in 1786 and common brewer in 1793, at the George and Dragon, Pickering [389] (Fig. 237), whilst successive members of the Potter family at the Black Swan, Kirkbymoorside [285], were innkeepers and malt-sters (*YG:* 6 Jan. 1838). More information concerning brewing is available for the town inns because they brewed for other inns or alehouses, as the phrase 'common brewer' above suggests. The inns which brewed their own beer can usually be identified from references to maltkilns or brewhouses, or both. In the middle years of the 18th century the Crown Inn, Helmsley [226] (Fig. 238), and the King's Arms (probably rebuilt as the King's Head), Kirkbymoorside [273], both had maltkilns, while the

White Horse, Kirkbymoorside [301], had a brewhouse as late as 1905. Little architectural evidence of this fragmented industry remains, one of the few brewhouses to survive being at the Black Swan, Kirkbymoorside [285], mentioned in 1815 and 1898.

Pickering was a major centre for brewing. The Black Swan [351], the Rose [353], the George and Dragon [389] and several others had brewhouses or malting kilns at various times in the 18th century, and details of the King's Arms, which stood on the east side of Burgate, include 'fixtures and brewing utensils' (*YG:* 8 Aug. 1846).

Some inns played a role in the sale of basic commodities. In the yard of the George and Dragon, Kirkbymoorside [286], was a corn exchange, and, since the Black Swan, Pickering, served as an Office for Corn Returns in the later 19th century (Bulmer 1890: 1009), the inn yard may have served a similar purpose to that of the Tontine. The Station Tavern, Grosmont [107], with stabling and warehouses adjacent, was described in 1848, when it was the Tunnel Inn, as in an 'eligible situation for corn, cattle and bacon trade' (*YG:* 9 Sept. 1848), trades also carried on at this period at the Tontine Inn, Kirkbymoorside [282] (*YG:* 3 Nov. 1849). The former Fat Ox, Houlsyke, Glaisdale [140], saw its heyday for the wholesale marketing of bacon, mutton and wool, somewhat later, *c.* 1860–5. These activities fit the descrip-tion of an inn in the period 1500–1700 as a 'place in which corn might be factored, bills exchanged and bonds entered into, forwards in commodities bought and sold and information on the state of trade passed on' (Patten 1978: 202), and it is clear that, whatever was usual elsewhere in England, in the North York Moors the inn's role was not limited to 'providing food, drink, accommodation and gossip' by the mid 18th century (Patten 1978). Its continuing commercial role is relevant to the nature and extent of the accommodation provided. Food, drink and a place to conduct business were evidently all that many of the buyers and sellers would require, so that the absence of the galleried ranges usual in inns on important roads is less surprising than appears at first sight.

Fig. 239 [449] The New Inn, Thornton Dale

The large public rooms available in inns made them suitable for a variety of functions. Petty Sessions were long held in Pickering inns but most meetings were less formal, as, for example, the ball given by the Bachelors of Helmsley at the Crown Inn, Helmsley [226], or the 'treat given by T. Marsden, Thornton paper mills, to workmen, at the New Inn of Mrs. Mercer', Thornton Dale [499] (Fig. 239) (*MNG:* 23 Feb. 1856; *MM*, 5 Jan. 1861). Sales of property at inns were frequently advertised. They also provided for the meetings and lectures which proliferated in the 19th century, notably those of agricultural societies which met at Pickering and Kirkbymoorside. Another early function of the Black Swan, Pickering, appears in an advertisement under its former name of the Globe, when it was an excise office besides being a 'well accustomed good inn' (*YC:* 27 Jan. 1729/30); but by 1823 the only excise office in the region was at the Black Swan, Helmsley [225].

Domestic buildings

No complete houses from before the middle of the 17th century have survived in any of the three towns, except for a few at the top of the social scale. The handful of such buildings were timber framed and either of manorial status or inns. In Helmsley the first category is represented by Canons Garth [187] and Rectory House [223], the second by the Crown Inn [226], the so-called Manor House, Castlegate [209], and Thorpe's Cottage [221], now part of the Feathers. Kirkbymoorside has one representative in each category, High Hall [259] and the Black Swan [285]. In Pickering only one timber-framed building has been identified, at Burgate Chambers, which combines box-frame construction with an apparently secondary cruck [363].

The scarcity of well-built timber-framed houses suggest that insubstantial forms of construction were normal. It may be implied in the complaint of 1448 by John Day against Sir

Edmund Hastynges and four others that they had demolished 'with force and armes two howses of your said beseecher' in Pickering (Turton 1894: 245–6). Much of whatever existed was swept away by fire in at least two of the three towns. Between 1578 and 1587, forty-six trees were delivered to tenants in the manor of Pickering whose houses were burnt (Survey of Woods, PRO: D.L.42/114) and in January 1607 great harm was done by extremity of fire in Helmsley, but the grant of £6.13s.4d. for rebuilding the houses does not suggest anything large or well built. The fire risk was less from the use of timber construction than from thatch, which survived as a roof covering in the towns until the 20th century. On the other hand, a rising standard of building construction may be implied by a survey of Kirkbymoorside in 1611 (PRO: L.R.2/186, ff. 70–91) which reported that 'Christopher Medd by his under tenant Robert Otterbourne holds a house erected within these 10 years, well built of 3 or 4 rooms of wood'; High Hall was built about this time or soon afterwards, and the Black Swan Inn in 1632. No timber-framed buildings seem to have been constructed in the towns after 1650.

Little is known about what the smaller houses were like before the mid 17th century. Most, no doubt, were single-storey cruck buildings, often longhouses. There is virtually no evidence for timber-framed outer walls in connection with crucks in any of the three towns, and whatever flimsy structures may have originally existed, cruck structures are generally associated with thick stone outer walls. In 1570 most of the households in Kirkbymoorside owned between one and three cows (*YAJ* 17 (1902–3): 146–7). This supports the impression of numerous longhouses in all three towns, rebuilt piecemeal at subsequent dates.

The towns were surrounded by common fields and, until enclosures took place, it was impossible to expand beyond the town boundaries. An increase in the housing stock was possible only by subdividing existing burgage plots, building behind the street frontages, converting farm buildings to domestic use, or encroaching on the waste. All these expedients were used from an early period, and can be demonstrated at frequent intervals up to the present day. The 1476 Rental of Pickering (PRO: D.L.43/11/5) includes entries for quarters and halves of cottages, one of three parts of one cottage, and another of two-and-a-half cottages. The description of Kirkbymoorside in 1570 as a 'market town inhabyted all with pore people' (*YAJ* 17 (1902–3): 146–7) suggests stagnation, but the 1611 Survey of Kirkbymoorside (PRO: L.R.2/186, ff. 70–91) mentions new buildings since 1567 'upon copyhold lands . . . upon old barns . . . and some upon land ends . . . some upon waste grounds as back houses and which are now made dwelling houses'. There are two vivid examples of types of urban change in the 1611 Survey; William Chapman had 'a house lately the end of a copyhold house' which seems to be the conversion of a byre end, and he made 'a fair dwelling house in the Marketstead' there which must surely, in the context of a list of encroachments, be the transformation of a stall into a permanent building. In 1623 a Survey of the Honour of Pickering (PRO: D.L.42/124) noted that 'Roger Lassells has built a house upon Potter Hill being part of the Prince's waste', while a generation later a Parliamentary Survey of Pickering of 1651 (PRO: E.317/43) reported twenty such encroachments. Enclosure around all three towns created a number of new isolated farmsteads and led in the towns to the conversion or abandonment of some older farmsteads based on the former town fields. As most of the earlier buildings were longhouses, it is only the presence of ancillary farm buildings, in particular barns, which can identify a particular example as a farmhouse rather than the home of a town-dweller with one or two cows.

The process of rebuilding and subdivision during the 18th century can be best followed in Pickering, where the mostly freehold properties feature in the county Register of Deeds kept after 1740, supplemented after 1795 by Duchy of Lancaster records. In Helmsley and Kirkbymoorside freehold properties were far fewer but the county Register of Deeds is still illuminating. The process of rebuilding is described in an Inquiry about Tithes and Rates in Kirbymoorside of 1815 (NYCRO; ZEW VII 3/13)in terms not dissimilar from those used in 1611. Houses had replaced barns, stables and cowhouses; gardens, orchards and yards had been divided and subdivided as appurtenances to them, and one or two new houses had been erected in orchards or garths where no buildings were before. This contrasts strongly with the picture presented in 1570.

The town of Helmsley was also almost entirely owned by the Duncombe estate, the freeholds being clearly marked on Tukes and Ayer's map of 1822. The buildings still reflect this ownership, for the freeholds stand out with superior or distinctive buildings. They include 19 Bridge Street [58], various other three-storey houses and a warehouse converted to domestic occupation in Church Street. The other houses in the town, owned by the estate, contrast with these houses in their size, form and date, just as they also contrast with the overall standards of housing in Kirkbymoorside and Pickering. The visual evidence of Helmsley is complemented by various written sources. Thomas Parker in his manuscript 'History of Kirkdale, with the towns and villages adjacent', described Helmsley in 1858: 'Since the accession of the present William Lord Feversham (Charles, 1st Baron Feversham, died in 1841) to the estates and possessions of the Duncombes, the Town of Helmsley has been greatly improved, old houses have been taken down and new and elegant ones erected in their stead . . . But in the year 1821 when I first visited it, "Far other scenes" were here: the houses low and covered with thatch . . . What kept the town in the state of existence at the time above mentioned was the unchangeable mind of the late Lord Feversham, an enemy to pride, extravagance and dress; but since his day, like the rest of the neighbourhood, its wings have become fledged' (Parker 1982: 18). There clearly had been room for improvement, but Parker perhaps exaggerated the amount. A valuation of 1868 (McDonnell 1963: 309–10) includes figures which show that, of 256 houses in the town, thirty-four were slated and therefore recent, sixty-six thatched and the remainder tiled. The thatched houses and cottages were well distributed throughout the town, and of the sixty-six no fewer than forty-five were indicated as being 'old', 'bad', 'very bad' or 'bad old'. Thirty-five of the 156 tiled houses were condemned under the same heading.

URBAN DOMESTIC HOUSE TYPES

Longhouses: from rural to urban forms

As the market towns were predominantly agricultural communities until at least the end of the 18th century, many longhouses can still be recognized as such although none are unaltered. The byre-end was seldom retained in agricultural use, being usually converted to domestic use or demolished. When converted, the low end either provided additional accommodation for the original house, in which case it corresponds to the parallel development of such houses in the countryside, or, in the characteristic urban mode of development, it became a separate dwelling. Occasionally the original house-part is still clearly recognizable, but usually a process of heightening, refacing or alternate rebuilding of both parts has taken place so that most houses, some from as late as the second half of the 19th century, do no more than hint externally at longhouse origins.

The general development of longhouse and linear plans is discussed above (Chapter 4) and the very few undivided examples in the towns underwent the same changes in use as those in the countryside. Though truncated, the byre-end at 22 Ryegate, Helmsley [232] (Fig. 240), retains unheated rooms. The original use of the third room at 38 Bondgate, Helmsley [196] (Fig. 241), another 17th-century single-storey building similarly heightened subsequently, is less certain: it became a bakehouse in the 19th century. Two-storey hearth-passage houses of one build, such

Fig. 240 [231] 22 Ryegate, Helmsley

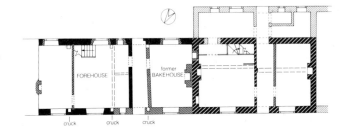

Fig. 241 [196, 195] 38, 36 Bondgate, Helmsley

139

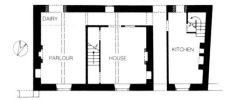

Fig. 242 [193] 20 Bondgate, Helmsley

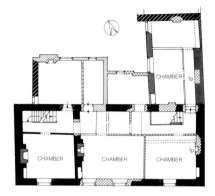

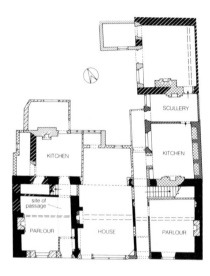

as 11 Castlegate, Pickering [365], and 20 Bondgate, Helmsley [193] (Fig. 242), are urban examples of fully domestic linear plans of late 18th or early 19th-century date.

Most urban longhouses and purpose-built hearth-passage houses were subdivided. The house and byre-ends of the former and the upper and lower ends of the latter usually became separate cottages, and either one or both ends might be rebuilt. Both cottages needed their own entrance doorway, and the simplest solution was to retain the hearth-passage as a common entrance, an arrangement which survives at 42–46 West End, Kirkbymoorside [296] (Fig. 243). This provided local precedent for pairs of cottages of equal size sharing a common passage entrance. Usually, however, the hearth-passage was retained as the entrance to only one cottage, and a new doorway was created on the street frontage for the other. The hearth-passage door usually survived in the customary position even when new ideas

Fig. 243 [296] 42–46 West End, Kirkbymoorside

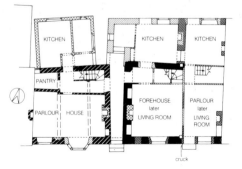

Fig. 244 [382] 30, 31 Hungate, Pickering: ground and first-floor plans

of planning caused the removal of the hearth-passage, as at 30, 31 Hungate, Pickering [382] (Fig. 244), or its metamorphosis to a staircase lobby. The main variations possible in these subdivided buildings are few, and are governed by two major factors: firstly, which cottage retains the hearth-passage, and secondly, the length of the byre or lower end. The door positions provided at the byre-end of a true longhouse during its conversion to a false longhouse (see Chapter 4) could be perpetuated in a subsequent conversion to domestic use, and retained on subdivision. Different planning and elevational treatments accordingly result from the former presence of a short or long byre. Most purpose-built hearth-passage houses in fully domestic use had a lower end corresponding in length to a short byre. Subdivisions resulting in two cottages are most widespread, and will be considered first.

The byre-end commonly retained the hearth-passage as the entrance, with a central doorway inserted in the house-part. With a former short byre this resulted in the classical solution to subdivision, adjacent double-fronted and single-fronted cottages, probably influenced by the growing popularity of central-entry and single-room width houses. At 86 and 86A Westgate, Pickering [411] (Fig. 103), alterations took place

Fig. 245 [203] 43, 45 Bridge Street, Helmsley

within the shell of the existing longhouse; at 21 and 23 Bondgate, Helmsley [190], the house-part was completely rebuilt (Fig. 181). Where a long byre was rebuilt, a two-room cottage was created. A hearth could be built backing onto the passage, which then separated stacks belonging to adjacent properties, as at 43, 45 Bridge Street, Helmsley [203] (Fig. 245). A simpler solution was to insert the stack between the two rooms, resulting in a passage-entrance house at the byre-end whose entrance was not a hearth-passage to that dwelling, as at Fern Cottage, 23 Piercy End (Fig. 246), and 3 West End, Kirkbymoorside [288, 302], and 70 Bondgate, Helmsley [199]. As with hearth-passage plans, such end-passage plans could have an independent development, but as most sites where they occur appear to be subdivisions of wider plots, and in view of the popularity of longhouses throughout the region, houses with such plans probably occupy the rebuilt byre-ends of longhouses, the passages representing the former hearth-passages which no longer provide access to the house-parts.

The retention of the hearth-passage by the house part was less common and could cause problems, especially in smaller longhouses. A staircase inserted between the two main rooms and reached directly by the new front door simplified the internal circulation but reduced the available room width, and a central door could not always be inserted conveniently in the existing front wall. Where there was insufficient room for a lobby the new door usually opens directly into the inner room.

Fig. 246 [288] 23 Piercy End, Kirkbymoorside

The inner room at 25, 27 Ryegate, Helmsley [230], is very narrow and so the doorway is in the main room. One mid 19th-century subdivision involved building a thick wall between the former house and parlour, thus reversing the customary classic arrangement. At 60, 61 Eastgate, Pickering [371] (Fig. 247), the passage door became the central entrance of the larger house, and the inserted door served the smaller.

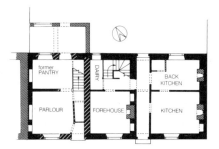

Fig. 247 [371] 60, 61 Eastgate, Pickering

As pressure on the available sites increased, further subdivision took place. Where space permitted, either end of a longhouse could be redeveloped more intensively as two separate, narrow cottages. The wider house-part was more appropriate for this treatment, and probably provided sites for 72, 74 West End, Kirkbymoorside [300] (Fig 248), and 53, 55 Eastgate,

Fig. 248 [300] 72, 74 West End, Kirkbymoorside

Pickering [369], which contrast markedly with their respective short and long rebuilt byre-ends, both of which retained the hearth-passage. In 14 and 15 Castlegate, Pickering [367] (Fig. 249), the hearth-passage is used as the entrance to one cottage in the house-part, and the inserted central door as the entrance to another. Alternatively, the site of a wide byre could be subdivided for cottages, as at 19, 20 Burgate, Pickering [358], and 37 West End, Kirkbymoorside [305] (Fig. 250), now a single dwelling. The houses at 55–57 Eastgate, Pickering [369], and 63, 65, 67 West End, Kirkbymoorside [310] (Fig. 180), are exceptional in accommodating passages providing rear access as well as separate doorways to each cottage on restricted frontages.

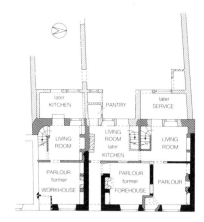

Fig. 249 [367] 14, 15 Castlegate, Pickering

Fig. 250 [305] 37 West End, Kirkbymoorside

The opportunity to combine entrances for two of the three cottages was realized at 42, 44 West End, Kirkbymoorside [296], where the existing hearth-passage served this purpose, and at 9 Ryegate, Helmsley [219] (Fig. 251), where the house-part was completely remodelled as a symmetrical passage-entry house.

Fig. 251 [229] 9 Ryegate, Helmsley

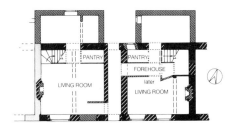

Houses with a two-room plan

The general difficulty of relating plan types to social classes or groups is increased by the urban process of consecutive rebuilding on adjacent sites which complicates even the identification of two-room houses. Gable-entry houses and hearth-passage houses with two-room plans are likely to be the surviving remnants of longhouses or three-room hearth-passage houses. Conversely, although most three-room hearth-passage plans are the product of alternate rebuilding, the existence of purpose-built gable-entry cottages raises the possibility that some hearth-passage houses may be the result of extensions of a two-room plan along a street frontage rather than of replacement by domestic accommodation of a byre. Building on an adjacent site can obliterate an original gable entry, so that the access must now be on the street frontage, resulting in a central-entry or end-lobby-entry plan. Sometimes the only evidence is an apparent cupboard recess the full depth of the original gable end wall.

One of the few gable-entry cottages unobscured by later additions in line is 2 Castlegate, Helmsley [208]. Its cruck construction and plan hints at a longhouse origin, but added rear wings suggest that the open passageway to the side which limits expansion marks an ancient site boundary, and the nearest building at the putative byre-end is set back from the street frontage of the cottage. However, this may only prove that subdivision took place a long time ago. A more likely case of a purpose-built two-room cottage is 24 High Street, Helmsley [216] (Fig. 252), which also retains its gable entry, but has been subdivided, a new central entry providing access to 26 High Street. The argument against any earlier building abutting the gable is stronger, as it would have blocked access to a cruck building on the adjacent plot. One feature present here but lacking in the two-room cottages derived from hearth-passage houses is the thick wall between the two rooms. This also appears at 32 High Street, Helmsley [218], where, despite the present central entry an earlier gable entry can be postulated from a walk-in cupboard the full depth of the gable wall.

Fig. 252 [216] 24 High Street, Helmsley

Fig. 253 [188] 1 Bondgate, Helmsley

Two-room hearth-passage houses may result from the covering in of an open alley: 1 Bondgate, Helmsley [188] (Fig. 253), appears to be all of one build, but the rendered front elevation could conceal constructional joints. Its decidedly wedge-shaped passage must be determined by a pre-existing site boundary. In 20 High Street, Helmsley [215] (Fig. 254), apparently the result of alternate rebuilds involving 8 High Street, is concealed a cruck structure apparently shared with 22 High Street, a three-room hearth-passage house where the existence of a projecting end gable stack suggests that the basic plan was reached no later than the 17th century. It is thus the result of an even earlier subdivision.

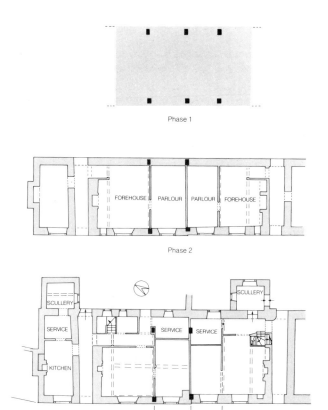

Phase 1

Phase 2

Fig. 254 [215] 20 High Street, Helmsley, and plan

Houses with a central entry

Urban central-entry houses cover a wide range of sizes and social status. The larger ones owned by professional men and the lesser gentry are discussed in Chapter 3; a scatter of small houses exists in each of the towns. A somewhat lower social level is represented by the nebulous term yeoman. Richard Ness was so described when he built 75 Eastgate, Pickering [374], in 1786, and sold it to Nicholas Piper, master mariner, the same year (NYCRO: Reg. Deeds BZ, 1785–6). The difficulty of relating houses to their owners' social positions is further illustrated by 27 Potter Hill, Pickering [396], a modest house owned by Richard Spenceley, labourer, in 1827 (NYCRO: Reg. Deeds FH, 1826–7), but inherited from his grandfather of the same name who was described as either a yeoman or a basket maker. Nevertheless, house size gives some indication of social status and must correspond broadly to economic position and social class; the difficulty is to define with sufficient precision what kind of people lived where.

The simplest form of central-entry plan, of which no unaltered example survives, would give a minimum of two rooms downstairs and two upstairs, equal to the accommodation of terrace houses two rooms deep. It is likely that one of the downstairs rooms would have been subdivided by a thin partition to create a pantry. Most central-entry houses have an outshut, as at 24 Dale End, Kirkbymoorside [267] (Fig. 255),

Fig. 256 [213] 21 High Street, Helmsley

Fig. 255 [267] 24 Dale End, Kirkbymoorside

and, at least on the ground floor, are two rooms deep, either by design or conversion; others have an added rear wing. They are rarely completely symmetrical. Differences in internal planning are indicated by the arrangement of the entrance door on the main elevation. This is either approximately on the axis, or to one side of it so that the door is wholly within one half of the elevation. Most of the smaller houses fall within the second category, although there is an overlap in size between the two types. In the simplest version of the second category the front door opens directly into one of the two front rooms, as at 13 and 21 High Street, Helmsley [212, 213] (Fig. 256). In most

cases, however, it now opens into a passage apparently taken out of one of the two front rooms, so that the doorway opening directly into the room must have been the norm earlier. At 23 Bondgate and 32 High Street, Helmsley [190 and 218] (Figs. 181, 257), this arrangement is explicable as the adaptation of the house-part of a longhouse to a central-entry plan, but at 36 and 40 Bondgate and 30 High Street [195, 197 and 217], the central-entry plan is probably primary. In most cases the staircase rises against the original back wall at the rear of the wider of the two front rooms. Plans of this kind can be deduced in Pickering, e.g., 27 Park Street, the house of a stonemason in 1857 and 1861. Probably many of the better-off independent craftsmen lived in such houses.

Fig. 257 [218] 32 High Street, Helmsley

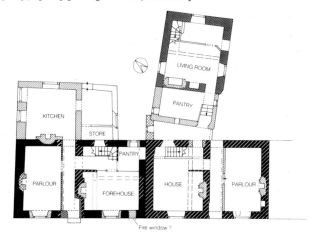

The symmetrical central-entry houses have front rooms of approximately equal width, usually with shallow service rooms behind at least one room. Smaller houses, most of them with only two first-floor windows, have a staircase rising directly from an entrance lobby serving the front rooms, the service rooms being reached from one front room, e.g., 10 and 85 West End, Kirkbymoorside [294, 308] (Fig. 258). A house at 36 Potter Hill, Pickering [398] (Fig. 259), with three first-floor windows,

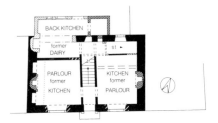

Fig. 258 [294] 10 West End, Kirkbymoorside

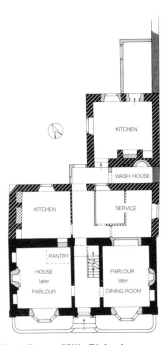

Fig. 259 [398] 36 Potter Hill, Pickering

Fig. 260 [290] 30 Piercy End, Kirkbymoorside

Fig. 261 [295] 14 West End, Kirkbymoorside

has a wider entrance hall to accommodate a dog-leg staircase. Like the White Swan, Pickering [385], which was built as a private house, it was originally only one room deep, with no obvious subdivision to create a service room. In most larger houses with three first-floor windows the entrance opens into a passage which widens at the back of the house to form a staircase hall, as at 30 Piercy End and 14 West End, Kirkbymoorside [290, 295] (Figs. 260, 261).

Occasionally the exact symmetry is impaired by a second doorway serving a passageway to the rear, needed only where there was no back lane access to the yard or garden. At 13 Undercliffe, Pickering [404] (Fig. 262), this gives the house the appearance of a pair of terrace houses, but without a window above the passage door to match that above the entrance.

Some houses have a carriageway to one side, resembling the entry to an inn yard. The room above it is usually several steps above the level of the first floor, and its restricted ceiling height suggests that it can only have been suitable for storage. Houses at 17 Hungate, Pickering [381], with two first-floor windows apart from the extra room, and at 34 Hungate [383], with three first-floor windows, were occupied by a yeoman and a horse dealer respectively. Yeomen, property owners and professional

Fig. 262 [404] 13 Undercliffe, Pickering

Fig. 263 [258] 20 Castlegate, Kirkbymoorside

men lived in both two and three-window versions of central-entry houses, and the difference in elevation no doubt reflects wealth rather than occupation.

More specifically urban types of building were developed in the last quarter of the 18th century. Maximum use was made of the building plots by means of double-room depths, and sometimes by increasing the height of three storeys. Although there are some groupings of paired central-entry houses, including a semi-detached 'mansion' of 1830, 40 and 41 Market Place, Pickering [390], terraces of houses one room wide but two deep gained in popularity in the early 19th century.

Houses with a one-room plan

The single-width house is found as a subdivision of an earlier building, as infill between existing buildings, and as a unit in a terrace or a pair of houses. Most such dwellings satisfied the modest needs of small tradesmen and town labourers, although there are examples of single-width houses with architectural pretensions which must have been influenced by the standards of the larger cities.

The simplest type had only one room on each floor, and was entered directly from the street. Although no unaltered examples have been recorded, the type can be illustrated by 20 Castlegate, Kirkbymoorside [258] (Fig. 263), which was probably built in the 18th century with one room on each floor, the corridor being inserted only in the 19th century when an extra room was added at the rear to give a plan similar to 21 Bondgate, Helmsley [190] (Fig. 181).

Where space was limited, development had to be upwards, producing three-storey houses. Although most were built as

terraces, individual three-storey houses are a feature of Kirkby-moorside; of brick at 5 Howe End [274], but of stone at 11 Howe End [275] and 37 West End [305].

Terraces and pairs of houses

The building of terraces and, in particular, the rebuilding or conversion of one house to make two on the same plot, is a product of population growth and indicates when the existing housing stock was becoming inadequate. In Pickering, the Napoleonic Wars were one such period. A newly erected house at 59 Eastgate [570] (Fig. 264), first mentioned in 1777, was in dual occupancy by 1804; 9 and 10 Castlegate [364], one-and-a-half storeys high, were rebuilt or converted after 1808; 66 and 67 Eastgate [373] probably replaced a single cottage documented in 1811. The property described as 'two messuages, lately one' in 1816, is probably 9 and 10 Undercliffe, Pickering [403], while 12 and 13 Castlegate [366] (Fig. 201) were erected as two cottages by one of the occupants, Robert Johnson, joiner, prior to 1818. A similar increase in density appears at Vine Cottage, Brant Hill [352], described on 7 November 1837 as 'two houses lately erected in the yard' of 25 Castlegate; it is in two unequal parts, capable of being mistaken for a subdivided three-room house. Like most purpose-built terraces and cottages produced by subdivision, these were intended to be rented. Evidently much of this kind of building was a form of investment, to obtain rent income.

In Helmsley and Kirkbymoorside, where in 1799 Sir Charles Duncombe owned 221 and 61 properties respectively, most rented accommodation was controlled by one man, but even in Pickering owner-occupiers possessing a single house were rare. The Land Tax returns for that year list three major owner-

Fig. 264 [370] 59 Eastgate, Pickering

occupiers in Pickering, Robert Kitching, William Piper and John Marshall, with Anthony Oates owning but not occupying a fourth large holding (PRO: I.R.22/177). The Register of Deeds shows that these land holdings could form the basis for large-scale investment in rented property. Robert Kitching, gent., was involved with twenty-five properties in the Pickering area during the first half of the 19th century and John Kitching, gent., with ten, mainly after 1842. John Watson, gent., 'of York' in 1816 and 'of Grays Inn' in 1818, probably brought money from a successful legal career to acquire the twenty-one properties with which he was involved between 1816 and 1855. His property investment is reflected to a lesser degree by that of the Petch family of Kirkbymoorside, based on a local solicitor's practice. More than one generation, and different branches of a small number of interrelated families, reappear in several transactions. In the 1851 Census, almost a third of those named as landowner or house proprietor, including both men and women, belonged to a dozen families, but other people, most of them women, invested in property on a much smaller scale. Nothing is known about the location of their property apart from their homes, which they presumably owned, but two 'house proprietors', Mary Champney at 8 Bridge Street, Pickering [355], and Christopher Lyon at 3 Undercliffe [402], lived in part of the property and rented out the other part, which was approximately equal in size. This was the type of investment open to a successful small tradesman.

How longer terraces were financed is unclear. Although the Duncombe Estate seems to have embarked on a major rebuilding programme from the mid 19th century onwards, earlier terraces were probably small-scale speculations. The main developments in the Pickering area were executed by George Green, a lime burner, who in 1841 and 1851 (Censuses) was living in terraces he had built himself; in 1841 at Westgate and in 1851 at New Bridge, Pickering [412 and 421]. He ceased his building activities in the region during 1851 on moving to Bedale (NYCRO: Reg. Deeds IA, 1851–3). He is variously described in deeds as builder or yeoman, although another George Green 'of London', who appears in some of the deeds, may also have been involved. It is clear that Green did not finance his building activities unaided; the gentry were either speculating in property development or creating an investment. Thomas Wrangler, gent., and his wife Mary appear in connection with the 'eleven newly erected cottages' in Westgate [412] and with other cottages erected by Green in Middleton [326]. Thomas Peirson, gent., appears with others in connection with 133 and 134 Westgate built by Green in 1842 (NYCRO: Reg. Deeds GX, 1841–2); they form the nucleus for a row of seven houses [413]. Peirson was also involved in 1843 with ten cottages at New Bridge as well as with other developments not by Green.

The vast majority of pairs of cottages or complete terraces comprise single-fronted houses. The main variations in the former are between mirror-image pairs with either back-to-back

Fig. 265 [204] 10 Bridge Street, Helmsley

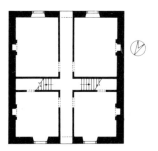

Fig. 266 [292] 4 Tinley Garth, Kirkbymoorside

Fig. 267 [194] 30–34 Bondgate, Helmsley

or gable stacks, and repeated units in series, the latter being usual in the longer terraces. Few single-fronted houses have a passageway to either the staircase or the back door, but have front doors which open either directly or from a small lobby into the front room. Double-fronted houses are occasionally found in terraces, usually in combination with single-fronted houses, and cover a wider timespan than the terraces of repeated single-fronted units, most of which date from the 19th century.

Pairs of double-fronted houses are unusual, and, apart from some mid to late 19th-century examples in Helmsley, ranges of this appearance usually prove to be composed of several houses with shared front doors. A pair of such houses can easily be mistaken for a central-entrance house with gable stacks. The least altered example is 9 Ryegate [229], but 10 Bridge Street and 7 High Street [204 and 211] (Fig. 265) were also of this type originally. The drawings for 34–46 High Street [219] (Fig. 171), a range of five houses of c. 1853 (NYCRO: ZEW M 88) show that the 'proposed cottages' were designed as a central-entry house flanked by two pairs of houses entered from shared passages. The resemblance to a terrace of three double-fronted houses, as as 14, 16 and 18 Bondgate [192], is belied by the paired windows over the doors to the two passages. Plans providing a common passage entrance to two houses are found earlier elsewhere, e.g., Blandford Forum (Dorset) where 7–17 East Street date from the first quarter of the 18th century (RCHM 1970: 19, 30), and nearer the area at 4 and 4A Precentor's Court, York, of similar date (RCHM 1981: 199, 200). The houses in Helmsley are shallower than these and the combined front-entrance type found in the West Midlands (Muthesius 1982: 102), whose closest parallel in the region is at 4 Tinley Garth, Kirkbymoorside [292] (Fig. 266). Shared front doors did not always conceal passages; both 13 and 14 Westgate, Pickering [406], built by 1811 (or 1806?) and 30, 32, 34 Bondgate, Helmsley [194] (Fig. 267), appear to be pairs of double-fronted houses, but were built with one half subdivided as two single-fronted houses entered from a lobby with a shared front door.

In the 18th century new-built terraces provided a combination of houses of different sizes and layout resembling that which arose naturally from the subdivision of former longhouses or three-room hearth-passage houses. The terrace at 6–9 Burgate, Pickering [356] (Fig. 268), is not composed of regular repeated units, although the present arrangement of two single-fronted and two double-fronted houses does not necessarily represent the original subdivision. They were probably built in the first half of the 18th century and are first mentioned in 1768 as four tenements in Boroughgate. The terrace 1–7 Train Lane, Pickering [401], built between 1800 and 1817, was constructed in stages and not to a standard plan, in order to provide basic accommodation, with one room on each floor, for some of the poorer inhabitants of the town. They included in 1841 a weaver, a stonemason, a butcher and a shoemaker, as well as a female labourer and four agricultural labourers. A more unusual mode of development appears at 33–36 Westgate [409], forming an unequal terrace described as five cottages in 1846, probably to be identified with the messuage with barns, stables, cottages and outbuildings adjoining described in 1838.

Fig. 268 [356] 6–9 Burgate, Pickering

At about the same time as this development in Westgate, Richard Boulton, a stonemason of Farmanby, who was in Castlegate, Pickering in 1823 (Baines 1823), and from 1831 in a farmhouse later the Sun Inn, Westgate [414], was building 62–65 Eastgate, Pickering [372] (Fig. 269). Of these, 62 and 63 are apparently two repeated units, and 64 and 65 a symmetrical pair with quoins, back-to-back stacks and probably fireplaces in the first-floor bedrooms served by end stacks. However, the houses are different sizes, and the two larger houses, 62 and 65, have entrance passages, while the smaller houses have direct entry into the front rooms. The differences are partly explained by the description of the houses in 1843 as two separate units: two houses lately erected by Richard Boulton on the site of a cottage with a gateway, and two cottages at the west end of the messuage then separated from the other part (NYCRO: Reg. Deeds HC, 1842–4). They were advertised for sale as four freehold cottages (YG: 5 Aug. 1843). The occupants in 1851 were a general dealer, a broom maker, and two agricultural labourers.

More complex layouts were developed in the 1850s. One example may stand for many. At the foot of Brant Hill, 19 and

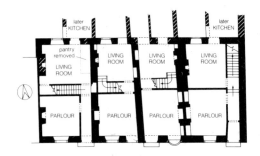

Fig. 269 [372] 62–65 Eastgate, Pickering

21 Park Street, Pickering [392], were built after 1855 as a single-fronted and a double-fronted house. A through-passage at the end of the block separates it from 14 Park Street, and provides access to 15 and 16, the survivors of a block of four houses one room wide and two deep constructed in the back yard.

Most 19th-century terraces are straightforward repeated units. 20–22 Westgate, Pickering [407], built in the 1840s, are only one-and-a-half storeys high. A straight joint between 20 and 21 suggests more than one period. Two-storey terraces were more common. A regular terrace of four cottages, 24–27 Westgate [408], was built between 1812 and 1818. The complexity of development is well illustrated by 23–25 Park Street [393], four newly erected cottages in 1857 replacing three of a row of five cottages in 1801, which probably in their turn replaced a house in four tenements after 1784.

Three-storey terraces of the early and mid 19th century became a feature of parts of Kirkbymoorside and Pickering, but not of Helmsley, and continued to be built until the end of the century. They are mostly composed of regularly repeated units, as is the development at New Bridge, Pickering [421], of which the surviving portion consists of two three-storey houses and five two-storey houses. The taller houses may have been occupied in 1851 by the builder George Green, and Anthony Dennis, a stone mason. The other tenants consisted of two farm labourers, five labourers, and a labourer's wife.

Monotony could be avoided by varying the grouping with a mixture of mirror-image and repeated units, or including in a group of three or more houses one pair with adjacent doorways. Pickering provides the greatest variety. A symmetrical treatment with repeated units either side of a central axis occurs at 52–55 Potter Hill [399] (Fig. 270), probably built in the 1850s, and at

Fig. 270 [399, 400] 52–56 Potter Hill, Pickering

14–19 Undercliffe, [405] (Fig. 271), a terrace built on the site of two cottages by 1848 (PRO: D.L.30/417/4; Pickering Court Rolls). Such terraces were not confined to urban settings: a similar grouping was used for a terrace of four cottages in Kildale [250]. An interesting indication of near-urbanity occurs at 6–11 Pickering Road, Thornton Dale [495] (Fig. 272), where two groups, each of three houses including one with adjacent doorways, are repeated on either side of a central passageway.

Fig. 271 [234]
14–19 Undercliffe,
Pickering

Fig. 272 [495]
6–11 Pickering Road,
Thornton Dale

CHAPTER 7

FARM BUILDINGS

The North York Moors region is rich in agricultural buildings. Numerous farmsteads form a conspicuous visual element in the landscape, especially in the dales which penetrate the moorland to north and south of the central watershed. The buildings of these farms are generally of modest size, reflecting the small size of the average holding. Though difficult to date with certainty, probably very few of those now standing are earlier than the second half of the 18th century. The absence of earlier buildings, however, does not mean that they did not exist, and documentary evidence testifies to their widespread occurrence. Many farmsteads were established before any of the surviving buildings were erected. In Bilsdale 75 per cent of farms named on the OS maps are identifiable in surveys of 1637 and 1642 (Ashcroft and Hill 1980). A survey of the manor of Kirkbymoorside of 1570 (PRO: E.164/37) names a number of farms in Farndale which still exist. Except in post-enclosure farmsteads, early 19th-century buildings may be merely the latest phase in a long process of alternate rebuilding.

A few mutilated purpose-built farm buildings containing crucks, probably of 16th or 17th-century date, provide fragmentary evidence for the bulk of farm buildings existing before the middle of the 18th century. The original form of cruck barns at Kingthorpe [253] and Holm Farm, Snainton [471], is complicated by later alterations, and an isolated one near Quarry Farm, Westerdale [516], which served a ruined longhouse at right angles to itself, is roofless. The presence of crucks in a byre or barn is not in itself proof of an early farm building. The cruck in the byre of Anthony House, Westerdale [519], was reused in one stage of the alternate rebuilding of a longhouse, while the byre at Westwood House, Ebberston [95] (Fig. 365), may have been the original farmhouse.

Purpose-built farm buildings from before the middle of the 18th century are hard to identify. At Caley Beck Farm, Eskdaleside cum Ugglebarnby [108], the constructional details of a former barn are similar to those of the late 17th-century farmhouse. Its proportions do not differ significantly from those of later barns. As functions did not alter, there may be no visible difference between 17th-century byres and small barns and their counterparts of a century later, especially if the roofs have been replaced. Firm dates on farm buildings begin to appear in the second half of the 18th century; one of the earliest, of 1767, is on a barn and byre at London House Farm, Glaisdale [160] (Fig. 295). Though limited in number, the dated buildings suggest that there was an increase in building activity towards the end of the 18th century and a decline after c. 1860.

The historical evidence

No farm buildings survive from the Middle Ages nor, except for an aisled barn at Murton Grange [328] and two dovecotes, from the farms associated with manor houses of the larger landowners during the 16th and 17th centuries. None of the earliest surviving houses below manorial status have separate contemporary farm buildings, but many were longhouses which originally combined dwelling with farming functions. These were primarily concerned with housing cattle, but crop storage under the same roof is shown by a reference of 1650 to a 'messuage house or mansion in Lastingham divided into a dwelling or firehouse, barn, and cow or beast house, all three divisions being under one roof and containing seven rooms or bays of building' (NYCRO: ZPF Box 7).

It is evident from a number of sources that farm buildings with specialized functions existed by the 16th century. A 1570 survey of Kirkbymoorside (PRO: E.164/37) mentions twelve barns, a barnstead, a dovecot, a forge and a 'waynehouse', and there were barns in Old Byland in 1592. Manor houses probably acquired specialized farm buildings earlier than yeoman farms did. At Hackness c. 1550 the manor house possessed a barn, stable and dovecot in addition to separate buildings for brewing and baking (NYCRO: ZF 4/3/1). In 1610 that at Kirkbymoorside had brewhouses, a stable, oxhouses and a dovecot, and the 'capital messuage' at Keldholme had a barn, kiln, dovecot, stable, cowhouse, calfhouse and hen house (PRO: L.R. 2/186).

The clearest impression of the variety of specialized farm buildings in the 17th century is provided by the 1637 survey of Bilsdale (Ashcroft and Hill 1980: 1–20), and associated surveys of the Helmsley estates of the Earl of Rutland (NYCRO: ZEW IV 1/4). In all of Bilsdale there were 89 barns, 66 hayhouses, 40 oxhouses, 40 cowhouses, 30½ backhouses, 9 kilns or kiln-houses, 8 calfhouses, 6 wainhouses, 5 turfhouses, 4 stables, 2 sheephouses and 1 beasthouse. The total for Harome (one of the Helmsley estates) is complicated by the ambiguous word 'lathe'. Apart from a haver lathe (for oats) and a hay lathe, there were 13 other lathes, 3 barns and 3 hayhouses there, and for livestock, only 1 oxhouse and 1 cowhouse, but 3 stables and 2 swine sties or cots. This relationship between crop storage and provision for draught-animals was worse than in Bilsdale. Most farms needed covered storage both for grain crops and fodder. In the whole area covered by these surveys, 50 farms had both barns and hayhouses, 44 barns only, 15 hayhouses only while 10 had lathes, including two with both a lathe or lathes and a hayhouse, and one fieldhouse. The lack of stables suggests that horses were rare. Where wainhouses existed, four were on farms with oxhouses, one with both oxhouse and stable, and one with a stable alone. Clearly the ox was the main beast of burden, doing most of the ploughing.

The terms 'lathe' and 'barn' could apparently be applied to either a corn barn or a hay barn: 'hayhouse' was not used to the exclusion of the other terms. Thirty loads of hay in the barn of John Thwing in Helmsley in 1571–2 seem to have been the only crop stored there (PRO: S.C.11/733). In Rosedale in 1649, 'barn' and 'lathe' are interchangeable, with a total of 39 barns or lathes, as well as 34 cowhouses, 3 stables, 2 backhouses or bakehouses and 1 kiln (PRO: E.317/50). Both a barn and a hay laith are mentioned, in 1667 and 1668 respectively, in the memoirs of Mrs Alice Thornton of East Newton, on the southern fringes of the area (Jackson 1873: 164, 170).

Evidence for farm buildings during the 18th century is provided by inventories, which contain useful information from *c.* 1690 onwards. Barns are frequently mentioned; beasthouses and cowhouses rather less often. Buildings for vehicles include helms and wainhouses.

The first survey for a period from which farm buildings survive in any quantity was made in 1792, covering the estate of Richard Bempde based on Hackness, in the south-east of the region (NYCRO: ZF 4/3/7). As on the Duncombe Estate in the south-west, oxen were much used and buildings to house them form the most numerous class; there were 101 oxhouses and 4 oxsheds. Other buildings included 48 barns, 39 stables, 22 hogsties and only 5 cowhouses. Wainhouses were now called cartlodges, of which there were twenty-six. Granaries were usually on upper floors: seven were over stables, three over oxhouses, and two over cartlodges.

Though mentioned from 1570 onwards, buildings to house wheeled vehicles formed a small proportion of all farm buildings up to 1800. The 'helm with wain' of William Marshall of Wykeham in 1737 implies some sort of waggon shed, but the precise purpose of other helms is uncertain; no surviving structure can be positively identified as such, and their appearance is difficult to visualize from passing references. The close of meadow called Helmefield in Bilsdale Kirkham in 1637 (Ashcroft and Hill 1980: 13) suggests the construction of some helms away from the main farmstead. Such isolated buildings may have been cattle shelters, as is implied by the subdivided farm in Bilsdale called Cowhellme; they could have formed the

nuclei of new settlements such as Helm House (North) and (South), Bilsdale West Side [32].

The conversion of houses is illustrated by Thorn Hill House, Goathland [165], of 1699, and Moor Houses, Bransdale [51], of 1714, both of which became farm buildings when new farmhouses were built. The process of conversion is rarely documented: one instance is a 'house, now converted into a stable or beasthouse, in Middleton', occupied by Thomas Suggitt, yeoman, in 1767 (NYCRO: Reg. Deeds AT, 1766-70).

Conversion was a two-way process and several dwellings began as farm buildings, although there is no documentary evidence for this before the 17th century. In 1610 Sir John Gibson the younger held a cottage, late a stable, adjoining the churchyard at Kirkbymoorside (PRO: L.R.2/186), and at Harome in 1637 there was 'one other little house which has been a stable' (NYCRO: ZEW IV 1/4). A conversion seems implied at Hart Hall, Glaisdale [153], in 1684 when Peter Cook, yeoman, left his sister Anne 'houserome in the turf house', and is explicit in the sale of a 'cottage formerly a kiln' in Fylingdales in 1750 (NYCRO: Reg. Deeds S, 1748–50). In 1786 David Cussons left to his wife Mary for life a 'house in yard or garth at backside of his present dwellinghouse now used for a stable to be converted into a comfortable place for her to live in'. The spaciousness of barns also provided potential for conversion. In 1796 John Allanson of Scalby bought a house in Pudding Lane, Snainton, which was 'late a barn purchased by John Stephenson of William Craven and converted into a house' (NYCRO: Reg. Deeds CN, 1796-7). In 1812 Johnson Robinson sold a 'house lately a barn' in West Ayton (NYCRO: Reg. Deeds DP, 1811–13).

The elements of the farmyard

THE LAYOUT OF FARMSTEADS

Every farmstead in the region is comprised of a limited number of buildings, each of which served a different specialized function connected with the business of running the farm. Buildings gathered together must inevitably have some sort of relationship to each other to constitute a layout, even if that relationship is one of irregularity. Though scarcely any two farmsteads have exactly identical layouts, a few major types can be distinguished. The principal differences lie in the extent to which buildings are separated from each other, or are joined together; in the degree to which they enclose the farmyard, and whether the relationships are orderly, in the sense of being laid out parallel or at right angles to each other, or irregular. Though many farmsteads occupy sites which have been settled since at least the 16th century and probably the medieval period, nearly all the buildings are no older than the late 18th century. There must have been a continual process of replacement of, and adding to, the older buildings, so that an understanding of the development of farmstead layout is hindered by only the later stages being available as evidence. From the later period, however, not only is there a great body of evidence provided by standing structures but it is supplemented, in some parishes, by the increasing number of estate and enclosure award maps from the late 18th century onwards.

The precise procedures by which farms were established and their buildings erected does not become clear until a relatively late date, by which time the basic system was that the tenant was responsible for the buildings. Where farms were of a similar size, not much difference is visible between a freehold farm and one belonging to a large estate but held on a long lease. On the Duncombe Park Estate, the few dated farm buildings before the middle of the 19th century bear the initials of the tenant, not the landlord. Responsibility for building work, and the employment of a full-time surveyor engaged on designing alterations and new buildings, was undertaken by the estate later in the century. Smaller farms could rarely afford more than piecemeal rebuilding of the farmstead: complete rebuilding, or the creation of a new farm by enclosure or the amalgamation of existing farms, called for the expenditure of capital usually only available to a major landlord.

The Parliamentary enclosures of the 18th and 19th centuries resulted in a number of new farms with the farmstead surrounded by its fields, but the rationalization of landholdings did not eliminate the urban and village farmsteads. Tuke's main complaint against places where the farmhouses were situated in villages was that the farms were 'made up of separate fields, widely dispersed over the face of the township, and of course inconveniently intermixed with each other' (Tuke 1800: 33). Enclosure awards at places such as Fadmoor nullified this particular argument: the village farmsteads remained, and the example of new farms stimulated new farm buildings on the old sites. These usually followed a regular layout, but the constraints imposed by the available sites of farms in both towns and villages resulted in marked differences from the plans exhibited by free-standing farmsteads.

Older enclosures seem to have resulted in a similar division between farmsteads in dispersed settlements and nucleated villages. At Thornton-le-Dale, where eighty-four oxgangs west of the beck were enclosed by 1685 (Beresford 1948–51: 362), working farmsteads survive in the village, and the 1851 census shows several farmers living there. The farmsteads planted in the surrounding former open fields were either created or completely rebuilt in the 19th century. Conversely, the dispersed farmsteads in several of the moorland dales predate the 18th-century enclosures. Bransdale, Farndale and Danby were occupied before the 19th century by scattered farmsteads and a small number of unimportant hamlets. Although enclosure gave the opportunity for the major landowners to build large, modern farmsteads, the biggest farms are not necessarily the most recent, as they include the former monastic granges and the pre-Parliamentary enclosure home farms of the large landowners. Centuries of rebuilding at both make it impossible to ascertain the original layouts.

Rearrangement of existing landholdings was another option open to the large landowners. The abandonment of deerparks

in the 17th century had made additional land available for agriculture. Blansby Park, the last major landholding near Pickering controlled by the Duchy of Lancaster, had been split into a number of different farms at that time. No trace of the 17th-century origin is now visible, as examination of the acreages belonging to each farm shows that a major redistribution of the landholdings took place in the 19th century, resulting in new farmsteads. A similar redistribution took place slightly earlier south of Thornton Dale at Newstead Grange, resulting in farmsteads dating from the later 18th century. This former grange of Rievaulx Abbey was divided into four in the 17th century, rearranged about 1790 by agreement between two related tenants, and further divided in the 19th century. On the Duncombe Park Estate, Middle Baxtons Farm, Helmsley [240], was created in the 19th century by combining land already improved from several other farms (Chapman 1961: 124).

Before the 18th century the longhouse was the most common type of farmhouse in the region. This combination of house and byre in a single building provided a basic form of farm layout. The decline of the true longhouse, and the adoption or rebuilding of the byre-end as part of the house itself, did not lead to the abandonment of the practice of linking house and farm buildings in a linear sequence, and other buildings were often added to one end or the other to produce an elongated range. A linear arrangement of house and buildings is quite common in farmsteads in the valleys both to north and south of the central watershed, and in every example the range is comprised of several building phases, indicating gradual development of an early site rather than the erection of a complete new farmstead; when the latter occurred, a different plan was adopted.

The longhouse origin of a linear layout is apparent at Raw Farm, Fylingdales [118]. The byre was rebuilt as a barn, leaving the hearth-passage remaining, with a new byre and, subsequently, a cartshed added beyond. More commonly the byre was converted into living accommodation and thus absorbed into the house. This alteration might have been preceded by the addition of further farm buildings. At Glaisdale Head [162] a new byre seems to have been added before the original one was divided into smaller rooms for domestic accommodation. Farm buildings were also added to the parlour end of the house, as at Bog House, Bransdale [54] (Fig. 273), where the original byre was rebuilt as a kitchen and two byres, a barn and boxes were built in separate phases at the other end. There

Fig. 273 [54] Bog House, Bransdale

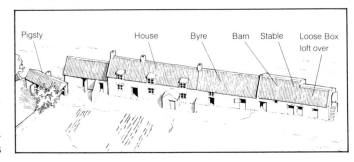

Fig. 274 [46] Cowl House, Bransdale

element, such as the barn at Hagg House Farm, Snilesworth [479] (Fig. 275). A linear arrangement was sometimes the result of joining together individual buildings or groups formerly not connected. Aumery Park, Fadmoor [114] (Fig. 276), has a very long range of which the major elements in the middle are house and barn; these are of different widths and not exactly on the same alignment, and seem to have been originally separate and later linked together by filling in the space between them.

Linear arrangements of farm buildings occur where the house is separate from them. In some of these it is probable that they developed from a longhouse by successive additions, a new detached farmhouse ultimately being built and the original one

Fig. 276 [14] Aumery Park, Fadmoor

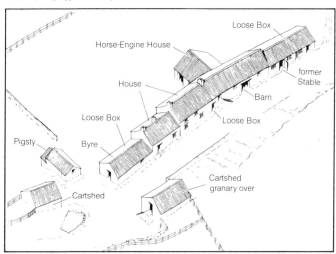

was also a small addition to the west end beyond the kitchen, but some other longhouses were extended equally at both sides. At Cowl House, Bransdale [46] (Fig. 274), despite being aligned up the sloping hillside, substantial additions were made at both ends to produce a range ultimately 50 metres long.

Though the origin of the linear arrangement may have been by making successive additions to the longhouse, the layout continued when the house itself was rebuilt to a new plan, generally with a central entry, as at Low Thwaites, Hawnby [181], where the house, with an attached cottage, is at one end of the range, or at Freeze Gill Farm, Troutsdale [505], with buildings to both sides of the house. Where the house has been rebuilt, other buildings in the range may be the earliest surviving

Fig. 275 [479] Hagg House Farm, Snilesworth

lost in a partial rebuilding of the range. This is probable at Botton Farm, Danby [80], which has a range of buildings with parts dated 1747 and 1806, and incorporates a reset arched lintel of 1679 which must surely have originally belonged to a house; the existing late 18th-century house stands on the other side of the farmyard.

Not all long ranges of building originated with a longhouse as a nucleus. Thirley Beck, Cloughton [63], has a range which provides for most of the farming functions and is separate from and at right angles to the late 17th-century house; this may be a rather exceptional case, as the house is distinctly superior to the average farmhouse of the period. At Hart Hall, Glaisdale [153], the farmhouse is an alternately rebuilt longhouse but the buildings are in two very long, nearly parallel ranges at right angles to it. Linear arrangements of farm buildings separate from the house were still being erected in the 19th century. One at Lockton, Bilsdale West Side [36], dated 1840, provides for byre, stable, barn and cartshed.

In most of the farms which have a linear arrangement there are also one or two other separate buildings or small groups, as at Low Thwaites, Hawnby [181], where, to the south of the main range, there is an isolated block comprising a small barn, a byre and a privy. Though detached buildings occur in this manner, subordinate to the main group, there are very few farmsteads entirely composed of them in a scattered or dispersed layout and even these often have a longhouse nucleus, as at Plumtree, Danby [78] (Fig. 277a), where there is a house with attached byre in addition to three separate buildings. Nor are detached buildings necessarily disposed irregularly; at Helm House South, Bilsdale West Side [32], a small group are placed parallel or at right angles to each other. At Orterley, Bilsdale Midcable [24], a longhouse extended in line with farm buildings forms the core of a much more extensive complex, including a second farmhouse of the late 18th century added at right angles to the earlier one. Both houses have farmyards and buildings serving similar functions, but differently planned due to piece-meal rebuilding (Fig. 278).

More common are farmyard arrangements consisting of a few blocks with two or three units in each. In the absence of documentary and archaeological evidence the precise develop-ment of such groupings can only be surmised, but they probably result from gradual enlargement of farmsteads. They may consist of a few fairly small blocks placed irregularly without any sense of formal relationship to each other, as at Houlsyke House, Glaisdale [141] (Fig. 277b). When closer together these blocks create a sense of enclosure, which can be completed by walls or fences to provide a secure foldyard, as at Forest Lodge, Danby [76] (Fig. 277c). The arrangement of a farmyard with buildings on most or all sides, though not connected to each other as in a courtyard farm, is one of the most characteristic in the region. The buildings may be around an irregularly shaped yard, at Moor Houses, Bransdale [51] (Fig. 277d), and at Stormy Hall, Danby [82] (Fig. 277e), where seven different inscribed dates testify to the gradual evolution or rebuilding of the farmstead; or at right angles like those at Low Wethercote, Bilsdale West Side [35] (Fig. 277f).

Comparative plans of farmyards

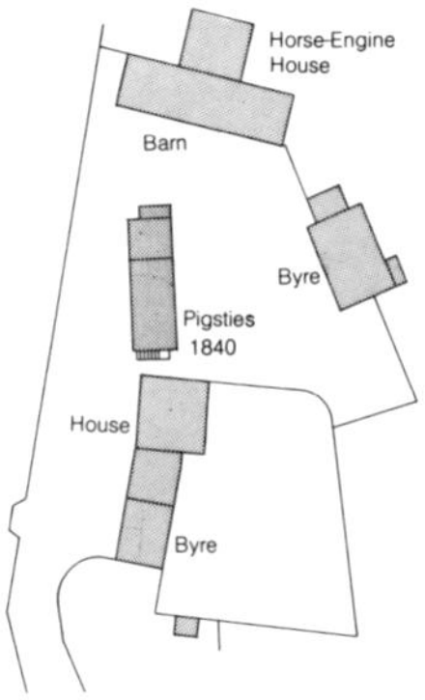

Fig. 277a
[78] Plumtree, Danby

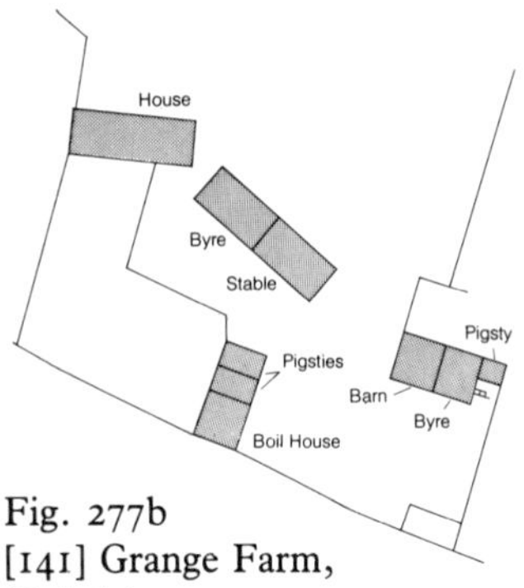

Fig. 277b
[141] Grange Farm, Glaisdale

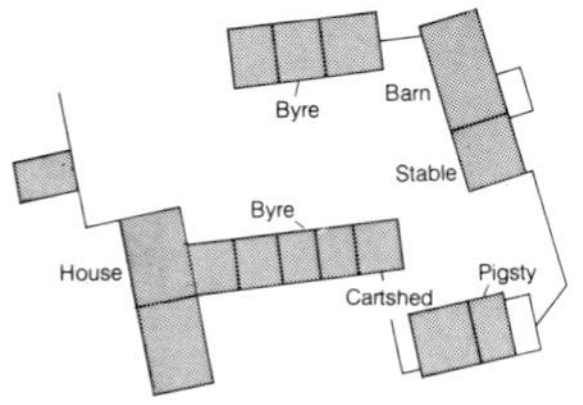

Fig. 277c [76] Forest Lodge, Danby

Fig. 277d
[41] Moor Houses, Bransdale

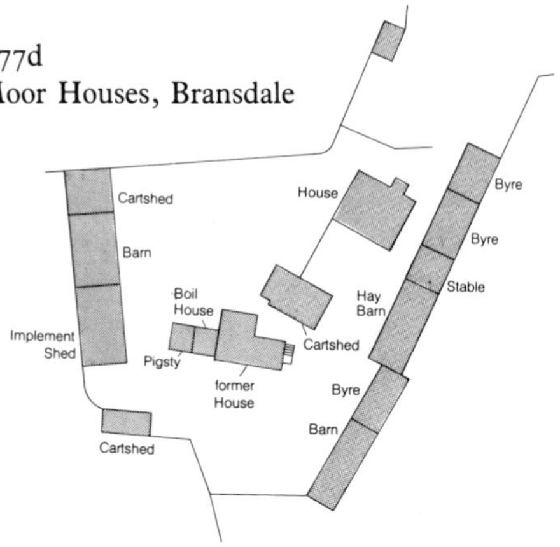

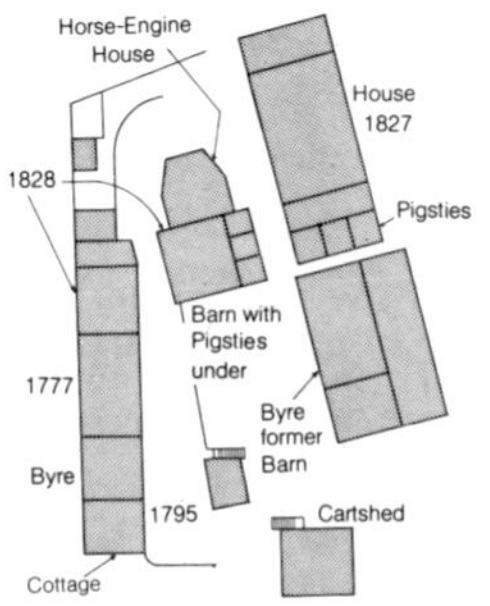

Fig. 277e
[82] Stormy Hall, Danby

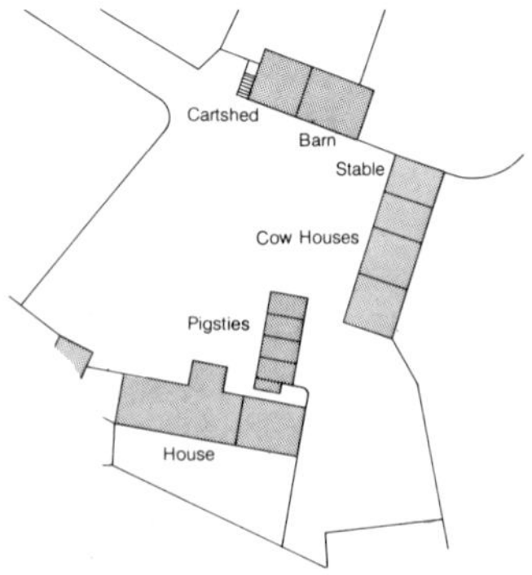

Fig. 277f [35] Low Wethercote, Bilsdale West Side

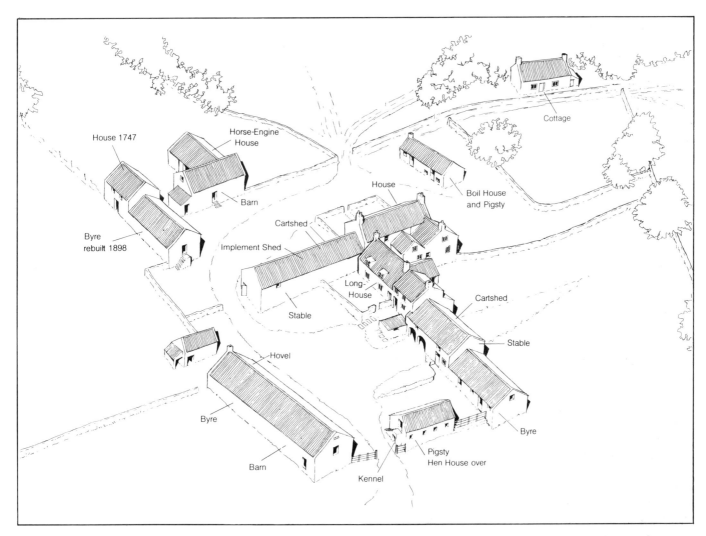

Fig. 278 [24] Orterley, Bilsdale Midcable

Occasionally the development of a farmstead can be followed using early maps, which show buildings that may now be demolished. In Rievaulx, maps of 1806 and 1822 (NYCRO: ZEW M 20, ZEW M 35) supplement the first edition OS map of 1853. At High Leys Farm, Rievaulx [448], a triangular arrangement of three separate blocks of 1806 had become more spread out, but less regular, by 1822. By 1853 the farm buildings had been regularized on three sides of an open courtyard related to the farmhouse: only the detached cartshed remained on a divergent diagonal.

Some irregular farms straddle a public road, with buildings on both sides of it. Hollins Farm, Farndale East [115], has the house gable-end to the road, with further buildings straggling up the hillside and creating a steep farmyard. This proved inadequate, and a further farm building was built in 1825 along the roadside on the opposite side of the road. West House, Kildale [252] (Fig. 279), has a scatter of buildings on both sides of the road, mainly set at an oblique angle to it. At White House Farm, Stainton Dale [488], and Low Cornfield House, Bransdale [44], the main farmstead is on one side of the road, with the farmhouse isolated on the other.

Fig. 279 [252] West House, Kildale

157

Farmsteads in towns and villages were subject to special constraints. The site was often rectangular, with a restricted frontage, a greater depth, and sometimes a back lane. In Kirkbymoorside the plots are narrow, with a street frontage equivalent to the length of a longhouse. This did not permit access from the front. The former farms grouped at the north end of the town include Dog and Duck Farm, 8 High Market Place, 14 High Market Place, and Manor Farm, Kirkbymoorside [269, 270, 275]. The farmyards are reached respectively from a back lane, a side lane and a side entrance in Castlegate. In Helmsley the farms are more scattered and the means of access varied. Town End Farm [199] has the house on the street frontage with access from the street to a long yard flanked by parallel ranges of buildings. Vicarage Farm [189] also has access from the street, but the house is set back from it, and there is a secondary entrance to the farmyard from a back lane. Church Farm and 44 Bondgate [198, 210] both have side access, from Pottergate and a lane to Rievaulx respectively.

A pattern is visible in the centre of Pickering, despite later rebuilding, of a longhouse and barn in line along the street frontage separated by the entrance to the farmyard. In Eastgate access was possible from the back lanes on both sides of the main road, and barns were also built along these back lanes. Constraints of an awkward urban site are probably responsible

for the irregular layout of the small 'model farmstead' built by William Marshall at Beck Isle, Pickering [346] (Fig. 280). It was probably the outcome of his advocacy of an agricultural college (Marshall 1788: 1–37), although on a smaller scale than would have been possible had the public funding he desired been forthcoming.

In villages there is more variety in plot sizes and shapes. The pattern of development is usually of the farmhouse facing the street, with other buildings on the frontage governed by the plot width: at the narrowest this only provides room for the entrance. Even though some villages, such as Middleton and Wombleton (Fig. 281), have back lanes to provide access to the yard, most farms also have an entry from the street. Carlton and Pockley have some wide frontages; Low Farm, Pockley [434], is very spread out, with separate groups of farm buildings on both sides of the house. Manor Farm, Pockley [427], is more restricted, with a street frontage comprising house and barn combined, the entry to the squarish farmyard, and the gable end of a range of right angles to the street. In Harome plots mainly have narrower frontages. The Farm [172] is wide enough for access from the street between a longhouse and a stable in line with parallel buildings behind forming an open courtyard. Two other farms there, however, only have room for the house and entrance to the street frontage. Greystones Farm and

Fig. 280 [346] Beck Isle, Pickering: cartshed and granary, flanked by stables

Fig. 281 Wombleton: village plan (farms shown solid; H=house)

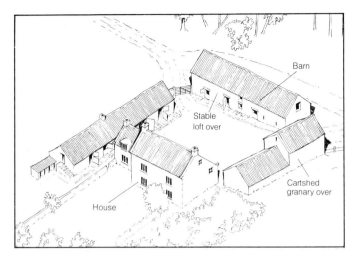

Fig. 282 [113] Cherry Tree Farm, Fadmoor

The simplest courtyard arrangement has separate ranges of buildings allowing gaps at the corners to be filled by fences and gates as at Cherry Tree Farm, Fadmoor [113] (Fig. 282). The plans become more regular as the different buildings coalesce, with linear ranges joining to form enclosures with right-angled corners, very often with an open side towards the south. Marshall remarks on this and adds: 'It is usual in planning a farmyard to place the main line of building with its front to the south; in which case two wings become necessary to screen the yard from north-east and north-west winds: and perhaps this has established the common practice of inclosing a farm-yard on three sides with buildings' (Marshall 1788: 131). The house itself may form one side of the yard, whether or not linked to the other buildings. Where all three wings around the yard were farm buildings, the house could form the fourth side. This was recommended by J. C. Loudon, the fifth edition of whose Encyclopedia, published in 1844, contained standardized farm layouts. The quadrangle was considered the norm, with the farmer's house on the south side where it enjoyed the best aspect and was also well placed for supervising the work of the farmyard, and the barn on the north in a convenient central position for supplying straw and hay to the flanking stables and cattle sheds (Robinson 1983: 69).

Lower Farm, Beadlam [23] (Fig. 283), founded after 1819, has this form with the farmhouse on the south, and farm build-

Rutland House both have a single range of farm buildings to the rear of the house, and at right angles to the street. The farm buildings at Rutland House are all later than 1830, and the large number of 19th-century farm buildings in village farms shows that these are not just survivals from before the Parliamentary enclosures.

The ultimate development of the farmstead before traditional farming methods were completely changed by mechanization was the courtyard farm, which in its most characteristic form has an approximately square yard mainly or completely enclosed by continuous ranges of buildings. As a consciously planned group it most commonly occurs among newly established farms built away from villages on land enclosed by parliamentary acts in the late 18th and early 19th centuries, particularly on the dip slopes of the Tabular Hills in the southern part of the region. The courtyard plan was also employed, though, on older sites in the valleys when the farms were comprehensively rebuilt. There is no clear distinction between the courtyard farm and the most regular examples of the farmyard with loose groupings of buildings around it, and on some farms the plan may have been achieved by gradual rebuilding, as at Wether Cote, Skiplam [462].

Fig. 283 [23] Lower Farm, Beadlam

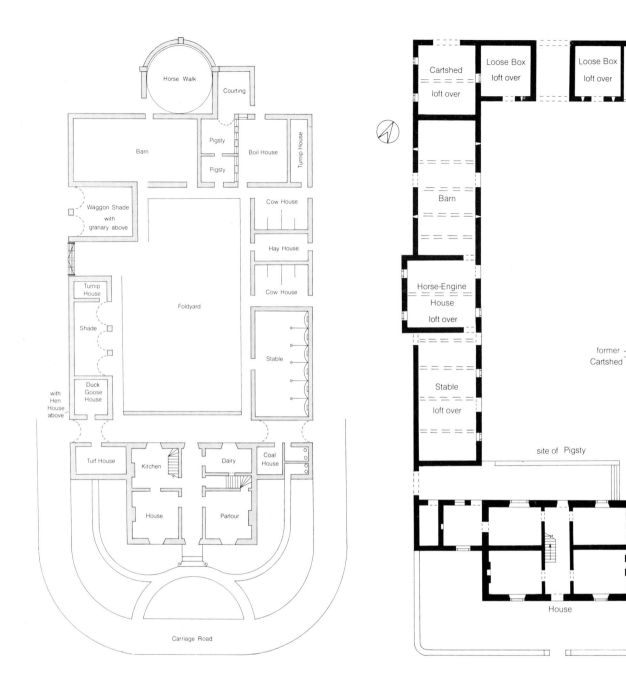

Fig. 284 [131] Howdale Farm, Fylingdales: proposed plan, 1828

Fig. 285 [126] Demesne Farm, Fylingdales

ings loosely grouped round three sides of the farmyard joined to the farmhouse by an enclosing wall. St Agnes House, Arden with Ardenside [13], does not have this wall, but is physically separated from a continuous range of farm buildings round three sides of the yard.

The most formal expression of the plan has the house enclosing the yard on one side and placed on the central axis. Designs for Howdale Farm, Fylingdales [131] (Fig. 284), dated 1828, and for White Hall Farm, Stainton Dale [486], are of this type (Whitby Museum: ZW(M)2/1). Demesne Farm, Fyling-

dales [126] (Fig. 285), is similar but has an axial entrance and the horse-engine house is integrated with the west range.

In many courtyard layouts the house stands apart from the farmyard, usually to one side of it; Stonebeck Gate Farm, Danby [86] (Fig. 286), is a particularly good example. Where the yard is only enclosed on three sides, both house and yard can have an open aspect to the south. Waterloo Farm, Sproxton [484], and High Baxtons Farm, Helmsley [239], have almost identical plans with the house west of, and in line with, the north range of the yard. At the former there are buildings on three sides of

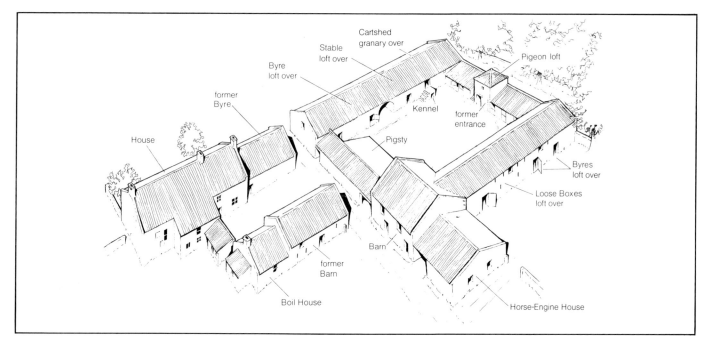

Fig. 286 [86] Stonebeck Gate Farm, Danby

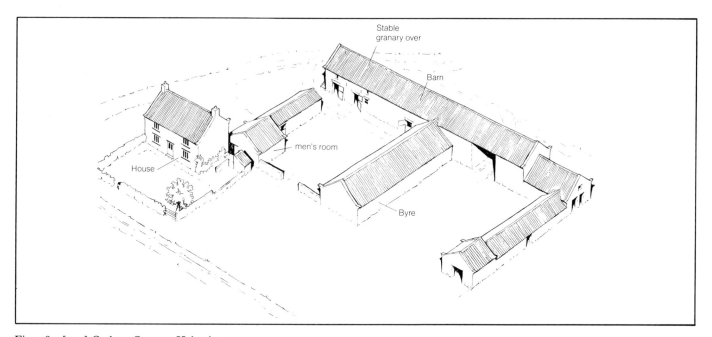

Fig. 287 [241] Carlton Grange, Helmsley

the yard and an enclosing wall on the fourth. At the latter the enclosing wall is replaced by a shelter shed. Both farms were on the Duncombe Park Estate, and High Baxtons was built on Baxtons Pasture following an enclosure award of 1816. At Cockmoor Hall, Snainton [275], and Carlton Grange, Helmsley [241] (Fig. 287), the houses are slightly farther apart, lying to the south-west of the farm buildings.

The courtyard used primarily as a fold yard may be only part of a complex. It is the dominant element at High Leys Farm, Rievaulx [448], but has been added to the mainly linear arrange-

ment at Ankness, Bransdale [53], and Abbot Hag Farm, Rievaulx [449].

Larger farms have more complex plans with two yards. At Carlton Grange, Helmsley [241], there are two south-facing foldyards and Coronation Farm, Cold Kirby [65], has the farmhouse backing on to one of two open farmyards. Brecks Farm, Pockley [439], has two separate farmyard areas and a detached house. Saintoft Grange, Pickering [416], has a tighter arrangement of two separate yards of different sizes and a further backyard to the farmhouse. Stiltons Farm, Rievaulx [451], has

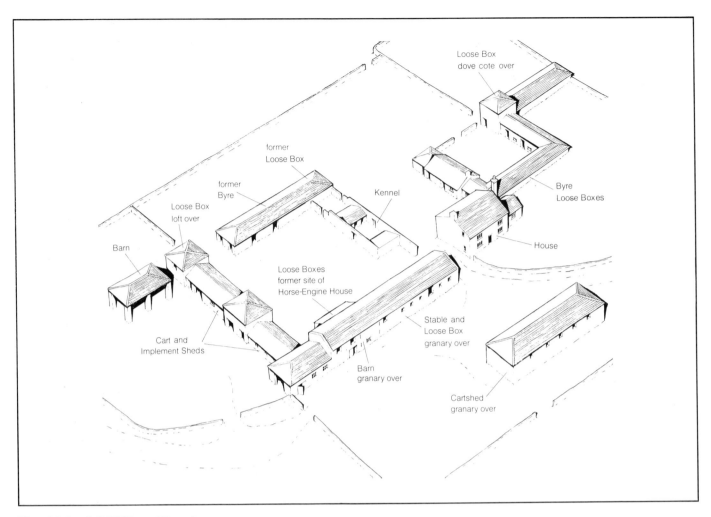

Fig. 288 [452] Griff Farm, Rievaulx

substantial buildings in addition to an enclosed yard. Griff Farm, Rievaulx [452] (Fig. 288), the home farm of the Duncombe Park Estate for a while, has two yards of differing sizes, one to either side of the farmhouse.

The influence of formal planning is visible in more modest farms. Wethead, Newton [338], unifies the living and farming requirements of a small farm of 43 acres in a single building of c. 1812. The stable and barn are disguised as wings of the main house, and provided with false windows. Bell Hill Farm, Stainton Dale [485] (Fig. 289), a larger farm with a separate farmyard between the house and two ranges of farm buildings at right angles to each other, incorporates service wings with farming functions in integral outshuts against both gables of the house, with further wings projecting at right angles to them to enclose the front garden. Certain landowners in the later 19th century imposed stylistic details and even alien architectural forms on their utilitarian farm buildings. The stone mullions on the false stable and barn windows at Wethead, and the 'Gothic' windows on William Marshall's stable block at Beck Isle [346] (Fig. 280) are the forerunners of the four-centred arched heads used for door and window openings in 1850 by John Allan for

Fig. 289 [485] Bell Hill Farm, Stainton Dale: with ranges flanking garden

his farm buildings at Hemp Syke [111]. The fine detailing of farm buildings rebuilt by the Foster Estate in 1886 at Lelum Hall, Egton [100], includes cross arrowslits serving as ventilation openings. The most eccentric structures were those commissioned by John Warren Barry, squire of Fyling Hall

Fig. 290 [125] Fyling Hall, Fylingdales: pigsty in form of Greek temple

from 1871, who had a pigsty built in the form of a Grecian temple (Fig. 290), and provided a cowbyre at Fyling Old Hall Farm, Fylingdales [128], with a complicated roof structure.

BUILDINGS FOR THE STORAGE AND PROCESSING OF CROPS

Barns

The barn, used for the storage and processing of the corn crop, is nearly always present in the farmyard in the region, though not such a dominant feature as in some parts of England. Although virtually no barns survive from before the second half of the 18th century, surveys of Bilsdale and Kirkbymoorside clearly indicate that they were common in the 17th century. Some farms had two or even three, suggesting that they were quite small, but to what extent these barns differed from later, surviving examples is not known.

Documentary evidence provides some impression of the size or arrangement of earlier barns, though the emphasis is on larger ones. The number of bays or 'rooms' is occasionally given but dimensions very rarely. In 1610 a barnstead in How End, Kirkbymoorside, measured 9 by 20 yards (PRO: L.R.2/186). The only comparable structure for which measurements are available was a hayhouse in Dalby erected in 1746, which was 13 by 28 feet and described as of two 'roomsteads' (Rushton 1976b: 83); if a roomstead was also a bay, the bay size would have been 14 feet. Another barn in Kirkbymoorside is described as of three rooms, and the conversion of two rooms of a barn into a cottage suggests that the barn had been of at least three bays. Other large barns also existed: in 1611 Richard Hunter was alleged to have taken down and carried away an ancient barn, of five bays, at Dalby (Rushton 1976b: 55). Apart from the 'great barn or lath' of Griff at Rievaulx, the tithe barns connected with the

rectory houses at Kirkbymoorside and Pickering were probably above the average size. The earliest barn still standing, at Murton Grange [328], has a large aisled structure and is almost certainly not typical.

Inventories give some evidence for the way in which barns were used. The storage of corn was paramount, some of it appearing as unthreshed, but the type of grain is rarely mentioned. Wheat appears in a number of inventories, such as that of Thomas Appleby of Welburn (1705). John Noddings of Wombleton had hard corn in 1734. Rye used for common, household brown bread (Tuke 1800: 117) was grown by George Sigsworth of Bransdale (1724), barley by William Bentley of Helmsley (1735), and oats by William Dobson of Sproxton (1756). The references to stouks, stoaks or stocks of oats, barley and rye in the inventories of William Sigsworth and Christopher Foxton (1727 and 1728) show that the crop was stored bound. After the corn had been threshed, straw was left in the barns of George Gayre of Kirkbymoorside (1764).

There is no visible evidence for separate stackyards in the region, even after the introduction of threshing machines in the 19th century. The practice of storing unthreshed corn in stacks, however, was not unknown earlier. As well as corn in the barn and hay in the house, William Bowlby of Helmsley had corn and hay in stacks in 1719. Jordan Wilson, also of Helmsley, Robert Barker of Wombleton and John Taylor of Bungdale Head, Scawton [456], all had corn stacks, in 1748, 1750 and 1782 respectively. John Rybie of Hutton Buscel had wheat and barley stacks in 1735. 'Corn in the barn', however, is a recurrent feature in most farmers' inventories.

Although haystacks are frequently mentioned, inventories from between 1699 and 1782 show that hay was also stored in barns. A specialized hay barn does not seem intended in most cases, although the barn was possibly a multi-purpose structure incorporating cattle stalls, the hay supplementing the straw obtained after threshing. Peas and beans were kept in barns by John Rybie of Hutton Buscel, and peas by Thomas Weetman of Scawton Croft, Scawton (1735, 1762), although George Beane of Kirkbymoorside stored his beans in two stacks (1734).

Despite their relative smallness, the rebuilding of so many barns in the later 18th century may be explained, at least for part of the region, by an increase in grain production. Marshall remarked that 'notwithstanding the goodness of the soil' in the Vale of Pickering 'and its fitness for WHEAT, very little of this grain has been carried out of the neighbourhood of its growth; having been wholly used in home-consumption. Of late years, however, there has been an overflow; and WHITBY has drawn part of its support from hence' (Marshall 1788: 294). The trend continued: 'About 20 years since, the upper part of Ryedale was chiefly supplied with wheat from Cleveland, many waggon-loads going weekly to Kirkbymoorside market: but this is now wholly supplied by its own neighbourhood, which, after satisfying the home demand, now sends some to Whitby and Malton markets; from the latter place it is conveyed by water to Leeds and Wakefield, and the manufacturing districts, there to be consumed' (Tuke 1800: 116). The demand for wheat tempted some farmers to neglect proper crop rotation, prompting the stipulation in the lease of an estate near Scarborough that no more than a quarter of the land in tillage was to be sown with wheat in any one year (Tuke 1800: 63).

The increased production of oats followed enclosures in the Vale of Pickering: 'Since the inclosure of common pastures great quantities of OATS have been sent out of the Vale' (Marshall 1788: 294). Friesland or Poland oats were sown in Ryedale, which was 'remarkable both for quantity and quality' of this cereal. In the 'almost inexhaustible fields of Ryedale, which are peculiarly adapted to the growth of oats', they could be grown for up to seven years in succession, alternating with a single crop of turnips or rape. They found a ready market in the West Riding (Marshall 1788: 108, 120, 127). Despite inventory evidence for their storage in barns, both Marshall and Tuke suggest that oats were normally threshed in the open air, either in the field or on a cloth in the stackyard. The straw was stacked loose, to be cut out as hay and consumed in the field.

Analysis of the crop returns for the North of the Vale of Pickering in 1810 showed that of the cereals, oats had become the main crop, with wheat second and barley third, and there were still only small quantities of rye. Only 25 per cent of the total acreage was arable (Musto 1963: 7–12).

Apart from the great majority of barns which stand within farmsteads, a few are exceptional because of their size and position. The earliest, at Murton Grange [328] on the site of a grange of Byland Abbey, was aisled and, though now much altered, must have been about 10 metres wide and probably over 20 metres long. Its timber arcades may date from after the Dissolution, but though the barn is possibly of the 17th century, because of its size and origins it gives no clue to the nature of the average farmyard barn of that period. The 18th-century Tile House Barn, Old Byland [343] (Fig. 299), also standing on former land of Byland Abbey, is isolated and some distance from the nearest farm. A slightly smaller barn at Low Hall, Brompton [56] (Fig. 291), was manorial. These last two buildings both have features which are uncharacteristic of barns in the region, notably wide opposed doorways.

The earliest surviving firmly dated barns are of the middle to late 18th century, possessing the main characteristics which continued into the 19th century. They must represent the tail-

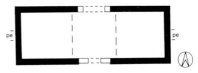

Fig. 291 [56] Low Hall, Brompton: barn

Fig. 292 [11] Cow Wath,
Arden with Ardenside: barn

end of a development which, by the late 18th century, was adequate for the needs of the time and did not change until the introduction of mechanical threshing.

Some barns stand detached from other buildings, though generally only in farmsteads with a scattered layout, as at Cow Wath, Arden with Ardenside [11] (Fig. 292), and Helm House, Bilsdale West Side [32] (Fig. 297). Others were originally detached but later had built against them an addition serving another function, such as the stable added to the barn at Cherry Tree Farm, Fadmoor [113] (Fig. 282). Most barns form part of a longer range or of a complete courtyard farmstead. In the latter, the barn is usually part of the range on the north side of the yard, occasionally with some degree of prominence by being taller than the buildings to which it is attached.

Where the barn is part of a linear range of buildings, it may be either at one end as at Cowl House, Bransdale [46] (Fig. 274), or towards the middle as at Hagg House Farm, Sniles-worth [479] (Fig. 275), and Lockton, Bilsdale West Side [36]. Many barns form half of a range, another function occupying the other part. The most common type has an attached cart-shed with granary above, as at Low Wethercote, Bilsdale West Side [35] (Fig. 293), and Hazel Green, Helmsley [238] (Fig.

Fig 293 [35] Low Wethercote, Bilsdale West Side: barn and cartshed, granary over

Fig. 294 [238] Hazel Green, Helmsley: barn

294). A barn may be attached to a byre with loft over, as at that of 1767 at London House Farm, Glaisdale [160] (Fig. 295). At Smout House, Bransdale [42], the barn is attached to a forge, though this is a rare occurrence, and at Toad Hole, Bransdale [41] (Fig. 296), it forms a single range with the farmhouse, as a result of alternate rebuilding of a longhouse.

The majority of barns are of moderate size, within a range of 9 to 12 metres long and 4 to 5.5 metres wide, with the general proportions of a length about twice the breadth. An example of the total volume within an average barn is provided by Helm

Fig 296 [41] Toad Hole, Bransdale: house and barn, stables and pigsties beyond

Fig. 295 [160] London House Farm, Glaisdale: barn

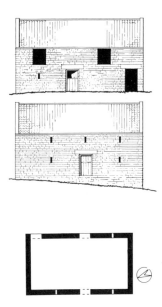

Fig. 297 [32] Helm House, Bilsdale West Side: barn

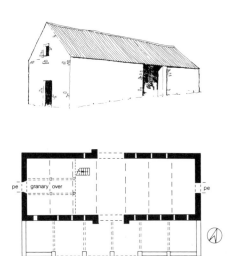

Fig. 299 [343] Tile House Barn, Old Byland: barn

House, Bilsdale West Side [32] (Fig. 297); this has a height of 4 metres to the wall-heads and a total capacity of 220 cubic metres, including the threshing floor. Apart from the few exceptional barns already mentioned, several larger ones stand in farmyards, and these are generally no wider than average but more elongated. Those at Cockmoor Hall, Snainton [475] (Fig. 298), and Leath House, Westerdale [515], are the largest. The smallest are at Low Thwaites, Hawnby [181], 5.5 metres long and 4.3 metres wide, and Head House, Snilesworth [478], 9.6 metres long but only 3.9 metres wide; these farms are in elevated positions on the margin of the moorland and, perhaps significantly, both have been abandoned.

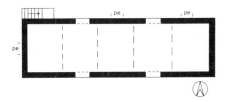

Fig. 298 [475] Cockmoor Hall, Snainton: barn

A distinguishing feature of barns in the North York Moors is the smallness of the doors. Doors large enough to accommodate a laden cart, common in other parts of England, are very rare. They occur at the exceptional Tile House Barn, Old Byland [343] (Fig. 299), and at Denham Grange, Thornton Dale [503] (Fig. 300), situated in the Vale of Pickering away from the upland area. The barn at Low Hall, Brompton [56] (Fig. 291), was built with large doorways which were later blocked and narrow ones provided. The vast majority of regional barns had doors only about 1.2 metres wide and little more than 2 metres high. Normally, doors opposite each other in the long sides gave access to the threshing floor: one was opened to provide light

Fig. 300 [503] Denham Grange, Thornton Dale: barn

for threshing, and the opening of both created a through draught while winnowing. It was not essential for both to be at ground level. In the barn at Helm House [32] (Fig. 297), built on a sloping site, one of the opposed doors is nearly 1 metre above the ground, with no provision for steps to it.

The most common arrangement was a pair of opposed doors exactly or nearly centrally in the barn, providing equal-sized spaces to each side of the threshing floor. But in some barns the doors are distinctly offset, occasionally being very close to one end as at Smout House, Bransdale [42]; this must have prevented the use of the threshing floor in the normal way, with unthreshed corn stacked to one side and threshed straw on the other. The large barn at Cockmoor Hall [475] (Fig. 298) has two threshing floors served by two pairs of opposed doors, an unusual arrangement among surviving barns. In the 1792 survey of the Hackness Estate, however, a number of barns were described as having two threshing floors, even though some were quite small and of only two bays (NYCRO: ZF 4/3/7). The word 'bay' may refer to a particular compartment or storage area in a barn rather than to a unit of space defined by roof

Fig. 301 [47] Low South House Farm, Bransdale

Fig. 302 [432] Bonfield Gill, Pockley: barn, stable to left

trusses; if this is so, however, a barn of three bays and one threshing floor is a type not apparent among existing structures, although five were mentioned at Hackness.

In addition to the usual pair of opposed doors, some barns had doors either at the end of the long walls or in the end walls, indicating that they served more than a storage function. A clue to this may be provided by the barns at Cowl House and Low South House Farm in Bransdale [46, 47] (Fig. 301), both of which have a byre with a loft over at one end. Though apparently later insertions in both cases, the arrangements may represent the continuation of an original purpose; certainly the doors to the byres, in the south wall only at Cowl House and in north and south walls at Low South House Farm, are original. However, drawings of *c.* 1828 for new buildings at Howdale Farm, Fylingdales [131] (Fig. 284), show a barn with a door at the end of the south wall, but no internal division or indication of separate usage of that part. Doors in gable-end walls are less frequent; that at Rutland House, Harome [173], was blocked by a later stable added to the north end. In barns which form only part of a longer range, a door may lead to the adjacent function; this occurs at the barn of 1767 at London House Farm, Glaisdale [160] (Fig. 295), which has a byre with loft over attached to it.

It is noteworthy that the few barns in the region with large cart entrances, such as Tile House Barn, Old Byland [343] (Fig. 299), Low Hall, Brompton [56] (Fig. 291), and Denham Grange, Thornton Dale [503] (Fig. 300), have loading doors in the gables only. The frequency of pitching holes in regional barns is associated with the smallness of the doors. As it was usually impossible to drive a cart into the barn for unloading, corn had to be passed through holes in the walls. Pitching holes (or eyes) are openings, about 1.2 metres square, closed by hinged shutters, and usually set high in the walls and in the gables. Some smaller barns have only one, in the north gable at Cow Wath, Arden [11] (Fig. 292), and in the east gable at Lower Farm, Beadlam [23]. There are often two just below the eaves level in one of the long walls, as at Helm House, Bilsdale West Side [32] (Fig. 297), Hazel Green, Helmsley [238], and many more examples. It was less common to have them in opposite walls of a barn, perhaps to avoid a through draught at the upper level, though they occur at Fryup Hall, Danby [90], and Aumery Park, Fadmoor [114].

As doorways and pitching holes could be closed, permanent ventilation was provided by slits, which are almost invariable features of barns in the region. The few barns without them have been mentioned as being exceptional in other respects, particularly doorways. That these barns either had large doorways, as Low Hall, Brompton [56], or four doors of average size, as Cockmoor Hall, Snainton [475], and High Baxtons,

Helmsley [239], suggests that doors were regarded as contributing towards ventilation. A few small barns, with only the two normal doors, however, have no ventilation slits; one is at Bonfield Gill, Pockley [435] (Fig. 302).

Ventilation slits are narrow openings about 10 centimetres wide and usually about 45 to 60 centimetres high, though a few are taller. They generally have splayed reveals and are therefore wider inside the barn. The minimum number normally provided was two, one to each side of a central door in a long wall, as at Cow Wath, Arden [11] (Fig. 292). More frequently, there were slits in the walls on both sides, and the numbers could be duplicated by providing two to each side of a door. If the end wall was not encumbered by another building, it also often had slits. A greater degree of ventilation was provided by two tiers, as at Beckside Farm, Danby [88] (Fig. 303). At Botton Farm, Danby [80], the barn is unusual in having slits at the higher level only.

Fig. 303 [88] Beck Side Farm, Danby

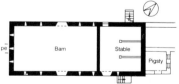

The invention by Andrew Meikle of a threshing machine (patented in 1788) revolutionized agricultural practice, and the horse-driven threshing machine was to achieve great popularity in the North York Moors. Its first appearance in North Yorkshire was at Nunnington in 1790, and many were in use in the region during the first half of the 19th century, as at Sinnington Lodge [460], where the sale particulars included a barn and threshing machine (*YG:* 15 Sept. 1821). 'They are constructed on several different plans, which are continually improved upon, and rendered more and more simple every year, and more efficacious with equal powers: none have yet been built here to go by water. The common wrights are beginning to make them, and there is no doubt but that in a short time they will construct them as generally and completely as they now do the winnowing machines' (Tuke 1800: 82). The machine, which separated the grain from the straw, was placed above a winnowing machine which removed the chaff. Both machines could be housed in existing barns, but the horse wheel, which transferred the power of horses, moving clockwise along a circular path, to the threshing machine inside the barn, needed more space. It was generally housed in an additional building attached to one side of the barn and was either square, polygonal or round-ended. As winnowing was now mechanized, the small opposing barn doors became obsolete, and the door nearest the horse-engine shed was often covered by the new construction.

The revolving central shaft in the horse-engine house was fixed at its head to a sturdy cross-beam which also served as the tie-beam of the roof truss. The cross-beam was strengthened by two beams jointed into it either side of the shaft, and supported at their other ends by the barn wall. These secondary beams often survive, but the drive-shaft and the remaining machinery have usually vanished. Where the cross-beam rests on the wall, the thickness is often increased by buttresses to take the weight; if there are openings to each side, support is provided by a substantial freestanding pier. The cross-beam usually supports a king-post truss, although queen-post and principal-rafter trusses are also found.

The most popular type of horse-engine house in the region was square on plan, with the wall furthest from the barn usually gabled. The main variations in the square plan concern the number of openings, and virtually every possible combination actually occurs.

Several horse-engine houses have a single opening adjacent to the barn wall which must have served as an entrance, and there are also unglazed windows to provide light and ventilation, as at the outfarm near Bridge Farm, Stainton Dale [487] (Fig. 304a). At Scawton Park [455] (Fig. 304b) and Fryup Lodge, Glaisdale [151], the horse-engine houses each have one wide opening and a narrow door, the latter perhaps only used by people tending the horses; that at Ouldray Farm, Rievaulx [446] (Fig. 304c), had two narrow doors in the gable, both now blocked. Where there is more than one large opening, they must have been as much for ventilation as to provide entrances. Two openings were arranged either in opposite walls, usually next to the barn wall, as at Higher Farm, Beadlam [22], or both in the

Fig. 304 Horse-engine houses: comparative plans and views (not to scale)

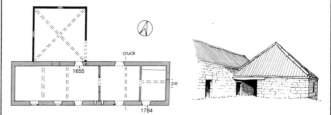

Fig. 304a [487] Outfarm, Stainton Dale

Fig. 304b [455] Scawton Park, Scawton

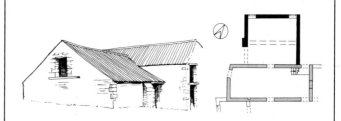

Fig. 304c [446] Ouldray Farm, Rievaulx

Fig. 304d [23] Lower Farm, Beadlam

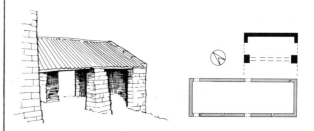

Fig. 304e [515] Leath House, Westerdale

Fig. 306 [426] West Farm, Pockley: horse-engine house

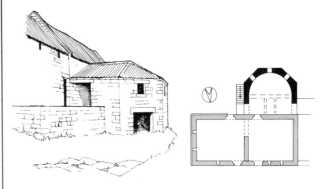

Fig. 305 Horse-engine houses: comparative plans and views (not to same scale)

Fig. 305a [156] Postgate Farm, Glaisdale

Fig. 305b [82] Stormy Hall, Danby

same side wall, of which West Farm, Pockley [426] (Fig. 306), is a good example.

At Low Farm, Pockley [434], there are three wide openings, two in one wall and one opposite. Horse-engine houses with four openings have them in pairs on each side wall, separated by piers; Lower Farm, Beadlam [23] (Fig. 304d), a farm in Gillamoor [133], and Middle Farm, Carlton, Helmsley [233], have three of the best surviving examples. Those at Leath House, Westerdale [515] (Fig. 304e), added to a barn of 1793, and at Crossley Side Farm, Danby [85], have tapering piers.

Polygonal or round-ended horse-engine houses are far less common in the region. The five-sided horse-engine houses at Postgate Farm, Glaisdale [156] (Fig. 305a), and Glaisdale Hall [152] (Fig. 307) are semicircular internally, but that at Stormy Hall, Danby [82] (Fig. 305b), lacks this refinement. A six-sided example in an isolated group of buildings at Nawton [336] (Fig. 305c) has openings on all sides and the roof is supported on piers, which are curved internally suggesting a notional semi-circular interior; there is a simpler version at West House, Kildale [252] (Fig. 305d).

The advent of the horse-engine meant that storage requirements for unthreshed grain were reduced, and it was possible to rethink the planning of barn and horse-engine house as a single unit. The opportunity was hardly ever taken. Nearly all horse-engine houses are additions to existing structures rather than of a single build with the barns to which they relate. Even in the 1818 design for Howdale Farm, Fylingdales [131] (Fig. 284), the relationship remained the same as that at other farms where the horse-engine house was added to the side of an existing barn. At Demesne Farm, Fylingdales [126] (Fig. 285), however, the horse-engine house was integrated into the design in a linear sequence of stable – horse-engine house – barn. Because the square space required by it was wider than the rest of the range, it was expressed externally by a projection beyond the line of the stable and barn walls, and to maintain a constant roof line with the barn a loft served by pitching eyes was introduced above the horse-engine house.

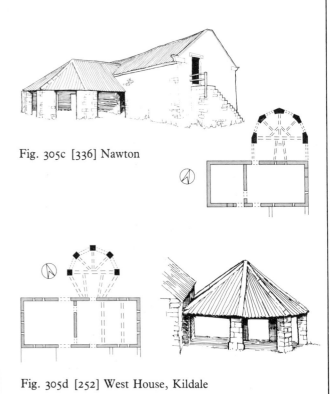

Fig. 305c [336] Nawton

Fig. 305d [252] West House, Kildale

Fig. 307 [152] Glaisdale Hall, Glaisdale: horse-engine house, exterior and interior

Ground wheels were probably introduced to the area after the horse-engine house. Horses were yoked to horizontal struts which rotated an upright shaft which transferred the movement by cast-iron gearing to a drive shaft at ground level, which the horses had to step over. They did not require an expensive superstructure, and were portable, but had the disadvantage of lack of protection for horses and machinery in bad weather. Carter's Foundry at Kirkbymoorside advertised portable thresh-ing machines in 1856 and 1857, but earlier models may have been introduced from the Midlands before this. The machinery from Stork House, Bransdale [52], is now in the Ryedale Folk Museum, and another example was recorded at Hollins Farm, Farndale East [115]. A detailed study covering much of the region shows that they were common in Bilsdale and at the head of Farndale (Harrison and Harrison 1973: 249, 263).

One class of farm building mentioned in the 17th-century surveys of which little trace survives is the hayhouse. Immediately north of Dalby, in Thornton Dale parish, a house called a hayhouse was built at Staindale in 1554/5. As a 'purpresture' it contravened an old forest rule and was ordered to be pulled down or the owner was to pay 40s (Rushton 1976b: 53). A hayhouse was mentioned in Kirkbymoorside in 1611 (PRO: Survey of Kirkbymoorside, L.R.2/186), and Robert Boddy, the farmer at High Dalby, Thornton Dale, had a cruck-built 'Hay House' made in 1746 from timber in Upper Dalby Wood, which consisted of two 'roomsteads' and measured 28 feet in length by 13 feet wide (Rushton 1976b: 82–3).

Hay was usually stored in stacks, which are often mentioned in inventories. The open-sided hay barn is relatively rare, though it was used by a few progressive and wealthy landowners and farmers. The Tancred family possessed one at the home farm at Arden. William Strickland had a hay barn at Bransdale Mill [40] (Fig. 308), built some time between 1820 and 1854. It has three wide arched openings in each long side, and solid gable walls but pierced with ventilation slits and pitching eyes.

Fig. 308 [40] Bransdale Mill, Bransdale: hay barn

Griff Farm, Rievaulx [452], the home farm to Duncombe Park, has a hay barn as part of a group of buildings built between 1806 and 1822. It consists of six tall stone piers supporting a slate roof, with a distinctive roof structure of king-post trusses. There is a similar, but larger, barn in the grounds of Duncombe Park itself, which has eight stone piers.

The fieldhouse is a small isolated building well away from the farmstead; it was not very common and was generally built on the sloping valley sides of the dales which penetrate the moorland heart of the region. It normally had two compartments, for haystore and byre, as at Bransdale [49] (Fig. 309a), where there are lofts over the byre and the western part of the larger compartment.

Fig. 309 Fieldhouses: comparative plans (at 1:400) and views

Fig. 309a [49] Bransdale

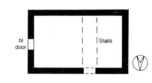

Fig. 309b [31] Bilsdale West Side

Fig. 309c [30] Bilsdale West Side

Fig. 309d [33] Bilsdale West Side

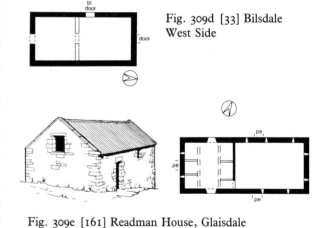

Fig. 309e [161] Readman House, Glaisdale

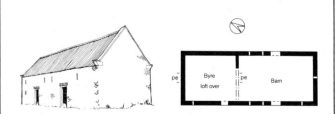

Fig. 309f [186] Red Barn, Hawsker

In Bilsdale West Side there are three fieldhouses which were all built to serve the top lands of farms on the lower valley slope. That serving Helm House [31] (Fig. 309b) was comparable in size to the Bransdale example but only had a timber partition between the compartments. It is too ruinous to determine whether there were lofts. The one which served Malkin Bower [30] (Fig. 309c) is much smaller and has two equal-sized compartments, each with a door in the south wall; there is an interconnecting door in the thick cross-wall, and a hay loft above with a door in the west gable. Two other fieldhouses with one gable door and one door in a long side also had two compartments. The third fieldhouse [33] (Fig. 309d) may have originally served Helm House (South) [32]. It is rather larger, and the stone partition wall is a later insertion.

Readman House, Glaisdale [161] (Fig. 309e), has a byre with opposed doors, and a door in the cross-wall leads from the byre to the haystore which is unusual in having no direct access from outside except for pitching eyes. Isolated farm buildings are not necessarily fieldhouses: Quarry Hill and Gilson House, Fylingdales [122, 127], are the remains of smallholdings where the house has been demolished. Red Barn, Hawsker cum Stainsacre [186] (Fig. 309f), combines a byre with loft over and a barn with opposed doors. The barn may not have been for hay, and the combined structure would fit into a farmyard as well as on to its isolated roadside site.

Fig. 310 [252] West House, Kildale: field barn with horse-engine house

Field barns are isolated threshing barns; they usually have associated horse-engine houses and are combined with provision for cattle. They were less isolated than the fieldhouses, and those serving West House, Kildale [252] (Fig. 310), Mount Pleasant, Nawton [337] (Fig. 305c), and West Farm, Pickering [420], were only a short distance away from the main farmstead. A larger development of the field barn was a small outfarm. This was virtually a complete farmstead without a house, with buildings around a foldyard, as at Nova Lodge, Pickering [417] (Fig. 311).

Fig. 311 [417] Nova Lodge, Pickering: buildings round foldyard

Until at least the late 18th century grain was frequently kept in the house between threshing and sale or use; the room used for storage is often specified in inventories as one of the chambers. The tradition of storing grain in chambers must have conflicted increasingly with their use as bedrooms, and was a factor in the heightening of some farmhouses. The grain was stored most conveniently in the roof space, preferably on a boarded floor, and there is evidence of external access being provided to granaries in farmhouse roofs.

At Cherry Tree Farm, Fadmoor [113], the present granary, built over a cartshed and appearing on a map of 1827 (NYCRO: ZEW M 51), probably replaces one in the farmhouse attic served by a door in the east gable wall. At West Sleightholmedale Farm, Skiplam [463], a surviving external staircase leads to the roof space above the men's room over the kitchen. This roof space was probably used as a granary until a purpose-built store with granary over was added to the barn in the early 19th century. The top floor of Fyling Old Hall [129] (Fig. 35) was converted to a granary, probably in the early 19th century when the garden front was refaced. An external staircase was provided

to the first floor, with a continuation indoors separate from the normal household circulation.

Separate granaries were rare before the late 18th century, though a 'garner' is mentioned at Harome in 1637 (NYCRO: ZEW IV 1/4), and John Sandwith, apothecary of Helmsley, kept corn in a granary in 1761. In 1792 Richard Bempde had thirteen granaries on his Hackness estate, all on upper floors of other farm buildings.

Most granaries were built as an upper storey over a cartshed, the free circulation of air below the floor helping to keep it dry. In the most common arrangement, with the cartshed openings in the long wall, the granary is usually approached by a flight of steps against the gable wall, as at High Wethercote, Bilsdale West Side [35] (Fig. 312). At Stiltons, Rievaulx [451] (Fig. 313), in the impressively long range of 1851, the granary steps are within the high bay at the east end. Occasionally, as at Park Gate, Fylingdales [124], there is a door centrally on the front which must have necessitated the use of a ladder. Where the cartshed entrance is in the end wall, the granary is entered from the long side, as at Breck House and Spout House, Bransdale [39, 45] (Figs. 314, 315). Granaries also occur above stables: the stable may be a separate building, as at Laskill Farm, Laskill

Fig. 312 [35] High Wethercote, Bilsdale West Side: cartshed and granary

Fig. 313 [451] Stiltons, Rievaulx: cartshed and granary

Fig. 314 [39] Breck House, Bransdale: cartshed and granary

Fig. 315 [45] Spout House, Bransdale: cartshed and granary

Fig. 316 [239] High Baxtons, Helmsley: stables and granary

Pasture [312], or part of a longer range including a barn, as at High Baxtons, Helmsley [239] (Fig. 316). Such granaries may have been used to store fodder for horses, to which oats were fed. Granaries above byres are unusual but in 1792 were mentioned above oxhouses at Hackness.

Ventilation in granaries was provided in one of the long walls by window-like openings, usually closed by hinged wooden shutters. Frequently fairly small, they may be set near to floor level, as at High Wethercote, Bilsdale West Side [35], or immediately below eaves level, as at Breck House, Bransdale [39]. There are some larger ones, such as those at Saintoft Grange, Pickering [416] (Fig. 317), which are glazed.

The storage of other crops

The use of root crops had more impact upon the buildings of the farmstead indirectly, through the greater numbers of animals which could be kept throughout the winter, than by the additional storage accommodation needed. Potatoes and turnips were slow to be adopted in the region. The former were first grown in the Vale of Pickering *c.* 1715, but not widely cultivated until the 1760s (Parker 1980: 23). Their storage did not usually entail any permanent structure, though a potato house near Mountain Ash Farm, Glaisdale, mentioned *c.* 1839, was 'made of stone, with large slabs for a roof and covered with earth, the interior was divided into 2 parts by a stone wall' (NYCRO: ZV 2/7). Turnips were even slower to gain popularity. Turnip houses, for storing food for cattle, appear in the 19th century. At High Baxtons Farm [239], a turnip store connects directly with the cow byre on one side, while that at Mount Pleasant, Old Byland [342], serves byres symmetrically arranged on either side of it.

SHELTERS FOR VEHICLES

Cartsheds

The cartshed, a common element in most farmsteads, is absent from some smaller farms. Although the earliest dated example is of 1768, most appear to be of the 19th century, reflecting an increase after 1800 in the number both of farms with carts and of carts used on individual farms. Tuke remarked on the scarcity of carts in the region: 'In the dales of the Eastern Moorlands very few carts are met with; generally small waggons, with low wheels, which do not contain more than from 12 to 20 bushels;

Fig. 317 [416] Saintoft Grange, Pickering: cartshed and granary

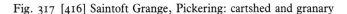

to these they yoke two pair of oxen, with one or two horses before them. But on the verge of these moors, and on the coast, more carts are kept, and both the carts and waggons are larger than in the dales' (Tuke 1800: 79).

Most cartsheds have granaries above them but a few have lofts, probably for hay, and some are of only one storey. They can be difficult to distinguish from implement sheds and possibly served either purpose. Sometimes they have double wooden doors but are generally left open; their openings may be spanned by lintels or arches. Timber lintels are found throughout the region but stone ones are limited to areas with suitable stone; they were used at the earliest known cartshed, at Fryup Hall, Danby [90] (Fig. 318). Sometimes the span was reduced slightly by corbelling the stones which directly support the lintel, as at Crossley Side Farm, Danby [85] (Fig. 319). Stone arches, either segmental, elliptical or three-centred, were used in those areas, such as Eskdale and the valleys to the south of the watershed, where sandstone occurs which could be cut to form shaped voussoirs. They seem to have been especially favoured on farms on the Duncombe Park Estate; dated examples occur in Bilsdale West Side at High Wethercote [35] of 1836, and Lockton [36] (Fig. 320) of 1840. The limestone of the southern margin of the moors was only suitable for rubble masonry and thereby less

Fig. 320 [36] Lockton, Bilsdale West Side: cartshed entrance

appropriate for constructing arches. In these areas, from *c.* 1840 onwards, brick was widely employed for arches and piers of cartshed openings, as at Boon Woods, Wombleton [529], dated 1841.

Some single-storeyed cartsheds have multiple openings in the long side, such as those at New House, Laskill Pasture [310], and Middle Baxtons, Helmsley [240]; the latter is a four-bay cartshed, each bay having double doors. Single-storeyed cartsheds with gable entrances are uncommon. That at Beck Side Farm, Danby [88] (Fig. 321), has a single semicircular arched opening in the gable with a blocked pitching eye above it, suggesting that some form of storage loft was intended. The cartshed added after 1854 at Smout House, Bransdale [42], has no such opening above the three-centred archway with chamfered voussoirs. High Normanby Farm, Fylingdales [119], has a freestanding cartshed with two segmental arched openings in the gable.

Fig. 318 [90] Fryup Hall, Danby: cartshed and horse-engine house

Fig. 319 [85] Crossley Side Farm, Danby: cartshed

Fig. 321 [88] Beck Side Farm, Danby: cartshed and pigsties

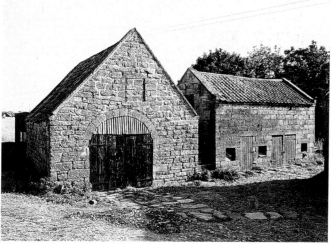

Fig. 322 [43] Cornfield House, Bransdale: cartshed to right

Cartsheds with granaries or lofts over may have access from the gable end of a long range. The most common form, however, has openings in one of the long sides, their number varying from one to six but usually two or three. While the number of cart openings can reflect variations in farm size, it may also indicate the growing complexity of farming techniques and the additional equipment to be stored.

All small cartsheds with only one door form part of a longer range, which may also contain a barn and stable or byre. They are usually at one end of the range as at Cornfield House, Bransdale [43] (Fig. 322), and at Lockton, Bilsdale West Side [36], built in 1840. Cartsheds with two openings are also usually combined with another building, though some are attached only to single-storeyed ranges. At three farms on the Duncombe Park Estate, in Bilsdale West Side, virtually identical two-bay cartsheds with granaries above are attached to barns: at Woolhouse Croft [37] built in 1835, at High Wethercote [35] (Fig. 312) of 1836, and at Low Wethercote (Fig. 293) which is undated but must be contemporary with the others. This arrangement is found elsewhere in the region, as at Glebe Farm, Sawdon [58].

Some three-bay cartsheds also form part of longer ranges as at Murkhead, Harwood Dale [177], and Lowfields Farm, Brompton [60]; one at Lower Farm, Beadlam [23], is attached to the farmhouse. More characteristically, they are detached as at The Mount, Wombleton [528] (Fig. 323); at Boon Woods

Fig. 323 [528] The Mount, Wombleton: three-bay cartshed

[529], an isolated farm in the same parish, a similar example is dated 1841.

Cartsheds with more openings are much less common, only occurring on larger farms. There are examples with four bays at Allerston Hall [8] and Wether Cote, Skiplam [462]. An impressive one dated 1851 at Stiltons, Rievaulx [451] (Fig. 313), with five openings, has a stable at one end and a loading bay at the other incorporating the stair to the granary. The largest is at Griff Farm, Rievaulx [452] (Fig. 324); built after 1850, this has six open bays with the granary wall supported by cast-iron columns, as well as two bays at one end and one at the other, all closed by doors.

Fig. 324 [452] Griff Farm, Rievaulx: detail of cartshed

Two-storeyed cartsheds with the entrance in the gable wall frequently have one or two openings; the only example with more, at Postgate Farm, Glaisdale [156], has paired openings to the main part of the building, and a further opening in the integral side outshut leading to a much shorter shed. Cartsheds of this type are frequently in a range, combined with another function such as a byre at Breck House and a stable at Spout House, both in Bransdale [39, 45] (Fig. 315); that at Hazel Green, Helmsley [238] (Fig. 294), backs on to a barn at its west end.

Gig and trap houses

In addition to farm carts, provision had to be made for the carriages used by the farmer and his family, if sufficiently wealthy not to rely on walking or horseriding. The gig house at Rutland House, Harome [173], is attached to a single-storey wash-house forming a rear wing to the house, and is obviously connected with domestic rather than farming functions. Trap houses shared this domestic connection. Those at Low Farm, Carlton, Helmsley [232], and Home Farm, Wilton [520], where the trap pony was kept next to the trap, are built in line with the farmhouse. Even where they are separated from the house, they are usually close to it. They usually are combined with other single-storey structures in a small block, and rarely have any architectural pretensions.

BUILDINGS FOR ANIMALS

Accommodation for cattle

Inventories show that cattle formed a major part of a farmer's wealth, although as he did not dispose of them every year they were not necessarily his principal source of income. On farms in the upland areas the breeding and rearing of cattle were of more significance than in the Vale of Pickering where dairying was more important, though until the improvement of transport and the growth of urban markets for fresh milk in the 19th century this involved the small-scale production of butter and cheese. The horse only gradually replaced the ox as a source of power; it is significant that in the 1637 survey of Bilsdale oxhouses far outnumber stables. Oxen were kept on the Duncombe Park Estate for ploughing until the present century. Their survival is matched by other, more 'progressive', farming areas. Oxen were used for ploughing in Norfolk throughout the 19th century, and answers to Bacon's questionnaire of 1844 showed that they were still being used by farmers on the Holkham Estate (Wade-Martins 1980: 174).

Cowhouses and oxhouses were mentioned in the several 17th-century surveys, although no separate buildings for cattle have been identified from that period. The longhouse was then predominant and cattle were normally kept in the byres attached to farmhouses. The detached or separate byre to house larger numbers of cattle over the winter was an 18th-century response to the opportunities provided by widespread cultivation of root crops and the introduction of artificial cattle foods (Robinson 1983: 85). As with so many other farm buildings, very few of those surviving are probably earlier in date than the late 18th century, and the majority are of the 19th.

A regional characteristic of the internal planning of byres is that cattle were usually stalled with their heads facing a wall, so that they had to be fed from behind. The arrangement with separate feeding and manure passages is a rare feature though it occurs at Church Farm, Aislaby [1], which has three pairs of doors in each of the long sides. Variations in plan tend to reflect the number of animals housed. The simplest arrangement, often found on smallholdings, is similar to a loose box on a larger farm and has a single door in a side wall near to a cross-wall, as at Ivy Cottage, Carlton [234]. If it was part of a range of farm buildings, there might be a connecting door in the cross-wall.

Byres with a single door placed centrally in a side wall are usually larger. At Keeper's Cottage, Pockley [428], the byre is almost square in plan, and has only two double stalls against the wall facing the entrance door. In most examples the byre is oblong, and although the stalls could form a single row along the wall opposite the entrance, all of the large byres with surviving fittings have two rows of stalls facing the cross-walls, with two pairs of stalls each side at Snaper House, Helmsley [236], and Street Gate Farm, Snilesworth [480].

Similar accommodation was provided by byres with opposed doors in the long sides, which bear a superficial resemblance to small barns. The simplest form has cattle on only one side of the passage between the doors, but there are many examples with stalls on both sides. They were quite often built in pairs, as at Low Wethercote Farm, Bilsdale West Side [35], and Winsley Hill Farm, Danby [69], where there is no structural division between them, and at The Elms, West Ayton [508], divided by a cross-wall. At Wether Cote, Skiplam [462] (Fig. 325), a pair of byres flank a covered entry to the farmyard, a particularly neat arrangement.

Fig. 325 [462] Wether Cote, Skiplam: byres flanking yard entrance

An alternative plan was to place the stalls facing a long wall, with the entrance in the opposite wall. This is probably a late development and is the normal modern method. By arranging the stalls this way it was possible to reach the cowhouse from adjacent buildings under cover, through doors in cross-walls which supplemented the entrance or entrances from the farmyard. The plan also made it possible to accommodate more cows in a single byre as it could be extended in length to the required size.

Many byres had no other openings in the walls other than the doors, which were split so that the upper half could be opened for ventilation. Further ventilation might be provided by slits, similar to those used in barns, as at Wether Cote, Skiplam [462]. Windows were not normally provided until after the middle of the 19th century, though many were subsequently inserted to comply with modern regulations.

Accommodation for cattle was also provided by shelter sheds. These were open-fronted buildings which afforded protection from the weather for loose cattle in foldyards, and occasionally in the fields, such as the one built against the isolated Tile House Barn, Old Byland [343]. None are closely dated but they are a late development and several can be shown from map evidence to have been added after 1850. The shelter shed sometimes forms an integral part of a farm layout. At High Baxtons Farm, Helmsley [239], it constitutes the whole range along the south side of the farmyard. In certain larger farms a separate yard was provided for cattle and the shelter shed faced on to that, as at Abbot Hag Farm, Rievaulx [449]. At Town End Farm, Beadlam [19], and Cockayne Lodge, Bransdale [38] (Fig. 326), small foldyards are enclosed on two adjacent sides by L-

Fig. 326 [38] Cockayne Lodge, Bransdale: shelter sheds round yard

shaped shelter sheds, and at Scawton Park [455] a detached group of buildings comprises a yard flanked by a shelter shed and byre.

Pinfolds

Pinfolds or pounds, used for confining stray cattle, were formerly common. They belonged to the local communities, not to individual farmsteads. Although not all survive, a number are marked on the first edition OS and later maps, usually in villages. The circular pinfolds at Hackness and Hutton Buscel (Fig. 327) are well-preserved examples. They also existed in the towns. There was a pinfold in Helmsley in the early 16th century (Belvoir: Misc. MS 105(3)), and in Pickering a pound mentioned in Hungate in 1651 survived until at least 1833 (PRO: E.317/43, D.L.30/417/5). Another 'common pound' on the west side of Potter Hill was mentioned in 1816 and 1819 (NYCRO: Reg. Deeds EB, 1816–17).

Stables

Although the 1637 Bilsdale Survey lists several stables, not all the farms mentioned possessed one. Similarly, only two of the three Newstead Grange leases mention stables. The 'waynehouses' of the Bilsdale Survey imply draught animals, but these may have been oxen rather than horses. On the evidence of surviving buildings there must have been an increase in the use of horse power during the 19th century, especially during its second quarter. Horses were gradually replacing oxen for ploughing, and with the advent of the horse-engine they also provided power for threshing and winnowing. Other horses were used for transport, either for riding or for drawing traps or gigs. This led to a greater diversity of specialized buildings to house the horse-operated implements, and it was necessary to construct coach-houses, cartsheds, traphouses and implement sheds.

Where few horses were kept, one or two loose boxes would be adequate, but these are not always easy to distinguish from the accommodation provided for cattle. The simplest stables are simple oblongs in plan, with a single door near a cross or end

Fig. 327 Pinfold, Hutton Buscel

wall and no window, as at 54 High Street, Helmsley [220].
Internal divisions rarely survive with this basic plan, but the
partition between two stalls is still in position in a stable at
Newgate Foot, Pockley [436], and at High Elm House,
Bransdale [48].

Unlike byres, purpose-built stables usually have windows.
Many are of two storeys, with a hay loft above, as at Harriet
Air Farm, Rievaulx [447] (Fig. 328), or a granary, at High
Baxtons Farm [239] (Fig. 316). At one side of the loft floor a
narrow gap was frequently provided so that feed could be
directly passed down to the horses below.

Most stables have stalls with the horses facing the long wall
on the opposite side to the entrance. Smaller ones are long
enough for two or at most three horses but larger examples have
as many as five stalls, as at Rea Garth Farm, Helmsley [242],
while West House, Kildale [252], has three sets of two stand-
ings, providing for six horses. Some stables resemble byres in
having opposed doors and stalls facing a cross-wall, as at Hart
Hall and Glaisdale Head, Glaisdale [153, 162]: there are usually
two or three stalls to each side.

Fig. 328 [447] Harriet Air Farm, Rievaulx: stable

Fig. 329 [490] Thornton Hall, Thornton Dale: stable range

Stables for riding and coach horses may seem out of place in the context of farm buildings, but most of the small manor houses also had farming functions. The stables at Thornton Hall [490] (Fig. 329) present the formal face of a group of utilitarian buildings including a barn and a cartshed. They have opposed doors serving a lobby to two sets of stables, entered through the cross-walls, which each have three stalls. The upper floors may have been used as sleeping quarters for the grooms. Similarly, the stable block at Kingthorpe House [254] has architectural pretensions which conceal humble origins as a barn. As large stables are rarely needed nowadays, several of the larger 19th-century stable blocks have undergone demolition or conversion. A castellated building near Woodlands, Aislaby, now converted to domestic use, contained stabling for fourteen horses (*The Yorkshireman:* 15 Aug. 1835). The stabling provided for racehorses at Hambleton House, Cold Kirby [66], still fulfils its original purpose. The ranges south and east of the house have lofts above the stables, which apparently are groups of units either with a door and adjacent window or a door flanked by windows. The north range consists of a row of single-storeyed boxes with no separate windows, and has a two-storeyed block at one end as accommodation for the stable lads (Fig. 330).

Fig. 330 [66] Hambleton House, Cold Kirby: north stable range

Smithies

The increased use of horses in the 19th century led to more work for blacksmiths. Not every farm would need a smithy of its own, and, because of the expense involved, purpose-built smithies served either individual village communities or particularly large or isolated farms. However, it is sometimes difficult to ascertain whether a farm building with a flue was designed as a smithy, a boilhouse, a wash-house or even as a 'slum', a heated room for farm labourers outside the farmhouse.

Smithies to serve village communities were normally built as self-contained units though that at Dial House Farm, Gillamoor [137] (Fig. 331), probably served both the village and the farm itself. An isolated roadside smithy in Danby [81] served the scattered dale farms while the forge at West Farm, Pickering [418], probably served the other farms on the Blansby Park Estate.

Fig. 331 [137] Dial House Farm, Gillamoor: smithy

The simplest smithy has an oblong plan and consists of a single room, with a door and window in one long side, additional doors or windows as required, and the forge against the gable wall. Most smithies consist of two rooms, and have been built on to a range of other farm buildings. In some the smithy is entered through a cross-wall from an adjacent cartshed, as at both the earlier smithy at Bransdale Mill [40] (Fig. 332a), which is dated 1818, and at Hasty Bank Farm, Pockley [438] (Fig. 332b), which was probably completed by 1822. Even where

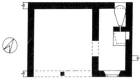

Fig. 332a [40] Bransdale Mill: smithy

Fig. 332b [438] Hasty Bank Farm, Pockley: smithy

there is no direct access, a cartshed is often the next structure to the forge. At Skiplam Grange [465] the smithy and a loose box are combined, without an interconnecting door.

Sheep

Sheep are not usually kept in buildings, and so leave few material remains that can be associated with them. The practice of sheep farming on the moors is attested by archaeological and historical evidence and by place-names such as Ewe Cote and Wether Cote attached to more remote settlements.

The medieval monasteries had extensive sheep farms on the moors. A large aisled barn, 8.5 metres wide and 33.5 metres long, excavated at Rudland Close, Hutton-le-Hole, has been identified as a sheephouse with an adjacent sheepfold belonging to St Mary's Abbey, York (Wilson and Hurst 1966: 20–43). Three similar aisled barns existed on Levisham Moor on land owned by Malton Priory (inf. J. McDonnell). Thomas de Westhorpe of Brompton owned 2723 sheep and 152 lambs in 1366 (Waites 1963–6: 448). Sir Roger Hastynges kept 400 sheep at one farm in Goathland and 300 sheep at another in Lockton in 1497 (Turton 1894: 186). The Duchy of Lancaster accounts for Dalby in 1325/6 show that the sheepfolds were roofed, as a thatcher was paid for ten days' work there (Rushton 1976b: 37).

A sheephouse and garth adjoining Doubting Castle, Clitherbeck, Danby, were leased in 1746 (NYCRO: ZDS I 1/6), and the sheephouse appears as a simple structure with a single door on a plan of 1781 (NYCRO: ZDS IV 6/3/1/6). In 1796, Thomas Todd was tenant of a farm at Lockton which included a close where there was an old sheephouse in Saltergate (PRO: D.L.30/399, Pickering Court Books 1795–1875). Arthur Young remarked on the importance of sheepkeeping to the farms about Kirkbymoorside: 'Their chief subsistence is keeping sheep on the moors; their stocks rise from 300 to 1000' (Young 1771: 90). Sheep were run on the moors during the summer and folded on the arable fields in winter. Their strong dung was highly valued.

Pigs

Pigs were an important source of household meat. 'Many of the labourers keep a pig, and some a cow' (Tuke 1800: 288). During the 17th and 18th centuries only one or two pigs appear to have been kept by each farm for domestic use, most of the exceptions such as the sow and 8 young pigs listed in an inventory of 1738 being newly born litters. Special buildings were not required; inventories usually refer to a 'pig in the yard' and this must often have been the situation until well into the 19th century.

Following the introduction of a new breed about 1750 and helped by the wider use of root crops, the number of pigs kept rose rapidly, reaching a peak in the 19th century. This local breed, the Bilsdale Blue, was very popular (Hartley and Ingilby 1972: 28), although 'the old long-eared kind' of pig with 'little to recommend it' remained prevalent (Tuke 1800: 282). Within a few years bacon was sent in quantity to West Yorkshire and some to London (Marshall 1788: 293). The boom in pig rearing is demonstrated by the large number of pigsties surviving throughout the region.

No surviving pigsty is known to have been built before the 19th century and the earliest that can be firmly dated are of 1818 and 1819. They are simple functional buildings which show no marked development during the century. The typical sty is small, sometimes square but more frequently rectangular, about 2 metres by 3 metres. Some farms had only one but more often there were two or three together in a single block. A few farms had larger groups; at Botton Grove, Danby [79], there are six in a single range, with doors in the same wall as the feeding troughs. Saintoft Grange, Pickering [416], has a long range with doors in the opposite wall to a row of ten feeding troughs (Fig. 333a.)

Pigs were fed on kitchen waste and sties were generally sited close to the farmhouse for convenience. Though some groups of sties were separate blocks, they were also quite often attached to a building serving another function, usually the boilhouse, where the feed was prepared. Another characteristic combination was with a hen house, which formed an upper storey above the sties, approached by a flight of steps against the gable-end wall (Figs. 333b and c). Sties were also attached to the farmhouse itself, and virtually every other type of farm building such as barn, byre, stable, cartshed, smithy and privy. An unusual method of combining functions is at Stormy Hall, Danby [82], where a barn built in 1828 on a sloping site has three sties forming a lower storey at one end. Pigsties may also be part of a larger complex of several buildings or integrated with one range of a courtyard farm, as at Stonebeck Gate, Danby [86], where they are at the corner of the yard closest to the farmhouse and with a passage proving easy access.

The feeding trough was normally the only opening in the walls of the pigsty, apart from the door. The vicious eating habits of pigs necessitated the use of a stone trough which would separate the pigs from the person pouring the swill. The trough was built into the wall with an inclined stone slab above it acting as a baffle (Fig. 333d). Normally each sty had only one feeding trough though sometimes there were two. Troughs were occasionally incorporated into the dividing walls between boilhouse and pigsty. At Cowl House, Bransdale [46], two sties on one side of a long boilhouse are served in this way.

Small enclosed yards outside the sty itself are rare in the region. Where they occur, feeding troughs are built into the walls of the yard as at Riddings Farm, Westerdale [514] (Fig. 333e). More ambitious examples, with long ranges of troughs, are at Lowdales, Hackness [168] (Fig. 333f), and Sledgates Farm, Fylingdales [123] (Fig. 333g). One even imitates a classical temple (Fig. 290).

Comparative views and details of pigsties

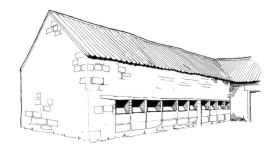

Fig. 333a [416] Saintoft Grange, Pickering

Fig. 333b [88] Beckside Farm, Danby

Fig. 333c [43] Cornfield House, Bransdale

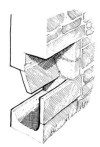

Fig. 333e [514] Riddings Farm, Westerdale

Fig. 333d Detail of pig trough

Fig. 333f [168] Lowdales, Hackness

Fig. 333g [123] Sledgates, Fylingdales

Poultry and pigeons

Hen houses were generally provided as lofts built over pigsties. Alternatively, nesting boxes were formed in the wall thickness of other buildings. They occur in the walls facing the farmyard at Stonebeck Gate [86], and in a cartshed at The Mount, Wombleton [528] (Fig. 334), where they are on the inner faces; this would not have been inconvenient in a building such as this with no doors.

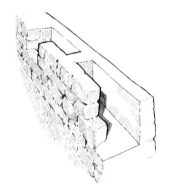

Fig. 335 [56] Low Hall, Brompton: dovecote

Fig. 334 [528] The Mount, Wombleton: nesting boxes, perspective sketch and cut-away view

Fig. 336 [61] Cloughton Hall, Cloughton: dovecote

The keeping of pigeons for food was for long a manorial prerogative. The few surviving freestanding dovecots are associated with houses of manorial status. The earliest and largest, at Low Hall, Brompton [56] (Fig. 335), is rectangular, with stepped gables, and is probably of 16th-century date. Others are at Low Hall, West Ayton [513], which is also square in plan and probably of the late 18th or early 19th century, and a circular one, of uncertain date, at The Hall, Cloughton [61] (Fig. 336).

The ownership of dovecots became more widespread during the 18th century, particularly in association with inns. The sale details of the George and Dragon, Kirkbymoorside [286], include dovecots among the outbuildings (*YH*: 26. Nov 1831), and a dovecot belonging to the Angel Inn, now 13 West End, Kirkbymoorside [303], is mentioned in the late 18th century (NYCRO: Deeds BS, 1781–3, ZRM/13).

From the middle of the 18th century onwards, and especially after Tuke's time, there is more evidence of pigeons being kept by farmers. The provision made for them was sometimes crude,

Fig. 337 [86] Stonebeck Gate Farm, Danby: dovecote and SW range

such as the openings pierced in a cowhouse gable at Ouldray, Rievaulx [446], which are probably for pigeons, and the pigeon house created in the roof of the barn at East Newton Hall [92]. Better-cut pigeon openings are probably contemporary with the building, such as pigeon openings in the gable of a building dated 1808 at Stonebeck Gate Farm, Danby [86]. A more substantial pigeon house added there after 1850 takes the form of a tower over an archway (Fig. 337). Less elaborate provision was made above the entrance archway to Demesne Farm, Fylingdales [126], of 1843, but pigeon holes exist in profusion in the gable of a farm range rebuilt after 1850 at Hart Hall, Glaisdale [153].

Pigeon lofts were also built over pigsties. Two dated examples, at Botton Grove and Plumtree, Danby [79, 78], are of 1819 and 1840 respectively. The most unusual combination occurs in

Fig. 338 [93] Cliff House, Ebberston: pigeon holes

a building with architectural pretensions at Cliff House, Ebberston [93], which has a a circular opening in the top of the gable wall, and a double arched opening below (Fig. 338). As there is a chimney against the far end, this may be a combination of boilhouse with pigeons above, and a double nesting box for poultry in the wall thickness.

Bees

The evidence provided by inventories shows that beekeeping was principally confined to Helmsley and a band of moorland parishes in the west of the region. Most beekeepers possessed between one and four hives, the only large-scale producers being Robert Foster of Fair Hill Farm, Laskill Pasture, with eight hives in 1689, and George Duck of Danby Lodge, with seven hives in 1720.

Honey was an additional source of income for many farmers, especially for those with access to the heather-covered moors. Swarms were kept in straw skeps, which were replaced by wooden hives from early in the 1880s onwards. The skeps were kept in bee boles, recesses in a wall, or on bee stones, flat circular stones with a projecting lip (Hartley and Ingilby 1972: 86–92). Dale Head, Westerdale [518], has a bee house with architectural pretensions, dated 1832. A series of stone slabs with chamfered arrises separate the bee boles, and support an arcade of three-centred arches cut in pairs from wide slabs. A projecting coping supported the lean-to roof (Hartley and Ingilby 1972: Pl. 223).

Dogs

Kennels for farm dogs were often provided by utilizing space beneath the external flights of stone steps which gave access to lofts and granaries on upper floors. The earliest dated example is probably that at Botton Grove, Danby [79], under the steps to a loft over a byre, combined with a barn of 1794. The opening for the dog was usually rebated for a hinged door, as at Spout House, Bransdale [45] (Fig. 339). The Kennels, Hutton Buscel [245] (Fig. 340), were built by George Osbaldeston for hunting dogs, which were kept on the ground floor, with an upper floor probably providing accommodation for kennel-hands, analogous to the arrangement at bigger riding stables.

Fig. 339 [45] Spout House, Bransdale: kennel below steps to stable loft

Fuel stores

Fuel used on farms was mainly wood, turf or peat, although some small mines provided a localized supply of coal. The turf stack, such as that mentioned at Eskdaleside in 1812 (Burnett: 47), was evidently adequate for most farms and was rarely far from the farmhouse. A turf house was mentioned at Hart Hall, Glaisdale [153], in 1684. Ankness, Bransdale [53], has a turf and stick house (identified as such on an estate plan) added to the house after 1850, and Demesne Farm, Fylingdales [126], has a small stick house added to the wash-house. At Beck Side Farm, Danby [88], a turf or peat house stands some way from the house, as does another, combined with a loose box, at High Farm, Pockley [425], datable before 1853. Turf was also used for fuel in towns. In 1730, buildings behind 1–3 Bridge Street, Helmsley, included a turfhouse (NYCRO: ZEW I 84), and another is mentioned in Pickering (NYCRO: Reg. Deeds AI, 1760–2).

Water mills

Water and water power played an important part in the development of local industry. The agriculture of the region produced grain crops for flour, and sheep and cattle provided wool and hides which formed the basis of small textile and leather industries. In addition, locally grown and imported flax was the foundation of a linen-weaving industry based on Helmsley. Hemp, grown in Brompton, Helmsley, Thornton Dale and elsewhere

Fig. 340 [245] The Kennels, Hutton Buscel

in the south of the region, was used for rope making as well as the manufacture of coarse cloth. Both flax and hemp were used in the production of paper. Tanning required large quantities of tree bark and a regular supply of water. In the Rievaulx area, iron ore was forged in furnaces using water power to work the bellows.

The textile industry has an early association with the use of water power, although cloth making in the region relied on hand weaving for both woollen and linen materials. Fulling mills existed in the region from at least the 14th century, increasing in numbers with the introduction of linen weaving and probably reaching a peak in the later 18th century. Several 18th-century fulling mills worked as such for only a short while. High Costa Mill, Aislaby [7], was used for fulling between 1755 and 1793, but for corn milling before and after that, while Low Costa Mill, Middleton [327], another corn mill, was a 'bitling mill' in 1785. Both were also referred to as bleaching mills. Flax spinning using water power began at Keldholme, Kirkbymoorside, in 1809, and at Boggle Hall or Esk Mill, north-west of Castleton in Danby parish, in 1813, but both had reverted to corn milling by 1827 and 1853 respectively. As spinning and weaving became more mechanized, the West Riding, with its large mills powered first by Pennine water and then by coal, captured the remaining trade.

The paper industry was introduced to the area by a silk weaver, John Blanchard of York, who in 1597 bought a new-built house in the the manor of Old Byland. By 1610 he had a paper mill, a house for drying paper, and tubs and troughs for working the paper, but by 1635 the mill was used for fulling (NYCRO: ZD VI/1/18). Paper making flourished for a longer period beside the beck upstream from Thornton Dale. An Ellerburn Paper Mill was in existence by 1680, and another, called the White Paper Mill, by 1696 (Rushton 1976b: 69–70). The High Paper Mill at Ellerburn [507] was rebuilt in 1733 and operated until c. 1869; only its farm and farmhouse survive. The Low Mill, renovated in 1789, was later rented to Thomas Marsden, who carried on business there until 1869; he also had works in Sheffield. He lived in Brook House, Thornton Dale [497], which had previously belonged to John Priestman (Jeffery 1931: 92), owner of the 18th-century tannery in the middle of the village (Rushton n.d.: 31). Other paper mills included one 'lately erected on the croft' of Bamford House, Lealholm [142], in 1766, and Vivis Mill, Pickering [423] (Fig. 341), which was used as a paper mill from 1768 to 1785 but was a corn mill before and after that period.

Tanners are recorded at Helmsley, Rievaulx, Bilsdale and Keldholme near Kirkbymoorside during the 14th century (Rushton 1976a: 26) and tanneries in several parts of the region

Fig. 341 [423] Vivis Mill, Pickering

during subsequent centuries. Helmsley remained a major tanning centre until the late 19th century. In Pickering there were tanneries on both sides of Pickering Beck in the 18th century (NYCRO: Reg. Deeds AD, 1757–8, AI, 1760–2, AN, 1763–8, AU, 1766–70). Tanneries were usually associated with water-powered machinery for dressing the leather, as at Calf Close Bank, Aislaby [5], described as a 'leather pelt or skinning mill' in 1796 (NYCRO: Reg. Deeds CO, 1796–7).

Lowna, Gillamoor [138] (Fig. 342), is the principal site in the region where buildings connected with a tanyard survive. The corn mill there also powered a pump circulating water through the soak pits, a bark crusher, a bone crusher for fertilizer and a wood saw. The property, described as a fulling mill in 1803 (NYCRO: Reg. Deeds CZ, 1803–5), was then occupied by Thomas Baxter, skinner and wool buyer, who started the tannery business.

Fig. 342 [138] Lowna, Gillamoor

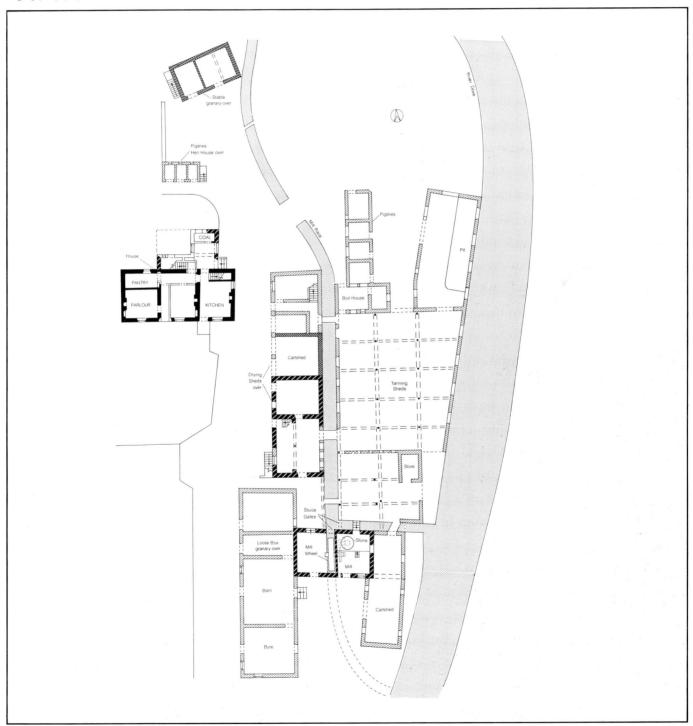

Most of the local industries which flourished during the 18th century died out during the 19th century, leaving little physical evidence of their former existence. The textile, iron and other mills were not usually abandoned but were converted or rebuilt as corn mills, supplementing the milling capacity of a number of smaller corn mills which continued to function. This suggests an increase in grain production resulting from a combination of improved agricultural techniques, intake of moorland, and a partial move away from pastoral farming.

Very few of the surviving corn mills still serve their original function. They tend to fit two main categories. In the first, the mill formed part of a smallholding and only provided a portion of the miller's livelihood. Sometimes it may only have served the farm itself. The farm is clearly the dominant element at Lower Askew, Lastingham [319], and Broad Gate Farm, Westerdale [517], which both possessed corn mills (Rutter 1970: 16, 1971: 27). The second category covers those larger mills,

mainly rebuilt or extended in the middle of the 19th century, which were easily adapted to modern milling or manufacturing techniques. Although still adjacent, the miller's house was not essential to the mill's survival as a working unit.

Many of the corn mills have ancient origins, although later rebuilt at the same or adjacent sites. Medieval corn mills in Ryedale (Rushton 1976a: 25) included Sproxton Mill [445], mentioned in Espec's second gift to Rievaulx Abbey of 1145, and Gillamoor Mill [139], in existence by 1154 (Hayes 1969: 16). As with farm buildings, the surviving mills mainly date from the last quarter of the 18th century and later, but must represent the last phase of a long period of development. Sproxton Mill was repaired in 1705/6, but a structure of that period is not suggested by photographs taken before its demolition. Rievaulx Mill [442] (Fig. 343), also rebuilt in 1706, must subsequently have been rebuilt again, as well as being heightened in 1875/6. The 1734 datestone at Hold Caldron Mill,

Fig. 343 [442] Rievaulx Mill, Rievaulx

Fig. 344 [466] Hold Caldron Mill, Skiplam: from NE

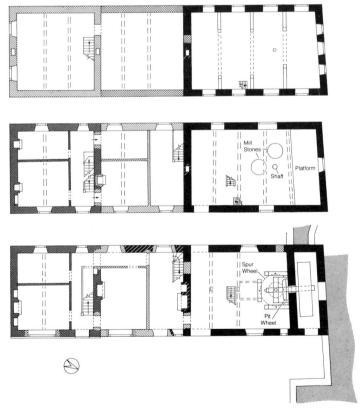

Skiplam [466] (Figs. 334, 345), probably came from a demolished mill upstream of the present structure. Some small mills of only one storey and a loft may be of early 18th-century date; these include that at Lastingham [318], which is earlier than the adjacent house of 1803, and Arden Mill [15] (Fig. 346), built before the attached mid 19th-century miller's house. Small mills satisfying local needs were, however, still being built in the 19th

Fig. 346 [15] Arden Mill, Arden with Ardenside, showing farm buildings

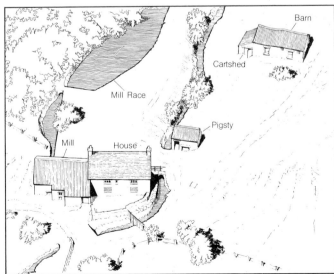

Fig. 345 [466] Hold Caldron Mill:
ground, first and second-floor plans

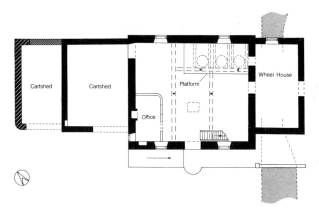
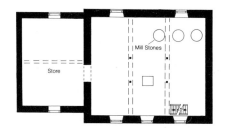
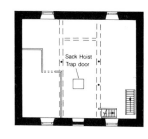
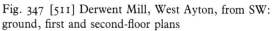

Fig. 347 [511] Derwent Mill, West Ayton, from SW: ground, first and second-floor plans

century along the smaller streams. A small mill might have only one pair of stones but the larger ones had two or three. The largest mills are three-storeyed and, in their ultimate form, of late date, such as the early 19th-century Derwent Mill, West Ayton [511] (Fig. 347), or Levisham Mill [322] of 1846. The largest complex is at Bransdale Mill [40] (Figs. 348–350), which comprises in addition to the mill itself, a house and cottage, and farm buildings including a smithy and haybarn. Sinnington Grange Mill [461] (Fig. 351), built in 1844, is exceptional in being four-storeyed and of brick.

Fig. 348 [40] Bransdale Mill, Bransdale, showing farm buildings

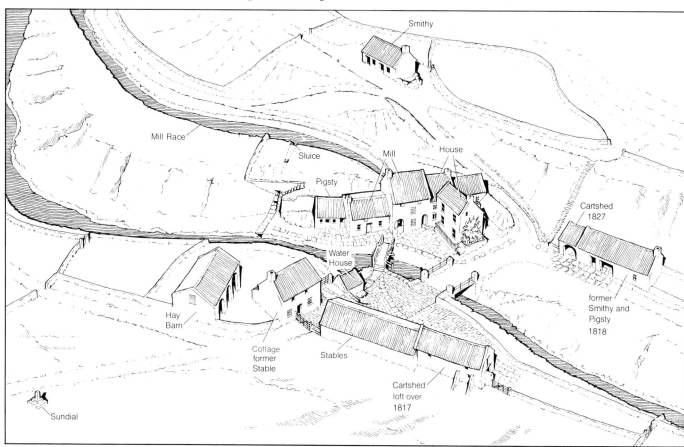

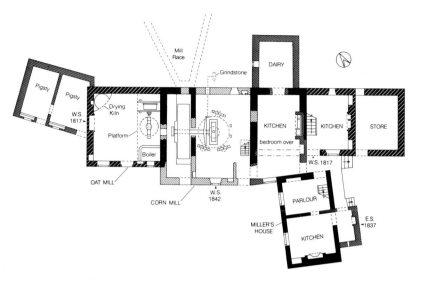

Fig. 349 [40] Bransdale Mill: plan

Fig. 350 [40] Bransdale Mill, showing machinery

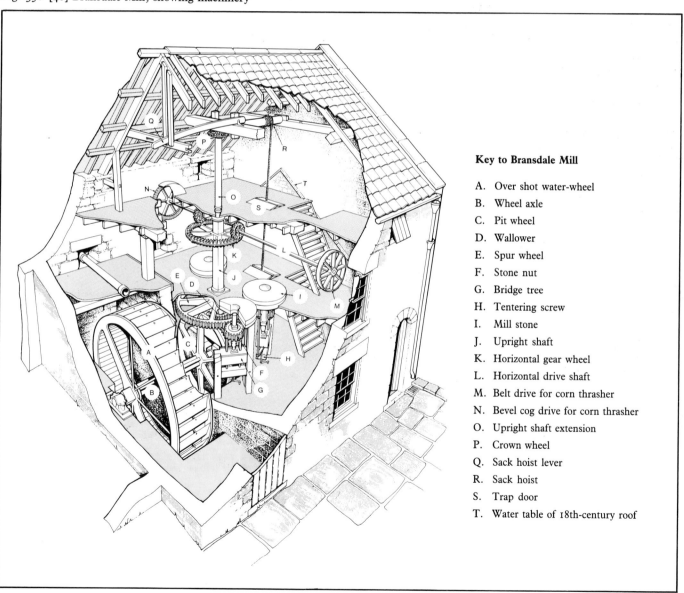

Key to Bransdale Mill

A. Over shot water-wheel

B. Wheel axle

C. Pit wheel

D. Wallower

E. Spur wheel

F. Stone nut

G. Bridge tree

H. Tentering screw

I. Mill stone

J. Upright shaft

K. Horizontal gear wheel

L. Horizontal drive shaft

M. Belt drive for corn thrasher

N. Bevel cog drive for corn thrasher

O. Upright shaft extension

P. Crown wheel

Q. Sack hoist lever

R. Sack hoist

S. Trap door

T. Water table of 18th-century roof

Fig. 351 [461] Sinnington Grange Mill, Sinnington

Fig. 352 [304] Windmill, Kirkbymoorside

The power for grinding corn was provided not only by water but also by animals and the wind. Windmills are rare in the region, though they existed by the 13th century: there was one at Appleton-le-Moors by 1266 (Rushton 1976*a*: 25), and a post mill on a carving at Rievaulx Abbey (McDonnell 1963: 119, Plate VI(a)) may be based on a local example. No other windmills are known before the 19th century. One was built of stone at Stainsacre *c*. 1816 (NYCRO: Reg. Deeds EA, 1816–17). A series of advertisements shows that windmills were also being built at Pickering.

The only surviving windmills are of brick: at Kirkbymoorside [304] (Fig. 352) of 1839, and at Green Lane, Low Hawsker [184], built between 1849 and 1863 by George Burnett (NYCRO: Reg. Deeds IY, 1862–3).

MILLERS' HOUSES

Millers' houses follow a similar development to that of farmhouses; many millers combined milling with farming and their purely domestic needs were not different from those of other men. The miller's house needed to be close to his work, so that many mill houses are adjacent to mills, and are often in line with them. This frequently resulted in a process of alternate rebuilding, with a straight joint between house and mill, as at Iburndale Mill [106]. The house and mill sometimes had a similar relationship to each other as the house and byre have in a longhouse. At High Costa Mill, Aislaby [7] (Fig. 353), two opposed doors in the rebuilt mill of 1819 may represent the position of a former hearth-passage, and another door provided direct access to the mill from the house.

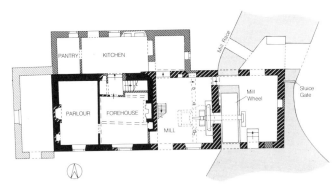

Fig. 353 [7] High Costa Mill, Aislaby

A linear arrangement, usually with intercommunication between the house and mill, was also possible with central-entry houses such as at Appleton Mill [10] (Fig. 354). Elsewhere, the mill and the house were initially separate, as at Bransdale Mill [40], and the desire to escape the smell and noise of their job must have persuaded many millers, including the one at West Ayton [510], that a sizeable gap between house and mill was

desirable. At Rievaulx the miller moved to a house a short distance away from the mill.

Standard forms of house plan were used by millers, as by others: longhouses, three-room linear houses and central-entry houses. Examples are at Kildale [249], Rievaulx [444] and Hawnby [180]. The millers at some of the larger mills could aspire to grander houses than those of the average yeoman farmer, although this may only be evident in the extra accommodation provided by large rear wings behind the central-entry millers' houses at Thornton Dale [496] and West Ayton [510], creating T-shaped plans (Fig. 355). The former was occupied for a time by the youngest son of the lord of the manor.

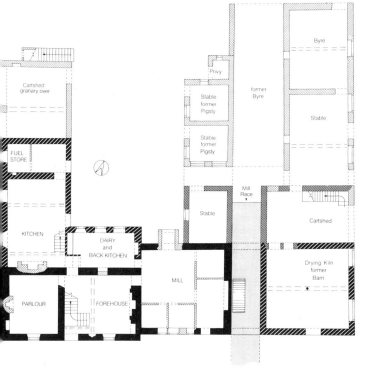

Fig. 354 [10] Appleton Mill, Appleton-le-Moors: from SW and plan

Fig. 355 [510] Derwent Mill Farm, West Ayton

CHAPTER 8

STRUCTURE AND FITTINGS

Regional methods of construction

TIMBER FRAMING

Timber-framed construction is rare in the region, though three conspicuous examples in Helmsley may give a false impression that it is more common. Only eight buildings containing elements of framed structures have been identified, some of them very fragmentary. From documentary or archaeological sources there is evidence of several more that have been demolished. All are in, or on the margins of, the Vale of Pickering, mostly in the three market towns. One less certain case, however, lying further to the north, is at Spout House, Bilsdale Midcable [28], where excavation produced the hint of a framed building earlier than the present cruck-built longhouse.

This limited evidence gives no firm indication of how extensively timber framing was employed in the medieval period, especially in smaller houses. It was certainly used in some of the most superior buildings. At the Duchy of Lancaster's Pickering Castle, Leland noted lodgings built of timber, and Norden's survey of 1619–21 describes the Mote Hall as being of 'postes and pan' construction. This, also known as the New Hall, was built in 1314 (Thompson 1958: 17) though the framing, probably limited to an upper storey, could have been a later addition. Some gentry houses were timber-framed. Excavations at several sites have revealed post holes, such as at the manor houses of Harome [174] and Wilton; they were also found at Neville Castle, Kirkbymoorside, but when a survey was made in 1570 all the buildings were of stone (Dornier 1967–70; Williams 1977). In the 16th and 17th centuries a number of substantial timber-framed houses were built, including Welburn Hall [506] (Fig. 13), High Hall, Kirkbymoorside [259] (Fig. 24), and Rectory House, Helmsley [223] (Fig. 23). Framing also occurs at three buildings which were inns by the 18th century and may have been so originally. Two are in Helmsley; the third, the Black Swan, Kirkbymoorside [285] (Fig. 356), has a timber, two-storeyed porch inscribed 1632, the only precisely dated use of framing in the region.

Jettied upper floors are found only in the porch of the Black Swan and at a building of uncertain purpose in Crown Square,

Fig. 356 [288] The Black Swan, Kirkbymoorside: dated porch

196

Fig. 357 [223] Rectory House, Helmsley: detail of framing of N. wall

Fig. 358 [506] Welburn Hall, Welburn: detail of W. wing

both in Kirkbymoorside. In the city of York all multi-storeyed timber buildings have jettied front walls (RCHM 1972; 1981), which also seems to be generally true of houses in other towns in North Yorkshire. Jettying is virtually unknown in the villages, however, and the unjettied houses in Helmsley and Kirkbymoorside seem to reflect a method of building more rural than urban. The technique of framing, with fairly closely spaced vertical studs and upward bracing from posts to wall-plates (Fig. 357), is similar to that found in the Vale of York (Hutton 1973). In town houses, Rectory House, Helmsley, and Welburn Hall, decorative patterns were created by the use of diagonal strutting (Fig. 358). They are unusual not simply in a local context but in a wider one embracing North Yorkshire generally; no parallels exist closer than West Yorkshire and the style only occurs more commonly in South Lancashire and the West Midlands.

CRUCK CONSTRUCTION

In the North York Moors at least 220 buildings are known where crucks either survive or where their former existence can reasonably be inferred. In only a minority of these is it certain that cruck trusses are preserved *in situ* but there are many instances of the reuse of cruck blades, probably from earlier buildings on the same site. The total also includes a number of buildings demolished within the last one hundred years where the presence of crucks was noted.

The region is the only upland area extending to the east coast of England, and is also the only part on that side of the country where crucks are known to occur in some numbers. To the south there is a scattering on the Yorkshire Wolds and in Holderness, and to the north two examples have been recorded at Sunderland, Tyne and Wear.

Cruck-framed buildings are found throughout the region, though relatively few are known in the parishes along the western margin and in a coastal belt extending about 10 kilometres inland. The thickest concentration is in the south-west where two villages in particular, Harome and Pockley, are notable for the number of cruck-framed houses which survive or are known to have existed until recent times. The greater number here is to some degree a matter of a differential survival rate, and the area was part of the Duncombe Park Estate which was reluctant to improve properties.

All the evidence points towards cruck framing as the normal method of construction in small houses before about the late 17th century, no early houses demonstrably having any other form of roof structure. The crucks are mostly in buildings of longhouse origin and only a few can be associated with a higher social level. Among English medieval buildings the cruck form particularly associated with houses of manorial status, especially those of the 13th and 14th centuries, is the base-cruck. The incomplete remains of the roof structure at Canons Garth, Helmsley [187], includes double tie-beams, one above the other, a feature associated elsewhere with base-crucks, of which the general distribution in England lies south of Yorkshire. The undoubted existence of an example only about 15 kilometres away at Baxby Manor, Husthwaite, North Yorkshire (Harrison and Hutton 1984: 21), however, makes it realistic to postulate one at Helmsley. Even so, the actual evidence at Canons Garth, particularly housings for braces in the lower tie-beams, suggests that an aisled construction is more likely. There is no evidence of cruck construction in any other of the houses of manorial or rectorial status in the region, though three pairs of *forks* were mentioned in 1502 at the Abbot of Whitby's house at Goathland (Turton 1894: 200).

There are other references to *forks* and *siles* in the Pickering area in the very late 15th century (Turton 1895: 204–7), showing that they were not uncommon at that time, whether or not the dominant form. With a lack of other documentary and archaeological evidence it is impossible to determine when crucks were first used in the region. In the absence of any marked sense of development in the surviving crucks, it is difficult to suggest which are the earliest examples and when they were built. The majority are probably of the 17th century but some may have been erected in the later part of the 16th.

The question of how late the method continued to be used before final abandonment is potentially capable of being answered more firmly since the period when this happened is within the date range of the standing buildings. The process is likely to have been gradual, spread over several decades, and it is not easy to identify the latest examples and assign dates to them. The abandonment of cruck construction is intimately connected with the introduction of two-storeyed houses. The cruck is pre-eminently a system suitable for single-storeyed buildings, as cruck blades are obtrusive features hindering free movement on the upper floor of two-storeyed houses. Houses that were two-storeyed throughout therefore represent a late stage in the use of crucks. One is at Wrelton [530], dated 1665; Thorn Hill House, Goathland [165], of 1699, is probably another. There is virtually no evidence of cruck building after 1700. Stangend, Danby [70], was dated 1704 but this probably represents an alteration to an existing cruck house. Timbers were cut for crucks for a hayhouse at Dalby, Thornton Dale, in 1746 (Rushton 1976*b*: 83), but this is an extremely late and isolated instance. By the early 18th century, houses were certainly being erected which were not cruck built.

All crucks in the region are basically similar in form. The form of the apex, for which the standard classification is by Alcock (1981: Fig. 49), is one of the most distinctive regional differences in Britain (Smith in Alcock 1981: 8). All crucks in the North York Moors which have not been altered or reset have the type C apex, with a saddle into which both blades of a truss are tenoned and which directly supports the ridge-piece. In most examples the feet of the blades are buried in the mass of the wall, though some may have been cut off. Where visible they stand on padstones, though whether there is a foundation below these is not known. The other normal components of a truss are a tie-beam and a collar, both of which are halved over the blades and fixed to them by two substantial pegs, driven in at different angles to provide greater resistance to any tendency for the members to pull apart. The frequent occurrence of these halvings and peg holes provides evidence for the reuse of members of cruck trusses.

The tie-beams, which also support the floors in houses with upper storeys, project at each end, presumably to support a wall-plate; this is the normal practice with cruck construction though this detail is invariably hidden in North York Moors buildings. Collars also protrude beyond the blades to support the purlins, an effective though rather unsophisticated method commonly found in crucks in Yorkshire and the East Midlands (Webster 1954), though rare in the West Midlands and Welsh border countries where crucks usually have a more distinctive curved or elbow shape, making it possible for purlins to be directly supported by the blades. Purlins rest directly on the protruding ends of collars, to which they are pegged, and are normally placed orthogonal to them in the attitude normally associated with arcade plates.

The height between tie-beam and collar is often less than 1.5 metres, a dimension not designed for two-storeyed houses except those having a chamber only over the parlour end. With a chamber also over the forehouse and the consequent need for first-floor circulation, a low collar is a distinct impediment. The low headroom of a doorway inserted into such a truss can be seen at Spout House, Bilsdale Midcable [28] (Fig. 165). In many other houses with inserted floors, collars were cut away to provide for a doorway with reasonable headroom, as at Orchard House, Harome [170].

In the relatively few cruck houses built with a complete upper floor, the proportions were arranged to ensure adequate headroom above the tie-beam. At Wrelton [530] (Fig. 359), the height of 2.3 metres even allows a doorway to have a separate head a short distance below the collar. In this and other two-storeyed cruck houses, the eaves level is above that of the tie-beam to allow for the provision of windows lighting the upper floor, and the trusses have spurs tying the blades to the wall-plates.

By the standards of crucks in some parts of Britain the blades of those in the North York Moors are not well shaped. The standards referred to here are primarily smoothness and regularity of outline but the actual shape itself should also be considered. A cruck blade with a greater degree of curvature or a more pronounced elbow shape than a nearly straight one is less intrusive in the interior space of a house and enables purlins to be directly supported on the backs of blades.

The smooth regular curves of the blades at Wrelton make this one of the best examples. That it also may be a fairly late cruck house is not necessarily significant, as a refined finish is probably more a product of wealth and social position rather than chronology. The Wrelton blades are of regular scantling, a quite common characteristic of crucks in the region, and the two blades of each truss are sufficiently mirror images to have been split from a single trunk. The two blades of most other cruck trusses, however, do not reflect each other's shape and have obviously been cut from different trees. It is quite common for blades to have a more distinct curvature in the lower half with a virtually straight part higher up such as at Delves Cottage, Egton [101] (Fig. 360), and Ivy Cottage, Pockley [433]; those at York House, Glaisdale [158] (Fig. 361), are straight apart from an elbow quite low down. Some trusses have blades with

Fig. 359 [530] Cruck Cottage, Wrelton: detail of E. cruck truss

Fig. 361 [158] York House, Glaisdale: cruck truss in House 1

Fig. 360 [101] Delves Cottage, Egton: cruck truss in forehouse

Fig. 362 [174] Old Manor House, Harome: interior as re-erected at Ryedale Folk Museum

a slightly reversed curve, a pair thus making a shape resembling an ogee arch, as at Forge House [169] and the Manor House [174], both in Harome (Fig. 362). Their presence at the latter, the most superior cruck house in the region, could indicate an element of display in the choice of their use; since these blades are large, over 8 metres long; however, they may simply underline the problems of finding timbers of sufficient length. Some crucks have irregularly shaped blades, indicating that even for use in smaller trusses it may not have been easy to find adequate timbers; at Barnclose House, Murton Grange [330] (Fig. 363), one truss has blades with a pronounced double bend in the middle, incidentally confirming that the pair have been split from a single trunk.

Fig. 363 [330] Barnclose House, Murton Grange: cruck truss in E. wall

The existing crucks are all in buildings with stone walls and almost all are internal, that is, they are not placed against gable ends. Because of the frequent and at times major alterations made to cruck buildings, there is no certainty that in those few exceptions where crucks are against a gable wall a further bay has not been removed. In the absence in most houses of firm dating criteria for both the crucks and the walling, it is uncertain whether they are contemporary with each other, but it would be unreasonable to expect that in every example the walling material is a later substitution for something else. In only one building, Spout House, Bilsdale Midcable [28], is there evidence to suggest an earlier timber-framed wall and it is by no means conclusive. The fundamental principle of cruck construction is that the roof load is transmitted directly to the ground by the cruck frame, not by the walls. When original walls were of clay or mud they could be rebuilt in masonry, leaving the roof in

position. Clay walls require cruck trusses in the gable ends, which do not generally occur in the region; in some houses they may have been removed in a later rebuilding, but this is unlikely in every case. It is probable that cruck buildings normally had walls of stone rubble, at least in the 17th century.

The thatched roof of White Cottage, Pockley [430], is unusual in having a hip at the south end. Inside, the ridge-piece extends beyond the southernmost cruck truss as far as the hip, and so that truss obviously does not represent the original gable end of the house. The hip could be a later alteration and a stone gable has been taken down, but its existence raises the question of whether hipped roofs were formerly more common in the region. This might be expected if earth walling had been a normal practice, but it may also be conjectured whether the end of the ridge was supported by an end cruck, or gavelfork, a form known to have existed elsewhere in North Yorkshire (Harrison and Hutton 1984: 7), though no examples have been discovered.

The reuse of crucks

A serious disadvantage of the cruck truss was its intrusion into interior space, hindering free movement. Those parts, especially collars, causing obstruction were frequently removed to allow upper floors to be used more effectively. But even in some houses where upper floors were not subsequently inserted, tie-beams proved to be too low and their centres were cut away; in Pockley this occurred at White Cottage [430] and Moorings [432], in both of which the lower ends of the blades were also sawn off and the trusses then supported on inserted posts below the stub ends of the tie-beams. In a few houses only the lower ends of the blades remain, the whole upper parts of the crucks having been removed; in these cases it was of course necessary to insert complete new roof trusses.

Though crucks became obsolete, they were composed of substantial timbers which, even when two or more centuries old, were capable of much serviceable use; it became common to reuse them, either as a modified form of truss or simply as individual timbers. This seems to have been already happening during the actual period of cruck building and was particularly common in the 18th century, though it probably never ceased, and a 20th-century instance has been recorded (Hayes and Rutter 1972: 50).

A common method of reuse of crucks in houses was as upper crucks. This form is normally defined as a cruck truss with blades rising from a beam at first-floor level in a two-storeyed building; the upper floor is generally a semi-attic with low walls and headroom within the roof space. Rose Marie Lodge, Appleton-le-Moors [9] (Fig. 364), illustrates the method; it was built in the middle of the 18th century and the roof trusses consist of thin cruck blades reused as upper crucks, crossing at the apex to clasp the ridge-piece. At Aspen Farm, Sproxton [483], two cruck trusses were reset when the farmhouse was altered and heightened in the 18th century. They retain saddles and appear to have been lifted up bodily, with the tie-beams removed. In their reset position they are most accurately

Fig. 364 [9] Rose Marie Lodge, Appleton-le-Moors: base of upper cruck truss

Fig. 365 [95] Westwood Farm, Ebberston: raised cruck truss

Fig. 366 [460] Sinnington Lodge, Sinnington: upper crucks

described as raised rather than upper crucks, with their feet built into the walls and not resting on transverse beams. Another example of crucks reset in a raised position is in a byre at Westwood Farm, Ebberston [95] (Fig. 365); at the apex the blades are halved over each other to provide a seating for the ridge, a common characteristic of reused blades.

An ambitious and surprising reuse of crucks in the late 18th century is at Sinnington Lodge [460] (Fig. 366). This superior farmhouse has a full double-pile plan and it might be expected that a truss derived from a pattern book would have been used for the roof, which has a considerable span. The trusses comprise two pairs of superimposed upper crucks. The blades are reused but have been cut back to the thinness more typical of late 18th-century roof members, and in the manner of base-crucks the blades of each do not meet but are connected by a collar which also supports the purlins. The trusses do not rise above the level of the upper collar so that the upper part of the roof is effectively of common-rafter construction.

The ultimate method of reuse of cruck blades was as principal rafters in otherwise normal roof trusses, as at Middle Farm, Cold Kirby [64], built in 1753. The reused blades are recognizable by their generally uneven form and by the housings for tie-beams and collars, cut diagonally across the face, and associated with peg holes; as with other reused cruck blades, they are usually halved across each other at the apex to support the ridge.

THE CONSTRUCTION OF ROOFS

The development of roof construction in the region, as elsewhere, was a matter of providing for certain needs within the limits of available resources, technical ability and imagination. The primary problem governing this development was the construction of a framework to support adequately the pitched roof necessary to cover the space enclosed by a building. In later centuries practical use was often made of the space immediately below the roof itself, necessitating the design of roof structures that were structurally sound but without members which unduly impeded movement around them.

Fig. 367 [477] Foulbridge, Snainton: roof structure of hall

Only two medieval roofs survive in the region, neither of them complete but both relatively early in date and connected with ecclesiastical establishments or patronage. At Foulbridge, Snainton [477], formerly a preceptory of the Knights Templars, there are remains of an aisled hall dated by dendrochronology to *c.* 1288. Of the four pairs of aisle posts, one retains the original arrangement of a slightly cambered tie-beam supporting a crown-post and, a little below, a strainer-beam with a more marked camber (Fig. 367). The rest of the original roof structure was later removed, when the pitch was lowered and the collar-purlin became the ridge. The other medieval roof is at Canons Garth, Helmsley [187], probably the medieval parsonage house built by Kirkham Priory, to which the church was appropriated. There are two trusses but not all that remains is visible, though the original pitch of the rafters is preserved. The most significant feature is a pair of tie-beams separated by what are now the wall-plates; though this method is used elsewhere in some base-cruck trusses, at Canons Garth an aisled structure was more probable. Above the tie-beams are crown-posts cut to an octagonal shape over most of their heights, and there was obviously a complex system of bracing.

Canons Garth was perhaps constructed in the early 14th century, a little later than Foulbridge. Both roofs represent a sophisticated level of construction, of national rather than local significance, by craftsmen familiar with techniques used elsewhere in buildings of elevated status. The roofs of the other major medieval buildings in the region have disappeared, for the halls of Pickering and Helmsley Castles are little more than foundations; even less survives at Cropton Castle, and the large building at Sinnington Hall [458] was re-roofed in the post-medieval period.

Roofs of the immediate post-medieval period, in the late 16th and early 17th centuries, provide a strong contrast in their simplicity, consisting of a simple triangle of principal rafters and tie-beam. They occur at Helmsley in the later wing at Canons Garth [187], the Manor House [209] and Rectory House [223], all timber-framed buildings. In these, purlins are trenched into the backs of the principal rafters and common rafters then laid on top. The visible gable ends are more elaborate with a decorative pattern of framing, also found in the east wing at High Hall, Kirkbymoorside [259] (Fig. 24).

Roofs with simple trusses formed of principal rafters and tie-beams, and sometimes with collars, continued in use as the common vernacular form until the 19th century. The most significant change during this period was an alteration in the method of supporting the purlins and the elimination of a separate common rafter laid on top of the principal; the latter was itself made deeper to support directly the roof laths. A roof of the older type with trenched purlins was used at Thorpe Hall, Fylingdales [117], in 1680, though having no tie-beam, the principals being housed into short sole-plates; another is at the Old Rectory, Pickering [379], built in 1698.

Purlins supported in an even more basic manner, on the backs of principal rafters with no, or only slight, trenching, were used throughout the 18th century, but often only where the principals are reused cruck blades, generally in farm buildings. This method of supporting purlins returned to favour in the later 19th century with the more widespread use of constructional textbooks.

By the later 18th century, the purlin fixing which became almost the only one employed was the tusk-tenon. In this the end of a purlin is cut down in thickness to form a tenon which is then pushed into a through-mortice in a principal rafter so that it protrudes beyond the other side; it is then secured in position by a peg driven through the projecting tenon. A requirement of this method is that each purlin only spans one bay of the roof structure between two pairs of trusses. Another

change, introduced at about the same time, was at the apex of the truss where the principal rafters are housed together; a slight notch was cut into the principal rafter containing the mortice, allowing a small seating to give extra support to the other principal in addition to that provided by the tenon (Fig. 368).

The use of thin, raking queen-struts without collars occurs in a number of trusses to which it must impart a slight extra stiffening, such as at an early 19th-century barn at Mount Pleasant, Nawton [337]. A more common practice was to use vertical queen-struts connecting the tie-beam with principal rafters at about their midpoint, with a strainer-beam spanning between the queen-struts near their heads. One example is in Ashton House, Nawton [334], which, though as late as the second quarter of the 19th century, still has a vernacular quality exemplified by thin timbers with a slightly irregular finish. It is in a usable attic and shows one advantage of this method of construction in that the centre part is clear of obstructions, allowing access. The trusses at Petch House, Kirkbymoorside [277], are very similar but have collars with queen-struts below (Fig. 369). In the town house of a professional man, built *c.* 1785, this hipped roof demonstrates the amount of space available when using this structural technique.

The maximum use of roof space was achieved by continuing the walls to about 1 metre above the attic floor level and using a truss arrangement at each side whereby the tie-beam is inter-

Fig. 368 [59] Rye Topping Farm, Brompton: roof truss

Fig. 369 [277] Petch House, Kirkbymoorside: roof structure

rupted by being housed into a queen-strut connecting principal rafter and floor beam, thereby tying the roof together; further strength is given by a strainer or collar and perhaps by diagonal bracing. An early instance in a domestic context is an 18th-century roof in the Old Vicarage, Kirkbymoorside [291], but the method was used most frequently in the early 19th century in mills and farm granaries; two examples in Skiplam are in Hold Caldron Mill [466] (Fig. 370), and in the granary at Ewe Cote Farm [464]. The truss of this type with the widest span, of 8.4 metres, is at the former Tontine Inn, Market Place, Kirkbymoorside [282], built in 1823.

The use of king-post trusses demonstrates the adoption of designs derived from pattern books rather than from local building practice, as it was not a form traditionally used in the North York Moors. The central uprights in the gable ends of the south-west wing at Canons Garth, Helmsley, and at High Hall, Kirkbymoorside, are not true king-posts as they do not support ridge beams but serve as part of the decorative herring-bone framing. At the Black Swan, Kirkbymoorside, there is, however, an isolated 17th-century example of a short king-post

standing on a collar and braced longitudinally to the ridge-piece, an arrangement more familiar in West Yorkshire.

King-post trusses came into use in the region in the late 18th century. Though the central post, and braces connected to its foot, caused an obstruction, making effective use of the roof space impossible, the soundness of the truss as a structural method was probably the reason for its popularity, especially over large spans. Among the examples recorded there is no sense of development, but sophisticated and complex designs were already available in pattern books, and could be used at will. One particular characteristic of the pattern-book truss is the enlargement of the head and foot of the vertical members with a splay at the points where diagonal struts meet them, to provide a less obtuse angle for the joint. Other features of this truss are the use of bolts, particularly one driven upwards through the tie-beam into the foot of the king-post, and occasionally of iron straps at junctions.

The simplest form of truss is that with a king-post braced to the principal rafters, as used at Low Hall, Kirkbymoorside [265], of c. 1797, and the late 18th-century Rutland House, Harome [173]; at the latter, the roof is not underdrawn but covers a low and unpartitioned second floor used like an attic. The trusses are also only partly underdrawn at Stiltons Farm, Rievaulx [451] (Fig. 167), a three-storeyed double-pile farm-house, where they have additionally a single queen-strut to each side. Similar trusses were also used in the late 18th century at 19 Bridge Street, Helmsley [200], but at Ryedale House, Helmsley [202], the full double-pile depth is spanned by trusses with a pair of queen-struts to each side of the king-post.

In farm buildings the king-post truss was commonly used in barns and horse-engine houses in the 19th century, and there is an elaborate adaptation of it for a polygonal engine-house at Nawton [336] (Fig. 371). In smaller 19th-century houses and cottages roof trusses often have no tie-beams, depending for rigidity on collars placed fairly low down. This was obviously to allow headroom while avoiding the use of a more complicated form of framing.

Fig. 370 [466] Hold Caldron Mill, Skiplam: roof structure

Fig. 371 [336] Mount Pleasant, Nawton: horse-engine house

Building materials of the region

THE USE OF STONE

The North York Moors have a good range of building stone (Fig. 2), although the type and nature of that stone, different techniques of quarrying and dressing, and the wealth and status of those who were building, all combined to influence the final appearance of the structures themselves. Over the northern part of the region, which includes the main moorland block, sandstones of brown to pale buff colour were the local building stone. Easily worked and capable of taking mouldings, they were strong enough to be used for lintels, window mullions and transoms, and for internal walls as thin as 20 centimetres. To the south, in contrast, the limestones and sandstones of the Tabular and Hambleton Hills were generally much less versatile, and mainly suitable only for use as rubble walling. The dominance of limestone in the south-west and sandstone in the south-east is indicated by the colour of the walls in each area, mainly grey-white in the west and brown-yellow in the east. Some better quality sandstone was quarried, particularly near Rievaulx and Hackness, but cost restricted its use to details, if at all, on smaller buildings.

Availability in itself was insufficient to ensure the use of stone. For economic reasons it was first adopted on a large scale in the medieval period only by major secular and ecclesiastical landowners, able to afford its quarrying and dressing. Nevertheless, for the bulk of walling stone, they still had to rely on what was available reasonably locally; only if none was suitable for such details as quoins, doors and windows was it brought from elsewhere. By the 12th century both rubble and ashlar masonry were being used for major buildings, but which was chosen depended very much on location, and this usage continued throughout the medieval period. Similar types of masonry were also employed for gentry houses in the 17th century (Figs. 31, 42), although the size of stone and nature of the tooling varies.

The earliest surviving houses below gentry status are principally of 17th-century date. In the south these have rubble walls of small roughly shaped stones of limestone or sandstone, either coursed (Fig. 103) or randomly laid (Fig. 94). To the north the better quality building stone is reflected in the almost universal use of coursed sandstone rubble, whether in the form of squared oblong stones with a roughly dressed surface (Fig. 87) or of more regularly squared stone with tooled faces (Fig. 101). Roughly dressed rubble continued in use in the 18th and 19th centuries but more regularly finished stone became much more common then. In the south, even the limestone was often cut into blocks of brick-like proportions which, as Marshall (1788: 106) observed, were sometimes combined with sandstone quoins and details (Fig. 148). Dressed squared sandstone rubble gave an even appearance to a wall, akin to that of ashlar, although the evenness varied with the type of tooling. Coarse diagonal tooling was often employed in the 17th century (Fig. 372a) and scutched tooling occurs sporadically from the late 17th century

Fig. 372a [158] York House, Glaisdale

Fig. 372b [179] Hawnby House, Hawnby

Fig. 372c [149] Bainley Bank Cottage, Glaisdale

onwards (Fig. 372b). In the mid to late 18th and 19th centuries, however, the most widespread type was herringbone tooling (Fig. 372c), at times restricted to the sandstone quoins and detailing of buildings otherwise of limestone. Rock-faced masonry became fashionable in the second half of the 19th century, and was extensively used on the rebuilt farms of the Foster Estate at Egton, as well as on contemporary villas, houses and cottages.

The widespread adoption of squared rubble in the 18th century was accompanied by a change in bonding material. Lime mortar was used for the major medieval buildings of the region and in the late 17th century also for structures of lesser social status, including the Old Rectory, Pickering [379], whose building accounts of 1698 include payment for eleven chaldrons of lime. Nevertheless, until it became more generally available in the 18th century, the stone walls of most buildings were bounded with earth. Marshall (1788: 109) wrote that 'formerly ordinary stone buildings were carried up entirely with 'mortar', that is, common earth beaten up with water, without the smallest admixture of lime. The stones themselves and the fillings (of stone) were depended upon as the bonds of union, the use of the 'mortar' being merely that of giving warmth to the building and a degree of stiffness to the wall'. The Danby stonemason, Joseph Ford, confirms this (Ford 1953: 63). Walls constructed in this way were perfectly adequate for cruck-trussed buildings, since they were not load-bearing and could easily be repaired. Buildings with earth mortar were not just of one storey, nor only of rough rubble. House 2 at York House, Glaisdale [158] (Fig. 120), and Caley Becks Farm [108] (Fig.

104) are both storeyed and of dressed rubble, their open joints showing where such mortar has been leached out; later repointing with lime mortar must disguise many other buildings originally built without it. The increased use of lime mortar in the 18th century is related to the spread of storeyed construction, to the associated use of trusses which put loads on to walls, and to the increased use of dressed squared rubble, for all of which its setting properties were invaluable.

THE USE OF BRICK

The shales of the region, and particularly the boulder clay and Kimmeridge clay of the Vale of Pickering and lower parts of Eskdale, were used for making bricks and tiles (Fox-Strangeways 1892: 472). However, because of its abundance, building stone continued to be employed even in some of these areas after the introduction of brick.

Brick was first adopted in the region in the mid 18th century by men of gentry or professional status, who built houses such as Middleton Hall [325], Hawsker Hall [183] (Fig. 52), and 26 Market Place, Kirkbymoorside [284]. At all but Hawsker Hall brick was restricted to the side and rear walls, stone being used at the front, but this usage soon changed in the late 18th and early 19th centuries as brick became a fashionable building material. In some houses, including Petch House [277] (Figs. 63, 65) and Vivers Lodge [278] (Fig. 73), only the front wall is of brick, but in general buildings were constructed entirely of brick (Figs. 72, 373). The differing use of brick in relation to stone probably reflects their comparative costs and accessibility.

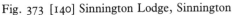

Fig. 373 [140] Sinnington Lodge, Sinnington

Marshall (1788: 109), writing of precisely the area in which most of these buildings occur, observed that 'where stones are far to be fetched, as towards the centre of the Vale [of Pickering], bricks are become a common material. If brick earth be found near the site of building, as it generally may in situations where stones are scarce, clamp bricks are considered in this country where coals may be had at a moderate price, as the readiest and (all things considered) the cheapest walling material'. Brick buildings occur mainly along the northern edge of the Vale of Pickering, and in Hawsker to the south of Whitby, both areas of naturally occurring brick earth, but not in any way to the exclusion of stone buildings. The late 18th and early 19th-century enclosure farms of the Duncombe Park Estate are of stone (Fig. 166), as are its town and village houses and cottages, and the cottages of the Wykeham Estate further east (Fig. 170). Stone maintained its ascendancy into the late 19th century and beyond because of its easy accessibility, in contrast to the expense of digging clay and firing bricks, and because there was a stock of existing stone houses which tended to be altered and extended in the same material.

Fig. 374 [59] Rye Topping Farm, Brompton

MATERIALS USED FOR ROOFING

The range of available roofing materials is indicated by William Marshall's observation that 'formerly straw and a heavy kind of slate were the common coverings; but of late years pantiles have become universal, and blue slate for better houses' (Marshall 1788: 107).

The roofs of most gentry houses in the region were covered with stone slates before the 18th century (Fig. 13), and this material was also used for The Old Rectory, Pickering [379], whose building accounts of 1698 include payment for 'eight rood and a halfe of slating att 16s: the road'. A few farmhouses, including Rye Topping Farm, Brompton [59] (Fig. 374), were similarly roofed, but until the introduction of pantiles, the roofs of most other buildings were thatched (Fig. 99) with heather, ling or rushes or sometimes bulrushes and bracken, all naturally occurring materials; in time, more durable rye and wheat straw was used, the former lasting twenty years, the latter ten (Ford 1953: 57; Hartley and Ingilby 1972: 5). Clearly until there was a surplus of straw not needed to feed animals, naturally occurring materials would have been employed.

The mid 18th century saw the introduction of pantiles (Fig. 138) to the region. From about 1740 they had been imported from northern ports to Whitby, where a tilery was eventually established (Charlton 1779: 340), and tiles were also made near Pickering (Hartley and Ingilby 1972: 6). Sewell (1923: 20) notes that from the Tile Yard at Cropton tiles were carried into Eskdale and its tributary dales, and in 1850 1450 tiles from Loftus were supplied for Lealholme Bridge Inn (Hartley and Ingilby 1972: 7). Parsonage terriers give some indication of the inroads which tiles made on thatch. The earliest detailed terriers for the region mostly date from 1764, but an earlier one for Hawnby describes the newly built parsonage house of 1733 [179] as having 'tiles'. That newly built in Sleights in 1765 [103] also

had 'tiles'. Of the seventeen other terriers of 1764, fifteen note thatched roofs, one of them specifically 'thatched with straw', while two, at Old Byland and nearby Scawton, are part slate, part thatch. That the slate was stone slate is confirmed by the 1817 terrier of Scawton which records a roof 'part tile, part thatch, part flag or thick slate'. The continuing use of thatch, however, is indicated by the terrier of Middleton which recorded in 1764 'the house is rebuilding', and in 1770 the house as 'stone built, thatched'. Thatch seems to have been retained on many parsonages into the 19th century, with rebuilding or renewal gradually taking its toll. Farm buildings were also thatched. The barn, stable and cowhouse at Hawsker, listed in 1777 as the property of Sleights chapelry, were built of stone and thatched; by 1857 they were tiled.

A valuation of Helmsley in 1868 (McDonnell 1963: 309–10) records that, of 256 houses in the town, 66 were thatched, 156 tiled and 34 slated. The nature of the roofing material of the thirty-four slated houses is uncertain; although historically in the region this term had referred to stone slates, by this late date Westmorland or Welsh slate is likely to have been meant (Fig. 230). Later renewal is a problem which besets the identification of original slate roofs, whether of Westmorland or of Welsh slate, but terriers are a valuable source of information, despite their frequent use of the ambiguous term 'slate'. The earliest mention is in a terrier of Glaisdale vicarage which in 1817 was 'built with stones and covered with Westmorland slates'. Three vicarages built in the south of the region in the 1840s, at Thornton Dale in 1841, Great Edstone of 1847 and Sinnington by 1849, all have Welsh slate roofs which the terriers of 1849 all describe as just 'slate'. The specifications drawn up by J. P. Pritchett for the Thornton Dale vicarage, now Comber House [489] (Figs. 59, 60), state that the roof should be 'covered with the best Welsh Countess slates', which were to be nailed with two copper nails each to half inch by one inch Memel laths, the whole to have double eaves and 'be pointed with good lime and hair' (Borthwick, MGA 1841/4).

The change in roofing materials is linked to changing building practices. Thatch was ideally suited to the steep roof pitch associated with crucks, but the more gentle slope of the types of truss replacing them required other materials. Stone slates were appropriate for these, but their weight and the expense of transport counted against them once pantiles became readily available. As Westmorland, Welsh and other slates became obtainable, largely as a result of the spread of railways, so they in turn provided an alternative to pantiles.

The external features of buildings

The principal external features are doors and windows, their forms varying with time, the location of a building, and the status and wealth of its owner. The surviving medieval buildings retain few external details. Only fragments remain from the grange at Laskill Farm [316], and a few doors and windows of various forms at Helmsley and Pickering Castles, Sinnington Hall [462] (Fig. 12), Ayton Castle [512] (Fig. 19) and Danby Castle. Buildings survive more completely from the 16th century onwards, when it becomes possible to trace the evolution of their external features in greater detail. At first the evidence comes entirely from houses of the nobility and gentry, but is later supplemented by buildings of those of inferior social status. From the 17th century onwards, there are the houses of yeomen farmers, from the mid 18th century those of the professional class, and from the late 18th or early 19th century those also of cottagers.

WINDOWS

The earliest surviving post-medieval windows are a few of 16th-century date at Danby Castle, most of them mullioned with arched lights. There are more substantial remains at Helmsley Castle, where the windows of the remodelling of 1563–87 are of two, three or four lights, some with mullions, others also transomed (Fig. 375). The different sizes and types of window reflect the relative importance of rooms, and their range is broadly typical of that found in 17th-century gentry houses, particularly those from early in the century such as Welburn Hall [506] (Fig. 15), Fyling Old Hall [129] (Fig. 35), and Riseborough Hall [504] (Fig. 31). By the middle of the century, however, a change occurred: East Newton Hall [92] has just one multiple-light mullioned and transomed window, the remainder being of two lights, some mullioned, others in the form of a mullioned and transomed window called a cross-window (Fig. 32). Other mid and late 17th-century houses have these smaller windows: Newbiggin Hall, Egton [99] (Fig. 28), originally had timber cross-windows, Thorpe Hall [118] (Fig. 43) just

Fig. 375 Helmsley Castle: west range

mullioned windows, and Thornton Hall [490] cross-windows of stone to the north and evidently timber to the south. Arden Hall [14] (Fig 44), built about 1700, also originally had timber cross-windows. The use of timber at these later buildings is of interest, since it seems to reflect fashionable influences outside the region. The Old Rectory, Pickering [379], built in 1698, reflects the same fashion at a lower social level, for here stone was restricted to the basement windows, timber being used elsewhere.

The mouldings of these windows changed with time, although most were recessed from the face of the wall. The late 16th-century windows at Helmsley Castle are all hollow-chamfered, the 17th-century windows elsewhere almost all splayed (Fig. 379). At two early 17th-century houses, Welburn Hall and Fyling Old Hall, some ovolo mouldings were also used. Some windows had hood mouldings over them; the latest of these occur at East Newton Hall (Fig. 33).

In contrast to the gentry houses, the 17th-century vernacular buildings of the area, mainly the houses of yeomen farmers, were more strongly influenced by local factors. In the mixed limestone and sandstone belt of the south, none has stone mullioned windows and the original windows probably had timber mullions. Almost all have been replaced, but one of the few to remain, the fire window at 86, 86A Westgate, Pickering [411], has a small octagonal timber mullion (Fig. 376). In the

Fig. 376 [411] 86, 86A Westgate, Pickering: fire-window, exterior and interior

north of the region, however, where good quality sandstone was freely available, stone was widely used for windows. Most have flat splayed mullions set flush with the wall-face, their sides either monolithic, composite or coursed in. They are generally of two or three lights (Fig. 101), although occasionally longer (Fig. 144). Recessed mullions are sometimes found; those at Spout House, Bilsdale Midcable [28] (Fig. 377a), as well as the arched lights there, are reused, probably from Helmsley Castle.

Mullioned windows with flush splayed mouldings continued in use in houses in the north of the region during the 18th century, dated examples including Fir Tree, Goathland [164], of 1728, and Street Farm, Glaisdale [144] (Fig. 377b), of 1749. They gradually became less common, however, eventually being relegated to less important parts of the elevation or to inferior buildings. At Crag House Farm, Danby [77], they were restricted to the service end of the farmhouse (Fig. 126), at Hart Hall, Glaisdale [153], to the rear elevation of the 1795 house, and in 1798 to the labourer's cottage at Stormy Hall, Danby [82] (Fig. 173). Square-cut mullions appear on a few buildings: those of 1740 at Brayton House, Goathland [163], are amongst the earliest, and cottages in Fylingdales [130] (Fig. 377c), of 1769, and High Farm, Danby [83], of 1775, also have them. This type never became popular, however, and by the end of the century was restricted to cellar windows, as at New Hambleton Farm, Pickering [419].

The heads of all mullioned windows, however disguised by mouldings, acted as rectangular lintels, and as the use of mullions ceased and timber frames were substituted, different forms of lintel evolved (Fig. 378), initially on gentry houses but later on other buildings. Rectangular stone lintels (Fig. 378a) were sometimes used, or an alternative, still rectangular but in three parts (Fig. 378b). During the 18th and 19th centuries the use of stone lintels spread throughout the region, although in the south they never completely supplanted timber ones. Most of them were basically rectangular and composed of either one or three pieces of stone. The tripartite lintel with projecting keyblock (Fig. 378c) was the commonest form. At times its side pieces are extremely long, at others they become an item of display as part of a rusticated window surround; most of the keyblocks are single, a few double. Monolithic versions of this lintel with the keyblock carved in relief (Fig. 378d) occur occasionally, almost all in the north of the region and of 18th-century date. Lintels with flush, level, but separate keyblocks (Fig. 378e) were used in the late 18th and early 19th centuries.

In the south of the region timber continued to be used for the lintels of houses, cottages and farm buildings in the 18th and 19th centuries. The mid 18th century, however, saw the adoption of the stone flat arch, a form ideally suited to the physical properties of both limestone and inferior quality sandstone. The flat arches were of individual stones, some little better than rubble, others cut into voussoir-like blocks (Fig. 378f). Similar arches, but with a keyblock, were occasionally used in the 18th century and are either entirely of stone or of brick with a stone keyblock. This particular shape was also used throughout the region in the form of a tripartite stone lintel (Fig. 378g).

Fig. 377a [28] Spout House, Bilsdale Midcable

Fig. 377b [144] Street Farm, Glaisdale

Fig. 377c [131] Browcote, Fylingdales

Various lintel shapes evolved from the stone flat arch, monolithic stone versions (Fig. 378h) being the most common. Rectangular lintels, with their ends often dressed back to simulate flat arches or just incised (Fig. 378i), occur in small numbers, mainly in the north; some have simulated voussoirs. A related lintel, also restricted to the north and only slightly more numerous, combined the flat arch and rectangular shapes into a dovetail form (Fig. 378j). Some have tooling simulating individual stones, a few have a projecting integral keyblock. The monolithic rectangular stone lintel (Fig. 378a) was already in use in the 17th century, but its widespread adoption seems to belong mainly to the 19th century, perhaps partly a consequence of larger scale quarrying and improved communications. Not infrequently, shaped lintels on the front elevation were combined with plain rectangular lintels at the rear, but by the end of the 18th century the latter also occur at the front, and during the 19th century became the most common lintel form throughout the region.

In the 19th century, segmental stone or brick arches (Fig. 378k) were used on a few buildings. A number of fire-windows and doors have round-headed arches, which are otherwise mainly restricted to stair and attic windows. Larger arches, most of them segmental, were used on farm buildings and over carriage entrances, often in the towns.

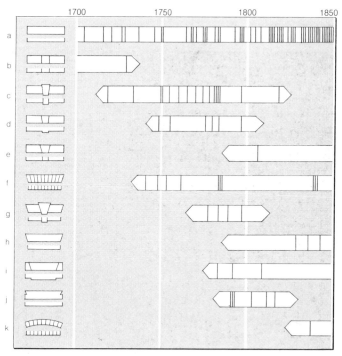

Fig. 378 Date range of lintel shapes, 1700 to 1850

Hood moulds and mouldings were lavished on some 16th and 17th-century windows; their equivalent in the 18th and early 19th centuries was the projecting surround, first used at gentry level (Fig. 47) before being adopted lower down the social scale (Fig. 442; also Figs. 67, 133). As window forms and their proportions changed, so did the type of frame within them.

211

Fig. 379 [117] Thorpe Hall, Fylingdales: casement window

Most mullioned, and mullioned and transomed, windows must have had casement frames (Fig. 379), although some hung-sash frames were introduced during and after the 18th century (Fig. 377c). The horizontally sliding Yorkshire sash was often adopted when mullions were dispensed with, and was also fitted into taller windows (Figs. 380a and b); the hung sash was usually used for narrower windows (Fig. 380c). The late 18th century saw the introduction of the tripartite window in some of the larger houses (Fig. 49), and the early 19th century that of the bow window (Fig. 51).

Fig. 380a [153] Hart Hall, Glaisdale

Fig. 380b [451] Stiltons, Rievaulx

Fig. 380c [2] Pond House, Aislaby

DOORWAYS

A number of doorways survive, in different states of completeness, in the medieval buildings of the region, but most are of later date. In the late 16th and 17th centuries the houses of the nobility and gentry of the region were built on a scale so different from that of contemporary yeoman houses that there was little scope for the filtering down and absorption of architectural forms at lower social levels. This was particularly true of window types and details but less so of doorways, whose similar size offered greater scope for forms to be copied or imitated. The earliest doorways are all derived from the sub-medieval type with its four-centred arch within a chamfered recess. Those of

the late 16th century at Helmsley Castle and of the 17th century at various gentry houses all have false four-centred arches, that is arches with straight rather than curved undersides. The earliest doorways, including one at Helmsley Castle (Fig. 381), have sunk spandrels, while the 17th-century ones (Fig. 382a) have plain spandrels. No house below gentry status has a lintel identical to either of these types but derivatives of them occur, mostly in the late 17th century, a few at the beginning of the 18th century. Two types retain the chamfered recess combined with either an angular underside (Fig. 382b) or one of triangular shape (Fig. 382c); most are plain but a few have scrolls, balls or other carved decoration. Another type has just a chamfered triangular head (Fig. 382d). A simpler form with a flat underside

Fig. 381

Fig. 382a

Fig. 382b

Fig. 381 Helmsley Castle:
doorway in W. range

Seventeenth-century doorways

Fig. 382a [117] Thorpe Hall,
Fylingdales

Fig. 382b [481] Woodman's Cottage,
Spaunton

Fig. 382c [163] Brayton House,
Goathland

Fig. 382d [46] Cowl House, Bransdale

Fig. 382c

Fig. 382d

chamfered to the opening (Fig. 383) came into use alongside these shaped lintels during the late 17th century. It appeared then at Newbiggin Hall [99] (Fig. 17), as well as on yeoman houses, and continued for much of the 18th century. The lintel with a segmental head (Fig. 384), often not chamfered, developed during the 17th century. In contrast to the other forms, it occurred mainly on farm buildings.

The 18th and 19th centuries saw other types of monolithic and multiple-form lintels (Fig. 378); simple timber lintels were used too. Identical types were often set over all openings, but the effect was sometimes relieved by having different forms for door and window (Fig. 236) or even for different windows (Fig. 139). External doorcases, which first appeared in the 18th century, were generally restricted to better quality houses. The earliest had simple mouldings (Fig. 385a) and some had flat hoods (Figs. 385b and c), but by the late 18th and 19th centuries most had semicircular fanlights and pedimented surrounds with pilasters or columns (Figs. 385d and e).

Fig. 383 [166] Hunt House, Goathland: lintel of 1685

Fig. 384 [148] Bainley Side Farm, Glaisdale: lintel of 1749

Fig. 385a [521] Carter Cl., Wombleton

Fig. 385b [62] Manor, Cloughton

Fig. 385c [103] Old Vicarage, Sleights

Fig. 385d [460] Sinnington Lodge

Fig. 385e [2] Pond House, Aislaby

Fig. 386 Helmsley Castle: chamber in W. range

The internal fittings of buildings

The internal fittings of buildings reflect, by their presence, quality and conformity to fashionable taste, the status, wealth and aspirations of their builders and succeeding occupiers. They are however, generally better indicators of changes in lifestyle and taste than are external features, since they were more readily adapted or added in response to variations in prosperity, social requirements or fashion.

THE 16TH AND 17TH-CENTURY HOUSES OF THE NOBILITY AND GENTRY

Little of note in the way of internal fittings survives in the region before those of the late 16th century at Helmsley Castle, which include the panelling, plasterwork and carved stone fireplaces of the great chamber and withdrawing chamber, both completed in 1582, and the fireplaces in the now semi-ruinous west tower. The fittings of the two chambers (Fig. 386) are similar to the almost contemporary but even more elaborate great chamber built by Sir William Fairfax at nearby Gilling Castle (Girouard 1978: Pl. 51; Bilson 1905–7); there, the use of strapwork and geometrical panels forms a link with a fireplace and overmantel at the early 17th-century Riseborough Hall (Fig. 387). The

Fig. 387 [504] Riseborough Hall, Thornton Riseborough: fireplace and overmantel

overmantel is associated with wainscotting of small square panels of characteristic early to mid 17th-century type found in a number of other gentry houses, including Arden Hall [14], Newbiggin Hall [99], Church House, Ebberston [96], East Newton Hall [92], and Low Hall, Brompton [56]. Much of this panelling has been subsequently reset but it is all moulded in one way or another, and some at Church House has a carved frieze. The panelling at East Newton Hall (Fig. 388), built 1656–62, is associated with an overmantel whose bolection-moulded oval panels reveal an awareness of contemporary fashion in internal decoration. There is no similar awareness at

Fig. 388 [92] East Newton Hall: fireplace, overmantel and panelling

Fig. 390a [129] Fyling Old Hall, Fylingdales

Fig. 389 [174] Old Manor House, Harome: decoration

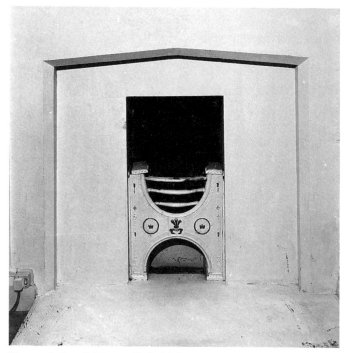

Fig. 390b [117] Thorpe Hall, Fylingdales

Thorpe Hall [117], built in 1680, which is conservative in its detailing if not in plan. Where used, panelling was almost certainly restricted to the principal rooms, the others having stud partitions or plastered walls. At the Manor House, Harome [174], the studs are stencilled with early 17th-century paintings (Fig. 389), a rare survival.

The late 16th and early 17th-century fireplaces at Helmsley Castle and Riseborough Hall (Figs. 386, 387) have more elaborately carved stone surrounds than those in 17th-century gentry houses, though most are derivatives of the same type. Lesser fireplaces remain from the 1629 remodelling at Fyling Old Hall

[129], both with false four-centred heads, one chamfered, the other within a wider moulded recess (Fig. 390a). The fireplaces at Church House, Ebberston [96], and New Hall, Arden with Ardenside [16], are of related forms; the chamber fireplaces at Thorpe Hall are simpler and just chamfered, one with a false four-centred head, the other a triangular head (Fig. 390b).

Few early staircases survive. There are some early 17th-century balusters, reset, at Arden Hall, and the altered staircase at Thorpe Hall incorporates others of 1680. The staircase at The Old Rectory, Pickering, built in 1698, has bulbous balusters of a more characteristic late 17th-century form (Fig. 391).

Fig. 391 [379]
The Old Rectory, Pickering:
staircase

The internal fittings of the various 17th-century gentry houses in the region were of little relevance to the majority of other houses, most of them the dwellings of men of yeoman status and below. These latter houses, mainly of 17th-century date, had comparatively plain interiors whose most notable features were frequently part of their basic structure. This applies particularly to fire areas, which in a majority of houses in the late 17th century contained the only fire. Bounded by a rear stone wall, heck and hearth beam, they were surmounted by a firehood and frequently lit by a fire-window. Hecks screening the fire from draughts were often entirely of timber, or of timber on a stone base, and sometimes formed the back of a narrow bench with a shaped end. All originally stopped against a heck post, some of which had a carved head, the carving usually a single saltire between or above a series of wide or narrow bands (Figs. 392a, b and c). This style of carving, the date of 1664 inscribed on one from Postgate Farm, Glaisdale [159], and the types of buildings in which some still remain, all indicate a 17th-century date. These 'witch posts', a term not used until the present century, are almost entirely restricted in their distribution to the North York Moors region (Hayes and Rutter 1972: 87–95; Hartley and Ingilby 1972: 8–10). Hearth beams supporting firehoods were sometimes chamfered and stopped; where the front of the fire area coincided with a cruck truss, as at Spout House [28] (Fig. 97) and Oak Crag [116] (Fig. 99), its tie-beam often served as the hearth beam, but when the fire area backed on to a cruck truss, as at Delves Cottage [101] (Fig. 102) and Cruck Cottage [530] (Fig. 123), tie-beam and collar might support the studs at the rear of a timber firehood. Funnel-shaped firehoods were built either of timber, with infill panels of wattle and daub between studs (Fig. 393), or of stone (Fig. 394); the former were more common. The stone walls at the back of fire areas, whether low or full height, were fire walls against which the fire burnt, and it became customary to set salt boxes and spice cupboards in them to keep their contents dry and close to hand. Stone salt boxes (Frank 1970), used to store salt for preserving meat and for cooking, were made from two hollowed-out blocks of sandstone, the upper with a square hole for a wooden door, the lower with a trough for the salt. They occur almost exclusively in the north of the region, where stone of appropriate size was readily available. None retains its original wooden door, although one at Carr Cote (Fig. 395) has the rebate for a door frame, and another at Stangend [70] the holes for the pivots. Spice cupboards for storage of spices and other dry foods occur more widely than salt boxes. These were generally small, often little larger than salt boxes but distinguishable from them in having no troughs. They often had carved wooden frames, some scratch-moulded like contemporary run-through panelling, others with more geometrical carving; the doors vary in their elaboration (Fig. 396). An inscribed stone surround at Laverock Hall (Fig. 396c) is unusual.

Fig. 392a [155] Quarry Farm, Glaisdale: heck post
Fig. 392b [101] Delves Cottage, Egton: detail of heck post
Fig. 392c [116] Oak Crag, Farndale East: detail of heck post

Fig. 392a

Fig. 392b

Fig. 392c

Fig. 393 [361] 35 Burgate, Pickering: timber firehood

Excluding the fire area and the limited contribution made by furniture and domestic fittings, house interiors were quite plain. Stud partitions relieved the blandness of lath and plaster in a few, panelling hardly ever being afforded; both, however, occur at Oak Crag, Farndale East (Fig. 160). Where not later insertions, beams rarely have more than a chamfer. Heated parlours were not particularly common in the 17th century; one of the few surviving parlour fireplaces is at Oak Crag (Fig. 397), its moulded surround, though cut into, similar to that on a doorway at Spaunton dated 1695 (Fig. 382b).

Spice cupboards

Fig. 396a [243] Mole End, Hutton Buscel

Fig. 396b [270] 14 High Market Place, Kirkbymoorside

Fig. 396c [314] Laverock Hall, Laskill Pasture

Fig. 394 [158] York House, Glaisdale: stone firehood, House 2

Fig. 395 [311] Carr Cote, Laskill Pasture: salt box

Fig. 397 [116] Oak Crag, Farndale East: parlour fireplace

THE 18TH-CENTURY HOUSES OF THE NOBILITY, GENTRY AND PROFESSIONAL CLASSES

Since there was little building activity by the gentry of the region in the late 17th century, the changing fashions in internal decoration in Restoration England are poorly represented. The early 18th century, however, saw a revival of building, and the established baroque style is reflected in the bolection-moulded doors (Fig. 398), chimney-pieces and panelling at Arden Hall, of about 1700. Its staircase (Fig. 399) with bulbous balusters is accomplished in design and construction, the profile of its blind ramped handrail being reflected in the raised panelling of its dado. East Newton Hall also underwent some refitting at this time, as indicated by bolection-moulded chimney-pieces (Fig. 388). As a result of fire, little is known of the fittings at Duncombe Park, built 1713–18, but those at Ebberston Hall of 1718 have bolection, cyma and other mouldings. They have much in common with such local and contemporary baroque craftsmanship, such as that at Beningbrough Hall. This is surprising in a house built to the design of Colen Campbell, one of the prime movers of the neo-Palladian movement in 18th-century Britain, but it accords with what is known at other houses of his design (Beard 1966: 51–4; Hall and Hall 1973: 53–4; Harris 1981: 120–1).

A number of slightly later gentry houses, including Hawsker Hall [183], Esk Hall [105], Thornton Hall [490] and the Manor House, Cloughton [62], indicate how different aspects of metropolitan styles were adopted locally with a varying time-lag and different emphases. All use bolection and raised mouldings to different degrees, at Hawsker Hall over the fire area of the 'house', on the parlour chimney-piece at Esk Hall and at Cloughton on fireplace overmantels (Fig. 400). All, however, make greater use of cyma-shaped and quarter-round mouldings for architraves and sometimes for chimney-pieces. Esk Hall and Cloughton have a simpler type of stone chimney-piece. Panelling, always recessed and often fielded, is either two or three panels high. No staircase now survives at Cloughton, and although those in the others have pedestals incorporating forms derived from 17th-century balusters, they are combined with columns in the most fashionable way (Fig. 401).

Not until the mid 18th century do the interiors of gentry houses show the influence of the neo-Palladian style. One of the earliest is Aislaby Hall [6], the Hayes' family mansion near Pickering. Its formal exterior is matched by an almost equally formal interior, its entrance hall with full Doric entablature (Fig. 48), staircase lit by a Venetian window with Ionic surround (Fig. 402), and doorcases with pulvinated friezes, some under

Fig. 398 [14] Arden Hall, Arden with Ardenside: door, c. 1700

Fig. 399 [14] Arden Hall: staircase

Fig. 400a [183] Hawsker Hall

Fig. 400b [105] Esk Hall, Sleights

Fig. 400c [62] Manor House, Cloughton

Fig. 401 [490] Thornton Hall, Thornton Dale: staircase

Fig. 402 [6] Aislaby Hall: staircase window

Fig. 403a Aislaby Hall: dining room

Fig. 403b Aislaby Hall: sitting room

Fig. 403c Aislaby Hall: first-floor room

Fig. 403d Thornton Hall: hall

broken pediments. The main rooms display a hierarchy of treatment: the dining room has an enriched chimney-piece and panelling above a carved dado rail (Fig. 403a), while other rooms have chimney-pieces of less elaboration and either dado panelling or only a dado rail (Figs. 403b and c). Doors are of six panels throughout: on the first floor they have the more fashionable narrow top panels, in contrast to the more traditional narrow centre panels of those on the ground floor. Aislaby Hall was completely rebuilt in the new style but some gentry houses were just partly refitted, as reflected by panelling and a staircase at Newbiggin Hall [99], a staircase at East Newton Hall [92], and

a chimney-piece at Thornton Hall [490] (Fig. 403d). Panelling of similar style was used a little lower down the social scale in the mid 18th century. The Bay Tree [120], built in 1764, has fully panelled ground and first-floor rooms, the panelling differing in detail and enrichment (Fig. 404); the chimney-pieces are as classical and correct as the Venetian window on the staircase with its Doric surround. The Old Vicarage, Sleights [103], built by the patron of the living in 1765, is understandably less elaborate internally than the Bay Tree, although the dining room, originally with dado panelling, has an arched side recess and an enriched stone chimney-piece (Fig. 405) which recalls

Fig. 404 [120]
The Bay Tree, Fylingdales:
panelled first-floor
room

Fig. 405 [103]
The Old Vicarage, Sleights:
dining room

223

Fig. 406a [200] 19 Bridge Street, Helmsley

Fig. 406b [277] Petch House, Kirkbymoorside: ground floor

Fig. 406c Petch House: first floor

one in Thornton Hall (Fig. 403d). Panelling was restricted elsewhere in the house to fireplace walls as was more commonly so in other buildings.

Following fashion elsewhere, panelling was used in a very limited way, if at all, in the late 18th century. A professional man's house at 19 Bridge Street, Helmsley [200], has just a dado rail to the staircase and its simple but elegant chimney-pieces (Fig. 406a) bear no trace of the neo-classical style of Robert Adam as reflected by the composition ornaments of the chimney-pieces in Petch House [277] (Figs. 406b and c), or the fittings of the parlour at Orchard House, Nawton [331] (Fig. 407). Woodlands [41], however, with its chimney-pieces, mahogany

doors with beaded panels, and moulded and enriched cornices and ceilings, is the finest manifestation of this style. The chimney-pieces in most of the principal rooms are enriched with applied composition ornament (Figs. 408 a to d), some of them motifs used by the York carver, Thomas Wolstenholme (RCHM 1975: liv, Pls. 110–15. The same motifs occur on a chimney-piece at nearby Pond House [2] which also has plasterwork ceilings and cornices with Adamesque detailing (Fig. 409), and at Kingthorpe House [254] (Fig. 410). Other craftsmen or sources are indicated by the completely different range of motifs on chimney-pieces at Cliff Grange, Snainton [473], and elsewhere.

Fig. 407 [331] Orchard House, Nawton: parlour

Fig. 408 [4] Woodlands, Aislaby: fireplaces

Fig. 408a Drawing room

Fig. 408b Library

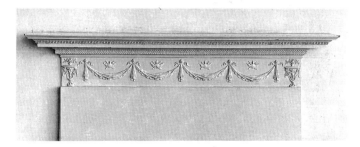

Fig. 408c SW first-floor room

Fig. 408d SE first-floor room

Fig. 409 [2] Pond House, Aislaby: details of entrance hall ceiling

Fig. 410 [254] Kingthorpe House: drawing-room fireplace

Fig. 411a [277] Petch House, Kirkbymoorside

Fig. 411b [103] The Old Vicarage, Sleights

The mid 18th-century change of style in internal decoration was reflected in staircases by the adoption of balusters with bulb-shaped or urn-shaped pedestals (Figs. 411a and b). The bulb-shaped pedestals are sometimes well proportioned, sometimes not, and the urn-shaped pedestals are generally simply moulded. Only at such high quality houses at Aislaby Hall [6] (Fig. 48) and Woodlands [4] were mouldings lavished on them. Both pedestal types continued in use until the end of the century, although some late 18th-century staircases have more fashionable square balusters. The compact form of staircase, rising in two flights separated by a half landing, which had been established earlier in the century, was used in many of these houses for the rest of the century. Most have open strings with shaped cheekpieces, and a few are cantilevered; close strings are rare.

18TH-CENTURY HOUSES OF THE YEOMEN AND COTTAGERS

Two main developments, the spread of storeyed construction and an increase in the number of heated rooms, affected the type of internal fittings in 18th-century farmhouses and cottages. The fire area continued to be incorporated in some houses, but with changes. As in the 17th century, its principal components were still the heck, hearth beam and firehood. Hecks, however, were of more varied construction, some plastered, others of plank and muntin construction (Fig. 392a), of panelling (Fig. 412) or of stone (Fig. 413); some still acted as the backs of benches, often with shaped ends. Heck posts were almost invariably plain. Hearth beams were often chamfered and stopped, and in the mid to late 18th century frequently had shelves on which family possessions, among other things, were displayed. Most shelves are moulded and dentilled, and contemporary with the hearth beam (Fig. 414), but some were added to existing beams as part of the continuing process of modernization and change. Firehoods, some concealed by partitions, were built of timber with a lath and plaster covering (Fig. 415), although use was still made of stone (Fig. 416).

A major change, however, was the replacement of the open fire by an iron range set within a stone fireplace. One of the earliest of these fireplaces, of mid 18th-century date (Fig. 417b), well illustrates how smoke was funnelled into the firehood, though the range has been removed. It is typical of those used for this purpose in the 18th and early 19th centuries, other 18th-century examples having either simple (Fig. 417a) or more elaborate (Fig. 417c) corbels. The corbel-headed form was

Fig. 412 [173] Rutland House, Harome: forehouse fireplace and heck

Fig. 414 [156] Postgate Farm, Glaisdale: forehouse, showing shelf over fireplace

Fig. 413 [314] Laverock Hall, Laskill Pasture: heck and bench in forehouse

Fig. 415 [290] 30 Piercy End, Kirkbymoorside: firehood behind panelling

Fig. 416 [311] Carr Cote, Laskill Pasture: fireplace and firehood

Fig. 417a [180] Mill House, Hawnby

Fig. 417b [290] 30 Piercy End, Kirkbymoorside

Fig. 417c [157] Low London, Glaisdale

particularly well suited for use with firehoods; it occurs much less frequently with ranges whose smoke was removed through flues incorporated in walls. The widespread use of the iron range had another effect on the area around the cooking hearth, for it restricted the amount of heat transmitted to walls and reduced the efficiency of salt boxes. Although the latter, as well as spice cupboards, were sometimes retained or reset, there was a marked increase in the number of larger cupboards set close to these new fireplaces (Fig. 418). They varied in form and in their number of panels, some having drawers at the base (Fig. 419).

Fig. 418 [95] Westwood Farm, Ebberston: fire area in house

Fig. 419a [77] Crag House, Danby: cupboards

Fig. 419b [91] Woodhead Farm, Danby

Fig. 419c [290] 30 Piercy End, Kirkbymoorside: cupboards in forehouse

Fig. 420a

Fig. 420b

Fig. 420c

Fig. 420d

Fig. 420e

Eighteenth-century staircases

Fig. 420a [190] 23 Bondgate, Helmsley

Fig. 420b [521] 1 Carter Close, Wombleton

Fig. 420c [154] Red House, Glaisdale

Fig. 420d [90] Fryup Hall, Danby

Fig. 420e [460] Sinnington Lodge

During the 17th century only a few houses were of two storeys, but as more were built or rebuilt as such, the staircase became increasingly important. In vernacular as in polite architecture, although beginning as a purely functional feature, it became a mode of display. Sometimes it was set in a common 17th-century position at the rear of the forehouse, often behind a partition (Fig. 105), and only rarely had balusters (Fig. 420a). During the first half of the 18th century, however, staircases were incorporated in entrance passages or halls (Fig. 145), or set in their own compartments, arrangements becoming commonplace later in the century (Fig. 149). Balustrades were at first commonly of splat balusters (Figs. 420a and b), but by the middle of the century the balusters were usually turned. Some of the latter (Fig. 420c) show an uncertain understanding of forms, while others (Figs. 420d and e) reflect the standardized forms in gentry and professional houses. There is variety in the arrangement, construction and form of these staircases, many rising with a half landing in the manner customary in gentry houses from the early 18th century. At the lower social level, however, close strings were often used in the mid 18th century and open strings later. Fashionable styles were being adopted but often with a delay, the length of which varied. The lattice

balustrade at Glaisdale Head (Fig. 162) must have been contemporary with others of its kind in York (RCHM 1981: lxxxix, 146, Fig. 88), and square balusters also appear in the late 18th century.

The internal walls and partitions of 18th-century houses and cottages were often of lath and plaster, less commonly of stone or brick; in some, timber was used for partitions and panelling. Plank and muntin partitions occur in a few houses in the mid 18th century, including the 1740 work at Brayton House, Goathland [163], and panelling, mostly in two heights, in others of mid to late 18th-century date. Few houses have fully panelled rooms, since panelling, evidently expensive, was used in a restricted way. It divides up ground and first floors at Westwood Farm, Ebberston [95] (Fig. 421), divides forehouse and inner room at Rose Marie Lodge, Appleton-le-Moors [9] (Fig. 142), screens off the staircase at Slidney Beck, Glaisdale [150] (Fig. 108), and creates first-floor landings or subdivides first floors at Street Farm [144], Crag House Farm [77], and Rutland House [173]. At 27, 29 Brook Lane, Danby [68] (Fig. 162), panels divide off a box bed on the ground floor. Red House, Glaisdale [154], has a plank dado in the parlour, 30 Piercy End, Kirkbymoorside [290], panelled parlour and stair dado. Panelled shut-

Fig. 421 [95] Westwood Farm, Ebberston: panelling in parlour

Fig. 422 [451] Stiltons, Rievaulx: window with panelled shutters and seat

ters, at times accompanied by window seats, were more common (Fig. 422). Plank panels divide off the box beds at Sinnington Lodge (Fig. 168). For much of the 18th century the doors in these houses were of two or four panels; though used from earlier in the century at a higher social level, six-panel doors were not adopted until the late 18th century.

The 18th century saw an increase in the number of heated rooms in houses, but few chimney-pieces survive from before the middle of the century. Those in the parlour and chamber over it at Westwood Farm, though simpler, are similar in form to those in some early 18th-century gentry houses (Figs. 400b and c); others of related type occur in the chambers over the parlours at Street Farm (Fig. 423a) and Red House, the latter without the fielded panel. Parlour fireplaces with simple segmental stone heads survive from the mid 18th century, including one at High Elm House, Bransdale [48]. A clumsy awareness of classical forms is shown by a number of chimney-pieces, including one of 1770 in the chamber over the parlour at Crag House Farm, Danby [77], and another of 1780 at York House (Fig. 423b). Both are of stone. Chimney-pieces of better form and proportion were by then common in other houses in the region (Fig. 423c). A few fireplaces have walk-in or wall cupboards beside them. Those in the parlour of 1797 at Hart Hall (Fig. 424) flank a chimney-piece of mid 18th-century style; in their form they recall a cupboard in the 'Dining Room' at Red House, built in 1748 (Fig. 145).

Fig. 424 [153] Hart Hall, Glaisdale: parlour fireplace and cupboards

Fig. 423a [144] Street Farm, Glaisdale

Fig. 423b [158] York House, Glaisdale

Fig. 423c [451] Stiltons, Rievaulx

Fig. 425a [129] Fyling Old Hall

Fig. 425b [125] Fyling Hall

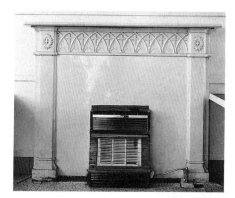

Fig. 425c [117] Thorpe Hall

Fig. 425d [56] Low Hall, Brompton

Fig. 425e [102] Carr View, Sleights

Fig. 425f [346] Beck Isle, Pickering

19TH-CENTURY INTERIORS

The interiors of various gentry and professional houses refitted in the very early 19th century, including Old Byland Hall [340], Kingthorpe House [254] and Cliff Grange, Snainton [473], show a continuation of the late 18th-century forms in their staircases, doors and chimney-pieces. There was soon a marked change in style, which is most completely demonstrated in the houses built or altered by professional men in the 1820s. Fyling Old Hall [129], Fyling Hall [125], Vivers Lodge [278], Carr View [102] and Esk Hall [105], although with some fittings of types already common in the late 18th century, also have doors, windows, chimney-pieces and cornices incorporating innovative convex mouldings and corner blocks. The mouldings are plain, fluted or reeded, and the corner blocks plain, carved with a roundel, or bearing an applied patera or lion's mask (Figs. 425a and b, 426a; also Fig. 46). Carr View also has some different, though related, fittings (Figs. 425e, 426b). Houses of equivalent status with similar fittings include Thorpe Hall [117] (Fig. 425c), High Hall, West Ayton [509], and Low Hall, Brompton [56] (Fig. 425d), and they are also found in some larger farmhouses, including Foulbridge [477]. Contemporary staircases include both established and more up-to-date forms. Esk Hall [105]

(Fig. 46) and Carr View [102] are among the houses with square balusters in the manner of late 18th-century examples, but more typically 19th-century turned forms occur at Fyling Hall [125] (Fig. 427a) and The Elms, West Ayton [508]. Comber House [494] has cast-iron balusters of a type used by the same architect elsewhere (Fig. 427b; RCHM 1981: xci, 52, Fig. 11x). The Gothic Revival is less well represented, its detailing rarely passing beyond the intersecting glazing bars of some stair windows. Beck Isle [346], however, has chimney-pieces, doors, windows and cornices in this style (Fig. 425f).

A number of farmhouses were partly refitted in simpler ways in the first half of the 19th century. In some the fire area was retained but heck, seat and fireplace were updated. Corbel-headed fireplaces continued to be used to house cooking ranges, some inserted in existing fire areas, others just against a wall (Figs. 428a and b). An increasing number lack corbels and have flat surrounds with simple mouldings (Fig. 428c). In many farmhouses, and in almost all cottages, doors and fireplaces were usually the only fittings of note, the former generally of four panels or just ledged and battened, the latter quite plain. Staircases frequently rose between walls or behind partitions, at times having a landing balustrade (Fig. 429).

Details of construction and fittings illustrate the gradual

233

Early 19th-century doorways

Fig. 426a [278] Vivers Lodge, Kirkbymoorside

Fig. 426b [102] Carr View, Sleights

Early 19th-century staircases

Fig. 427a [125] Fyling Hall

Fig. 427b [489] Comber House, Thornton Dale

Fig. 426a

Fig. 426b

Fig. 427a

Fig. 427b

234

Fig. 428a [18] Cliff Cottage, Beadlam

Fig. 428b [157] Low London, Glaisdale

Fig. 428c [46] Cowl House, Bransdale

Fig. 429 [333] Manor Farm, Nawton: landing balustrade

Fig. 430 [419] New Hambleton, Pickering: staircase

235

decline of vernacular building under the influence of polite architecture, a process which can be readily observed in the North York Moors. The longhouse, formerly predominant in the region, could not be made symmetrical in appearance, and its asymmetry was accentuated by the introduction of the fire-window and the separate byre door. The centralized plan, introduced in the 17th century for the houses of wealthy yeomen, was not adopted on a wide scale in the region until after 1750. As the farmhouse with a central doorway and symmetrical elevation became widespread, internal details improved and staircases were introduced, often set at the rear of an entrance hall as a display feature. Dressed stonework, moulded doorway and window surrounds accompanied improvements in plan. However, only a few buildings in the area, such as Duncombe Park, Ebberston Hall and Hackness Hall, were designed by known architects. Elsewhere, even at gentry level, masons using copybooks were probably the designers, working on or influencing the farmhouses of the yeomen and the town houses of the professional classes. Most of the buildings discussed in this book are, in their plans, appearance and details, even though often much altered, true examples of vernacular architecture.

LIST OF BUILDINGS RECORDED

Arranged by civil parishes and containing buildings discussed in the volume with their national grid references, as well as all others in the survey area which have been recorded in detail. The Commission record cards also have information on over 3000 other pre-1850 houses and farms in the North York Moors which were photographed and briefly described in the preliminary survey for the volume. For many of these, particularly in the towns, documentary sources are also noted.

AISLABY near Whitby
[1]   Church Farm (NZ 860086)
[2]   Pond House (NZ 85830878)
[3]   White Row, 36–44 Main Road (NZ 85830873)
[4]   Woodlands (NZ 861080)
[5]   Groves Mill (NZ 866082)

AISLABY near Pickering
[6]   Aislaby Hall (SE 77588568)
[7]   High Costa Mill (SE 777839)

ALLERSTON
[8]   Allerston Hall (SE 87778297)

APPLETON-LE-MOORS
[9]   Rose Marie Lodge (SE 73548782)
[10] Appleton Mill (SE 746879)
Also recorded: Hamley; Ridings Barn

ARDEN WITH ARDENSIDE
[11] Cow Wath (SE 523931)
[12] Harker Gates (SE 526916)
[13] St Agnes House (SE 529914)
[14] Arden Hall (SE 519906)
[15] Arden Mill (SE 521907)
[16] New Hall (SE 531904)
Also recorded: Far House; Lower Locker Farm; Brewster Mill

BEADLAM
[17] White Cottage (SE 65228479)
[18] Cliff Cottage (SE 65308461)
[19] Town End Farm (SE 65348465)
[20] The White Horse Public House (SE 65438461)
[21] Old Vicarage (SE 65498460)
[22] Higher Farm (SE 636891)
[23] Lower Farm (SE 638875)
Also recorded: Pretty Cottage; The Laundry; South View; Rose Cottage; High Farm; Manor Farm; Middle Farm: Hill Crest; Southfields; Gale House

BILSDALE MIDCABLE
[24] Orterley (SE 558984)
[25] Stingamires (SE 563958)
[26] High Crosset (SE 576949)
[27] Low Crosset (SE 576946)
[28] Spout House, formerly The Sun Inn (SE 574936)
Also recorded: Raisdale Mill; East Bank House

BILSDALE WEST SIDE
[29] Malkin Bower (SE 571944)
[30] Fieldhouse (SE 568942)
[31] Fieldhouse (SE 566937)
[32] Helm House (SE 568934)
[33] Fieldhouse (SE 564934)
[34] Bumper Castle (SE 551924)
[35] Low Wethercote and High Wethercote (SE 561298)
[36] Lockton (SE 565918)
[37] Woolhouse Croft (SE 564914)
Also recorded: Low Banniscue; Little Banniscue; High Banniscue; Crow Nest; Howe Cliff; Wether House; Ewe Cote; Timber Holme; Grimes Holme

BRANSDALE
[38] Cockayne Lodge (SE 619985)
[39] Breck House (SE 615980)
[40] Bransdale Mill (SE 621979)
[41] Toad Hole (SE 625979)
[42] Smout House (SE 626976)
[43] Cornfield House (SE 616972)
[44] Low Cornfield House (SE 617970)
[45] Spout House (SE 626970)
[46] Cowl House (SE 616967)
[47] Low South House Farm (SE 617961)
[48] High Elm House (SE 618956)
[49] Fieldhouse (SE 616954)
[50] Catherine House (SE 620953)
[51] Moor Houses (SE 632948)
[52] Stork House (SE 623945)
[53] Ankness (SE 639935)
[54] Bog House (SE 653934)
Also recorded: Cockayne; Cow Sike; Colt House; South House; Clegret; Low Barn; Low Lidmoor; Rudland House; Coronation Cottage

BROMPTON
[55] High Hall (SE 94278218)
[56] Low Hall (SE 939817)
[57] Butts Farm (SE 942816)
[58] Glebe Farm, Sawdon (SE 943848)
[59] Rye Topping Farm (SE 946805)
[60] Lowfields Farm (SE 945799)
Also recorded: Manor House; Rose Cottage; Carr Farm; Green Farm; Dale House Farm, Sawdon

CLOUGHTON
[61] Cloughton Hall or White Hall (TA 008942)
[62] Manor House (TA 00969453)
[63] Thirley Beck Farm (SE 984947)

COLD KIRBY
[64] Middle Farm (SE 53238457)
[65] Coronation Farm (SE 53238450)
[66] Hambleton House (SE 524835)
Also recorded: School House; East Farm; High House Farm

CROPTON
Also recorded: The Old Cottage; Cruck Cottage; White Cottage; Nutholm

DALE TOWN
Also recorded: Sunnybank Farm; Gowerdale House; Daleside Cottage; Dale Town

DANBY
[67] Beech Farm, Ainthorpe (NZ 70450806)
[68] 27 & 29 Brook Lane, Ainthorpe (NZ 70460794)
[69] Winsley Hill Farm (NZ 702086)
[70] Stangend (NZ 703084)
[71] Clitherbeck Cottages (NZ 717099)
[72] Rose Cottage (NZ 715098)
[73] Danby Lodge Farm (NZ 715084)
[74] Danby Lodge (NZ 716084)
[75] High Butterwitts (NZ 724080)
[76] Forest Lodge (NZ 685067)
[77] Crag House (NZ 687062)
[78] Plumtree (NZ 689055)
[79] Botton Grove (NZ 698054)
[80] Botton Farm (NZ 697045)
[81] Smithy (NZ 693045)
[82] Stormy Hall (NZ 688044)
[83] High Farm (NZ 694037)
[84] Castlehouses (NZ 716074)
[85] Crossley Side Farm (NZ 713059)
[86] Stonebeck Gate Farm (NZ 715053)
[87] Brook Side Farm (NZ 739061)
[88] Beck Side Farm (NZ 738060)
[89] Fir Tree House (NZ 734055)
[90] Fryup Hall (NZ 722044)
[91] Woodhead Farm (NZ 716041)
Also recorded: Doubting Castle; Lumley House; Fairy Cross Plain

Fig. 431 [73] Danby Lodge Farm, Danby

EAST AYTON
Also recorded: Manor House

EAST NEWTON AND LAYSTHORPE
[92] East Newton Hall (SE 645794)

EBBERSTON
[93] Cliff House (SE 899830)
[94] Peartree Cottage (SE 89898247)
[95] Westwood Farm (SE 89858246)
[96] Church House (SE 898828)
[97] Scamridge Farm (SE 896857)
[98] Welldale House (SE 913826)
Also recorded: Beckus; Manor Farm

EGTON
[99] Newbiggin Hall (NZ 841068)
[100] Lelum Hall (NZ 803055)
[101] Delves Cottage (NZ 791045)
Also recorded: Dalton Cottage; Egton Manor; Orchard Cottage; Bank House Farm

ESKDALESIDE CUM UGGLEBARNBY
[102] Carr View, 71 Coach Road, Sleights (NZ 86670729)
[103] The Old Vicarage, 115 Coach Road, Sleights (NZ 86670729)
[104] Midge Hall, 125–127 Coach Road, Sleights (NZ 86650723)
[105] Esk Hall, Sleights (NZ 86560778)
[106] Corn Mill, Iburndale (NZ 872070)
[107] Post Office, Station Tavern, warehouse, stabling and cottages, Grosmont (NZ 828053)
[108] Caley Becks Farm (NZ 85610654)
[109] 1–6 Hollins Cottages (NZ 833054)
[110] Dean Hall (NZ 883064)
[111] Hemp Syke (NZ 884060)
Also recorded: Eskdale Gate; Foster's Farm; Browcote

FADMOOR
[112] Laburnum Cottage (SE 67678943)
[113] Cherry Tree Farm (SE 654903)
[114] Aumery Park (SE 660896)
Also recorded: The Plough Inn and Moorland View; Pennyholme; The Green; Westfield Farm; North Farm

FARNDALE EAST
[115] Hollins Farm (SE 661984)
[116] Oak Crag (SE 678962)

FARNDALE WEST
Also recorded: White House (formerly Harland Head)

FYLINGDALES
[117] Thorpe Hall, Fyling Thorpe (NZ 94410494)
[118] Raw Farm, Raw (NZ 93420568)
[119] High Normanby Farm (NZ 932060)
[120] The Bay Tree (NZ 951053)
[121] Lingers Hill (NZ 956052)
[122] Quarry Hill (NZ 934052)
[123] Sledgates Farm (NZ 937047)
[124] Park Gate (NZ 938046)
[125] Fyling Hall (NZ 937043)
[126] Demesne Farm (NZ 940033)
[127] Gilson House (NZ 942034)
[128] Fyling Old Hall Farm (NZ 943029)

[129] Fyling Old Hall (NZ 944028)
[130] Browcote (NZ 965022)
[131] Howdale Farm (NZ 952018)
Also recorded: Rosslyn House and Cottage; Oak Tree House and
Oak Dene; Bay Ness; Ramsdale: White House

GILLAMOOR
[132] Manor Farm (SE 68379004)
[133] Barn (SE 68318997)
[134] Highfield Farm (SE 68158997)
[135] The Row (SE 68229002)
[136] Reckon Forge (SE 68249002)
[137] Dial House Farm (SE 68309006)
[138] Lowna (SE 687910)
[139] Gillamoor Mill (SE 687904)
Also recorded: Pinfold; Southlands

Fig. 432 [149] Bainley Bank Cottage, Glaisdale

GLAISDALE
[140] Fat Ox Farm, Houlsyke (NZ 736089)
[141] Grange Farm, Houlsyke (NZ 73810794)
[142] Bamford House, Lealholm (NZ 76250769)
[143] Longstones (NZ 76900799)
[144] Street Farm, Street (NZ 73420471)
[145] Lawns Farm (NZ 744079)
[146] Lane Head Farm (NZ 753063)
[147] Prospect House (NZ 740054)
[148] Bainley Side Farm (NZ 736050)
[149] Bainley Bank Cottage (NZ 738043)
[150] Slidney Beck Farm (NZ 721038)
[151] Fryup Lodge (NZ 721031)
[152] Glaisdale Hall (NZ 773055)
[153] Hart Hall (NZ 774049)
[154] Red House (NZ 771049)
[155] Quarry Farm (NZ 769048)
[156] Postgate Farm (NZ 758044)
[157] Low London (NZ 756043)
[158] York House (NZ 747037)
[159] Highdale Farm (NZ 735032)
[160] London House Farm (NZ 744032)
[161] Readman House (NZ 743021)
[162] Glaisdale Head (NZ 744021)
Also recorded: Horse How Farm; Hilltop Farm; Morgan Intakes;
Dale Head

GOATHLAND
[163] Brayton House (NZ 832013)
[164] Fir Tree House, Beck Hole (NZ 821022)
[165] Thorn Hill House (NZ 840001)
[166] Hunt House (SE 815987)
Also recorded: Ellers Farm

GREAT EDSTONE
[167] Vicarage (SE 70618498)

HACKNESS
[168] Lowdales (SE 954916)
Also recorded: Hackness Mill

HAROME
[169] Forge House (SE 64918208)
[170] Orchard House (SE 64888209)
[171] Greystones Farm (SE 64838208)
[172] The Farm (SE 64828206)
[173] Rutland House (SE 64728200)
[174] Old Manor House (SE 64628206)
[175] Star Inn (SE 64618215)
[176] Mill Cottage (SE 64728170)
Also recorded: Appletree Cottage; house and cottage, Main Street;
Headland Cottage; Cruck Cottage; Lancaster House; Mill Green

HARWOOD DALE
[177] Murkhead (SE 951951)

HAWNBY
[178] Daniel Steps (SE 54328983)
[179] Hawnby House (SE 54208973)
[180] Mill House (SE 54268939)
[181] Low Thwaites (SE 543944)
[182] Nova Scotia Farm (SE 543913)
Also recorded: Sike House; Honey Hill; Hazelshaw House; Carr
House; Parci Gill; Low Hazel Heads; Gill End; Hawnby Hall;
Dial Cottage; Pear Tree Cottage; cottage near Hawnby Hotel; Ivy
Cottage; Tancred Cottage; South Farm; cottage near Post Office;
Village Hall

HAWSKER-CUM-STAINSACRE
[183] Hawsker Hall (NZ 92200753)
[184] House and windmill, Green Lane, Low Hawsker (NZ
       92510758)
[185] Highgate House (NZ 918100)
[186] Red Barn (NZ 922088)
Also recorded: Stainsacre Hall

HELMSLEY
[187] Canons Garth
[188] 1 Bondgate
[189] Vicarage Farm, Bondgate
[190] 21, 23 Bondgate
[191] 8, 10, 12 Bondgate
[192] 14, 16, 18 Bondgate
[193] 20 Bondgate
[194] 30, 32, 34 Bondgate
[195] 36 Bondgate
[196] 38 Bondgate
[197] 40 Bondgate
[198] 44 Bondgate
[199] 70 Bondgate

Fig. 433 [205] 3–4 Buckingham Square, Helmsley

[200] 19 Bridge Street
[201] Buckingham House, 33 Bridge Street
[202] Ryedale House, 39 Bridge Street
[203] 43, 45 Bridge Street
[204] 10 Bridge Street
[205] 3–4 Buckingham Square
[206] Estate Office, Buckingham Square
[207] 9 Castlegate
[208] 2 Castlegate
[209] Old Manor House, 18 Castlegate
[210] Church Farm, 1 High Street
[211] 7 High Street
[212] 13 High Street
[213] 21 High Street
[214] 8 High Street
[215] 20, 22 High Street
[216] 24, 26. High Street
[217] 30 High Street
[218] 32 High Street
[219] 36–46 High Street
[220] 54 High Street
[221] 5 Market Place
[222] Warehouse behind 14 Market Place
[223] Rectory House, Market Place
[224] Bankins, Market Place
[225] The Black Swan Hotel, Market Place
[226] The Crown Hotel, Market Place
[227] 6, 8, 10 Pottergate
[228] 5, 7 Ryegate
[229] 9 Ryegate
[230] 25, 27 Ryegate
[231] 22 Ryegate
[232] Low Farm, Carlton (SE 610865)
[233] Middle Farm, Carlton (SE 60978657)
[234] Ivy Cottage, Carlton (SE 61008647)
[235] Cottage, Carlton (SE 61008670)
[236] Snaper House (SE 598915)
[237] Old Kiln (SE 604924)

[238] Hazel Green (SE 608918)
[239] High Baxtons Farm (SE 598878)
[240] Middle Baxtons Farm (SE 600867)
[241] Carlton Grange (SE 608879)
[242] Rea Garth Farm (SE 625858)
Also recorded: 19, 42 Bondgate; Farm, Bondgate; 1, 5, 18–22, 27 Bridge Street; 14, 15, 17, 35 Church Street; 18, 52 High Street; 1, 2, 3, 4, 13 Market Place; 1, 9, 11 Pottergate; 2 Ryegate; High Farm, Carlton; High House; Piethorn; Old Fold; Lund; Cowhouse Bank Farm; Carlton Park Farm

HUTTON BUSCEL
[243] Mole End (SE 97148402)
[244] Martin Garth (SE 97158404)
[245] The Kennels (SE 974846)
Also recorded: The Holt (former vicarage); Smithy and Forge Cottage; Simonside; Church Lane Cottage

HUTTON-LE-HOLE
[246] Hammer and Hand (SE 70539006)

KILDALE
[247] Rectory (NZ 607094)
[248] Lounsdale Farm (NZ 605108)
[249] Bleach Mill Farm (NZ 596093)
[250] Little Kildale (NZ 615092)
[251] East Green Beck Farm (NZ 620098)
[252] West House (NZ 635094)
Also recorded: Wood End

KINGTHORPE
[253] Cruck Barn (SE 836859)
[254] Kingthorpe House (SE 834857)

KIRKBYMOORSIDE
[255] Tolbooth, Market Place
[256] Old Police Station, Tinley Garth
[257] 4, 6, 8 Castlegate
[258] 20 Castlegate
[259] High Hall, Castlegate
[260] 5 Church Street
[261] The Green, Church Street
[262] 8 Crown Square
[263] East end of Crown Square
[264] Market stalls, Crown Square
[265] Low Hall, Dale End
[266] 12–20 Dale End
[267] 24 Dale End
[268] 30, 32 Dale End
[269] Dog and Duck Farm, 8 High Market Place
[270] 14 High Market Place
[271] Manor House, formerly Manor Farm, High Market Place
[272] Buckingham House, High Market Place
[273] King's Head, High Market Place
[274] 5 Howe End
[275] 7, 9, 11 Howe End
[276] 2 Howe End
[277] Petch House, Howe End
[278] Vivers Lodge, Howe End
[279] 4 Market Place
[280] 6 Market Place
[281] 8 Market Place
[282] 10 Market Place, formerly the Tontine Inn

[283] 14 Market Place
[284] 26 Market Place
[285] The Black Swan Hotel, Market Place
[286] The George and Dragon and 19 Market Place
[287] 17, 19 Piercy End
[288] Fern Cottage, 23 Piercy End
[289] 47, 49 Piercy End
[290] 30 Piercy End
[291] Old Vicarage, Tinley Garth
[292] 4 Tinley Garth
[293] 8 West End
[294] 10 West End
[295] 14 West End
[296] 42, 44 and 46 West End
[297] 48 West End
[298] 58, 60, 62 West End
[299] 64, 66, 68 West End
[300] 70, 72, 74 West End
[301] The White House Public House, at junction of West End with Piercy End
[302] 3 West End
[303] 11, 13 West End, formerly The Angel Inn
[304] Windmill, West End
[305] 37 West End
[306] 63, 65, 67 West End
[307] 73, 75, 77 West End
[308] 85 West End
Also recorded: Little Garth; Job Hole; Mount Pleasant, Dale End; 23 Dale End; 16, 18 High Market Place; 1, 3 Howe End; 2, 12 Market Place; 28, 36 Piercy End; 56, 76, 79, 83 West End; The Cricketers' Arms, West End; Huntsmans House, West Lund Lane; Corn Mills, Kirkby Mills

LASKILL PASTURE
[309] Laverock Hall and Laverock Hall Farm (SE 572928)
[310] New House (SE 576920)
[311] Carr Cote (SE 575918)
[312] Laskill Farm (SE 563907)
[313] Newgate Foot (SE 567898)
[314] Broadway Foot (SE 560887)
Also recorded: Oak House; Feather House Farm; Snilegate Head

LASTINGHAM
[315] April Cottage (SE 72959038)
[316] The Shop (SE 72959041)
[317] The Vicarage (SE 72729050)
[318] Corn Mill (SE 728904)
[319] Lower Askew (SE 744898)

LEVISHAM
[320] Levisham Hall (SE 832906)
[321] The Green Farm (SE 83349050)
[322] Levisham Mill (SE 835201)
Also recorded: Newton House Farm

LOCKTON
[323] Saltersgate Public House (SE 851943)

MARTON
Also recorded; The Cottage; Rosedene

MIDDLETON
[324] Vicarage (SE 78248541)
[325] Middleton Hall (SE 78278535)
[326] Terrace (SE 78188533)
[327] Low Costa Mill (SE 775837)
Also recorded: Prospect House

MURTON GRANGE
[328] Murton Grange Farm (SE 535880)
[329] Shaken Bridge Farm (SE 558883)
[330] Barnclose House (SE 566871)

NAWTON
[331] Orchard House (SE 65518488)
[332] 1–4 East View (SE 65578467)
[333] Manor Farm (SE 65598468)
[334] Ashton House (SE 65718477)
[335] Prospect House (SE 65588484)
[336] Farm buildings, N. of Mount Pleasant (SE 649865)
[337] Mount Pleasant (SE 649864)
Also recorded: Pasture House; Pasture Cottage; Rose Cottage; Beech Cottage; South View; The Cottage; Plumpton Court; Middle Farm; Stoneycroft; The Rose and Crown

Fig. 434 [331] Orchard House, Nawton

NEWTON
[338] Wethead (SE 812926)
[339] Mill Cottage (SE 813923)

OLD BYLAND
[340] Old Byland Hall (SE 55058578)
[341] House (SE 55048580)
[342] Mount Pleasant (SE 543864)
[343] Tile House Barn (SE 561866)
[344] Ashberry Farm (SE 571844)
Also recorded: King Spring House; farm buildings, Ashberry Hill; Wethercote; Old Byland Grange Farm; Tylas Farm; Reins Farm; Caydale Mill; Green Lea; Valley View Farm

PICKERING
[345] Market Hall, 11, 12, 13 Birdgate
[346] Beck Isle Museum
[347] Rose Cottage, Beck Isle

[348] 4, 5, 6 Birdgate
[349] 7 Birdgate
[350] 15–17 Birdgate
[351] The Black Swan Inn, 18 Birdgate
[352] Vine Cottage, Brant Hill
[353] The Rose Public House, Bridge Street
[354] 6, 7 Bridge Street
[355] 8 Bridge Street
[356] 6–9 Burgate
[357] 12 Burgate
[358] 18–20 Burgate
[359] 31 Burgate
[360] 33 Burgate
[361] 34, 35 Burgate, once The Crown Inn
[362] 36 Burgate
[363] 40 Burgate and Burgate Chambers
[364] 9, 10 Castlegate
[365] 11, Castlegate
[366] 12, 13 Castlegate
[367] 14, 15 Castlegate
[368] 25 Castlegate
[369] 55, 56, 57 Eastgate
[370] 59 Eastgate
[371] 60, 61 Eastgate
[372] 62–65 Eastgate
[373] 66 and 67 Eastgate
[374] 75 Eastgate
[375] 118 Eastgate
[376] Eastgate House, 132 Eastgate
[377] The Horse Shoe Inn, Hall Garth
[378] 7 Hall Garth
[379] Old Rectory, Hall Garth
[380] 25 Hall Garth
[381] 17 Hungate
[382] 30, 31 Hungate
[383] 34 Hungate
[384] Low Hall, now Forest and Vale Hotel, Malton Road
[385] The White Swan, on N. side of Market Place
[386] The Bay Horse Inn, Market Place
[387] 17–22 Market Place
[388] 37 Market Place
[389] St George's House, formerly The George Inn, Market Place
[390] 40, 41 Market Place
[391] 42 Market Place
[392] 14, 15, 16, 19, 21 Park Street
[393] 23–25 Park Street
[394] 26, 27 Park Street
[395] 15, 15A Potter Hill
[396] 27 Potter Hill
[397] 34 Potter Hill
[398] 36 Potter Hill
[399] 52–55 Potter Hill
[400] 56 Potter Hill
[401] 1–7 Train Lane
[402] 3 Undercliffe
[403] 9, 10 Undercliffe
[404] 13 Undercliffe
[405] 14–19 Undercliffe
[406] 13, 14 Westgate
[407] 20–23 Westgate

[408] 24–27 Westgate
[409] 33–36 Westgate
[410] 65–68 Westgate
[411] 86, 86A Westgate
[412] 87–96 Westgate
[413] 128–134 Westgate
[414] The Sun ph, Westgate
[415] 1 Willowgate, formerly the King's Arms Inn
[416] Saintoft Grange (SE 792893)
[417] Nova Lodge (SE 793876)
[418] West Farm (SE 818866)
[419] New Hambleton (SE 800864)
[420] Field Barn (SE 812861)
[421] Former New Cottages, New Bridge (SE 802853)
[422] Scalla Moor House Farm (SE 818850)
[423] Vivis Mill (SE 795834)
[424] Black Bull ph (SE 802815)
Also recorded: Beck Isle Cottage; 3 Birdgate; 5 Bridge Street; 43, 44 Market Place; 14, 25, 37, 38, 39 Potter Hill; 104 Westgate; Barn, Willowgate; Carter's House; Ivy Cottage byre; former Hare and Hounds, Stape; Pickering Low Mill; Wray House; Low Carr Farm

POCKLEY
[425] High Farm (SE 63748633)
[426] West Farm (SE 63708624)
[427] Manor Farm (SE 63768620)
[428] Keepers Cottage (SE 63708614)
[429] West View (SE 63718596)
[430] White Cottage (SE 63598578)
[431] The Old Forge (SE 63578575)
[432] Moorings, formerly Post Office (SE 63588573)
[433] Ivy Cottage (SE 63548572)
[434] Low Farm (SE 63528556)
[435] Bonfield Gill (SE 608947)
[436] Newgate Foot (SE 620902)
[437] Pockley Grange (SE 624899)
[438] Hasty Bank Farm (SE 625884)
[439] Brecks Farm (SE 638849)
Also recorded: Birk Nab Farm; Blaiskey Barn; Oxclose Farm; Auburn House; Rose Cottage; South View and Sunny View; Middle Farm

RIEVAULX
[440] Swiss Cottage (SE 57638513)
[441] Alexandra Cottage (SE 57598512)
[442] Rievaulx Mill (SE 576851)
[443] Mill Cottage (SE 57528516)
[444] Mill House (SE 57548507)
[445] Sproxton Mill (SE 607824)
[446] Ouldray Farm (SE 591865)
[447] Harriet Air Farm (SE 575855
[448] High Leys Farm (SE 586855)
[449] Abbot Hag Farm (SE 578843)
[450] Forge Cottage (SE 576842)
[451] Stiltons (SE 599846)
[452] Griff Farm (SE 588838)
Also recorded: Severadus and Beck Cottage; Beck House; Woodlands; Spring Cottage; Rose Tree Cottage; Abbey Cottage; Furnace Mill; School House; Wood View; Verbena Cottage; Rye House; Smithy; Cringle Carr; Sour Leys Farm; Oscar Park; New Leys Farms; Middle Heads Farm; Crabtree Hall

ROSEDALE EAST SIDE
[453] Milburn Arms Hotel, formerly The Crown Hotel (SE 72519596)

SCAWTON
[454] Rose Cottage (SE 54878345)
[455] Scawton Park (SE 549840)
[456] Bungdale Head Farm (SE 559837)
[457] Scawton Croft (SE 572841)
Also recorded: Hay Hall; Crow Green; Antofts; Church Farm; Vicarage Farm; The Cottage; Hare Inn

SINNINGTON
[458] Old Hall (SE 74588610)
[459] Vicarage (SE 74448603)
[460] Sinnington Lodge (SE 742847)
[461] Sinnington Grange Mill (SE 739841)

SKIPLAM
[462] Wether Cote (SE 648894)
[463] West Sleightholmedale Farm (SE 651898)
[464] Ewe Cote Farm (SE 651877)
[465] Skiplam Grange (SE 657874)
[466] Hold Caldron Mill (SE 669869)
Also recorded: Otter Hill

SNAINTON
[467] The Coachman, formerly The New Inn (SE 91488235)
[468] Hill Crest (SE 92008232)
[469] Cottage in High Street (SE 92228224)
[470] Oakwood Cottage (SE 91958208)
[471] Holm Farm House, West Lane (SE 91698216)
[472] Cottage, West Lane (SE 91808215)
[473] Cliff Grange (SE 91778214)
[474] The Old Hall (SE 91748210)
[475] Cockmoor Hall (SE 911864)
[476] Wydale Hall (SE 928833)
[477] Foulbridge (SE 914795)
Also recorded: Forge House; Prospect Farm; 47 High Street; Pippin (formerly Grosvenor House), Pudding Lane

SNEATON
Also recorded: 1, 2 Sea View Cottages; Ivy Cottage

SNILESWORTH
[478] Head House (SE 534971)
[479] Hagg House Farm (SE 523937)
[480] Street Gate Farm (SE 527934)
Also recorded: Lane House Farm; Plane Tree Hall Farm; Hill End Farm; Low Cote Farm; Blow Gill Farm; Scotland Farm; Cragg Farm; High Arngill; Low Arngill

SPAUNTON
[481] Woodman's Cottage (SE 72418992)

SPROXTON
[482] Cottages (SE 61518155)
[483] Aspen Farm (SE 6138148)
[484] Waterloo Farm (SE 579813)
Also recorded: Rose Cottage; Forge Cottage; Cottage, Chapel Lane; Middle Farm

STAINTON DALE
[485] Bell Hill Farm (SE 985998)
[486] White Hall Farm (SE 99808875)
[487] Outfarm near Bridge Farm (SE 997978)
[488] White House Farm (TA 003977)
Also recorded: Low Peak Farm; Stainton Farm

SUFFIELD-CUM-EVERLEY
Also recorded: Everley Hotel; Forest Lodge

THORNTON DALE
[489] Comber House (SE 83768310)
[490] Thornton Hall (SE 83638307)
[491] Welcome Cafe and The Gift Box, Cross Street (SE 83438305)
[492] Church Farm House (SE 83928312)
[493] The Old Vicarage, two cottages and Oban Cottage, Malton Gate (SE 83368292)
[494] Roxby House and Roxby Cottage, Malton Gate (SE 83378385)
[495] 6–11 Pickering Road (SE 83358305)
[496] Thornton Mill (SE 83658347)
[497] Brook House, Priestman's Lane (SE 83758327)
[498] Beck Hall, Priestman's Lane (SE 83758322)
[499] The New Inn (SE 83388303)
[500] Shop, The Square (SE 83388301)
[501] Old Ellers, Ellerburn (SE 842842)
[502] High Paper Mill Farm (SE 852844)
[503] Denham Grange (SE 822795)
Also recorded: The Buck; High Hall; High Dalby; Hagg House; Derwent House; Skelton Wath

THORNTON RISEBOROUGH
[504] Riseborough Hall (SE 752830)

TROUTSDALE
[505] Freeze Gill Farm (SE 92509000)

WELBURN
[506] Welburn Hall (SE 682846)

WEST AYTON
[507] Ayton Castle (SE 98818505)
[508] The Elms (SE 986848)
[509] High Hall (SE 98698478)
[510] Derwent Mill Farm (SE 987849)
[511] Derwent Mill or High Mill (SE 988849)
[512] House and shop (SE 98688468)
[513] Low Hall (SE 98738430)
Also recorded: Low Yedmandale

WESTERDALE
[514] Riddings Farm (NZ 660048)
[515] Leath House (NZ 648042)
[516] Barn (NZ 679058)
[517] Broad Gate Farm (NZ 671050)
[518] Dale Head (NZ 678044)
[519] Anthony House (NZ 676040)
Also recorded: Fir Trees House; Park House; New House; Hill House

WILTON
[520] Home Farm (SE 86108280)
Also recorded: Prospect House; Grange Farm

Fig. 435 The Plough, Wombleton

WOMBLETON
[521]   1–7 Carter Close (SE 66908407)
[522]   Rose Cottage (SE 66908403)
[523]   Greenside Hill and Hornby Cottage (SE 66918398)
[524]   Ivy Cottage (SE 66928397)
[525]   Woods Cottage, Beech Cottage and adjoining cottage (SE 66918395)
[526]   Fir Tree Farm (SE 66958383)
[527]   Cottage behind Penn Cottage (SE 66888387)
[528]   The Mount (SE 66858412)
[529]   Boon Woods (SE 653869)
Also recorded: School; The Plough Inn; Hillcrest; Ryecroft; South View Farm; barn near Rosslyn; Penn Cottage; White House Farm; Manor Farm

WRELTON
[530]   Cruck Cottage (SE 76508596)

WYKEHAM
[531]   Downe Arms (SE 96438335)
[532]   Lora Terrace (SE 95908316)
Also recorded: Methodist House, Ruston

BIBLIOGRAPHICAL SOURCES AND ABBREVIATIONS

ALCOCK, N. W. 1981. Cruck construction: an introduction and catalogue. *Counc. Brit. Archaeol. Rep.* **42**

ALCOCK, N. W. and LAITHWAITE, M. 1973. Medieval houses in Devon and their modernisation. *Medieval Archaeol.* **17**, 100–25

ALLERSTON, P. 1970. English village development: findings from the Pickering district of North Yorkshire. *Trans. Inst. Brit. Geogr.* **51**, 95–109

AMBLER, L. 1913. *The Old Halls and Manor Houses of Yorkshire*

ANDREWS, D. D. and MILNE, G. (eds.) 1979. Vol. I. Domestic Settlement, I: Areas 10 and 6. In *Wharram. A Study of Settlement on the Yorkshire Wolds*, ed. J. G. Hurst, *Soc. Medieval Archaeol. monogr. ser.* **8**

ASHCROFT, M. Y. and HILL, A. M. 1980. *Bilsdale Surveys 1637–1851*. NYCRO Publ. **23**. Northallerton

ATKINSON, J. C. 1891. *Forty Years in a Moorland Parish*. London

BAILDON, W. P. (ed.) 1920. Compositions for not taking knighthood at the Coronation of Charles I. In Miscellanea I, *YASRS* **61**, 84–107

BAINES, E. 1823. *History, Directory and Gazetteer of the County of York. Vol. II: East and North Ridings*. Leeds

BAKER, G. 1906. *Unhistoric Acts: some Records of early Friends in North-East Yorkshire*. London

BARKER, T. E. 1980. The Eure Family. *NYCRO Journal* **7**, 21–66

BARLEY, M. W. 1961. *The English Farmhouse and Cottage*. London
1963. A glossary of names for rooms in houses of the sixteenth and seventeenth centuries. In *Culture and Environment: Essays in Honour of Sir Cyril Fox*, eds. I. Ll. Foster and L. Alcock, pp. 479–501. London
1979. The double pile house. *Archaeol. J.* **136**, 253–64

BASS Documents in possession of Bass North Ltd., United House, Piccadilly, York

BEARD, G. 1966. *Georgian Craftsmen and their Work*. London

BELVOIR Archives of the Duke of Rutland in Belvoir Castle

BERESFORD, G. 1979. Three deserted medieval settlements on Dartmoor: a report on the late E. Marie Minter's excavations. *Medieval Archaeol.* **23**, 98–158

BERESFORD, M. W. 1948–51. Glebe Terriers and Open Field, Yorkshire. *YAJ* **37**, 325–68
1957. *History on the Ground*. Lutterworth (revised Gloucester 1971)

BERESFORD, M. W. and HURST, J. G. (eds.) 1971. *Deserted Medieval Villages*. London

BERESFORD, M. W. and ST JOSEPH, J. K. S. 1979. *Medieval England* 2nd edn. Cambridge

BETTEY, J. H. 1982. Seventeenth-century squatters' dwellings: some documentary evidence. *Vernacular Architect.* **13**, 28–30

BILSON, J. 1905–7. Gilling Castle. *YAJ* **19**, 105–92

BIRDSALL Archives in Birdsall House, North Yorkshire

BORTHWICK Documents in Borthwick Institute of Historical Research, St Anthony's Hall, Peasholme Green, York

BREARS, P. C. D. (ed.) 1972. Yorkshire probate inventories 1542–1689. *YASRS* **134**

BREARS, P. and HARRISON, S. 1979. *The Dairy Catalogue*. York

BLKG Drawings in the office of Brierley, Leckenby, Keighley and Groom, architects, York

BROWN, W. 1885–8. Descriptions of the buildings of twelve small Yorkshire priories at the Reformation. *YAJ* **9**, 197–215, 320–33

BROWN, W. (ed.) 1897. Yorkshire Lay Subsidy (1301). *YASRS* **21**
1902. Yorkshire Inquisitions III. *YASRS* **31**, 72–5

BULMER, T. & CO. 1890. *History, Topography, and Directory of North Yorkshire. Part II*. Ashton-on-Ribble

BURNETT Burnett Papers in Whitby Museum

BURNETT, J. 1978. *A Social History of Housing 1815–1970*. Newton Abbot

CCHR 1903. *Calendar of the Charter Rolls preserved in the Public Record Office 1226–57*. London

CCHR 1906. *Calendar of the Charter Rolls preserved in the Public Record Office 1257–1300*. London

CCHR 1927. *Calendar of the Charter Rolls preserved in the Public Record Office 1300–1326*. London

CHR 1837. *Rotuli Chartarum in Turri Londiniensi asservati 1199–1216*. London

CAMERON Documents in possession of Messrs J. W. Cameron & Co. Ltd., Hartlepool, Cleveland

CAMP, A. J. 1974. *Wills and their Whereabouts*

CARTWRIGHT, R. n.d. *Spout House – The Old Sun Inn*

CHAPMAN, J. 1961. *Changing Agriculture and the Moorland Edge in the North Yorkshire Moors, 1750–1960*. MA thesis, University of London
1976. Parliamentary enclosure in the uplands: the case of the North York Moors. *Agr. Hist. Rev.* **24**, 1–17

CHARLTON, L. 1779. *The History of Whitby and of Whitby Abbey*. York

CHOLMLEY, H. 1777. *The Memoirs of Sir Hugh Cholmley Knt and Bart. . . .* London

CLAY, C. (ed.) 1893. Early Yorkshire Charters Vol. X. *YRS* Extra Series, Vol. VIII

CLAY, J. W. (ed.) 1893. *Yorkshire Royalist Composition Papers.* *YASRS* **15**

COLGRAVE, B. and MYNORS, R. A. B. 1969. *Bede's Ecclesiastical History of the English People.* Oxford

COOPER, I. n.d. *Helmsley, or Reminiscences of 100 Years Ago. To which is added a Guide to the Locality with Descriptive Notes* (reprint of articles in *YG* during 1887)

COOPER, R. G. 1976–7. Quarrying in the Hambleton Hills, North Yorkshire: the problem of identifying disused workings. *Ind. Archaeol. Rev.* **1**, 164–70

CROSSLEY, E. W. 1940–3. Pickering Parsonage House and Tithe Barn. *YAJ* **35**, 217–21

CUMING, E. D. (ed.) 1926. *Squire Osbaldeston: his Autobiography.* London

DORNIER, A. M. 1967–70. Neville Castle, Kirkbymoorside. Excavations 1963 and 1965. *YAJ* **42**, 98–102

EASTMEAD, W. 1824. *Historia Rievallensis.* London

FIRST REPORT 1867. *First Report from the Commissioners on the Employment of Children, Young Persons, and Women in Agriculture.* London

FORD, J. 1953. *Some Reminiscences and Folk Lore of Danby Parish and District.* Whitby

FOSTER, I. Ll. and ALCOCK, L. (eds.) 1963. *Culture and Environment: Essays in Honour of Sir Cyril Fox.* London

FOX-STRANGEWAYS, C. 1982. *The Jurassic Rocks of Britain. Vol. I: Yorkshire.* London

FRANK, B. 1970. Salt boxes of the North York Moors. *Dalesman* **32**, 775–8

FLHG 1976. Fylingdales Local History Group. The parish of Fylingdales in 1841: an analysis of census returns. *NYCRO Journal* **3**, 34–76

1979. Fylingdales Local History Group. *Fylingdales Census Returns, 1851–1861.* NYCRO Publ. **20**. Northallerton

GIROUARD, M. 1978. *Life in the English Country House.* London

GRANVILLE, A. B. 1841. *Spas of England. Vol. I. The North.* Bath (reprinted 1971)

GRAVES, J. 1808. *The History of Cleveland in the North Riding of the County of York.* Carlisle

HAGGARD, H. RIDER. 1902. *Rural England. Vol. II.* London

HAIGH, D. H. 1879. Yorkshire dials. *YAJ* **5**, 134–222

HALL, I. 1979. *Samuel Buck's Yorkshire Sketchbook.* Reproduced in facsimile from Lansdowne MS 914. Ilkley

HALL, I. and HALL, E. 1973. *A New Picture of Georgian Hull.* York

HARRIS, J. 1981. *The Palladians.* London

HARRISON, A. and HARRISON, J. K. 1970. A field survey of horse wheels and wheel houses in Cleveland and the North Yorkshire Moor dales. *Cleveland and Tees-side Local Hist. Soc. Bull.* **8**, 13–23

1973. The horse wheel in North Yorkshire. *Ind. Archaeol.* **10**, 247–65

HARRISON, B. 1970. The linen industry in the Northallerton district. *Cleveland and Tees-side Local Hist. Soc. Bull.* **9**, 22–3

HARRISON, B. J. D. and HUTTON, B. 1984. *Vernacular Houses in North Yorkshire and Cleveland.* Edinburgh

HARTLEY, M. and INGILBY, J. 1972. *Life in the Moorlands of North-East Yorkshire.* London

HARVEY, J. 1954. *English Medieval Architects.* London

HASTINGS, R. P. 1980. The North Riding linen industry. *NYCRO Journal* **7**, 67–86

1981. *Essays in North Riding History.* NYCRO Publ. **28**. Northallerton

1982. *Poverty and the Poor Law in the North Riding of Yorkshire c. 1780–1837*, Borthwick Papers 62. York

1984. *More Essays in North Riding History.* NYCRO Publ. **34**. Northallerton

HAYES, R. H. 1969. The story of Gillamoor and Fadmoor. *Ryedale Historian* **4**, 7–24

n.d. *Excavations at Harome Hall, The Old Manor House*

HAYES, R. H. and HURST, J. n.d. *A History of Hutton-le-Hole in the Manor of Spaunton.* Helmsley

HAYES, R. H. and RUTTER, J. G. 1972. Cruck-framed Buildings in Ryedale and Eskdale. *Scarborough Dist. Archaeol. Soc. Res. Rep.* **8**

1974. Rosedale Mines and Railway. *Scarborough Dist. Archaeol. Soc. Res. Rep.* **9**

HEAVISIDES, M. 1909. *Rambles in Cleveland.* Stockton on Tees

HELLEN, J. A. 1972. Agricultural innovation and detectable landscape margins: the case of wheelhouses in Northumberland. *Agr. Hist. Rev.* **20**, 140–54

HEMP, W. J. and GRESHAM, C. 1942–3. Park, Llanfoothen, and the unit system. *Archaeol. Cambrensis* **97**, 98–112

HOBSBAWM, E. J. 1969. *Industry and Empire.* Harmondsworth

HODGSON, R. I. 1980. Medieval colonisation in Northern Ryedale. *Ryedale Historian* **10**, 47–62

HOLLAND, S. 1855. *A Memoir of the Rev. Sidney Smith*, Vols. I and II. London

HOLLINGS, A. 1971. *Goathland. The Story of a Moorland Village.* Whitby

HOSKINS, W. G. 1953. The rebuilding of rural England. *Past and Present* **4**, 44–59. (reprinted in Hoskins, W. G. 1963. *Provincial England: Essays in Social and Economic History*, pp. 131–48)

1955. *The Making of the English Landscape.* London (republished 1976)

HULL UL   Hull University Library

HUTTON, B. 1973. Timber-framed houses in the Vale of York. *Medieval Archaeol* **17**, 87–99

1977. Rebuilding in Yorkshire: the evidence of inscribed dates. *Vernacular Architect.* **8**, 19–24

I'ANSON, W. M. 1912–13. The castles of the North Riding. *YAJ* **87**, 303–99

JACKSON, C. (ed.) 1873. The Autobiography of Mrs. Alice Thornton, of East Newton, Co. York. *Surtees Soc. Pub.* **62**

JARRETT, M. G. and WRATHMELL, S. 1977. Sixteenth and seventeenth-century farmsteads: West Whelpington, Northumberland. *Agr. Hist. Rev.* **25**, 108–19

JEFFERY, R. W. 1931. *Thornton-le-Dale.* Wakefield

JONES, S. R. and SMITH, J. T. 1963. The houses of Breconshire. Part I. *Brycheiniog* **9**, 1–77

1964. The houses of Breconshire. Part II. *Brycheiniog* **10**, 69–183

1965. The houses of Breconshire. Part III. *Brycheiniog* **11**, 1–149

1966–7. The houses of Breconshire. Part IV. *Brycheiniog* **12**, 1–91

JOURDAIN, M. 1950. *English Interior Decoration 1500 to 1830.* London

JSTB   Documents in possession of John Smith's Tadcaster Brewery, Estate Department, Tadcaster, North Yorkshire

LAING, D. 1800. *Hints for Dwellings. Original Designs for Cottages, Farmhouses, Villas.* London

LANDOWNERS 1873. *England and Wales (exclusive of the Metropolis) Return of Owners of Land 1873. Vol. II.* London

MCCUTCHEN, K. L. 1940. Yorkshire fairs and markets. *Thoresby Soc.* **39**

MACDONALD, S. 1975. The progress of the early threshing machine. *Agr. Hist. Rev.* **23**, 63–77

MCDONNELL, J. (ed.) 1963. *A History of Helmsley, Rievaulx and District.* York

1975. The evolution of a monastic grange. *NYCRO Journal* **2**, 78–95

MACHIN, R. 1975. The unit system: some historical explanations. *Archaeol. J.* **132**, 187–94

1977a. The Great Rebuilding: a reassessment. *Past and Present* **77**, 33–56

1977b. The mechanism of the pre-industrial building cycle. *Vernacular Architect.* **8**, 15–19

1978. *The Houses of Yetminster.* Bristol

MG *Malton Gazette*

MM *Malton Messenger*

MNG *Malton and Norton Gazette*

MARCHAND, J. (ed.) 1933. *A Frenchman in England, 1784.* Cambridge

MARSHALL, W. 1788. *The Rural Economy of Yorkshire.* London

MARTIN, E. J. 1927–9. The Templars in Yorkshire. *YAJ* **29**, 366–85

MASON, K. 1968. Yorkshire cheese-making. *Folk Life* **6**, 7–17

MEADS, D. M. (ed.) 1930. *Diary of Lady Margaret Hoby 1599–1605.* London

MERCER, E. 1975. *English Vernacular Houses. A Study of Traditional Farmhouses and Cottages.* London

MINGAY, G. E. 1977. *Rural Life in Victorian England.* London

MITCHELL, W. R. (ed.) 1981. *Life on the North York Moors. A Pictorial Review.* Clapham

MOORMAN, M. (ed.) 1971. *Journals of Dorothy Wordsworth* 2nd edn

MUSTO, N. M. 1963. Farming in the North of the Vale of Pickering, *Trans. SDAS* **6**, 7–12; **7**, 8–11

MUTHESIUS, S. 1982. *The English Terraced House.* Yale University

NMR National Monuments Record

NATTRASS, M. 1956–8. Witch posts and early dwellings in Cleveland. *YAJ* **39**, 136–46

1960–2. Witch posts. *Gwerin* **3**, 254–67

1974–5. Some freehold farms and the Manor of Danby. *Cleveland and Tees-side Local Hist. Soc. Bull.* **27**, 19–26

NEAVE, V. 1971. Living-in in the East Riding. *Vernacular Architect.* **2**, 18–19

NICHOLS, J. G. (ed.) 1853. *The Topographer and Genealogist II.* London

NIELSON, V. C. 1968. Cheese making and cheese chambers in Gloucestershire. *Industrial Archaeol.* **5**, 162–70

NRRS *North Riding Record Series*

NYCRO North Yorkshire County Record Office

ORD, J. W. 1846. *The History and Antiquities of Cleveland.* London

OS Ordnance Survey

PARKER, J. W. R. 1929. Lay Subsidy Rolls I Edward II, 1327/8. In Miscellanea II, *YASRS* **74**

PARKER, T. 1885–8. Welburn Hall. *YAJ* **9**, 380–4

PARKER, T. 1980. History of Kirkdale with the towns and villages adjacent. *Ryedale Historian* **10**, 4–46

1982. History of Kirkdale with the towns and villages adjacent (cont.). *Ryedale Historian* **11**, 10–25

PR 1908. *Patent Rolls of the reign of Henry III preserved in the Public Record Office.* London

PATTEN, J. 1978. *English Towns 1500–1700.* Chatham

PICKUP, A. 1983. *Pickering in Old Picture Postcards.* Zaltbommel, Netherlands

PRITCHARD, J. L. 1961. *Sir George Cayley.* London

PRO Public Record Office

PURDY, J. D. 1975. The Hearth Tax Returns for Yorkshire. MA thesis, University of Leeds

PURVIS, J. S. 1944–7. Dilapidations in parsonage property. *YAJ* **26**, 36–7

RAHTZ, P. (ed.) 1971. *Medieval Village Research Group Report* **19**

REPORTS 1843 *Reports of Special Assistant Poor Law Commissioners on the Employment of Woman and Children in Agriculture.* London

REYNOLDS, S. 1977. *An Introduction to the History of English Medieval Towns.* Oxford

RICKMAN, T. H. 1968. The Farmhouse, Thorpeacre, Loughborough. *Medieval Archaeol.* **12**, 150–3

RIMINGTON, F. C. 1966. Excavations at the Allerston Manor site, 1962–4. *Trans. SDAS* **9**, 19–28

1970–8. The early deer parks of North-East Yorkshire. *Trans. SDAS* **13–21**

RIMINGTON, F. C. and RUTTER, J. G. 1967. Ayton Castle. *Scarborough Dist. Archaeol. Soc. Res. Rep.* **5**

ROBERTS, D. L. 1972. The legal significance of fragmentary survival. *Vernacular Architect.* **3**, 24–6

ROBINSON, J. M. 1983. *Georgian Model Farms. A Study of Decorative and Model Farm Buildings in the Age of Improvement 1700–1846.* Oxford

ROWNTREE, A. (ed.) 1931. *The History of Scarborough.* London

ROWNTREE, S. and KENDALL, M. 1913. *How the Labourer Lives.* London

RCHM(E) 1936. *An Inventory of the Historical Monuments in the County of Westmorland.* London

1970. *An Inventory of the Historical Monuments in the County of Dorset. Vol. III: Central Dorset.* London

1972. *An Inventory of the Historical Monuments in the City of York. Vol. III: South-West of the Ouse.* London

1975. *An Inventory of the Historical Monuments in the City of York. Vol. IV: Outside the City Walls East of the Ouse.* London

1981. *An Inventory of the Historical Monuments in the City of York. Vol. V: The Central Area.* London

RUSHTON, J. H. 1969. Helmsley inns and alehouses in the Victorian age. *Ryedale Historian* **4**, 47–54

1976a. Life in Ryedale in the 14th century (Part 1). *Ryedale Historian* **8**, 19–29

1976b. *Dalby – Valley of Change*

n.d. *The Ryedale Story.* York

RUTTER, J. G. 1969. Industrial archaeology in North-East Yorkshire; list of sites – Area I, Scarborough. *Trans. SDAS* **12**, 17–33

1970. Industrial archaeology in North-East Yorkshire: list of sites – Area II, Ryedale and the Hambletons. *Trans. SDAS* **13**, 23–51

1971. Industrial archaeology in North-East Yorkshire: list of sites – Area III, Whitby and Eskdale. *Trans. SDAS* **14**, 17–48

RYDER, P. F. and COLEMAN, S. 1983. Paull Holme Tower. *E. Riding Archaeol.* **7**, 85–90

SALMON, D. J. (ed.) 1981. *Malton in the early Nineteenth Century.* NYCRO Publ. **26**. Northallerton

SALZMAN, L. F. 1952. *Building in England down to 1540.* Oxford

SDAS Scarborough and District Archaeological Society

SEWELL, J. T. 1923. *An Account of some Medieval Roads crossing the Moors South and South West of Whitby.* Whitby

SHEFFIELD 1914. Sheffield City Libraries. *Descriptive Catalogue of The Charters . . . forming the Jackson Collection . . . by T. W. Hall and A. H. Thomas.* Sheffield

SHEPPARD, J. A. 1974. Metrological analysis of regular village plans in Yorkshire. *Agr. Hist. Rev.* **22**, 118–35

—— 1976. Medieval village planning in northern England: some evidence from Yorkshire. *J. Hist. Geogr.* **21**, 3–20

SINGER *et al.* 1957. Singer, C., Holmyard, E. J., Hall, A. R. and Williams, T. I. (eds.). *A History of Technology. Vol. III: From the Renaissance to the Industrial Revolution c. 1500–c. 1750.* Oxford

SMITH, J. T. 1963. The long-house in Monmouthshire: a re-appraisal. In *Culture and Environment: Essays in Honour of Sir Cyril Fox*, eds. I. Ll. Foster and L. Alcock, pp. 389–414. London

—— 1964. Cruck construction: a survey of the problems. *Medieval Archaeol.* **8**, 119–51.

—— 1971. The architecture of the domestic system in south-east Lancashire and the adjoining Pennines. In *The History of Working-class Housing*, ed. S. D. Chapman, pp. 247–76. Newton Abbot

STILL, L. and PALLISTER, A. 1964. The excavation of one house site in the deserted village of West Hartburn, Co. Durham. *Archaeol. Aeliana 4 ser.* **42**, 187–206

TATE, W. E. 1965–70. A cottage and four acres. *The Amateur Historian* **7**, 13–16

TAYLOR, C. C. 1974. *Fieldwork in Medieval Archaeology.* London

—— 1983. *Village and Farmstead.* London

THIRSK, J. 1967. *The Agrarian History of England and Wales. Vol. IV: 1500–1640.* Cambridge

THOMPSON, M. W. 1958. *Pickering Castle.* London

THORN, J. C. 1979. The camera in Area 10. In *Vol. I. Domestic Settlement, I: Areas 10 and 6*, eds. D. D. Andrews and G. Milne. In *Wharram. A Study of Settlement on the Yorkshire Wolds*, ed. J. G. Hurst, *Soc. Medieval Archaeol. monogr. ser.* **8**

TRADITIONAL 1986. History Distilled. *Traditional Homes* **March 1986**, pp. 18–27

TUKE, J. 1800. *General View of the Agriculture of the North Riding of Yorkshire.* London

TURTON, R. B. (ed.) 1894–7. Documents relating to the Forest and Honor of Pickering. *NRRS n.s.*, **1–4**

TYSON, B. 1982. Some traditional buildings in the Troutbeck Valley: a documentary study. *Trans. Cumberland Westmorland Antiq. Archaeol. Soc.* **82**, 151–76

VCH 1914. *The Victoria County History of the County of York. North Riding: Vol. I.* London

—— 1923. *The Victoria County History of the County of York. North Riding: Vol. II.* London

—— 1974. *The Victoria County History of the County of York. Vol. I.* London (reprint of volume first published in 1907)

WACHER, J. 1963–6. Excavations at Riplingham, East Yorkshire, 1956–7. *YAJ* **41**, 608–69

WADE-MARTINS, S. 1980. *A great estate at work: the Holkham estate and its inhabitants in the nineteenth century.* Cambridge

WAITES, B. 1959–62a. The monastic settlement of North-East Yorkshire. *YAJ* **40**, 478–95

—— 1959–62b. The monastic grange as a factor in the settlement of North-East Yorkshire. *YAJ* **40**, 627–56

—— 1963–6. A Yorkshire farmer in the Memoranda Rolls. *YAJ* **41**, 445–8

—— 1967. *Moorland and Vale-land Farming in North-East Yorkshire.* York

—— 1972. Medieval assessments and agricultural prosperity in North-East Yorkshire, 1292–1342. *YAJ* **44**, 134–45

—— 1977. The medieval ports and trade of North-East Yorkshire. *Mariner's Mirror* **63** part 2, 137–49

WEBSTER, V. R. 1954. Cruck-Framed Buildings of Leicestershire. *Trans. Leicestershire Archaeol. Hist. Soc.* **30**, 26–58

WHELLAN, T. & CO. 1859. *History and Topography of the City of York and the North Riding of Yorkshire. Vol. II.* Beverley

WG. *Whitby Gazette*

WT *Whitby Times*

WHITING, C. E. (ed.) 1946–7. The Autobiographies and Letters of Thomas Comber Parts I and II. *Surtees Soc. Pub.* **156** (1946 for 1941); **157** (1947 for 1942)

WILLAN, T. S. 1932–4. The Parliamentary Surveys for the North Riding of Yorkshire. *YAJ* **31**, 224–89

WILLIAMS, R. A. H. 1977. An excavation at Neville Castle, Kirkbymoorside, North Yorkshire, 1974. *YAJ* **49**, 87–96

WILSON, D. M. and HURST, D. G. 1966. Medieval Britain in 1965. *Medieval Archaeol.* **10**, 168–219

—— 1967. Medieval Britain in 1966. *Medieval Archaeol.* **11**, 262–319

WINDSOR Documents in possession of the Church Commissioners relating to property of the Chapel of St George in Windsor Castle

WOOD, M. E. 1974. *Norman Domestic Architecture.* London

YCA York City Archives

YC *York Courant*

YH *York Herald*

YAJ *Yorkshire Archaeological Journal*

YAS Yorkshire Archaeological Society

YASRS *Yorkshire Archaeological Society Record Series*

YG *Yorkshire Gazette*

YOUNG, A. 1770. *A Six Months Tour through the the North of England. Vol. 1.* London

—— 1771. *A Six Months Tour through the North of England. Vol. 2.* London

YOUNG, G. 1817. *A History of Whitby.*

INDEX